D1430334

Life Under the "Peculiar Institution"

Selections from the Slave Narrative Collection

Life Under the "Peculiar Institution"

Selections from the Slave Narrative Collection

NORMAN R. YETMAN

University of Kansas

Holt, Rinehart and Winston Inc.

New York   Chicago   San Francisco   Atlanta
Dallas   Montreal   Toronto   London   Sydney

ACKNOWLEDGMENTS

I am grateful to W. Austin Bishop, Joel O. Conarroe, Robert A. Jones, Geoffrey H. Steere, and my wife, Anne, for their assistance —both evaluative and supportive—at various stages of this book's preparation. I am especially indebted to Benjamin A. Botkin, who graciously permitted me to examine his extensive personal files, whose conversations and correspondence with me were invaluable to my becoming familiar with the Collection, and whose many other kindnesses will always be warmly remembered.

N. R. Y.

CONTENTS

LIST OF NARRATIVES

INTRODUCTION

IN 1855 JOHN LITTLE, a fugitive slave who had escaped to Canada, uttered this perceptive commentary upon attempts to convey the realities of the existence that he had fled: "Tisn't he who has stood and looked on, that can tell you what slavery is—'tis he who has endured." The view that slavery could be best described by those who had themselves experienced it has found expression in a voluminous number—over 6,000—of commentaries, autobiographies, narratives, and interviews with those who had "endured." Although most of these accounts appeared prior to the Civil War, about one-third of them are the result of the ambitious efforts of the Federal Writers' project of the Works Progress Administration to interview surviving ex-slaves during the 1930's. The result of the efforts of the Federal Writers was the Slave Narrative Collection, a group of autobiographical accounts of former slaves that today stands as one of the most enduring and unheralded achievements of the Writers' Project.[1] Compiled in seventeen states during the years 1936–38, the Collection consists of over 2,000 interviews with ex-slaves. The interviews, almost exclusively verbatim testimonies concerning ante-bellum slave life and the respondents' personal reactions to bondage, afforded aged ex-slaves an unparalleled opportunity to give their personal account of life under the "peculiar institution," to describe in their own words what it felt like to be a slave. The Collection constitutes an illuminating source of data about ante-bellum Southern life, about the institution of slavery, and, most importantly, about the reactions and perspectives of those who had been enslaved.

The Collection provides a unique and virtually unsurpassed group portrait of a historical population. Aside from the large number of autobiographies contained in it, its most attractive feature is the composition of the sample of the slave population represented. Whereas the antebellum slave narratives had been employed primarily as abolitionist propaganda and represented a skewed sample of the total slave

---

[1] Federal Writers' Project, *Slave Narratives, A Folk History of Slavery in the United States from Interviews with Former Slaves* (Typewritten Records Prepared by the Federal Writers' Project, Washington, D.C., 1941).

population, the Collection achieved great diversity and inclusiveness. The ex-slaves ranged in age from one to over fifty at the time of emancipation in 1865.

Their ages were distributed as follows:

Age	Percentage Composition of the Collection
1– 5	16
6–10	27
11–15	24
16–20	16
21–30	13
over 30	3

This meant that over two-thirds were over eighty when interviewed. Almost all had experienced slavery within the states of the Confederacy and still resided there. The major categories of slave occupations were all adequately represented. The slave holdings of an ex-slave's owner varied considerably, ranging from over a thousand slaves to situations in which the informant was the only slave owned by the master. The treatment these individuals received ran the gamut from the most harsh, impersonal and exploitative to the extremely indulgent, intimate and benevolent. Except for the fact that the informants were relatively young when they experienced slavery and that older slaves had died before these interviews were undertaken, all the major categories of the slave population appear to have been well represented in the collection.[2]

Since the actual occupational distribution of the slave population is unknown, assurance of total randomness of this sample is a priori impossible. It is further precluded by the fact that the number of interviews obtained by each of the participating state Writers' Projects varied considerably — ranging from three in Kansas to over 600 in Arkansas.[3] But there appears little reason to believe that the processes involved in the selection of informants for interview produced a sample that systematically diverged from the parent population. At least the sample biases — the disproportionate number of runaways, individuals who had purchased their freedom or had been freed, young males, craftsmen, and individuals from

---

[2] The number of individuals interviewed represented approximately 2 percent of the total ex-slave population in the United States at the time. The 1930 Census revealed a total of 118,446 Blacks in the age categories seventy-five and over. There is no reason to assume that the number in this category was significantly different in 1937, the year in which most of the narratives were compiled. Assuming that approximately 10 percent of these had been free Blacks before Emancipation, the number of former slaves still exceeded 100,000 in 1937. United States Bureau of the Census, Fifteenth Census of the United States, 1930, Population. General Report, Statistics by Subjects, II; 577

[3] For an enumeration of the number of narratives obtained in each of the participating states, see Appendix I, page 000.

the border states—that characterized the universe of antebellum slave narratives is absent.[4] The methodological problem of sample bias that inevitably confronts the historian, while not totally eliminated, is substantially reduced in this sample of the slave universe. This remarkable collection of personal documents provides an invaluable source of sociohistorical data, one that warrants a much closer examination than it has previously been accorded.

Neglect of the Collection stems from several factors. Very important among these factors has been the Collection's inaccessibility. Although the original transcripts are available for reference in the Rare Book Division of the Library of Congress, the Collection does not circulate. Few laymen are aware of its existence, and most scholars acquainted with it have relied upon the accounts contained in Benjamin A. Botkin's *Lay My Burden Down*, which is comprised of excerpts and selections from it and, until the appearance of this volume, was the sole publication derived primarily from these autobiographies. But the material as a whole has been virtually unexploited during the three decades that have elapsed since the narratives were obtained.

The Collection's sheer bulk (more than 10,000 unindexed pages) undoubtedly has discouraged efforts to make effective use of its data. Moreover, the quality of the accounts is grossly uneven, reflecting the varied caliber of the Federal Writers, most of whom were white-collar workers on relief. Many of them were unsophisticated in the use of interview techniques, expressed little concern for the sources of distortion inherent in the interview process, and were insensitive to the nuances of interview procedure. A questionnaire, devised to suggest possible categories of discussion, was often partially or totally ignored, and this resulted in rambling and trivia. When it was too closely followed, the result was stylized and superficial responses, devoid of spontaneity. Although the narratives range in length from one to twenty-five typewritten pages, the use of a substantial number of them is precluded by their brevity.

Perhaps the most significant cause of the neglect of the Slave Narrative Collection, however, has been the circumspection with which historians have generally regarded the use of personal reminiscences. The recollection of the past is always a highly subjective phenomenon, one continually subject to modification and distortion. The alleged untrustworthiness of slave narratives has therefore been a frequent and not inconsequential

---

[4] That some sample error was operating is shown by the fact that according to the 1930 Census, aged Blacks lived primarily in rural areas, whereas those whose accounts are found in the Collection were overwhelmingly urban residents. The primary basis for selection was apparently availability. Those in closest proximity to the cities in which the Federal Writers were based were most likely to the interviewed.

Males were also disproportionately represented in the Collection. Whereas the Black population eighty-five and over was characterized by an extremely low ratio of males to females (.74), the ratio in the Collection is unaccountably high (1.43). This will account for the fact that more males than females have been included in the narratives selected for this volume.

objection to their use in historical research.[5] Yet a blanket indictment of the narratives is as unjustified as their indiscriminate or uncritical use. Each kind of historical document has its own particular uses for providing an understanding of the past as well as its own inherent limitations. Therefore, the utility of the narratives cannot be determined a priori, but only in the context of the objectives of the researcher.

Several uses for the Collection are immediately apparent. First, it provides important source materials for an understanding of antebellum life, the nature and effects of the institution of slavery, and the impact of Emancipation and Reconstruction. The Collection, by virtue of its representing a broad sample of the slave population, provides an invaluable reference source for testing historical and social scientific generalizations. In addition, it can serve to suggest new subjects for research.

The Collection has relevance to literary as well as to historical and social-scientific analyses. As sensitive literary scholars have increasingly recognized, the narrative represents a unique literary style and a once flourishing cultural form that is today rapidly becoming extinct under the impact of modern mass communications. The former slaves interviewed by the Federal Writers were among the most able practitioners of this style. More specifically, the recording of the recollections of these aged Black people has preserved an important component of the oral tradition of Black Americans. In these interviews folk speech, idiom, and vernacular storytelling are fused with folk images, symbols, and myths to convey a sense of the experiential significance and reality of life in bondage. The Collection thus contributes to an understanding of the "folk" or ethnohistory of Black America and can become an integral component in the task of reconstructing the rich heritage of Black people.

Finally, the recent publication of such controversial works as Stanley M. Elkins' *Slavery* and William Styron's best-selling *The Confessions of Nat Turner* has stimulated an enormous interest in the reality of slavery as perceived from the perspective of the slave. As new questions — especially those concerning the effects of the institution of slavery upon the psyche of the enslaved — are raised, these highly personal and subjective accounts assume a new significance and become an appropriate, even essential, source of data.

The publication of this volume grew out of my conviction that the Slave Narrative Collection should be made more widely available. Botkin's *Lay My Burden Down*, while vividly capturing its flavor, represents only a small sampling of its contents. Less than twenty of the more than 2,000 narratives are printed in their entirety. Moreover, since the book is comprised primarily of excerpts and selections from individual accounts, the

[5] See, for example, Ulrich B. Phillips, *American Negro Slavery* (New York, 1929), vii and *Life and Labor in the Old South* (Boston, 1929), 218–219. See also Kenneth M. Stampp, *The Peculiar Institution* (New York, 1956), 74–75. For one of the sensitive uses of the Slave Narrative Collection, see Willie Lee Rose, *Rehearsal for Reconstruction* (New York, 1964).

narrative and experiential quality of the accounts is often lost. The absence of complete narratives, furthermore, precludes the possibility of systematically analyzing and correlating different facets of slave life (for example, the relation between runaways and occupational status, geographical location, and motivation; between family structure and postemancipation activity).

This book, then, is substantially different from *Lay My Burden Down*. Since my primary objective has been to make the contents of the Collection more accessible, any narratives previously reprinted in their entirety, or substantially so, were not included. Consequently, except in a few instances where small portions of a complete narrative were used, those reprinted in this volume have never been published previously. The most distinctive feature, however, is its format—each item included is a complete narrative, so that the focus is upon the individual former slave as well as upon the collective experience. Only minor editing, designed to improve readability and continuity, has been employed. This has included an attempt to achieve some uniformity of dialect spelling, which varied greatly among the more than 300 interviewers. At no point, however, have the metaphors or the patterns of speech themselves been changed. Since the primary objective of the Federal Writers' Project in interviewing the former slave was to gain information concerning his perspective of slave life and his reactions to emancipation, I have likewise eliminated those comments, usually very brief, that concerned the informant's situation when interviewed. Such editorial omissions were minor, however. Each narrative has been reprinted substantially intact.

Given its size and its varied quality, it would have been impossible in a single volume to reprint the Collection in its entirety. Therefore some means of selection has been necessary. I have attempted to avoid, as much as possible, subjective judgments in this process so that the selections contained in the volume would be representative of the Collection. I have employed several criteria in this selection process. First, as mentioned, those narratives that had already been previously published in their entirety were excluded. Since many of the individuals whose accounts are found in the Collection were still children at Emancipation, the second criterion was that the sample be restricted to individuals who had reached a minimum age of thirteen, or adolescence, by the time of Emancipation. This requirement substantially reduced the size of the sample, since a majority of the former slaves had not yet reached this age when Emancipation was proclaimed. Many of the narratives of poorer quality were thus eliminated, because many of the accounts of individuals who were young children when Emancipation occurred are not so detailed as those obtained from older former slaves.

Not only was some factual information concerning each informant desirable (for example, occupation, residence under slavery, size of owner's holdings), but a minimum amount of discussion on the part of the informant was essential if the narrative was to effectively convey the feeling of "what it was like to be a slave." As previously noted, one of the primary deficiencies of many of the narratives is their brevity, for without enabling the informant to elaborate upon the questions posed by the interviewer the uniqueness of each individual and his experiential world under slavery cannot begin to emerge. Accordingly, the decision was made to restrict the sample to those narratives that comprised at least three typewritten pages.

About 300 of the narratives conformed to these criteria. Since a single volume employing all of them would be unwieldy, some further means of selection was necessary. Personal bias could have been eliminated from the selection process by the use of a random sample, and this alternative was considered. But this procedure would have eliminated a large number of excellent accounts while including many that were not so rich in content. To prevent this, I have had to employ some kind of subjective judgment. The narratives that I have selected were rated according to the following criteria: readability and interest; detail of content; continuity of narrative; prominence of personal experience, as contrasted to mere description of slave life. The narratives that were judged to be the finest according to these criteria were then selected for this volume. Because the caliber of the Federal Writers and their dedication to the task of interviewing the former slaves varied widely from state to state, those individuals interviewed in several states — most notably Oklahoma, North Carolina, and Texas — have necessarily been disproportionately represented.

The decision to arrange the narratives alphabetically was deliberate. The categories by which data is organized can be coercive to the point of rigidifying and impeding research. To minimize the effect of imposing on the reader my perceptions and organization of the data, I have chosen what I feel is the most simple and least coercive means of organization in the hope that the narratives will "speak for themselves." The reader is then free to organize the data in his own manner.

NARRATIVES

ISAAC ADAMS

Interviewed at Tulsa, Oklahoma
Interviewer not identified
Age when interviewed: 87

I WAS BORN IN LOUISIANA, way before the War. I think it was about
ten years before, because I can remember everything so well
about the start of the War, and I believe I was about ten years old.

My mammy belonged to Mr. Sack P. Gee. I don't know what his real
given name was, but it maybe was Saxon. Anyways we all called him
Master Sack. He was a kind of youngish man, and was mighty rich. I
think he was born in England. Anyway his pappy was from England,
and I think he went back before I was born.

Master Sack had a big plantation ten miles north of Arcadia, Louisiana,
and his land run ten miles along both sides. He would leave in a buggy
and be gone all day and still not get all over it. There was all kinds of
land on it, and he raised cane and oats and wheat and lots of corn and
cotton. His cotton fields was the biggest anywheres in that part, and
when chopping and picking times come he would get Negroes from
other people to help out. I never was no good at picking, but I was a
terror with a hoe!

I was the only child my mammy had. She was just a young girl,
and my master did not own her very long. He got her from Mr. Addison
Hilliard, where my pappy belonged. I think she was going to have me
when he got her. Anyways, I come along pretty soon, and my mammy
never was very well afterwards. Maybe Master Sack sent her back over to
my pappy. I don't know.

Mammy was the house girl at Mr. Sack's because she wasn't very
strong, and when I was four or five years old she died. I was big enough
to do little things for Mr. Sack and his daughter, so they kept me at the
mansion, and I helped the house boys. Time I was nine or ten Mr. Sack's
daughter was getting to be a young woman—fifteen or sixteen years old
—and that was old enough to get married off in them days. They had a lot
of company just before the War, and they had a whole bunch of house
Negroes around all the time.

Old Mistress died when I was a baby, so I don't remember anything
about her, but Young Mistress was a winder! She would ride horseback

8

nearly all the time, and I had to go along with her when I got big enough. She never did go around the quarters, so I don't know nothing much about the Negroes Mr. Sack had for the fields. They all looked pretty clean and healthy, though, when they would come up to the Big House. He fed them all good and they all liked him.

He had so much different kinds of land that they could raise anything they wanted, and he had more mules and horses and cattle than anybody around there. Some of the boys worked with his fillies all the time. And he went off to New Orleans every once in a while with his race horses. He took his daughter but they never took me.

Some of his land was in pasture but most of it was all open fields, with just miles and miles of cotton rows. There was a pretty good strip along one side he called the "old" fields. That's what they called the land that was wore out and turned back. It was all growed up in young trees, and that's where he kept his horses most of the time.

The first I knowed about the War coming on was when Mr. Sack had a whole bunch of white folks at the Big House at a function. They didn't talk about anything else all evening and then the next time they come nearly all their menfolks wasn't there—just the womenfolks. It wasn't very long till Mr. Sack went off to Houma with some other men, and pretty soon we know he was in the War. I don't remember ever seeing him come home. I don't think he did until it was nearly over.

Next thing we knowed they was Confederate soldiers riding by pretty nearly every day in big droves. Sometimes they would come and buy corn and wheat and hogs. But they never did take any anyhow, like the Yankees done later on. They would pay with billets, Young Missy called them, and she didn't send them to get cashed but saved them a long time. Then she got them cashed, but you couldn't buy anything with the money she got for them.

That Confederate money she got wasn't no good. I was in Arcadia with her at a store, and she had to pay seventy-five cents for a can of sardines for me to eat with some bread I had, and before the War you could get a can like that for two cents. Things was even higher then than later on, but that's the only time I saw her buy anything.

When the Yankees got down in that country most of the big men paid for all the corn and meat and things they got, but some of the little bunches of them would ride up and take hogs and things like that and just ride off. They wasn't anybody at our place but the womenfolks and the Negroes. Some of Mr. Sack's women kinfolks stayed there with Young Mistress.

Along at the last the Negroes on our place didn't put in much stuff—just what they would need, and could hide from the Yankees, because they would get it all took away from them if the Yankees found out they had plenty of corn and oats.

The Yankees was mighty nice about their manners, though. They camped all around our place for a while. There was three camps of them close by at one time, but they never did come and use any of our houses or cabins. There was lots of poor whites and Cajuns that lived down below us, between us and the Gulf, and the Yankees just moved into their houses and cabins and used them to camp in.

The Negroes at our place and all of them around there didn't try to get away or leave when the Yankees come in. They wasn't no place to go, anyway, so they all stayed on. But they didn't do very much work. Just enough to take care of themselves and their white folks.

Master Sack come home before the War was quite over. I think he had been sick, because he looked thin and old and worried. All the Negroes picked up and worked mighty hard after he come home, too. One day he went into Arcadia and come home and told us the War was over and we was all free. The Negroes didn't know what to make of it, and didn't know where to go, so he told all that wanted to stay on that they could just go on like they had been and pay him shares.

About half of his Negroes stayed on, and he marked off land for them to farm and made arrangements with them to let them use their cabins, and let them have mules and tools. They paid him out of their shares, and some of them finally bought the mules and some of the land. But about half went on off and tried to do better somewheres else. I didn't stay with him because I was just a boy and he didn't need me at the house anyway.

Late in the War my pappy belonged to a man named Sander or Zander. Might been Alexander, but the Negroes called him Mr. Sander. When Pappy got free he come and asked me to go with him, and I went along and lived with him. He had a sharecropper deal with Mr. Sander and I helped him work his patch. That place was just a little east of Houma, a few miles.

When my pappy was born his parents belonged to a Mr. Adams, so he took Adams for his last name, and I did too, because I was his son. I don't know where Mr. Adams lived, but I don't think my pappy was born in Louisiana. Alabama, maybe. I think his parents come off the boat, because he was very black—even blacker than I am.

I lived there with my pappy until I was about eighteen and then I married and moved around all over Louisiana from time to time. My wife give me twelve boys and five girls, but all my children are dead now but five. My wife died in 1920 and I come up here to Tulsa to live. One of my daughters takes care and looks out for me now.

LUCRETIA ALEXANDER

Interviewed at Little Rock, Arkansas
Interviewed by Samuel S. Taylor
Age when interviewed: 89

BEEN MARRIED three times and my last name was Lucretia Alexander. I was twelve years old when the War began. My mother died at seventy-three or seventy-five. That was in August, 1865 — August the ninth. She was buried August twelfth. The reason they kept her was they had refugeed her children off to different places to keep them from the Yankees. They couldn't get them back. My mother and her children were heir property. Her first master was Tolliver. My mother was named Agnes Tolliver. She had a boy and a girl both older than I were. My brother come home in '65. I never got to see my sister till 1869. When my mother died she left four living children. I was the youngest. My father died in 1881 and some say he was 112 and some say 106. His name was Beasley, John Beasley, and he went by John Beasley till he died. I ain't got nary living child. My oldest child would have been sixty-four if he were living. They claim my baby boy is living, but I don't know. I had four children. I got religion in 1865. I was baptized seventy-three years ago this August.

The first overseer I remember was named Kurt Johnson. The next was named Mack McKenzie. The next one was named Phil Womack. And the next was named Tom Phipps. Mean! Liked meanness! Mean a man as he could be! I've seen him take them down and whip them till the blood run out of them.

I got ten head of grandchildren. And I been grandmother to eleven head. I been great-grandmother to twelve of great-grandchildren. I got one twenty-three and another nineteen or twenty. Her father's father was in the army. She is the oldest. Lotas Robinson, my granddaughter, has four children that are my great-grandchildren. Gayden Jenkins, my grandson, has two girls. I got a grandson named Don Jenkins. He is the father of three boys. He lives in Cleveland. He got a grandson named Mark Jenkins in Memphis who has one boy. The youngest granddaughter—I don't remember her husband's name—has one boy. There are four generations of us.

My mother was treated well in slavery times. My father was sold five times. Wouldn't take nothin'. So they sold him. They beat him and knocked him about. They put him on the block and they sold him about beatin' up his master. He was a native of Virginia. The last time they sold him they sold him down in Claiborne County, Mississippi, just below where I was born at. I was born in Copiah County near Hazlehurst, about fifteen miles from Hazlehurst. My mother was born in Washington County, Virginia. Her first master was Qualls Tolliver. Qualls moved to Mississippi and married a woman down there and he had one son, Peach Tolliver. After he died, he willed her to Peachy. Then Peachy went to the Rebel army and got killed.

My mother's father was a free Indian named Washington. Her mother was a slave. I don't know my father's father. He moved about so much and was sold so many times he never did tell me his father. He got his name from the white folks. When you're a slave you have to go by your owner's name.

My master's mother took me to the house after my mother died. And the first thing I remember doing was cleaning up. Bringing water, putting up mosquito-bars, cooking. My master's mother was Susan Reed. I have done everything but saw. I never sawed in my life. The hardest work I did was after slavery. I never did no hard work during slavery. I used to pack water for the plow hands and all such as that. But when my mother died, my mistress took me up to the house.

But Lord! I've seen such brutish doin's—runnin' niggers with hounds and whippin' them till they was bloody. They used to put 'em in stocks, used to be two people would whip 'em—the overseer and the driver. The overseer would be a man named Elijah at our house. He was just a poor white man. He had a whip they called the BLACKSNAKE.

I remember one time they caught a man named George Tinsley. They put the dogs on him and they bit him and tore all his clothes off of him. Then they put him in the stocks. The stocks was a big piece of timber with hinges in it. It had a hole in it for your head. They would lift it up and put your head in it. There was holes for your head, hands and feet in it. Then they would shut it up and they would lay the whip on you and you couldn't do nothin' but wiggle and holler, "Pray, Master, pray!" But when they'd let that man out, he'd run away again.

They would make the slaves work till twelve o'clock on Sunday, and then they would let them go to church. The first time I was sprinkled, a white preacher did it. I think his name was Williams. The preacher would preach to the white folks in the forenoon and to the colored folks in the evening. The white folks had them hired. One of them preachers was named Hackett; another, Williams; and another, Gowan. There was five of them but I just remember three. One man used to hold the slaves so late that they had to go to the church dirty from their work. They would be sweaty and smelly. So the preacher rebuked them about it. That was old man Bill Rose.

The niggers didn't go to the church building. The preacher came and preached to them in their quarters. He'd just say, "Serve your masters. Don't steal your master's turkey. Don't steal your master's chickens. Don't steal your master's hogs. Don't steal your master's meat. Do whatsomeever your master tell you to do." Same old thing all de time.

My father would have church in dwelling houses and they had to whisper. My mother was dead and I would go with him. Sometimes they would have church at his house. That would be when they would want a real meetin' with some real preachin'. It would have to be durin' the week nights. You couldn't tell the difference between Baptists and Methodists then. They was all Christians. I never saw them turn nobody down at the communion, but I heard of it. They used to sing their songs in a whisper and pray in a whisper. There was a prayer-meeting from house to house once or twice—once or twice a week.

Old Phipps whipped me once. He aimed to kill me but I got loose. He whipped me about a colored girl of his'n that he had by a colored woman. Phipps went with a colored woman before he married his wife. He had a girl named Martha Ann Phipps. I beat Martha about a pair of stockings. Mistress bought me a nice pair of stockings from the store. You see, they used to knit the stockings. I wore the stockings once; then I washed them and put them on the fence to dry. Martha stole them and put them on. I beat her and took them off of her. She ran and told her father and he ran me home. He couldn't catch me, and he told me he'd get me. I didn't run to my father. I run to my mistress, and he knew he'd better not do nothin' then. He said, "I'll get you, you little old black somethin'." Only he didn't say "somethin'." He didn't get me then.

But one day he caught me out by his house. I had gone over that way on an errand I needn't have done. He had two girls hold me. They was Angeline and Nancy. They didn't much want to hold me anyhow. Some niggers would catch you and kill you for the white folks; and then there was some that wouldn't. I got loose from them. He tried to hold me hisself but he couldn't. I got away and went back to my old mistress and she wrote him a note never to lay his dirty hands on me again. A little later her brother, Johnson Chatman, came there and ran him off the place. My old mistress' name was Susan Chatman before she married. Then she married Tolliver. Then she married Reed. She married Reed last—after Tolliver died.

One old lady named Emily Moorehead runned in and held my mother once for Phipps to whip her. And my mother was down with consumption too. I aimed to get old Phipps for that. But then I got religion and I couldn't do it. Religion makes you forget a heap of things.

Susan Reed, my old mistress, bought my father and paid fifteen hundred dollars for him and she hadn't never seen him. Advertising. He had run away so much that they had to advertise and sell him. He never would run away from Miss Susan. She was good to him till she got that old nigger beater—Phipps. Her husband, Reed, was called a nigger spoiler. My father was an old man when Phipps was an overseer and wasn't able to fight much.

Phipps sure was a bad man. He wasn't so bad neither; but the niggers was scared of him. You know in slave times, sometimes when a master would get too bad, the niggers would kill him — took him off out in the woods somewhere and get rid of him. Two or three of them would get together and scheme it out, and then two or three of them would get him way out and kill him. But they didn't nobody ever pull nothin' like that on Phipps. They was scared of him.

One time I saw the Yankees a long way off. They had on blue uniforms and was on coal black horses. I hollered out, "Oh, I see somethin'." My mistress said, "What?" I told her, and she said, "Them's the Yankees." She went on in the house and I went with her. She sacked up all the valuables in the house. She said, "Here," and she threw a sack of silver on me that was so heavy that I went right on down to the ground. Then she took hold of it and helped me up and helped me carry it out. I carried it out and hid it. She had three buckskin sacks—all full of silver. That wasn't now; that was in slavery times. During the War, Jeff Davis gave out Confederate money. It died out on the folks' hands. But there wasn't nothin' but gold and silver in them sacks.

I heard them tell the slaves they were free. A man named Captain Barkus who had his arm off at the elbow called for the three nearby plantations to meet at our place. Then he got up on a platform with another man beside him and declared peace and freedom. He pointed to a colored man and yelled, "You're free as I am." Old colored folks, old as I am now, that was on sticks, throwed them sticks away and shouted.

Right after freedom I stayed with that white woman I told you about. I was with her about four years. I worked for twelve dollars a month and my food and clothes. Then I figured that twelve dollars wasn't enough and I went to work in the field. It was a mighty nice woman. Never hit me in her life. I never have been whipped by a white woman. She was good to me till she died. She died after I had my second child—a girl child.

I have been living in this city fifteen years. I come from Chicot County when I come here. We came to Arkansas in slavery times. They brought me from Copiah County when I was six or eight years old. When Mrs. Tolliver married she came up here and brought my mother. My mother belonged to her son and she said, "Agnes (that was my mother's name), will you follow me if I buy your husband?" Her husband's name was John Beasley. She said, "Yes." Then her old mistress bought Beasley and paid fifteen hundred dollars to get my mother to come with her. Then Peachy went to war and was shot because he come home of a furlough and stayed too long. So when he went back they killed him. My mother nursed him when he was a baby. Mother really belonged to Peachy, but when Peachy died, then she fell to her mistress. Old man Tolliver said he didn't want none of us to be sold; so they wasn't none of us sold. Maybe there would have been if slavery had lasted longer; but there wasn't.

MARY ANDERSON

Interviewed near Raleigh, North Carolina
Interviewed by Pat Matthews
Age when interviewed: 86

M Y NAME IS Mary Anderson. I was born on a plantation near
Franklinton, Wake County, North Carolina, May 10, 1851. I was a
slave belonging to Sam Brodie, who owned the plantation at this place.
My missus was Evaline. My father was Alfred Brodie and my mother was
Bertha Brodie.

We had good food, plenty of warm homemade clothes, and comfortable
houses. The slave houses were called the quarters, and the house where
Marster lived was called the Great House. Our houses had two rooms
each, and Marster's house had twelve rooms. Both the slave and white
folks buildings were located in a large grove one mile square covered with
oak and hickory nut trees. Marster's house was exactly one mile from the
main Louisburg Road and there was a wide avenue leading through the
plantation and grove to Marster's house. The house fronted the avenue
east and in going down the avenue from the main road you traveled
directly west.

The plantation was very large and there were about two hundred acres
of cleared land that was farmed each year. A pond was located on the
place and in winter ice was gathered there for summer use and stored in
an ice house which was built in the grove where the other buildings were.
A large hole about ten feet deep was dug in the ground; the ice was put
in that hole and covered. A large frame building was built over it. At the
top of the earth there was an entrance door and steps leading down to the
bottom of the hole. Other things besides ice were stored there. There was
a still on the plantation and barrels of brandy were stored in the ice house,
also pickles, preserves, and cider. Many of the things we used were made
on the place. There was a grist mill, tannery, shoe shop, blacksmith shop,
and looms for weaving cloth.

There were about one hundred and sixty-two slaves on the plantation.
Every Sunday morning all the children had to be bathed, dressed, and
their hair combed, and carried down to Marster's for breakfast. It was a
rule that all the little colored children eat at the Great House every Sunday
morning in order that Marster and Missus could watch them eat so they
could know which ones were sickly and have them doctored.

15

Sunday was a great day on the plantation. Everybody got biscuits, Sundays. The slave women went down to Marster's for their Sunday allowance of flour. All the children ate breakfast at the Great House and Marster and Missus gave out fruit to all. The slaves looked forward to Sunday as they labored through the week. It was a great day. Slaves received good treatment from Marster and all his family.

The slave children all carried a mussel shell in their hands to eat with up to the Great House. The food was put on large trays and the children all gathered around and ate, dipping up their food with their mussel shells which they used for spoons. Those who refused to eat or those who were ailing in any way had to come back to the Great House for their meals and medicine until they were well.

Marster had a large apple orchard in the Tar River low grounds and up on higher ground and nearer the plantation house there was on one side of the road a large plum orchard and on the other side was an orchard of peaches, cherries, quinces, and grapes. We picked the quinces in August and used them for preserving. Marster and Missus believed in giving the slaves plenty of fruit, especially the children.

Marster had three children, one boy named Dallas, and two girls, Bettie and Carrie. He would not allow slave children to call his children "Marster" and "Missus" unless the slave said "Little Marster" or "Little Missus." He had four white overseers, but they were not allowed to whip a slave. If there was any whipping to be done he always said he would do it. He didn't believe in whipping, so when a slave get so bad he could not manage him, he sold him.

Marster didn't quarrel with anybody; Missus would not speak short to a slave, but both Marster and Missus taught slaves to be obedient in a nice quiet way. The slaves were taught to take their hats and bonnets off before going into the house, and to bow and say, "Good mornin' Marster Sam and Missus Evaline." Some of the little Negroes would go down to the Great House and ask them when it was going to rain, and when Marster or Missus walked in the grove the little Negroes would follow along after them like a gang of kiddies. Some of the slave children wanted to stay with them at the Great House all the time. They knew no better, of course, and seemed to love Marster and Missus as much as they did their own mother and father. Marster and Missus always used gentle means to get the children out of their way when they bothered them and the way the children loved and trusted them was a beautiful sight to see.

Patterrollers were not allowed on the place unless they came peacefully, and I never knew of them whipping any slaves on Marster's place. Slaves were carried off on two horse wagons to be sold. I have seen several loads leave. They were the unruly ones. Sometimes he would bring back slaves; once he brought back two boys and three girls from the slave market.

We were allowed to have prayer meetings in our homes and we also went to the white folks' church. But they would not teach any of us to read and write. Books and papers were forbidden. Marster's children and the slave children played together. I went around with the baby girl

Carrie to other plantations visiting. She taught me how to talk low and how to act in company. My association with white folks and my training while I was a slave is why I talk like white folks.

The War was begun and there were stories of fights and freedom. The news went from plantation to plantation and while the slaves acted natural and some even more polite than usual, they prayed for freedom.

Then one day I heard something that sounded like thunder and Marster and Missus began to walk around and act queer. The grown slaves were whispering to each other. Sometimes they gathered in little gangs in the grove. Next day I heard it again, boom, boom, boom. I went and asked Missus, "Is it going to rain?" She said, "Mary, go to the icehouse and bring me some pickles and preserves." I went and got them. She ate a little and gave me some. Then she said, "You run along and play."

In a day or two everybody on the plantation seemed to be disturbed and Marster and Missus were crying. Marster ordered all the slaves to come to the Great House at nine o'clock. Nobody was working and slaves were walking over the grove in every direction. At nine o'clock all the slaves gathered at the Great House and Marster and Missus came out on the porch and stood side by side. You could hear a pin drop everything was so quiet. Then Marster said, "Good morning," and Missus said, "Good morning, children." They were both crying. Then Marster said, "Men, women, and children, you are free. You are no longer my slaves. The Yankees will soon be here." Marster and Missus then went into the house; got two large arm chairs and put them on the porch facing the avenue and sat down side by side and remained there watching.

It about an hour there was one of the blackest clouds coming up the avenue from the main road. It was the Yankee soldiers. They finally filled the mile long avenue reaching from Marster's house to the main Louisburg Road and spread out over the mile square grove. The mounted men dismounted. The footmen stacked their shining guns and began to build fires and cook. They called the slaves, saying, "You are free."

Slaves were whooping and laughing and acting like they were crazy. Yankee soldiers were shaking hands with the Negroes and calling them Sam, Dinah, Sarah, and asking them questions. They busted the door to the smokehouse and got all the hams. They went to the icehouse and got several barrels of brandy: such a time! The Negroes and Yankees were cooking and eating together. The Yankees told them to come on and join them, they were free. Master and Missus sat on the porch and they were so humble no Yankee bothered anything in the Great House.

The slaves were awfully excited. The Yankees stayed there, cooked, ate, drank, and played music until about night. Then a bugle began to blow and you never saw such getting on horses and lining up in your life. In a few minutes they began to march, leaving the grove which was soon silent as a graveyard. They took Marster's horses and cattle with them and joined the main army and camped just across Cypress Creek one and one-half miles from my marster's place on the Louisburg Road.

When they left the county, lot of the slaves went with them and soon there were none of Marster's slaves left. They wandered around for a year from place to place, fed and working most of the time at some other slave owner's plantation and getting more homesick every day.

The second year after the surrender our Marster and Missus got on their carriage and went and looked up all the Negroes they heard of who ever belonged to them. Some who went off with the Yankees were never heard from again. When Marster and Missus found any of theirs they would say, "Well, come on back home." My father and mother, two uncles and their families moved back. Also Lorenze Brodie and John Brodie and their families moved back. Several of the young men and women who once belonged to him came back. Some were so glad to get back they cried, 'cause fare had been mighty bad part of the time they were rambling around and they were hungry.

When they got back Marster would say, "Well, you have come back, have you?" And the Negroes would say, "Yes, Marster." Most all spoke of them as "Missus" and "Marster" as they did before the surrender, and getting back home was the greatest pleasure of all. We stayed with Marster and Missus and went to their church, the Maple Springs Baptist Church, until they died.

Since the surrender I married James Anderson. I had four children, one boy and three girls.

MARY ARMSTRONG

Interviewed at Houston, Texas
Interviewer not identified
Age when interviewed: 91

YOU ALL has to 'cuse me if I don't talk so good, 'cause I'se been feelin' poorly for a spell and I ain't so young no more. Law me, when I think back what I used to do, and now it's all I can do to hobble round a little. Why, Miss Olivia, my mistress, used to put a glass plumb full of water on my head and then have me waltz round the room, and I'd dance so smoothlike, I don't spill nary drop.

That was in St. Louis, where I'se born. You see my mama belong to Old William Cleveland and Old Polly Cleveland, and they was the meanest two white folks whatever live, cause they was always beatin' on their slaves. I know, cause Mama told me, and I hears about it other places, and besides, Old Polly, she was a Polly devil if there ever was one, and she whipped my little sister what was only nine months old, and just a baby, to death. She come and took the diaper offen my little sister and whipped till the blood just ran—just 'cause she cry like all babies do, and it kilt my sister. I never forgot that, but I got some even with that Old Polly devil and it's this-a-way.

You see, I'se 'bout ten year old and I belongs to Miss Olivia, what was that old Polly's daughter, and one day Old Polly devil comes to where Miss Olivia lives after she marries, and tries to give me a lick out in the yard, and I picks up a rock about as big as half your fist and hits her right in the eye and busted the eyeball, and tells her that's for whippin' my baby sister to death. You could hear her holler for five miles, but Miss Olivia, when I tells her, says, "Well, I guess Mama has learnt her lesson at last." But that Old Polly was mean like her husband, Old Cleveland, till she die, and I hopes they is burnin' in torment now.

I don't 'member 'bout the start of things so much, 'cept what Miss Olivia and my mama, her name was Silvy, tells me. 'Course, it's powerful cold in winter times and the farm was lots different from down here. They calls 'em plantations down here, but up at St. Louis they was just called farms, and that's what they were 'cause we raises wheat and barley and rye and oats and corn and fruit.

The houses was builded with brick and heavy wood, too, 'cause it's cold up there, and we has to wear them warm clothes and they's wove on the place, and we works at it in the evenin's.

Old Cleveland takes a lot of his slaves what was in "custom" and brings 'em to Texas to sell. You know he wasn't 'sposed to do that, 'cause when you's in "custom," that's 'cause he borrowed money on you, and you's not 'sposed to leave the place till he paid up. 'Course, Old Cleveland just tells the one he owed the money to, you had run off, or squirmed out some way, he was that mean.

Mama say she was in one bunch and me in 'nother. Mama had been put before this with my papa, Sam Adams, but that makes no difference to Old Cleveland. He's so mean he never would sell the man and woman and chillen the same one. He'd sell the man here and the woman there and if they's chillen he'd sell them some place else. Oh, old Satan in torment couldn't be no meaner than what he and Old Polly was to they slaves. He'd chain a nigger up to whip 'em and rub salt and pepper on him, like he said, "to season him up." And when he'd sell a slave, he'd grease their mouth all up to make it look like they'd been fed good and was strong and healthy.

Well, Mama say they hadn't no more'n got to Shreveport before some law man catch Old Cleveland and takes 'em all back to St. Louis. Then my little sister's born, the one Old Polly devil kilt, and I'se about four year old then.

Miss Olivia takes a likin' to me and though her papa and mamma so mean, she's kind to everyone, and they just love her. She marries to Mr. Will Adams what was a fine man, and has about five farms and five hundred slaves, and he buys me for her from Old Cleveland and pays him twenty-five hundred dollars, and gives him George Henry, a nigger, to boot. Lawsy, I'se sure happy to be with Miss Olivia and away from Old Cleveland and Old Polly, 'cause they kilt my little sister.

We lives in St. Louis on Chinqua Hill, and I'se house girl, and when the babies starts to come I nusses 'em and spins thread for clothes on the loom. I spins six cuts of thread a week, but I has plenty of time for myself and that's where I larns to dance so good. Law, I sure just crazy about dancin'. If I'se settin' eatin' my victuals and hears a fiddle play, I gets up and dances.

Mr. Will and Miss Olivia sure is good to me, and I never calls Mr. Will "Massa" neither, but when they's company I calls him Mr. Will and round the house by ourselves I calls them "Pappy" and "Mammy," 'cause they raises me up from the little girl. I hears Old Cleveland done took my mamma to Texas again but I couldn't do nothin', 'cause Miss Olivia wouldn't have much truck with her folks. Once in a while Old Polly comes over, but Miss Olivia tells her not to touch me or the others. Old Polly tries to buy me back from Miss Olivia, and if they had they'd kilt me sure. But Miss Olivia say, "I'd wade in blood as deep as hell before I'd let you have Mary." That just the very words she told 'em.

Then I hears my papa is sold some place I don't know where. 'Course I didn't know him so well, just what mamma done told me, so that didn't worry me like Mamma being took so far away.

One day Mr. Will say, "Mary, you want to go to the river and see the boat race," Law me, I never won't forget that. Where we live it ain't far to the Miss'sippi River and pretty soon here they comes, the *Natchez* and the *Eclipse,* with smoke and fire just pourin' out of they smokestacks. That old captain on the *Eclipse* starts puttin' in bacon meat in the boiler and the grease just comes out a-blazin' and it beat the *Natchez* to pieces.

I stays with Miss Olivia till '63 when Mr. Will set us all free. I was 'bout seventeen year old then or more. Away I goin' to find my mamma. Mr. Will fixes me up two papers, one 'bout a yard long and the other some smaller, but both has big gold seals what he says is the seal of the State of Missouri. He gives me money and buys my fare ticket to Texas and tells me they is still slave time down there and to put the papers in my bosom but to do whatever the white folks tells me, even if they wants to sell me. But he say, "Before you gets off the block, just pull out the papers, but just hold 'em up to let folks see and don't let 'em out of your hands, and when they sees them they has to let you alone."

Miss Olivia cry and carry on and say be careful of myself 'cause it sure is rough in Texas. She give me a big basket what had so much to eat in it I could hardly heft it and another with clothes in it. They puts me in the back end of the boat where the big, old wheel what run the boat was and I goes to New Orleans and the captain puts me on another boat and I comes to Galveston, and that captain puts me on another boat and I comes up this here Buffalo Bayou to Houston.

I looks round Houston, but not long. It sure was a dumpy little place then and I gets the stagecoach to Austin. It takes us two days to get there and I thinks my back busted sure enough, it was such rough ridin'.

Then I has trouble sure. A man ask me where I goin' and says to come along and he takes me to a Mr. Charley Crosby. They takes me to the block what they sells slaves on. I gets right up like they tells me, 'cause I 'lects what Mr. Will done told me to do, and they starts biddin' on me. And when they cried off and this Mr. Crosby come up to get me, I just pulled out my papers and helt 'em up high and when he sees 'em he say, "Let me see them." But I says, "You just look at it up here." He squints up and say, "This gal am free and has papers." And tells me he a legislature man and takes me and lets me stay with his slaves. He is a good man.

He tells me there's a slave refugee camp in Wharton County but I didn't have no money left, but he pays me some for workin' and when the War's over I starts to hunt Mama again, and finds her in Wharton County near where Wharton is. Law me, talk about cryin' and singin' and cryin' some more, we sure done it. I stays with Mama till I gets married in 1871 to John Armstrong. And then we all comes to Houston.

I gets me a job nussin' for Dr. Rellaford and was all through the yellow fever epidemic. I 'lects in '75 people die just like sheep with the rots. I'se seen folks with the fever jump from their bed with death on 'em and grab other folks. The doctor saved lots of folks, white and black, 'cause he sweat it out of 'em. He mixed up hot water and vinegar and mustard and some else in it.

But, law me, so much is gone out of my mind, 'cause I'se ninety-one year old now and my mind just like my legs, just kinda hobble round a bit.

FRANK BELL

Interviewed at Madisonville, Texas
Interviewer not identified
Age when interviewed: 86+

I WAS OWNED by Johnson Bell and born in New Orleans, in Louisiana. Accordin' to the bill of sale, I'm eighty-six years old, and my master was a Frenchman and was real mean to me. He run saloon and kept bad women. I don't know nothing about my folks, if I even had any, 'cept Mama. They done tell me she was a bad woman and a French Creole.

I worked round master's saloon, kept everything cleaned up after they'd have all night drinkin' parties, men and women. I earned nickels to tip off where to go, so's they could sow wild oats. I buried the nickels under rocks. If Master done cotch me with money, he'd take it and beat me nearly to death. All I had to eat was old stuff those people left, all scraps what was left.

One time some bad men come to Master's and gets in a shootin' scrape and they was two men kilt. I sure did run. But Marster cotch me and make me take them men to the river and tie a weight on them, so they'd sink and the law wouldn't get him.

The clothes I wore was some Master's old ones. They always had holes in them. Master he stay drunk nearly all time and was mean to his slave. I'm the only one he had, and didn't cost him nothing. He have bill of sale made, 'cause the law say he done stole me when I'm small child. Master kept me in chains sometimes. He shot several men. I didn't have no quarters but stays round the place and throw old sack down and lay there and sleep. I'm afraid to run, 'couse Marster say he'd hunt me and kill nigger.

When I'm about seventeen I marries a gal while Master on drunk spell. Master he run her off, and I slips off at night to see her, but he finds it out. He takes a big, long knife and cuts her head plumb off, and ties a great, heavy weight to her and makes me throw her in the river. Then he puts me in chains and every night he come give me a whippin' for a long time.

When war come, Master swear he not gwine fight, but the Yankees they captures New Orleans and throws Marster in a pen and guards him. He gets a chance and escapes.

When war am over he won't free me, says I'm valuable to him in his trade. He say, "Nigger, you's supposed to be free but I'll pay you a dollar a week and if you runs off I'll kill you." So he makes me do like before the War, but gives me about a dollar month, 'stead week. He says I cost more'n I'm worth, but he won't let me go. Times I don't know why I didn't die before I'm growed, sleepin' on the ground, winter and summer, rain and snow. But not much snow there.

Master helt me long years after the War. If anybody get after him, he told them I stay 'cause I wants to stay, but told me if I left he'd kill him another nigger. I stayed till he gits in a drunk brawl one night with men and women and they gits to shootin' and some kilt. Master got kilt.

Then I'm left to live or die, so I wanders from place to place. I nearly starved to death before I'd leave New Orleans, 'cause I couldn't think Master am dead and I afraid. Finally I gets up nerve to leave town and stays the first night in white man's barn. I never slept. Every time I hears something I jumps up and Master be standin' there, lookin' at me, but soon's I get up he'd leave.

Next night I slept out in a hay field, and Marster he get right top of a tree and start hollerin' at me. I never stays in that place. I gets gone from that place. I gets back to town fast as my legs carry me.

Then I gets locked up in jail. I didn't know what for, never did know. One the men says to me to come with him and takes me to the woods and gives me an ax. I cuts rails till I nearly falls, all with chain locked round feet, So I couldn't run off. He turns me loose and I wanders again. Never had a home. Works for men long 'nough to get fifty, sixty cents, then starts roamin' again, like a stray dog.

After long time I marries Feline Graham. Then I has a home and we has a white preacher marry us. We has one boy and he farms and I lives with him. I worked at sawmill and farms all my life, but never could make much money.

You know, the nigger was wild till the white man made what he has out of the nigger. He done educate them real smart.

MARY A. BELL
Interviewed at St. Louis, Missouri
Interviewed by Grace E. White
Age when interviewed: 85

I WAS BORN in Missouri, May 1, 1852, and owned by an old maid named Miss Kitty Diggs. I had two sisters and three brothers. One of my brothers was killed in de Civil War, and one died here in St. Louis in 1919. His name was Spot. My other brother, four years younger than I, died in October, 1925, in Colorado Springs.

Slavery was a mighty hard life. Kitty Diggs hired me out to a Presbyterian minister when I was seven years old, to take care of three children. I nursed in dat family one year. Den Miss Diggs hired me out to a baker named Henry Tillman to nurse three children. I nursed there two years. Neither family was nice to me. De preacher had a big farm. I was only seven years old so dey put me on a pony at meal time to ride out to de field and call de hands to dinner. After the meals were finished, I helped in the kitchen, gathered the eggs, and kept plenty busy. My father was owned by de Lewis family out in the country, but Miss Diggs owned my mother and all her children.

I never attended school until I came to St. Louis. When Abraham Lincoln was assassinated I had never been to school. Dat same year I attended school at Benton Barracks and went about six or seven months with de soldiers. There was no Negro schools in St. Louis in dat time. The next school I attended was St. Paul Chapel. I went there about six months. De next place I went to school was Eighteenth and Warren. I went there about two years. My next school was Twenty-third and Morgan, now Delmar Boulevard, in a store building. I went there between two and three years. I was very apt and learned fast. My father at de time I was going from school to school, was a nurse in Benton

Barracks and my mother taken in washing and ironing. I had to help her in de home with de laundry.

I so often think of de hard times my parents had in their slave days, more than I feel in my own hard times, because my father was not allowed to come to see my mother but two nights a week. Dat was Wednesday and Saturday. So often he came home all bloody from beatings his old nigger overseer would give him. My mother would take those bloody clothes off of him, bathe de sore places and grease them good and wash and iron his clothes, so he could go back clean.

But once he came home bloody after a beating he did not deserve and he run away. He scared my mother most to death because he had run away, and she done all in her power to persuade him to go back. He said he would die first, so he hid three days and three nights, under houses and in the woods, looking for a chance to cross the line, but de patterollers were so hot on his trail he couldn't make it. He could see de riders hunting him, but dey didn't see him. After three days and three nights he was so weak and hungry he came out and gave himself up to a nigger trader dat he knew. He begged de nigger trader to buy him from his owner, Mr. Lewis, because Marse Lewis was so mean to him and de nigger trader knew how valuable he was to his owner. De nigger trader promised he would try to make a deal with his owner for him, because de nigger trader wanted him.

So when dey brought Father back to his owner and asked to buy him, Mr. Lewis said there wasn't a plantation owner with money enough to pay him for Spot. Dat was my father's name, so of course that put my father back in de hands of Marse Lewis. Lewis owned a large tobacco plantation and my father was de head man on dat plantation. He cured all de tobacco, as it was brought in from the field, made all the twists and plugs of tobacco. His owner's son taught him to read, and dat made his owner so mad, because my father read de emancipation for freedom to de other slaves, and it made dem so happy, dey could not work well, and dey got so no one could manage dem when dey found out dey were to be freed in such a short time.

Father told his owner after he found out he wouldn't sell him, dat if he whipped him again, he would run away again, and keep on running away until he made de free state land. So de nigger trader begged my father not to run away from Marse Lewis, because if he did Lewis would be a ruined man, because he did not have another man who could manage de workers as Father did. So the owner knew freedom was about to be declared and my father would have de privilege of leaving, whether his owner liked it or not. So Lewis knew my father knew it as well as he did, so he sat down and talked with my father about the future and promised my father if he would stay with him and ship his tobacco for him and look after all of his business on his plantation after freedom was declared, he would give him a nice house and lot for his family right on his plantation. And Father had such influence over de other slaves he wanted him to convince de others dat it would be better to stay with their former owner and work for him for their living dan take a chance on strangers they did not know and who did not know dem. He pleaded so hard with my father dat Father told him all right to get rid of him. But Lewis had been so mean to Father dat down in Father's heart he felt Lewis did not have a spot of good in him. No place for a black man.

So Father stayed just six months after dat promise and taken eleven of the best slaves on de plantation and went to Kansas City and all of dem joined the U.S. Army. Dey enlisted de very night dey got to Kansas City and de very next morning de patterrollers were there on de trail after dem to take dem back home, but de officers said dey were now enlisted U.S. soldiers and not slaves and could not be touched.

In de county where I was raised de white people went to church in de morning and de slaves went in de afternoon. I was converted at the age of fourteen, and married in 1873. My husband died May 27, 1896, and I have been a widow ever since. I do get a pension now. I never started buying dis little old four-room frame dwelling until I was sixty-four years old and paid for it in full in six years and six months.

I told you my father's name was Spot, but that was his nickname in slavery. His full name was Spottwood Rice.

I married at de age of twenty-one and was de mother of seven children, but only have two living. My son's full name is William A. Bell. He is enlisted in de army in the Philippine Islands. I love army men; my father, brother, husband, and son were all army men. I love a man who will fight for his rights, and any person that wants to be something.

VIRGINIA BELL
Interviewed at Houston, Texas
Interviewer not identified
Age when interviewed: 88

I DON'T KNOW 'zackly how old I is. You see it ain't like things is today. The young folks can tell you their 'zact age and everything, but in those days we didn' pay much 'tention to such things. But I knows I was born in slavery times and my pappy told me I was born on a Christmas Day, but didn' 'member just what year.

We was owned by Massa Lewis. Thomas Lewis was his name, and he was a United States Lawyer. I ain't goin' to talk against my white folks like some cullud folks do, 'cause Massa Lewis was a mighty fine man and so was Miss Mary, and they treated us mighty good.

Massa had a big plantation near Opelousas and I was born there. I 'member the neighbor folks used to bring their cotton to the gin on his farm for ginnin' and balin'. My mother's name was Della. That was all, just Della. My pappy's name was Jim Blair. Both of them was from Virginny, but from diff'rent places, and was brought to Louisiana by nigger traders and sold to Massa Lewis. I know my pappy was lots older than my mother and he had a wife and five chillen back in Virginny and had been sold away from them out here. Then he and my mother started a family out here. I don' know what become of his family back in Virginny, 'cause when we was freed he stayed with us.

When I got old enough I was house girl and used to carry notes for Miss Mary to the neighbors and bring back answers. Miss Mary would say, "Now, Virginny, you take this note to such and such place and be sure and be back in such and such time." And I always was.

Massa Lewis had four or five families of us slaves, but we used to have some fun after work and us young folks would skip rope and play ring games. Durin' week days the field hands would work till the sun was just goin' down and then the overseer would holler "All right!" and that was the signal to quit. All hands knocked off Saturday noon.

We didn' have no schoolin' or preachin'. Only the white folks had them, but sometimes on Sundays we'd go up to the house and listen to the white folks singin'.

Iffen any of the slave hands wanted to get married, Massa Lewis would get them up to the house after supper time, have the man and woman join hands and then read to them outen a book. I guess it was the Scriptures. Then he'd tell 'em they was married but to be ready for work in the mornin'. Massa Lewis married us accordin' to Gospel.

Massa used to feed us good, too, and we had plenty clothes. Iffen we got sick, we had doctor treatment, too. Iffen a hand took sick in the field with a misery, they was carried to their quarters and Massa or Miss Mary would give them a dose of epecac and make them vomit and would send for the doctor. They wouldn' fool none iffen one of us took sick, but would clean us out and take care of us till we was well.

There was mighty little whippin' goin' on at our place, 'cause Massa Lewis and Miss Mary treated us good. They wasn't no overseer goin' to whip, 'cause Massa wouldn' allow him to. Let's see, I don' rec'lec' more than two whippin's I see anyone get from Massa, and that has been so long ago I don' rec'lec' what they was for.

When the War done come 'long it sure changed things, and we heerd this and that, but we didn't know much what it was about. Then one day Massa Lewis had all the wagons loaded with food and chairs and beds and other things from the house and our quarters, and I heerd him say we was movin' to Polk County, way over in Texas. I know it took us a long time to get there, and when we did I never see so much woods. It sure was diff'rent from the plantation.

I had to work in the fields, same as the rest, and we stayed there three years and made three crops of cotton, but not so much as on our old place, 'cause there wasn't so much clearin'. Then one day Massa Lewis told us we was free, just as free as he was—just like you take the bridle offen a hoss and turn him loose. We just looked 'roun as iffen we hadn' good sense. We didn' have nothin' nor nowhere to go, and Massa Lewis say iffen we finish makin' de crop, he would take us back to Opelousas and give us a place to stay and feed us. So after pickin' we goes back and when we git there we sees where those rascal Yankees 'stroyed everything —houses burned, sugar kettles broke up. It looked mighty bad.

Massa Lewis hadn' no money, but he fixed us up a place to stay and give us what he could to eat, but things was mighty hard for a while. I know pappy used to catch rabbits and take them to town and sell them or trade them for somethin' to eat, and you know that wasn't much, 'cause you can't get much for a little ol' rabbit.

Then the Provo' Marshal, that was his name, give us a order for things to put in a crop with and to live till we made the crop. 'Course, I guess we wasn' as bad off as some, 'cause white folks knew we was Massa Lewis' folks and didn' bother us none.

Then I got married to John Bell, and it was a Scripture weddin', too. He died twenty-eight years ago, but I has stayed married to him ever since. We had thirteen chillen, but they is all dead now 'cept four, but they was raised up right and they is mighty good to they ole mammy.

BOSTON BLACKWELL

Interviewed at North Little Rock, Arkansas
Interviewed by Beulah Sherwood Hagg
Age when interviewed: 98

I KNOWS MY AGE, good. Old Miss, she told me when I got sold— "Boss, you is thirteen—borned Christmas. Be sure to tell your new mistress and she put you down in her book." My borned name was Pruitt 'cause I got borned on Robert Pruitt's plantation in Georgia— Franklin County, Georgia. But Blackwell is my freed name. You see, after my mammy got sold down to Augusta—I wished I could tell you the man what brought her; I ain't never seed him since—I was sold to go to Arkansas, Jefferson County, Arkansas. Then was when Old Miss telled me I am thirteen. It was before the Civil War I come here. The onliest auction of slaves I ever seed was in Memphis, coming on to Arkansas. I heerd a girl bid off for eight hundred dollars. She was about fifteen, I reckon. I heerd a woman—a breeding woman—bid off for fifteen hundred dollars. They always brought good money. I'm telling you, it was when we was coming from Atlanta.

I'll tell you how I runned away and joined the Yankees. You know Abraham Lincoln declared freedom in '63, first day of January. In October '63, I runned away and went to Pine Bluff to get to the Yankees. I was on the Blackwell plantation south of Pine Bluff in '68. They was building a new house; I wanted to feel some putty in my hand. One early morning I climb a ladder to get a little chunk and the overseer man, he seed me. Here he come, yelling me to get down; he gwine whip me 'cause I's a thief, he say. He call a slave boy and tell him cut ten willer whips; he gwine wear every one out on me. When he's gone to eat breakfast, I runs to my cabin and tells my sister, "I'se leaving this here place for good." She cry and say, "Overseer man, he kill you." I says, "He kill me anyhow." The young boy what cut the whips—he named Jerry—he come along with me, and we wade the stream for long piece. Heerd the hounds a-howling, getting ready for to chase us. Then we hide in dark woods. It was cold, frosty weather. Two days and two nights we traveled. That boy, he so cold and hunngry, he want to fall out by the way, but I drug him on. When we gets to the Yankee camp all our troubles was over. We gets all the contraband we could eat. They was hundreds of runaways there. The Yankees feeds all them refugees on contraband. They made me a driver of a team in the quartermaster's department. I was always careful to do everything they told me. They told me I was free when I gets to the Yankee camp, but I couldn't go outside much. Iffen you could get to the Yankee's camp you was free right now.

That old story about forty acres and a mule, it make me laugh. They sure did tell us that, but I never knowed any person which got it. The officers telled us we would all get slave pension. That just exactly what they tell. They sure did tell me I would get a parcel of ground to farm. Nothing ever hatched out of that, neither.

When I got to Pine Bluff I stayed contraband. When the battle come, Captain Manly carried me down to the battleground and I stay there till fighting was over. I was a soldier that day. I didn't shoot no gun nor cannon. I carried water from the river for to put out the fire in the cotton bales what made the breastworks. Every time the 'Federates shoot, the cotton, it come on fire. So after the battle, they transfer me back to quartermaster driver. Captain Dodridge was his name. I served in Little Rock under Captain Haskell. I was swored in for during the War. It was on the corner of Main and Markham Street in Little Rock I was swored in. Year of '64. I was 5 feet, 8 inches high. Living in the army was purty good. Iffen you obeyed them Yankee officers they treated you purty good, but iffen you didn't they sure went rough on you.

After the soldiers all go away, the first thing, I work on the railroad. They was just beginning to come here. I digged pits out, going along front of where the tracks was to go. I get one dollar a day. I felt like the richest man in the world! I boarded with a white family. Always I was a-watching for my slave pension to begin coming. Before I left the army my captain, he telled me to file. My file number, it is 1,115,857. After I keeped them paper for so many years, white and black folks both telled me it ain't never coming—my slave pension—and I reckon the children tored up the papers. That number for me is filed in Washington.

After the railroad I went steamboating. First one was a little one; they call her *Fort Smith* 'cause she go from Little Rock to Fort Smith. It was funny, too, her captain was name Smith. Captain Eugene Smith was his name. He was good, but the mate was sure rough. They's plenty to do on a riverboat. Never is no time for rest. Load, unload, scrub. Just you do whatever you is told to do and do it right now, and you'll keep outen trouble, on a steamboat, or a railroad, or in the army, or wherever you is. That's what I knows.

I reckon they was right smart old masters what didn't want to let they slaves go after freedom. They hated to turn them loose. Just let them work on. Heap of them didn't know freedom come. I used to hear tell how the government had to send soldiers away down in the far back country to make them turn the slaves loose. I can't tell you how them free niggers was living; I was too busy looking out for myself. Heaps of them went to farming. They was sharecroppers.

Them Ku Kluxers was terrible—what they done to people. Oh, God, they was bad. They come sneaking up and runned you outen your house and take everything you had. They was rough on the women and children. People all wanted to stay close by where soldiers was. I sure knowed they was my friend.

After peace, I got with my sister. She's the onliest of all my people I ever seed again. She told me she was scared all that day I runned away She couldn't work, she shake so bad. She heerd overseer man getting ready to chase me and Jerry. He saddle his horse, take his gun and pistol, both. He gwine kill me on sight, but Jerry, he say he bring him back, dead or alive, tied to his horse's tail. But he didn't get us, Ha, Ha, Ha. Yankees got us.

Now you wants to know about this voting business. I voted for General Grant. Army men come around and registered you before voting time. It wasn't no trouble to vote them days; white and black all voted together. All you had to do was tell who you was vote for and they give you a colored ticket. All the men up had different colored tickets. Iffen you're voting for Grant, you get his color. It was easy. They was colored men in office, plenty. Colored legislators, and colored circuit clerks, and colored county clerks. They sure was some big officers colored in them times. They was all my friends. This here used to be a good county, but I tell you it sure is tough now. I think it's wrong— exactly wrong that we can't vote now. The Jim Crow law, it put us out. The Constitution of the United States, it give us the right to vote. It made us citizens, it did.

You just keeps on asking about me, lady. I ain't never been asked about myself in my *whole* life! Now you wants to know after railroading and steamboating what. They was still work the Yankee army wanted done. The War had been gone for long time. All over every place was bodies buried. They was bringing them to Little Rock to put in government graveyard. They sent me all over the state to help bring them here. Major Forsythe was my quartermaster then.

After that was done, they put me to work at St. John's hospital. The work I done there liked to ruin me for life. I cleaned out the water closets. After a while I took down sick from the work—the scent, you know —but I keep on till I get so far gone I can't stay on my feets no more. A misery got me in the chest; right here, and it been with me all through life; it with me now.

I filed for a pension on this ailment. I never did get it. The government never took care of me like it did some soldiers. They said I was not an enlisted man, that I was a employed man, so I couldn't get no pension. I give my whole life to the government for many years. White and black both always telling me I should have a pension. I stood on the battlefield just like other soldiers. Iffen I could of had some help when I been sick, I might not be so no account now.

DAVID BLONT
Interviewed in North Carolina
Interviewed by Mary Hicks
Age when interviewed: 90+

DE DAYS on de plantation was de happy days. De marster made us work through de week, but on Saturdays we used to go swimmin' in de river and do a lot of other things dat we like to do.

We didn't mind de work so much 'cause de ground was soft as ashes and de marster let us stop and rest when we got tired. We planted 'taters in de uplands and corn in de low grounds next de river. It was on de Cape Fear and on hot days when we was a-pullin' de fodder we'd all stop work about three o'clock in de evenin' and go swimmin'. After we come out'n de water we would work harder dan ever and de marster was good to us, 'cause we did work and we done what he asked us.

I 'members once de marster had a overseer dere dat was meaner dan a mean nigger. He always hired good overseers and a whole lot of times he let some Negro slave oversee. Well, dis overseer beat some of de half grown boys till de blood run down to dere heels and he told de rest of us dat if we told on him dat he'd kill us. We don't dare ask de marster to get rid of de man so dis went on for a long time.

It was as cold as de devil one day and dis overseer had a gang of us a-clearin' new ground. One boy ask if he could warm by de brush heap. De overseer said no, and after awhile de boy had a chill. De overseer don't care, but dat night de boy am a sick nigger. De next mornin' de marster gets de doctor, and de doctor say dat de boy has got pneumonia. He tells 'em to take off de boy's shirt and grease him with some tar, turpentine, and kerosene, and when dey starts to take de shirt off dey finds dat it am stuck. Dey had to grease de shirt to get it off 'cause de blood where de overseer beat him had stuck de shirt tight to de skin. De marster was in de room and he asked de boy how come it, and de boy told him.

De marster sorta turns white and he says to me, "Will you go and ask de overseer to stop here a minute, please?" When de overseer comes up de steps he asks sorta sassy-like, "What you want?" De marster says, "Pack you things and get off'en my place as fast as you can, you pesky varmint." De overseer sasses de marster some more, and den I sees de marster fairly lose his temper for de first time. He don't say a word, but he walks over, grabs de overseer by de shoulder, sets his boot right hard 'gainst de seat of his pants and sends him, all drawed up, out in de yard on his face. He close up like an umbrella for a minute, den he pulls hisself all together and he limps outen dat yard and we ain't never seed him no more.

Dere wasn't no marryin' on de plantation dem days, and as one old woman raised all of de chillens, me and my brother Johnnie ain't never knowed who our folks was. Johnnie was a little feller when de War ended, but I was in most of de things dat happen on de plantation for a good while.

One time dere, I done forgot de year, some white mens comes down de river on a boat and dey comes into de fields and talks to a gang of us and dey says dat our masters ain't treatin' us right. Dey tells us dat we oughta be paid for our work, and dat we hadn't oughta have passes to go anywhere. Dey also tells us dat we oughta be allowed to tote guns if we wants 'em. Dey says too dat sometime our masters was gwine to kill us all.

I laughs at 'em, but some dem fool niggers listens to em, and it 'pears dat dese men give de niggers some guns after I left and promised to bring em more de next week. I finds out de next day about dis and I goes and tells de marster. He sorta laughs and scratches his head. "Dem niggers am headed for trouble, Dave," he says to me, "and I wants you to help me." I says, "Yes sir, Marster." And he goes on, "You finds out when de rest of de guns comes, Dave, and let me know."

When de men brings back de guns I tells de marster, and I also tells him dat dey wants to hold a meetin'. "All right," he says, and laughs, "Dey can have de meetin'. You tell 'em, Dave, dat I said dat dey can meet on Tuesday in de pack house."

Tuesday evenin' he send dem all off to de low grounds but me, and he tells me to nail up de shutters to de pack house and to nail 'em up good. I does like he tells me to do and dat night de niggers marches in and sneaks deir guns in too. I is lyin' up in de loft and I hears dem say dat after de meetin' dey is gwine to go up to de big house and kill de whole family. I gets out of de winder and I runs to de house and tells de marster. Den me and him and de young marster goes out, and quick as lightnin', I slams de pack house door and I locks it. Den de marster yells at dem, "I'se got men and guns out here," he yells, "and if you don't throw dem guns of de hole up dere in de loft, and throw dem every one out I'se gwine to stick fire to dat pack house." De niggers 'liberates for a few minutes and den dey throws de guns out. I know how many dey has got so I counts till dey throw all out, den I gathers up dem guns and I totes 'em off to de Big House.

Well, sir, we keeps dem niggers shut up for about a week on short rations, and at de end of dat time dem niggers am cured for good. When dey comes out dey had three overseers 'stead of one, and de rules am stricter dan ever before, and den de marster goes off to de War. I reckon I was about fifteen or sixteen den and de marster carries me along for his personal servant and bodyguard and he leaves de rest of dem niggers in de fields to work like de dickens while I laughs at dem Yankees.

Jim belonged to Mr. Harley who lived in New Hanover County durin' de War; In fact, he was young Massa Harley's slave. So when young Massa Tom went to de War Jim went along too. Dey was at Manassas, dey tells me, when Massa Tom got kilt, and de orders was not to take no bodies off de field right den. Course Old Massa down near Wilmington don't know about young Massa Tom, but one night dey hears Jim holler at de gate. Dey goes runnin' out, and Jim has brung Massa Tom's body all dat long ways home so dat he can be buried in de family burying gound. De massa frees Jim dat night, but he stays on a long time after de War, and till de day he died he hated de Yankees for killin' Massa Tom. In fact we all hated de Yankees, 'specially after we near about starve dat first winter. I tried to make a livin' for me and Johnnie, but it was bad goin'. Den I comes to Raleigh and I gets along better. After I gets settled I brings Johnnie, and so we done purty good.

ANDREW BOONE

Interviewed in rural Wake County, North Carolina
Interviewed by Pat Matthews
Age when interviewed: 90

I BELONGED to Billy Boone in slavery time. He was a preacher. He lived and owned a plantation in Northampton County. The plantation was near woodland. The nearest river to the place was the Roanoke. My ole missus' name was Nancy. When Old Marster died I stayed around with first one, then another, of the chillens, 'cause Marster told me just before he died for me to stay with any of 'em I wanted to stay with. All dem ole people done dead and gone on.

Niggers had to go through thick and thin in slavery time, with rough rations most of de time, with just enough clothin' to make out with. Our houses were built of logs and covered with slabs. Dey was rived out of blocks of trees about eight feet in length. De chimleys was built of sticks and mud, den a coat of clay mud daubed over 'em. De cracks in de slave houses was daubed with mud too.

We worked from sun to sun. If we had a fire in cold weather where we was workin' Marster or de overseer would come and put it out. We et frozn meat and bread many times in cold weather. After de day's work in de fields was over we had a task of pickin' de seed from cotton till we had two ounces of lint or spin two ounces of cotton on a spinnin' wheel. I spun cotton on a spinnin' wheel. Dats de way people got clothes in slavery time.

I can't read and write but dey learned us to count. Dey learned us to count dis way. "Ought is an ought, and a figger is a figger, all for de white man an' nothin' for de nigger."

Dey sold slaves just like people sell hosses now. I saw a lot of slaves sold on de auction block. Dey would strip 'em stark naked. A nigger scarred up or whaled and welted up was considered a bad nigger and did not bring much. If his body was not scarred, he brought a good price. I saw a lot of slaves whipped and I was whipped myself. Dey whipped me with de cat-o'-nine-tails. It had nine lashes on it. Some of de slaves was whipped wid a cobbin paddle. De had forty hole in 'em and when you was buckled to a barrel dey hit your naked flesh with de paddle and everywhere dere was a hole in de paddle it drawed a blister. When de whippin' with de paddle was over, dey took de cat-o'-nine-tails and busted de blisters. By dis time de blood sometimes would be runnin' down deir heels. Den de next thing was a wash in salt water strong enough to hold up an egg. Slaves was punished dat way for runnin' away and such.

If you was out without a pass dey would sure get you. De patterrollers sure looked after you. Dey would come to de house at night to see who was there. If you was out of place, dey would wear you out.

Sam Joyner, a slave, belonged to Marster. He was runnin' from de patterrollers and he fell in a ole well. De patterroller went after Marster. Marster told 'em to get ole Sam out and whip him just as much as dey wanted to. Dey got him out of de well and he was all wet and muddy. Sam began takin' off his shoes, den he took off his pants and got in his shirttail. Marster, he say, "What you takin' off you clothes for, Sam?" Sam, he say, "Marster, you know you all can't whip dis nigger right over all dese wet clothes." Den Sam lit out. He run so fast he nearly flew. De patterrollers got on deir hosses and run him but dey could not ketch him. He got away. Marster got Sam's clothes and carried 'em to de house. Sam slipped up next morning, put his clothes on, and Marster said no more about it.

I was a great big boy when de Yankees come through. I was drivin' a two mule team and doin' other work on de farm. I drove a two hoss wagon when dey carried slaves to market. I went to a lot of different places.

My marster was a preacher, Billy Boone. He sold and bought niggers. He had fifty or more. He worked the grown niggers in two squads. My father was named Isham and my mother was Sarah Boone. Marster Boone whipped with de cobbin paddle and de cat-o'-nine-tails and used the salt bath and dat was 'nough. Plenty besides him whipped dat way.

Marster had one son, named Solomon, and two girls, Elsie and Alice. My mother had four children, three boys and one girl. The boys were named Sam, Walter, and Andrew, dats me, and de girl was Cherry.

My father had several children, 'cause he had several women besides Mother. Mollie and Lila Lassiter, two sisters, were also his women. Dese women was given to him and no other man was allowed to have anything to do with 'em. Mollie an' Lila both had chillens by him. Dere names wus Jim, Mollie, Liza, Rosa, Pete, and I can't remember no more of 'em.

De Yankees took just what dey wanted and nothin' stopped em', 'cause de surrender had come. Before de surrender de slave owners begun to scatter de slaves about from place to place to keep de Yankees from gettin' 'em. If de Yankees took a place de slaves nearby was moved to a place further off.

All I done was for de Rebels. I was with 'em and I just done what I was told. I was afraid of de Yankees cause de Rebels had told us dat de Yankees would kill us. Dey told us dat de Yankees would bore holes in our shoulders and work us to carts. Dey told us we would be treated a lot worser den dey was treating us. Well, de Yankees got here but they treated us fine. Den a story went 'round and 'round dat de marster would have to give de slaves a mule and a year's provisions and some land, about forty acres, but dat was not so. Dey never did give us anything. When de War ended and we was told we was free, we stayed on with Marster 'cause we had nothin' and nowhere to go.

We moved about from farm to farm. Mother died and Father married Maria Edwards after de surrender. He did not live with any of his other slave wives dat I knows of.

I have worked as a hand on de farm most of de time since de surrender and Daddy worked most of de time as a hand, but he had gardens and patches most everywhere he worked. I worked in New York City for fifteen years with Crawford and Banhay in de show business. I advertised for 'em. I dressed in a white suit, white shirt, and white straw hat, and wore tan shoes. I had to be a purty boy. I had to have my shoes shined twice a day. I lived at 18 Manilla Lane, New York City. It is between McDougall Street and Sixth Avenue. I married Clara Taylor in New York City. We had two children. The oldest one lives in New York. The other died and is buried in Raleigh.

W. L. BOST
Interviewed at Asheville, North Carolina
Interviewed by Marjorie Jones
Age when interviewed: 88

M Y MASSA'S NAME was Jonas Bost. He had a hotel in Newton, North Carolina. My mother and grandmother both belonged to the Bost family. My ole massa had two large plantations, one about three miles from Newton and another four miles away. It took a lot of niggers to keep work a-goin' on them both. The womenfolks had to work in the hotel and in the Big House in town. Ole Missus she was a good woman. She never allowed the massa to buy or sell any slaves. There never was an overseer on the whole plantation. The oldest colored man always looked after the niggers. We niggers lived better than the niggers on the other plantations.

I remember when I was a little boy, about ten years, the speculators come through Newton with droves of slaves. They always stay at our place. The poor critters nearly froze to death. They always come 'long on the last of December so that the niggers would be ready for sale on the first day of January. Many the time I see four or five of them chained together. They never had enough clothes on to keep a cat warm. The women never wore anything but a thin dress and a petticoat and one underwear. I've seen the ice balls hangin' on to the bottom of their dresses as they ran along, just like sheep in a pasture before they are sheared. They never wore any shoes. Just run along on the ground, all spewed up with ice. The speculators always rode on horses and drove the poor niggers. When they get cold, they make 'em run till they are warm again.

The speculators stayed in the hotel and put the niggers in the quarters just like droves of hogs. All through the night I could hear them mournin' and prayin'. I didn't know the Lord would let people live who were so cruel. The gates were always locked and they was a guard on the outside to shoot anyone who tried to run away. Them slaves look just like droves of turkey runnin' along in front of them horses.

I remember when they put 'em on the block to sell 'em. The ones 'tween eighteen and thirty always bring the most money. The auctioneer he stand off at a distance and cry 'em off as they stand on the block. I can hear his voice as long at I live.

If the one they going to sell was a young Negro man this is what he says: "Now gentlemen and fellow citizens here is a big black buck Negro. He's stout as a mule. Good for any kind o' work and he never gives any trouble. How much am I offered for him?" And then the sale would commence and the nigger would be sold to the highest bidder.

If they put up a young nigger woman, the auctioneer cry out: "Here's a young nigger wench, how much am I offered for her?" The poor thing stand on the block a shiverin' and a shakin' nearly froze to death. The poor mothers beg the speculators to sell 'em with their husbands, but the speculator only take what he want. So maybe the poor thing never see her husband again.

Old Massa always see that we get plenty to eat. O' course it was no fancy rations. Just corn bread, milk, fat meat, and 'lasses, but the Lord knows that was lots more than other poor niggers got. Some of them had such bad masters.

Us poor niggers never allowed to learn anything. All the readin' they ever hear was when they was carried through the big Bible. The massa say that keep the slaves in they places. They was one nigger boy in Newton who was terrible smart. He learn to read and write. He take other colored children out in the fields and teach em' about the Bible, but they forget it before the next Sunday.

Then the patterrollers they keep close watch on the poor niggers so they have no chance to do anything or go anywhere. They just like policemen, only worser, 'cause they never let the niggers go anywhere without a pass from his master. If you wasn't in your proper place when the patterrollers come they lash you till you was black and blue. The women got fifteen lashes and the men thirty. That is for just bein' out without a pass. If the nigger done anything worse he was taken to the jail and put in the whippin' post. They was two holes cut for the arms stretch up in the air and a block to put your feet in, then they whip you with cowhide whip. And the clothes sure never get any of them licks.

I remember how they kill one nigger whippin' him with the bullwhip. Many the poor nigger nearly killed with the bullwhip. But this one die. He was a stubborn Negro and didn't do as much work as his massa thought he ought to. He been lashed lot before. So they take him to the whippin' post, and then they strip his clothes off and then the man stand off and cut him with the whip. His back was cut all to pieces. The cuts about half inch apart. Then after they whip him they tie him down and put salt on him. Then after he lie in the sun awhile they whip him agin. But when they finish with he, he was dead.

Plenty of the colored women have children by the white men. She know better than to not do what he say. Didn't have much of that until the men from South Carolina come up here and settle and bring slaves. Then they take them very same children what have they own blood and make slaves out of them. If the missus find out she raise revolution. But she hardly find out. The white men not going to tell and the nigger women were always afraid to. So they just go on hopin' that things won't be that way always.

I remember how the driver, he was the man who did most of the whippin', used to whip some of the niggers. He would tie their hands together and then put their hands down over their knees, then take a stick and stick it 'tween they hands and knees. Then he take hold of them and beat 'em first on one side, then on the other.

Us niggers never have chance to go to Sunday school and church. The white folks feared for niggers to get any religion and education, but I reckon somethin' inside just told us about God and that there was a better place hereafter. We would sneak off and have prayer meetin'. Sometimes the patterrollers catch us and beat us good but that didn't keep us from tryin'. I remember one old song we used to sing when we meet down in the woods back of the barn. My mother she sing and pray to the Lord to deliver us out o' slavery. She always say she thankful she was never sold from her children, and that our massa not so mean as some of the others. But the old song it went something like this:

> Oh, Mother lets go down, lets go down, lets go down, lets go down.
> Oh, Mother lets go down, down in the valley to pray.
> As I went down in the valley to pray,
> Studyin' about that good ole way,
> Who shall wear that starry crown?
> Good Lord, show me the way.

Then the other part was just like that except it said "Father" instead of "Mother," and then "Sister" and then "Brother." Then they sing sometime:

> We camp awhile in the wilderness, in the wilderness, in the wilderness.
> We camp awhile in the wilderness, where the Lord makes me happy,
> And then I'm a-goin' home.

I don't remember much about the War. There was no fightin' done in Newton. Just a skirmish or two. Most of the people get everything just ready to run when the Yankee soldiers come through the town. This was toward the last of the War. 'Course the niggers knew what all the fightin' was about, but they didn't dare say anything. The man who owned the slaves was too mad as it was, and if the niggers said anything they get shot right then and there. The soldiers tell us after the War that we get food, clothes, and wages from our massas else we leave. But they was very few that ever got anything. Our ole massa say he not gwine pay us anything. 'Course his money was no good, but he wouldn't pay us if it had been.

Then the Ku Klux Klan came along. They were terrible dangerous. They wear long gowns, touch the ground. They ride horses through the town at night and if they find a Negro that tries to get nervy or have a little bit for himself, they lash him nearly to death and gag him and leave him to do the best he can. Sometime they put sticks in the top of the tall thing they wear and then put an extra head up there with scary eyes and great big mouth. Then they stick it clear up in the air to scare the poor Negroes to death.

They had another thing they call the "Donkey Devil" that was just as bad. They take the skin of a donkey and get inside of it and run after the poor Negroes. Them was bad times, them was bad times. I know folks think the books tell the truth but they sure don't. Us poor niggers had to take it all.

Then after the War was over we was afraid to move. Just like tarpins or turtles after 'mancipation. Just stick our heads out to see how the land lay. My mammy stay with Marse Jonah for about a year after freedom, then Ole Solomon Hall made her an offer. Ole man Hall was a good man if there ever was one. He freed all of his slaves about two years before 'mancipation and gave each of them so much money when he died; that is, he put that in his will. But when he die his sons and daughters never give anything to the poor Negroes.

My mother went to live on the place belongin' to the nephew of Solomon Hall. All of her six children went with her. Mother she cook for the white folks and the children make crop. When the first year was up us children got the first money we had in our lives. My mother certainly was happy.

We live on this place for over four years. When I was about twenty year old I married a girl from West Virginia, but she didn't live but just about a year. I stayed down there for a year or so and then I met Mamie. We came here and both of us went to work. We work at the same place.

We bought this little piece of ground about forty-two years ago. We gave one hundred twenty-five dollars for it. We had to buy the lumber to build the house a little at a time but finally we got the house done. It's been a good home for us and the children.

We have two daughters and one adopted son. Both of the girls are good cooks. One of them lives in New Jersey and cooks in a big hotel.

She and her husband come to see us about once a year. But the adopted boy, he was part white. We took him when he was small and did the best we could by him. He never did like to associate with colored people. I remember one time when he was a small child I took him to town and the conductor made me put him in the front of the streetcar 'cause he thought I was just caring for him and that he was a white boy. Well, we sent him to school until he finished. Then he joined the navy. I ain't seen him in several years. The last letter I got from him he say he ain't spoke to a colored girl since he has been there. This made me mad so I took his insurance policy and cashed it. I didn't want nothin' to do with him, if he deny his own color.

JACOB BRANCH
Interviewed at Double Bayou Settlement
   near Houston, Texas
Interviewer not identified
Age when interviewed: 86

I'SE BOUGHT and fetched here to Double Bayou when I'se just three year old. I and my half-brother, Eleck, he de baby, was both born in Louisiana on de Van Loos place, but I go by de name of Branch, 'cause my daddy name Branch. My mama name Renee. Dey split up us family and Elisha Stevenson buy my mama and de two chillen. I ain't never see my daddy no more and don't 'member him at all.

Old 'Lisha Stevenson he a great one for to raise pigs. He sell sometime five hundred hogs at one time. He take he dogs and drive dem hogs 'cross de Neches River all by hisself, to sell dem. Dat how he git money to buy niggers, sellin' hogs and cowhides.

Old Massa he sure a good old man, but de old missy, she a tornado. Her name Miss 'Liza. She could be terrible mean. But sometime she take her old morrel — dat a sack make for to carry things in — and go out and come back with plenty joints of sugarcane. She take a knife and sit on de gallery and peel dat cane and give a joint to every one de li'l chillen.

Mama, she work up in de Big House, doin' cookin' and washin'. Old Massa go buy a cullud man name Uncle Charley Fenner. He a good old cullud man. Massa brung him to de quarters and say, "Renee, here you husband," and den he turn to Uncle and say, "Charley, dis you woman." Den dey consider dem married. Dat de way dey marry den, by de massa's word. Uncle Charley, he good step-pa to us.

De white folks have de good house with a brick chimney. Us quarters dey good, snug li'l house with flue and oven. Dey didn't bother to have much furniture, 'cause us in dere only to sleep. Us have homemake bench and "Georgia Hoss" bed with hay mattress. All us cookin' and eatin' done in de kitchen of de Big House. Us have plenty to eat, too. De smokehouse always full of white 'taters and cracklin's hangin' on de wall. Us get dem most any time us want, just so long us didn't waste nothin'. Dey have big jar with buttermilk and allow us drink all us want.

Old lady 'Liza, she have three women to spin when she get ready make de clothes for everybody. Dey spin and weave and make all us clothes. Us all wear shirttail till us about twelve or fourteen, boys and gals, too. You couldn't tell us apart.

Us chillen start to work soon's us could toddle. First us gather firewood. Iffen it freezin' or hot us have to go to toughen us up. When us get li'l bigger us tend de cattle and feed hosses and hogs. By time us good sprouts us pickin' cotton and pullin' cane. Us ain't never idle. Sometime us get far out in de field and lay down in de corn row and nap. But, lawdy, iffen dey catch you, dey sure wore you out! Sunday de onliest rest day and den de white folks allow us play.

Massa never whip Uncle Charley, 'cause he good nigger and work hard. It make Missy mad and one time when Massa gone she go down in de field. Uncle Charley hoein' corn just like Massa done told him, just singin' and happy. Old Missy she say, "Nigger, I'se sho' gwine to whip you." He say, "What for you whip me, I doin' every bit what old Massa done tell me." But Missy think he gettin' it too good, 'cause he ain't never been whipped. She clumb over de fence and start down de row with de cowhide. Uncle Charley, he ain't even raise he voice, but he cut de last weed outen dat corn and commence to wave he hoe in de air, and he say, "Missey, I ain't 'vise you come any step closer." Dat sure make her mad, but she afraid to do nothin'.

One time she have another nigger named Charlie. Massa go on de trip and she tell dis Charley iffen he ain't finished grindin' all de cornmeal by Monday she gwine to give him a t'ousand lashes. He try, but he ain't able make dat much meal, so come Monday he runned off in de bayou. Dat night come de big freeze and he down dere with water up to he knees and when Massa come home and go get him, he so froze he couldn't walk. Dey brung him in de kitchen and Old Missy cuss him out. Soon's he thaw out, he done die right dere on de spot.

My pore mama! Every washday old Missy give her de beatin'. She couldn't keep de files from speckin' de clothes overnight. Old Missy get up soon in de mornin', before Mama have time get dem specks off. She snort and say, "Renee, I'se gwine to teach you how to wash." Den she beat Mama with de cowhide. Look like she cut my mama in two. Many's de time I edges up and tries take some dem licks off my mama. Slavery, one to nother, was purty rough. Every plantation have to answer for itself.

When I 'bout ten dey sets me ginnin' cotton. Old massa he done make de cotton with de hand crank. It built on a bench like. I gin de cotton by turnin' dat crank. When I gets a lapful I puts it in de tow sack and dey take it to Miss Susan to make de twine with it. I warm and damp de cotton before de fireplace before I start ginnin' it.

Dere school for de white chillen in Double Bayou and I used to go meet de chillen comin' home and dey stop 'longside de way and teach me my ABC. Dey done carry me as far as Baker in de book when Old Missy find it out and make dem stop. De War comin' on den and us darsn't even pick up a piece of paper. De white folks didn't want us to learn to read for fear us find out things.

One mornin' Eleck and me git up at crack of dawn to milk. All at once come a shock what shake de earth. De big fish jump clean out de bay and turtles and alligators run out deir ponds. Dey plumb ruint Galveston! Us runned in de house and all de dishes and things done jump out de shelf. Dat de first bombardment of Galveston. De soldiers put powder under people's houses and blowin' up Galveston.

Young Massa Shake Stevenson he volunteer and get kilt somewheres in Virginny. Young Massa Tucker Stevenson, he ain't believe in war and he say he never gwine fight. He hide in de woods so de conscrip' men can't find him. Old man LaCour come 'round and say he have orders for find Tucker and bring him in dead or alive. But 'cause he Old Massa's friend, he say, "Why don't you buy de boy's services off?" So Old Massa take de boat, *Catrig*, us calls it, and loads it with corn and such and us pole it down to Galveston. De people need dat food so much, dat load supplies done buy off Massa Tucker from fightin'.

After war starts lots of slaves runned off to get to de Yankees. All dem in dis part heads for de Rio Grande river. De Mexicans rig up flatboats out in de middle de river, tied to stakes with rope. When de cullud people gets to de rope de can pull deyself 'cross de rest de way on dem boats. De white folks rode de 'Merican side dat river all de time, but plenty slaves git through, anyway.

I wait on lots of soldiers. I have to get smartweed and boil it in salt water to bathe dem in. Dat help de rheumatism. Dem soldiers have rheumatism so bad for standin' day and night in de water.

Us sure in good health dem days. Iffen a cullud man weak dey move de muscles in he arms, bleed him, and give him plenty bacon and corn bread, and he git so strong he could lift a log. Dey didn't go in for cuttin' like dey do now. Dey get herbs out de woods, blue moss and quinine and calomel. I think people just die under pills, now. Old lady Field she make medicine with snakeroot and larkspur and marshroot and redroot.

After war am over Massa Tucker brung de freedom papers and read dem. He say us all am free as hell. Old man Charley so happy he just roll on de floor like a hoss and kick he heels. De next mornin' Mama start do somethin' and Missy cuss her out. I runned to Missy and say "Us free as de birds." She sure whip me for dat, but no more, 'cause she so mean us all leave.

Dat funny. Old man LaFour, what de head de patterrollers and so mean, he de first to help us niggers after freedom. He loan us he ox team and pay Uncle Charley a dollar de day for work and a dollar every time my mama wash for he wife.

Old Massa and Missy split up. She so mad she ain't give him no better show dan she done us. Old Massa gettin' some peaches one day and she come after him with de buggy whip. He git on he hoss and say, "Liz, you's gettin' broad as de beef. You too big for me." She so mad she spit fire. Lightnin' done kill her. She upstairs and de big streak hits her. It knock her under de bed.

De first freedom work I done am pullin' up potato hills at two bits a hunnerd. 'Bout two bits de most us could make in one day. I work two days to buy Mama de turkey hen for Christmas. Anything Mama want I think she got to have. I'se growed before I gets much as four bits a day. I'se done earn as much as a dollar fifty in my time, though.

When I'se twenty-five year old I marries Betty Baker, but she dead now. De Reverend Patterson he marry us. Us has four chillen livin'. Turah and Renee, dat my gals, Enrichs and Milton, dat my boys. Milton work in Houston and Enrich help me farm. I'se a Mason thirty year.

WILLIAM BRANCH
Interviewed at San Antonio, Texas
Interviewer not identified
Age when interviewed: 87

I WAS A slave. I was born May 13, 1850, on the place of Lawyer Woodson in Lunenburg County, Virginia. It was about seventy-five miles southwest of Richmond. They was two big plantations, one on one side the road, yother the yother. My marster owned seventy-five slaves. He raised tobacco and cotton. I worked tobacco sometime, sometime cotton. Dere wasn't no whippin' or switchin'. We had to work hard. Marster Woodson was a rich man. He live in a great big house, a lumber house painted white. And it had a great big garden.

De slaves lives in a long string of log houses. Dey had dirt floors and shingle roofs. Marster Woodson's house was shingle roof too. We had home cured bacon and veg'tables, dried corn, string beans, and dey give us hoecakes baked in hot ashes. Dere always was lots of fresh milk.

How's us slaves get de clothes? We carded de cotton, den de women spin it on a spinnin' wheel. After dat dey sew de garment together on a sewin' machine. We's got sewin' machine, wid a big wheel and a handle. One woman turn de handle and de yother woman do de sewin'. Dat's how we git de clothes for de seventy-five slaves. We makes clothes for de marster's whole family. De missis send de pattern and de slaves makes de clothes. Over nigh Richmond a friend of Marster Woodson has three hundred slaves. Dey makes all de clothes for dem.

I was with Marster till de Yankees come down to Virginia in 1861. De sergeant of de Yankees takes me up on his hoss and I goes to Washington wid de Yankees. I got to stay dere 'cause I'd run away from my marster.

I stay at de house of Marse Frank Cayler. He's an old time hack driver. I was his houseboy. I stay dere till de year 1870, den I goes to Baltimore and joins de United States Army. We's sent to Texas 'count of de Indians bein' so bad. Dey put us on a boat at Baltimore and we landed at Galveston.

Den we marches from Galveston to Fort Duncan. It was up, up, de whole time. We ties our bedclothes and rolls dem in a bundle wid a strap. We walks wid our guns and bedclothes on our backs, and de wagons wid de rations follows us. Dey is pulled by mules. We goes fifteen miles every day. We got no tents; night come, we unrolls de blankets and sleeps under de trees, sometime under de brush.

For rations, we got canned beans, milk, and hardtack. De hardtacks is three or four in a box; we wets 'em in water and cooks 'em in a skillet. We gets meat purty often. When we camps for de night de captain say, "You all kin go huntin'." Before we git to de mountains dere's deer and rabbits and dey ain't no fences. Often in de dark we sees a big animal and we shoots. When we bring him to camp, de captain say, "Iffen de cow got iron burns de rancher gwine to shoot hisself a nigger scout." But de cow ain't got no iron, it's—what de name of de cow what ain't feel de iron? Maverick. Yes sir, we gets lots of dem mavericks. We's goin' along de river bottom, and before we comes to Fort Duncan we sees de cactus and muskeet. Dere ain't much cattle, but one colored scout shoots hisself a bear. Den we eats high. Fort Duncan were made of slab lumber and de roof was gravel and grass.

Den we's ordered to Fort Davis and we's in de mountains now. Climb, climb all day, and de Indians give us a fit° every day. We kills some Indians and dey kills a few soldiers. We was at Fort Clark awhile. At Fort Davis I joins de colored Indian Scouts. I was in Captain George L. Andrew's Company K.

We's told de northern Cheyennes is on a rampus and we's goin' to Fort Sill in Indian Territory. Before we gits to Fort Concho°° de Comanches and de Apaches give us a fit. We fitten' 'em all de time and when we gets away from de Comanches and Apaches we fitten de Cheyennes. Dey's seven feet tall. Dey couldn't come through that door.

When we gits to Fort Sill, General Davidson say de Cheyennes is off deir reservation, and he say, "You boys is got to get dem back. Iffen you kill 'em, dey can't get back to the reservation." Den we goes scoutin' for de Cheyennes and dey is scoutin' for us. Dey gets us first. On de Wichita River was five hundred of 'em and we got seventy-five colored Indian

° Fight.
°° Now San Angelo.

Scouts. Den Red Foot, de chief of de Cheyennes, he come to see Captain Lawson and say he want rations for his Indians. De captain say he can't give no rations to Indians off de reservation. Red Foot say he don't care about no reservation and he say he take what we got. Captain Lawson allow we gotter git reinforcements.

We got a guide in de scout troop, he calls hisself Jack Kilmartin. De captain say, "Jack, I'se in trouble, how kin I get a dispatch to General Davidson?" Jack says, "I kin get it through." And Jack, he crawl on his belly and through de brush and he lead a pony, and when he gets clear he rides de pony bareback till he get to Fort Sill. Den General Davidson he sound de general alarm and he send two companies of cavalry to reinforce us. But de Cheyennes give 'em a fit all de way, dey's gotter cut deir way through de Cheyennes.

And Colonel Shafter comes up, and goes out in de hills in his shirt sleeves jus' like you's sittin' dere. Dey's snow on de ground and de wind's cold, but de colonel don't care, and he say, "What's dis order General Davidson give? Don't kill de Cheyennes? You kill 'em all from de cradle to de Cross."

And den we starts de attack. De Cheyennes got Winchesters and rifles and repeaters from de government. Yes sir, de government give 'em de guys dey used to shoot us. We got de old fashion muzzle loaders. You puts one ball in de muzzle and shove de powder down wid de ramrod. Den we went in and fit 'em and 'twas like fightin' a wasp's nest. Dey kills a lot of our boys and we nearly wipes 'em out. Den we disarms de Cheyennes we captures, and turns deir guns to de regiment.

I come to San Antonio after I'se mustered out and goes to work for de Bell Jewelry Company and stays dere till I can't work no more. Did I like de army? I'd rather be in de army dan a plantation slave.

JOHN BROWN
Interviewed in Tulsa, Oklahoma
Interviewer not identified
Age when interviewed: 87

MOST OF the folks have themselves a regular birthday but this old colored man just pick out any of the days during the year—one day just about as good as another. I been around a long time but I don't know when I got here. That's the truth. Nearest I figures it the year was 1850—the month don't make no difference nohow. But I know the borning was down in Talledega County, Alabama, near the county seat town.

Miss Abby was with my mammy that day. She was the wife of Master John Brown. She was with all the slave women every time a baby was born. Or, when a plague of misery hit the folks she knew what to do and what kind of medicine to chase off the aches and pains. God bless her! She sure loved us Negroes.

Most of the time there was more'n three hundred slaves on the plantation. The oldest ones come right from Africa. My grandmother was one of them. A savage in Africa—a slave in America. Mammy told it to me. Over there all the natives dressed naked and lived on fruits and nuts. Never see many white mens. One day a big ship stopped off the shore and the natives hid in the brush along the beach. Grandmother was there. The ship men sent a little boat to the shore and scattered bright things and trinkets on the beach. The natives were curious. Grandmother said everybody made a rush for them things soon as the boat left. The trinkets was fewer than the peoples. Next day the white folks scatter some more. There was another scramble. The natives was feeling less scared, and the next day some of them walked up the gangplank to get things off the plank and off the deck. The deck was covered with things like they'd found on the beach. Two-three hundred natives on the ship when they feel it move. They rush to the side but the plank was gone. Just dropped in the water when the ship moved away.

Folks on the beach started to crying and shouting. The ones on the boat was wild with fear. Grandmother was one of them who got fooled, and she say the last thing seen of that place was the natives running up and down the beach waving their arms and shouting like they was mad. The boat men come up from below where they had been hiding and drive the slaves down in the bottom and keep them quiet with the whips and clubs. The slaves was landed at Charleston. The town folks was mighty mad 'cause the blacks was driven through the streets without any clothes, and drove off the boat men after the slaves was sold on the market. Most of that load was sold to the Brown plantation in Alabama. Grandmother was one of the bunch.

The Browns taught them to work. Made clothes for them. For a long time the natives didn't like the clothes and try to shake them off. There was three Brown boys—John, Charley, and Henry. Nephews of old lady Hyatt who was the real owner of the plantation, but the boys run the place. The old lady, she lived in the town. Come out in the spring and fall to see how is the plantation doing. She was a fine woman. The Brown boys and their wives was just as good. Wouldn't let nobody mistreat the slaves. Whippings was few and nobody got the whip unless he need it bad. They teach the young ones how to read and write; say it was good for the Negroes to know about such things.

Sunday was a great day around the plantation. The fields was forgotten, the light chores was hurried through, and everybody got ready for the church meeting. It was out of the doors, in the yard fronting the big lot where the Browns all lived. Master John's wife would start the meeting with a prayer and then would come the singing — the old timey songs.

But the white folks on the next plantation would lick their slaves for trying to do like we did. No praying there, and no singing.

The master gave out the week's supply on Saturday. Plenty of hams, lean bacon, flour, cornmeal, coffee, and more'n enough for the week. Nobody go hungry on that place! During the growing season all the slaves have a garden spot all their own. Three thousand acres on that place — plenty of room for gardens and field crops.

Even during the War foods was plentiful. One time the Yankee soldiers visited the place. The white folks gone and I talks with them. Ask me lots of questions—got any meats—got any potatoes—got any this—some of that—but I just shake my head and they don't look around. The old cook fixes them up though. She fry all the eggs on the place, skillet the ham and pan the biscuits! Them soldiers fill up and leave the house friendly as anybody I ever see!

The Browns wasn't bothered with the Ku Klux Klan either. The Negroes minded their own business just like before they was free. I stayed on the plantation till the last Brown die. Then I come to Oklahoma and works on the railroad till I was too old to hustle the grips and packages.

JULIA BROWN
Interviewed at Atlanta, Georgia
Interviewed by Geneva Tonsill
Age when interviewed: 85

I WAS BORN four miles from Commerce, Georgia, and was thirteen year old at surrender. I belonged to the Nash family—three old maid sisters. My mama belonged to the Nashes and my papa belonged to General Burns; he was a officer in the War. There was six of us chillens, Lucy, Melvina, Johnnie, Callie, Joe, and me. We didn't stay together long, as we was give out to different people. The Nashes didn't believe in selling slaves and we was known as their niggers. They sold one once 'cause the other slaves said they would kill him 'cause he had a baby by his own daughter. So to keep him from bein' kilt, they sold him.

My mama died the year of surrender. I didn't fare well after her death. I had such a hard time. I was give to the Mitchell family and they done every cruel thing they could to me. I slept on the floor nine years, winter and summer, sick or well. I never wore anything but a cotton dress, a shimmy, and drawers. That woman didn't care what happened to the niggers. Sometime she would take us to church. We'd walk to the church house. I never went nowhere else. That woman took delight in callin' slaves. She'd lash us with a cowhide whip. I had to shift for myself.

They didn't mind the slaves matin', but they wanted their niggers to marry only amongst them on their place. They didn't allow 'em to mate with other slaves from other places. When the women had babies they was treated kind and they let 'em stay in. We called it "lay-in," just about like they do now. We didn't go to no hospitals as they do now. We just had our babies and a granny to catch 'em. We didn't have all the pain-easin' medicines then. The granny would put a rusty piece of tin or a ax under the mattress and this would ease the pain. The granny put a ax under my mattress once. This was to cut off the after-pains and it sure did, too. We'd set up the fifth day and after the "layin-in" time was up we was allowed to walk outdoors and they told us to walk around the house just once and come in the house. This was to keep us from takin' a 'lapse.

We wasn't allowed to go around and have pleasure as the folks does today. We had to have passes to go wherever we wanted. When we'd get out there was a bunch of white men called the "patty rollers." They'd come in and see if all us had passes, and if they found any who didn't have a pass, he was whipped, give fifty or more lashes—and they'd count them lashes. If they said a hundred, you got a hundred. They was somethin' like the Klu Klux. We was 'fraid to tell our masters about the patty rollers because we was scared they'd whip up again, for we was told not to tell. They'd sing a little ditty; it went somethin' like this:

> Run, nigger, run. De patty rollers'll get you.
> Run, nigger, run. You'd better get away.

We was 'fraid to go any place.

Slaves was treated in most cases like cattle. A man went about the country buyin' up slaves like buyin' up cattle and the like, and he was called a "speculator." Then he'd sell 'em to the highest bidder. Oh! it was pitiful to see chillen taken from their mothers' breasts, mothers sold, husbands sold from wives. One woman he was to buy had a baby, and of course the baby come before he bought her and he wouldn't buy the baby, said he hadn't bargained to buy the baby, too, and he just wouldn't.

My uncle was married, but he was owned by one master and his wife was owned by another. He was allowed to visit his wife on Wednesday and Saturday, that's the onliest time he could get off. He went on Wednesday and when he went back on Saturday his wife had been bought by the speculator and he never did know where she was.

I worked hard always. You can't imagine what a hard time I had. I split rails like a man. I used a huge glut and a iron wedge drove into the wood with a maul, and this would split the wood. I help spin the cotton into thread for our clothes. The thread was made into big broaches—four broaches made four cuts, or one hank. After the thread was made we used a loom to weave the cloth. We had no sewin' machine—had to sew by hand. My mistress had a big silver bird and she would always catch the cloth in the bird's bill and this would hold it for her to sew.

I didn't get to handle money when I was young. I worked from sunup to sundown. We never had overseers like some of the slaves. We was give so much work to do in a day and if the white folks went off on a vacation they would give us so much work to do while they was gone and we better have all of that done, too, when they'd come home.

They made me hoe when I was a child and I'd keep right up with the others, 'cause they'd tell me that if I got behind a runaway nigger would get me and split open my head and get the milk outen it. Of course, I didn't know then that weren't true. I believed everything they told me and that made me work the harder.

Some of the white folks was very kind to their slaves. Some did not believe in slavery and some freed them before the War and even give 'em land and homes. Some would give the niggers meal, lard, and like that.

There was a white man, Mister Jim, that was very mean to the slaves. He'd go round and beat 'em. He'd even go to the little homes, tear down the chimneys, and do all sorts of cruel things. The chimneys was made of mud and straw and sticks; they was powerful strong, too. Mister Jim was just a mean man, and when he died we all said God got tired of Mister Jim being so mean and kilt him.

When they laid him out on the coolin' board, everybody was settin' round, moanin' over his death, and all of a sudden Mister Jim rolled offen the coolin' board. Such a-runnin' and gettin' outen that room you never saw! We said Mister Jim was tryin' to run the niggers and we was 'fraid to go about at night. I believe it then. Now that they's embalmin' I know that must have been gas and he was purgin', for they didn't know nothin' about embalmin' then. They didn't keep dead folks outen the ground long in them days.

Doctors wasn't so plentiful then. They'd go round in buggies and on hosses. Them that rode on a hoss had saddle pockets just filled with little bottles and lots of them. He'd try one medicine and if it didn't do no good he'd try another until it did do good. And when the doctor went to see a sick person he'd stay right there until he was better. He didn't just come in and write a prescription for somebody to take to a drugstore.

We used herbs a lot in them days. When a body had dropsy we'd set him in a tepid bath made of mullein leaves. There was a jimsonweed we'd use for rheumatism, and for asthma we'd use tea made of chestnut leaves. We'd get the chestnut leaves, dry them in the sun just like tea leaves, and we wouldn't let them leaves get wet for nothin' in the world while they was dryin'. We'd take poke collard roots, boil them, and then take sugar and make a syrup. This was the best thing for asthma. It was known to cure it, too. For colds and such we used horehound; made candy outen it with brown sugar. We used a lots of rock candy and whiskey for colds, too. They had a remedy that they used for consumption — take dry cow manure, make a tea of this, and flavor it with mint and give it to the sick person. We didn't need many doctors then for we didn't have so much sickness in them days, and naturally they didn't die so fast. Folks lived a long time then. They used a lot of peach tree leaves, too, for fever, and when the stomach got upset we'd crush the leaves, pour water over them, and wouldn't let them drink any other kind of water till they was better. I still believes in them old homemade medicines, too, and I don't believe in so many doctors.

We didn't have stoves plentiful then; just ovens we set in the fireplace. I'se toted a many a armful of bark—good old hickory bark to cook with. We'd cook light bread—both flour and corn. The yeast for this bread was made from hops. Coals of fire was put on top of the oven and under the bottom, too. Everything was cooked on coals from a wood fire — coffee and all. The victuals was good in them days. We got our vegetables outen the garden in season and didn't have all the hothouse vegetables. There was racks fitted in the fireplace to put pots on. Once there was a big pot settin' on the fire, just boilin' away with a big roast in it. As the water boiled, the meat turned over and over, comin' up to the top and goin' down again. Old Sandy, the dog, come into the kitchen. He set there awhile and watched that meat roll over and over in the pot, and all of a sudden-like he grabbed at that meat and pulls it outen the pot. Course he couldn't eat it 'cause it was hot and they got the meat before he et it.

The kitchen was away from the Big House, so the victuals was cooked and carried up to the house. I'd carry it up myself. We couldn't eat all the different kinds of victuals the white folks et and one mornin' when I was carryin' the breakfast to the Big House we had waffles that was a pretty golden brown and pipin' hot. They was a picture to look at and I just couldn't keep from takin' one, and that was the hardest waffle for me to eat before I got to the Big House I ever saw. I just couldn't get rid of that waffle 'cause my conscience whipped me so.

They taught me to do everything. I'd use battlin' blocks and battlin' sticks to wash the clothes. We all did. The clothes was taken out of the water and put on the block and beat with a battlin' stick, which was made like a paddle. On wash days you could hear them battlin' sticks poundin' every which way. We made our own soap, used old meat and grease, and poured water over wood ashes which was kept in a rack-like thing, and the water would drip through the ashes. This made strong lye. We used a lot of such lye, too, to boil with.

Sometimes the slaves would run away. Their masters was mean to them that caused them to run away. Sometimes they would live in caves. They got along all right—what with other people slippin' things into 'em. And, too, they'd steal hogs, chickens, and anything else they could get their hands on. Some white people would help, too, for there was some white people who didn't believe in slavery.

They would always try to find them slaves that run away, and if they was found they'd be beat or sold to somebody else. My grandmother run away from her master. She stayed in the woods and she washed her clothes in the branches. She used sand for soap.

I stayed with the Mitchells till Miss Hannah died. I even helped to lay her out. I didn't go to the graveyard, though. I didn't have a home after she died and I wandered from place to place, stayin' with a white family this time and then a nigger family the next time. I moved to Jackson County and stayed with a Mister Frank Dowdy. I didn't stay there long, though. Then I moved to Winder, Georgia. They called it "Jug Tavern" in them days, 'cause jugs was made there.

I married Green Hinton in Winder. Got along well after marryin' him. He farmed for a livin' and made a good livin' for me and the eight chillens, all born in Winder. The chillens was grown nearly when he died and was able to help me with the smallest ones. I got along all right after his death and didn't have such a hard time raisin' the chillens. Then I married Jim Brown and moved to Atlanta. Jim farmed at first for a livin' and then he worked on the railroad—the seaboard. He helped to grade the first railroad track for that line. He was a sand-dryer.

After he moved here he bought this home. I'se lived here twenty years. Jim was killed on the railroad. He was comin' in the railroad yard one day and stepped off the little engine they used for the workers right in the path of the L & N train. He was cut up and crushed to pieces. He didn't have a sign of a head. They used a rake to get up the pieces they did get. A man brought a few pieces out here in a bundle and I wouldn't even look at them.

I got a little money from the railroad, but the lawyer got most of it. He brought me a few dollars out and told me not to discuss it with anyone nor tell how much I got. I tried to get some of the men that worked with him to tell me just how it all happened, but they wouldn't talk, and it was scandalous how them niggers held their peace and wouldn't tell me anything. The boss man came out later but he didn't seem interested in it at all, so I got little or nothing for his death. The lawyer got it for hisself.

JAMES CAPE
Interviewed at Fort Worth, Texas
Interviewer not identified
Age when interviewed: 100

I'SE BORN in yonder Southeast Texas and I don't know what month or de year for sure, but 'twas more dan a hundred years ago. My mammy and pappy was born in Africa, dats what dey's told me. Dey was owned by Marster Bob Houston and him had de ranch down dere, where dey have cattle and hosses.

When I'se old 'nough to set on de hoss, dey larned me to ride, tendin' hosses. 'Cause I'se good hoss rider, dey uses me all de time gwine after hosses. I goes with dem to Mexico. We crosses de river lots of times. I 'members once when we was a drivin' about two hundred hosses north-wards. Dey was a bad hailstorm comes into de face of de herd and dat herd turns and starts de other way. Dere was five of us riders and we had to keep dem hosses from scatterment. I was de leader and do you know what happens to dis nigger if my hoss stumbles? Right dere's where I'd still be! Marster give me a new saddle for savin' de hosses.

One day Marster Bob comes to me and says, "Jim, how you like to join de army?" You see, de War had started. I says to him, "What does I have to do?" And he says, "Tend hosses and ride 'em." I was young den and thought it would be lots of fun, so I says I'd go. So de first thing I knows, I'se in de army away off east from here, somewhere dis side of St. Louis, and in Tennessee and Arkansas and other places. I goes in de army 'stead of Dr. Carroll.

After I gets in de army, it wasn't so much fun, 'cause tendin' hosses and ridin' wasn't all I does. No sir, I has to do shootin' and get shooted at! One time we stops de train, takes Yankee money and lots of other things off dat train. Dat was way up de other side of Tennessee.

You's heard of de battle of Independence? Dat's where we fights for three days and nights. I'se not tendin' hosses dat time. Dey gives me a rifle and sends me up front fightin' when we wasn't runnin'. We does a heap of runnin' and dat suits dis nigger. I could do dat better'n advance. When de order comes to retreat, I'se all ready.

I gets shot in de shoulder in dat fight and lots of our soldiers gets killed and we loses our supply, just leaves it and runs. Another time we fights two days and nights and de Yankees was bad dat time, too, and we had to run through de river. I sure thought I'se gwine get drowned den. Dat's de time we tries to get in St. Louis, but de Yankee mans stop us.

I'se free after de War and goes back to Texas, to Gonzales County, and gets a job doin' cowboy work for Marster Ross herdin' cattle. And right dere's where I'se lucky for not gettin' in jail or hanged. It was dis way: I'se in town and dat man, Ross, says to me, "I understand you's a good cowhand," and he hires me and takes me way out. No house for miles before we comes to de ranch with cattle and I goes to work. After I'se workin' awhile, I wonders how come dey brings in such fine steers so often and I says to myself, "Marster Ross must have heaps of money for to buy all dem steers." Dey pays no attention to de raisin' of cattle, just brings 'em in and drives dem 'way.

One time Marster Ross and six mens was gone a week and when dey comes back, one of 'em was missin'. Dey had no steers dat time and dey talks about gettin' frusterated and how one man gets shot. I says to myself, "What for was dey chased and shot at?" Den I 'members Marster Bob Houston done told me about rustlers and how dey's hanged when dey's caught, and I know den dat's how come all dem fine steers is drove in and out all de time. But how to get away, dere's de puzzlement. I not know which way to go and dere's no houses anywhere near. I keeps gettin' scareter, and every time somebody comes, I thinks it's de law. But Marster Ross drives de cattle north and I says to him, "I'se good hand at de drive.

Kin I go with you next time you goes North?" And not long after dat we starts and we gets to Kansas City. After Marster Ross gets shut of de critters, he says, "We'll rest for couple days, den starts back." I says to me, "Not dis nigger."

I sneaks away and was settin' on a bench when along comes a white man and he's tall, had dark hair, and was fine lookin'. He says to me, "Is you a cowhand?" So I tells him I is, and he says he wants a hand on his farm in Missouri and he says, "Come with me." He tells me his name was James and takes me to his farm where I tends cattle and hosses for three years and he pays me well. He gives me more'n I earns. After three years I leaves, but not 'cause I learned he was outlaw, 'cause I learned dat long time afterwards. I'se lonesome for Texas and dat's how I comes to Fort Worth and here's where I'se stayed ever since.

I'se married about forty years ago to a woman dat had eight chillens. We separated 'cause dem chillens cause arguments. I can fight one, but not de army.

RICHARD CARRUTHERS
Interviewed in rural area near Houston, Texas
Interviewer not identified
Age when interviewed: 100

I WANTS TO tell the Gospel truth. My mammy's name was Melia Carruthers and my papa's name was Max. My papa's papa's name was Carruthers, too. My brothers' names was Charlie and Frank and Willie and John and Tom and Adam.

When I was still little, Mr. Billy Coats bought my mama and us and with about five hundred of his slaves we set out to come to Texas. We goes to Bastrop County and starts to work. My old missy—her name was Missy Myra—was ninety-nine year old and her head was bald as a egg and had wens on it as big as eggs, too.

In them days the boss men had good houses but the niggers had log cabins and they burned down oftentimes. The chimney would catch fire, 'cause it was made out of sticks and clay and moss. Many the time we have to get up at midnight and push the chimney away from the house to keep the house from burnin' up.

The chairs was mostly chunks of cordwood put on end, or slabs, just rough, and the beds was built like scaffoldin'. We made a sort of mattress out of corn shucks or moss.

My missy, she was good, but the overseer, he was rough. His temper born of the devil, himse'f. His name was Tom Hill, but us called him "Devil Hill."

Old Devil Hill, he used to whip me and the other niggers if we don't jump quick enough when he holler and he stake us out like you stake out a hide and whip till we bleed. Many the time I set down and made a eight-plait whip, so he could whip from the heels to the back of the head till he figger he get the proper retribution. Sometime he take salt and rub on the nigger so he smart and burn proper and suffer misery. They was a calaboose right on the plantation, what look like a icehouse, and it was sure bad to get locked up in it.

Us got provisions allowanced to us every Saturday night. If you had two in the family, they allowanced you one-half gallon 'lasses and twelve to fifteen pounds bacon and a peck of meal. We have to take the meal and parch it and make coffee out of it. We had our flours. One of them we called biscuit flour and we called it "shorts." We had rye and wheat and buck grain.

If they didn't provision you 'nough, you just had to slip round and get a chicken. That easy 'nough, but grabbin' a pig sure 'nough problem. You have to catch him by the snoot so he wont squeal, and clomp him tight while you knife him. That ain't stealin', is it? You has to keep right on workin' in the field, if you ain't allowanced 'nough, and no nigger like to work with his belly groanin'.

When the white preacher come he preach and pick up his Bible and claim he gettin' the text right out from the good Book and he preach: "The Lord say, don't you niggers steal chickens from your missus. Don't you steal your master's hogs." That would be all he preach.

Us niggers used to have a prayin' ground down in the hollow and sometime we come out of the field, between eleven and twelve at night, scorchin' and burnin' up with nothin to eat, and we wants to ask the good Lord to have mercy. We puts grease in a snuff pan or bottle and make a lamp. We takes a pine torch, too, and goes down in the hollow to pray. Some gets so joyous they starts to holler loud and we has to stop up they mouth. I see niggers get so full of the Lord and so happy they drops unconscious.

I kept a eye on the niggers down in the cotton patch. Sometime they lazy round and if I see the overseer comin' from the Big House I sings a song to warn 'em, so they not get whipped, and it go like this:

> Hold up, hold up, American Spirit!
> Hold up, hold up, H-O-O-O-O-O-O-O!

We used to go huntin' and they was lots of game—bears and panthers and coons. We have bear dog, fox dog, and rabbit dog that mostly just go by the name of houn' dog. Then they have a dog to run niggers.

I never tried the conjure, but they would take hair and brass nails and thimbles and needles and mix them up in a conjure bag. But I knows one thing. They was a old gin between Wilbarger and Colorado and it was haunted with spirits of kilt niggers. Us used to hear that old mill hummin' when dark come and we slip up easy, but it stop. Then when you slip away it start up.

I 'member when the stars fell. We runs and prays, 'cause we thinks it Judgment day. It sure scared dumb old Devil Hill, them stars was over his power.

On Sundays we put shoes on our feet and they was brass toed. They was so hard and stiff they go "tump, tump, tump," when we walk. That's the only day we got 'cept Christmas and then we just got somethin' extry to eat. All them women sure knowed how to cook! I often tell my wife how glad I was one mornin' when my missy give me a hot, butter biscuit. I goes down and shows it to all the other boys. We didn't get them hot, butter biscuits in them days.

I used to dance the pigeon wing, and swing my partners round. Was them womenfolks knock-kneed? You sure couldn't tell, even when you swung 'em round, 'cause they dresses was so long.

I'se been all 'round the mountain and up on top of it in my day. Durin' slave time I been so cold I most turn white and they set me before the fire and poultice me with sliced turnips. Come a norther and it blow with snow and sleet and I didn't have 'nough clothes to keep me warm.

When a nigger marry, he slick up his lowers and put on his brass-toed shoes, then the preacher marry him out of the Bible. My pappy have a pass to visit my mammy and if he don't have one, the patteroller conk him on the head. My grandma and grandpa come here in a steamboat. The man come to Africa and say, "Man and woman, does you want a job?" So they gets on the boat and then he has the 'vantage.

When I was twenty-one and some more, I don't know just how old, I was a free man. That was the day I shouted. We niggers scattered like partridges. I had a fiddle and I'd play for the white folks wherever I went, when they has the balls. I marries after 'while, but I don't know what year, 'cause we never done paid no 'tention to years. My first wife died after a long time, I think about thirty-four year and I married another and she died this very year. Just three months later I marries my housekeeper, named Luvena Dixon, 'cause I always lived a upright life and I knowed the Lord wouldn't like it if I went on livin' in the same house with Luvena without we was married. She is fifty-two year old, and we is happy.

HENRY CHEATAM

Interviewed at Marysville, Alabama
Interviewed by Ila B. Prine
Age when interveiwed: 87

I SURE 'MEMBERS plenty about de slave days. I was born in 1850 near West Point. Dat's in Clay County, Mississippi, you know. I belonged to Mr. Tom Hollingshead who was killed in de Civil War. I 'members all de slaves agoin' in to take a last look at him after dey done brung his body home. My mammy's name was Emmeline Cheatam, and my pappy's was Sam Cheatam. I don't remember my grandpappy and grandmammy at all.

Us slaves lived in log cabins what was daubed with clay to keep de rain and wind out, and de chimneys was made of clay and sticks. De beds was homemade and nailed agin' de wall with legs on de outer side. De massa's house was built of logs too, but it much bigger'n de nigger cabins and set way out in front of ours. After Massa was kilt, Old Miss had a nigger overseer and dat was de meanest devil dat ever lived on de Lord's green earth. I promise myself when I growed up dat I was a-goin' to kill dat nigger if it was de last thing I ever done. Lots of times I'se seen him beat my mammy, and one day I seen him beat my auntie who was big with a child, and dat man dug a round hole in de ground and put her stomach in it, and beat and beat her for a half hour straight till de baby come out right dere in de hole.

Mistis allow such treatment only 'cause a heap of times she didn't know nothin' about it, and de slaves better not tell her, 'cause dat overseer whip 'em if he finds out dat dey done gone and told. I'se seed some terrible things in my time. When de slaves would try to run away our overseer would put chains on deir legs with big long spikes between deir feets, so dey couldn't get away. Den Ise' seen great bunches of slaves put up on de block and sold just like dey was cows. Sometimes de chillens would be separated from dere maws and paws.

I come pretty near to bein took away from my maw. When de slaves was bein' divided, one of Old Miss' daughters was a-goin' to Texas, and I was goin' to have to go when somebody hollered "Freedom!" and I sure was glad 'cause I could stay with my mammy now.

In does days us had plenty of good plain food, such as pot likker, greens, cornbread, 'taters, peas, pears, and at hog killin' us had chittlin's and pig jowls and back bone. Den us would cotch possums at night when dey come up in de corn field. Us never seed no flour, though.

As for fishin', we never did none, 'cause we hadda work too hard. We worked from can to can't. Get up at sunrise, go to de field, and stay till dark. In de middle of de day dey would send out somethin' to eat to de field, with a barrel of water. But for breakfast and supper, us hadda cook our own grub dey give us.

Our clothes weren't many. Us chillens wore a one-piece suit made outen ausenberg, and us would have to take dat off at night, wash it, and put it back on de next day. As for shoes, chillen never had none. You see, I was just a chile, just big enough to tote water to de fields.

I 'members when de Yankees was a-comin' through I helped to carry be hosses to de woods and helped to hide de meat and bury de valuables, 'cause dem Yankees took whatever dey wanted, and you better not say nothin', neither, 'cause dey had dem long swords a-hangin' at deir sides.

In dem days, de slaves done all de work and carried all de news. De marsters sent notes from one plantation to another, and when dey wanted de niggers to come to de Big House dey would blow an old cow horn. Dey had certain number of blows for certain niggers. Dat is, de niggers dat was somethin'. Dey would also use dis horn for possom and coon huntin' at night. De li'l niggers at night went to de Big House to spin and weave. I'se spun a many roll and carded a many bat of cotton. I'se also made a many taller candle by tyin' strings onto a long stick and droppin' dem down into moulds filled with taller. I'se hid many a night in de fence corners when I'd be a-goin' somewheres to get my mammy some tobacco. De patterrollers would be out lookin' for slaves dat didn't have no pass from deir overseer and I'd hear dem a-comin' and I'd hide till dey pass on, 'cause if dey cotch me I sure gwine have a sound beatin'.

De owners always took care of us, and when us got sick dey would get a doctor, and Old Miss was all right, but dat overseer was a devil. He wouldn't allow no meetin' on de place. Sometimes us would slip down de hill and turn de wash pot bottom upwards so de sound of our voices would go under de pot, and us'd have a singin' and prayin' right dere. Most of de slaves could go sometimes to de white folks' church when dey gets a pass from deir massa, but dat mean overseer always tried to keep us from goin' so's us couldn't learn nothin'. He didn't want us to learn to read or write neither. Us didn't have nothin' but food and clothes. We didn't have no garden of our own and dere weren't no celebratin', 'ceptin' at hog killin'. Dat was de biggest day of de year.

On Saturday afternoon we was allowed to play, but I can't 'member none of de games. Us just played like all li'l niggers did den. At nighttime us just went to our cabins and went to bed, 'cause we weren't allowed to do no singin'. Most of de singin' was done in de fields.

About funerals and weddin's. Us niggers never married and I don't 'member any big weddin's of de white folks. But dey buried folks den de same as dey does now, in a box. Dey would bury de slaves as dey done de white folks, but us didn't even have no baptizin' on account of dat overseer. He didn't like for us to get religion. 'Course, all slaves didn't have hard treatment like us did, 'cause deir overseer and marster weren't as mean as ours.

We didn't know nothin' about no hoodoo stuff in dem days. Dey only had homemade medicines, dat is unless dey got sure 'nough powerful sick, and den dey would go to see a doctor. Us used boneset tea made from a weed. Lord, it was bitterer dan quinine, and it were good for de chills and fever, and it would purge you too. Den us used life-everlastin' tea for fever, and Jerusalem brush weed to get rid of worms.

But I knows dere is ghosts, 'cause when I was a little boy my mammy come in from de field and laid across de bed and I was sittin' in front of de fireplace and a big somethin' like a cow without no head come in de door and I commence to beat on it with my fists. Den my mammy say: "What matter with you, nigger?" Den dat critter he walk right out de door. I looked outen de window and dere it was a-goin' in Aunt Martha's cabin. I never did see it no more. Den another time a white man died and my mammy was to stay with his sister; and dis spirit like an angel come to my mammy and told her to tell de white lady to read de Bible backwards three times, 'cause dere was one talent between her and Jesus. After dat she were comforted. Another time, my pappy, Sam Cheatam, who was a wicked man, was a-sittin' in front of de fire and a big brindle dog come to de door and started barkin'. My pappy say: "What in de hell am dat?" and snapped his fingers at de dog. De dog he den dropped dead. Some folks say dat dere ain't no such things as ghosts, but I know dere is, 'cause dere is good spirits and bad spirits.

I'se had two wives, but I was only a young nigger when I had de first one, and had two chillens by her. Den I left her 'cause she weren't no account. Dats been forty year ago, and I ain't never seen my chillens in all dem years. My second wife I got when I lived thirty miles below Birmingham, Alabama, at de old Bank Mines. Dats been thirty-five year ago and us is still together. Us ain't never had no chillens.

PETER CLIFTON
Interviewed at Winnsboro, South Carolina
Interviewed by W. W. Dixon
Age when interviewed: 89

YOU WANT me to start with my first memory and touch de high spots till dis very day? Dat'll take a long time but I glad to find someone to tell dat to. I 'members when I was a boy, drivin' de calves to de pasture, a highland moccasin snake rise up in de path. I see dat forked tongue and them bright eyes right now. I so scared I couldn't move out my tracks. De mercy of de Lord cover me with His wings. Dat snake uncoil, drop his head, and silently crawl away. Dat was on de Biggers Mobley place 'tween Kershaw and Camden, where I was born, in 1848.

My pappy named Ned; my mammy named Jane. My brothers and sisters was Tom, Lizzie, Mary, and Gill. Us live in a log house with a plank floor and a wooden chimney dat was always catchin' afire and de wind comin' through and fillin' de room with smoke and cinders. It was just one of many others, just like it, dat made up de quarters. Us had peg beds for de old folks and just pallets on de floor for de chillen. Mattresses was made of wheat straw but de pillows on de bed was cotton. I does 'member dat Mammy had a chicken feather pillow she made from de feathers she saved at de kitchen.

My grandpappy was named Warren and Grandmammy name Maria. De rule on de place was: "Wake up de slaves at daylight, begin work when they can see, and quit work when they can't see." But they was careful of de rule dat say: "You mustn't work a child, under twelve years old, in de field."

My master's first wife, I heard him say, was Mistress Gilmore. Dere was two chillen by her. Was Master Ed, dat live in a palace dat last time I visit Rock Hill and go to 'member myself to him; then dere was Miss Mary dat marry her cousin, Dr. Jim Mobley. They had one child, Captain Fred, dat took de Catawba rifles to Cuba and whip Spain for blowin' up de Maine. Master Biggers had a big plantation and a big mansion four miles southeast of Chester. He buy my mammy and her chillen in front of de courthouse door in Chester, at de sale of de Clifton estate. Then he turn round and buy my pappy dere, 'cause my mammy and sister Lizzie cryin' about him have to leave them. I wasn't born then. Marster Biggers was a widower then and went down and courted de widow Gibson, who had a plantation and fifty slaves 'tween Kershaw and Camden. Dere is where I was born.

Marster had one child, a boy, by my mistress, Miss Sallie. They call him Black George. Him live long enough to marry a angel, Miss Kate Mc-Crorey. They had four chillen. Dere got to be ninety slaves on de place before war come on. One time I go with Pappy to de Chester place. Seem like more slaves dere than on de Gibson place. Us was fed up to de neck all de time, though us never had a change of clothes. Us smell pretty rancid maybe, in de winter time, but in de summer us no wear very much. Girls had a slip on and de boys happy in their shirt tails.

De overseer on de place was named Mr. Mike Melton. He poor man but him come from good folks, not poor white trash. But they was cussed by Marster, when after de War they took up with de Republican party. Sad day for old Marster when him didn't hold his mouth.

Marster Biggers believe in whippin' and workin' his slaves long and hard; then a man was scared all de time of being sold away from his wife and chillen. His bark was worse than his bite, though, for I never knowed him to do a wicked thing like dat. To whip a slave, they put de foots in a stock and clamp them together. Then they have a crosspiece go right across de breast high as de shoulder. Dat crosspiece long enough to bind de hands of a slave to it at each end. They always strip them naked and sometime they lay on de lashes with a whip, a switch, or a strap.

I see Marster buy a many a slave. I never saw him sell but one and he sold dat one to a drover for four hundred fifty dollars, cash down on de table, and he did dat at de request of de overseer and de mistress. They was uneasy about him.

They give us Christmas Day. Every woman got a handkerchief to tie up her hair. Every girl got a ribbon, every boy a Barlow knife, and every man a shin plaster. De neighbors call de place, de Shin Plaster, Barlow, Bandanna place. Us always have a dance in de Christmas.

After freedom when us was told us had to have names, Pappy say he love his old Marster Ben Clifton de best and him took dat titlement, and I'se been a Clifton ever since.

I meets Christina and seek her out for to marry. Dere was somethin' about dat gal dat day I meets her, though her hair had about a pound of cotton thread in it, dat just attracted me to her like a fly will sail 'round and light on a 'lasses pitcher. I kept de Ashford Ferry Road hot till I got her. I had to ask her old folks for her before she consent. Dis took about six months. Everything had to be regular. At last I got de preacher, Reverend Ray Shelby, to go down dere and marry us. Her have been a blessin' to me every day since. Us have seven chillen. They's scattered east, west, north, and south. De only one left is just David, our baby, and him is a baby six foot high and fifty-one years old.

Yes sir, us had a bold, drivin', pushin', marster, but not a hard-hearted one. I sorry when the military come and arrest him. It was dis a way. Him try to carry on with free labor about like him did in slavery. Chester was in military district number two. De whole state was under dat military government. Old Marster went to de field and cuss a nigger woman for de way she was workin', choppin' cotton. She turnt on him with de hoe and gashed him about de head with it. Him pull out his pistol and shot her.

Dr. Babcock say de wound in de woman not serious. They swore out a warrant for Marster Biggers, arrest him with a squad, and take him to Charleston, where him had nigger jailers and was kicked and cuffed about like a dog. They say de only thing he had to eat was cornmeal mush brought 'round to him and other nice white folks in a tub and it was ladled out to them through de iron railin' into de palms of deir hands. Mistress stuck by him, went and stayed down dere. The filthy prison and hard treatments broke him down, and when he did get out and come home, him passed over de river of Jordan, where I hopes and prays his soul finds rest. Mistress say one time they threatened her down dere dat if she didn't get up ten thousand dollars they would send him where she would never see him again.

MARTHA COLQUITT

Interviewed at Athens, Georgia
Interviewed by Sarah H. Hall
Age when interviewed: 85

WHEN I WAS BORN, my ma belonged to Marse Billie Glen and us lived on his big plantation way down below Lexington. My pa was Anderson Mitchell. He come from Milledgeville and belonged to Mr. D. Smith. The Smithies lived close by Marse Billie's place. My ma was Healon Mitchell. I don't know what her last name was before she married. She was born in Virginny, and her and my grandma was sold and brought to Georgia when Ma was a baby. Grandma never did see none of her other chillen or her husband no more, and us never did hear nothin' about 'em.

Ma had four chillen. Lucy was my onliest sister. Mr. Deavenport bought her and she growed up at his place, what was called "De Glade." It was a big fine place at Point Peter, Georgia. Lucy married a Taylor. My brother, Isaac, was raised at Mr. Hamilton's place at Point Peter. After he growed up, he worked in Atlanta and bought him a home dere. He got in a fight with a man what had done stabbed his mule, and de man hurt Isaac so bad he went crazy and died in de asylum in Milledgeville, but dey took him back and buried him in Atlanta.

My older brother was Anderson Mitchell, and after freedom come he got work in Athens at de compress. His boss man moved to Augusta and took Anderson with him to work in de compress dere. One day somethin' blowed up and he was scalded so bad it paralyzed him. Dey brought him back here, but he soon died.

Ma's house was right on de edge of Marse Billie's yard, 'cause she was de cook. Grandma lived in de same house with Ma and us chillen, and she worked in de loom house and wove cloth all de time. She wove de checkedy cloth for de slaves clothes, and she made flannel cloth too, leastways, it was part flannel. She made heaps of kinds of cloth.

Our beds had big homemade posties and frames, and us used ropes for springs. Grandma brought her featherbed with her from Virginny, and she used to piece up a heap of quilts out of our old clothes and any kind of scraps she could get a hold of. I don't know what de others had in dey cabins 'cause Ma didn't allow her chillen to visit round de other folkses none.

60

Ma's chillen all had victuals from de white folkses kitchen. After Marse Billie's family done et and left de table, de cook was supposed to take what was left to feed de house niggers and her own chillen, and us did have sure 'nough good victuals. All de other slave folks had dey rations weighed out to 'em every week and dey cooked in dey own cabins. When de wheat was ground at de mill it made white flour, and shorts, and seconds. Most of de shorts was weighed out in rations for de slave folks. Now and den at Christmas and special times dey got a little white flour. Dey liked corn bread for regular eatin'. Dey was always lots of hogs on Marse Billie's plantation, and his colored folkses had plenty of side meat. Slaves never had no time to hunt in de daytime, but dey sure could catch lots of possums at night, and dey knowed how to get catfish at night, too.

'Cross de road from de Big House, Marse Bill had a big garden, and he seed dat his help had plenty of somethin' good to boil. Dey weren't no separate gardens. Dey didn't have time to work no gardens of dey own.

In summertime us chillen wore just one piece of clothes. It was a sack apron. In winter Grandma made us yarn underskirts and yarn drawers buttoned down over our knees. Ma made our home-knit stockings. Dey called our brass toed shoes "brogans." I don't 'spect you ever seed a brass toed shoe!

Our Big House sure was one grand fine place. Why, it must have been as big as de Mill Stone Baptist Church. It was all painted white with green blinds and had a big old high porch dat went nigh all 'round de house.

If I ever did hear what Marse Billie's wife was named, I done plumb clear forgot. Us called her "Mistress" long as she lived and I don't re-collect hearin' her called nothin' else. Marster and Mistress never had no chillen whilst I was dere. Miss Lizzie was dey youngest child and she was most grown when I was born.

Marse Billie's overseer lived in a four-room house up de road a piece from the Big House. Nobody thought about none of Marse Billie's over seers as poor white folkses. Every overseer he ever had was decent and respectable. 'Course, dey weren't in de same class with Marse Billie's family, but dey was all right. Dey was four or five homes nigh our planta-tion, but all of 'em belonged to rich white folkses. If dey was any part white folkses round us chillen never heard nothin' of 'em.

I don't know just how many slaves Marse Billie had, but dey sure was a drove of 'em. Sometimes he had 'em all get together in de back yard at de Big House, and dey just filled up de yard.

De overseer blowed a horn to wake 'em up just before day, so as everybody could cook, eat, and get out to de fields by sunrise. Dey quit nigh sundown, in time for 'em to feed the stock, do de milkin', tend to bringin' in de wood, and all sorts of other little jobs dat had to be done before it got too dark to see. Dey never was no work done at night on our plantation.

If any of Marse Billie's help was whipped, I never knowed nothin' about it. Dey used to say dat if any of 'em didn't work right de overseer would take 'em to de workshop. Us chillen never did know what happened when dey took 'em to de workshop. It was too far away for us to hear what happened dere. De workshop was a big lone shed off to itself, where dey had de blacksmith place, and where harness was mended, and all sorts of fixin' done to de tools and things.

Us never heard of no jail. Marse Billie bossed his place and us never knowed about no trouble. De workshop was de nighest thing to a jail or a court dat anybody on our plantation knowed anything about. Us never seed nobody in chains till long after de War, when us was livin' in Lexington, and Mr. Jim Smith come through dere with some colored folkses all chained up, but us never did know how come dey was chained.

No slave never runned away from Marse Billies plantation. Dey never even wanted to try. Dey was always afraid dey might not be able to take as good care of deyselves as Marse Billie did for 'em, and dey didn't know what would happen to 'em off de plantation.

I heared 'em talkin' about patterrollers, but I never did see one. Folkses said dey would get you and beat you if dey catch you off de plantation where you belonged without no pass. If any of Marse Billie's slaves got catched by de patterrollers, I never knowed nothin' about it.

I never heared of no trouble 'twixt de white folkses and de colored folkses. Grandma and Ma never allowed us to go to no other cabins, and us didn't hear about what was goin' on amongst de others. At night Ma always spinned and knit, and Grandma, she sewed, making clothes for us chillen. Dey done it 'cause dey wanted to. Dey was workin' for deyselves den. Dey weren't no work at night. On Saturday night, Ma bathed all her chillen. I don't know what de other families done den. Slaves was allowed to frolic Saturday night, if dey behaved deyselves. On Sunday nights dey most always had prayer meetings.

On Christmas mornin' all of us would come up to de yard back of de Big House and Marse Billie and de overseer handed out presents for all. Dey was a little dram and cake too. Us chillen got dolls, and dresses, and aprons. Them stuffed rag dolls was de prettiest things! On New Year's day all de mens would come up to de Big House early in de mornin' and would work lively as dey could a-cuttin' wood and doing all sorts of little jobs till de dinner bell rung. Den Marse Billie would come out and tell 'em dey was startin' de New Year right a-workin' lively and fast. Den he would say dat dey would be fed good and looked after good, long as dey worked good. He give 'em a good taste of dram and cake all round, and let 'em go back to dey cabins for dinner, and dey could have de rest of de day to frolic.

Dem corn shuckin's us used to have sure was a sight. Corn would be piled up high as dis house, and de folkses would dance round and holler and whoop. Ma allowed us chillen to watch 'em about a half hour; den made us come back inside our cabin, 'cause dey always give de corn shuckin' folkses some dram, and things would get mighty lively and rough by de time all de corn was shucked.

On bright moonshiny nights folkses would invite de neighbors to come for cotton pickin's. After the cotton was picked dey would eat barbecue, and dance, and have a big time.

I never seed but one weddin' before freedom come, and dat was when Marse Billie's daughter, Miss Lizzie Glenn, married Mr. Detweiler. Dey had everything at dat weddin', just everything. Miss Lizzie had on a white silk dress a-trailin' so far behind her dat it took two ladies to tote her train. Her veil was floatin' all about her, and she was just de prettiest thing I ever did see in my whole life. A long time after dat, Mr. Detweiler, he died, and left Miss Lizzie with two chillen, and she married Mr. Roan.

I never seed no slave marriage. Ma went to 'em sometimes, but she never allowed us to go, 'cause she said us was too little. Marse Billie sent after his own preacher, and de couple would come up to de Big House and stand in de parlor door to be married before Master and Mistess. Den de colored folkses would go back down to de cabins and have a weddin' supper and frolic and dance. Dat's what Ma told me about 'em.

Us used to play lots, but us never did have no special name for our playin'. "Swingin' in de corner," was when us all joined hands in a long row, and de leader would begin to run round in circles, and at de other end of de line dey would soon be runnin' so fast dey was most flyin'.

Us all de time heard folkses talkin' about voodoo, but my grandma was powerful religious, and her and Ma told us chillen voodoo was a no 'count doin' of de devil, and Christians was never to pay it no attention. Us was to be happy in de Lord, and let voodoo and de devil alone. None of us liked to hear screech owls holler, 'cause everybody thought it means somebody in dat house was goin' to die if a scheech owl lit on your chimney and hollered, so us would stir up de fire to make de smoke drive him away. I always runned out and tried to see 'em, but old as I is, nigh eighty-six, I ain't never seed no screech owl.

I sure does believe in haunts, 'cause I done heard one and I seed it too, leastwise I seed its light. It was about thirty years ago, and us had just moved in a house where a white family had moved out. The ma had died a few days after a little baby was born, and de baby had died too. One night I heard a strange sound like somebody movin' round in de house, and pretty soon a dim light come a-movin' into my room real slow and after goin' round de room it went out of sight in de closet.

Next day I went to see de white folkses what had lived dere before us moved in, and de husband told me not to worry, dat it was his wife's haunt. He said she was huntin' for some money she had hid in de house, 'cause she wanted her chillen what was still livin' to have it. I went back home and almost tore dat house down lookin' for dat money. Long as us lived dere, I would see dat light now and den at night, and I always hoped it would lead me to de money but it never did.

When folkses got sick, Marse Billie had 'em looked after. Mistess would come every day to see about 'em, and if she thought dey was bad off, she sent after Dr. Davenport. Dr. Davenport come dere so much till he courted and married Marse Billie's daughter, Miss Martha Glenn. I was named for Miss Martha.

Dey sure did take special good care of the mammies and de babies. Dey had a separate house for 'em, and a granny woman who didn't have nothin' else to do but look after colored babies and mammies. De granny woman took de place of a doctor when de babies was born, but if she found a mammy in a bad fix she would ask Mistess to send for Dr. Davenport.

Us didn't have no separate church for colored folkses. De white folkses had a big Baptist church dey called Mill Stone Church down at Goosepond, a good ways down de road from Marse Billie's plantation. It sure was a pretty sight to see, dat church, all painted white and set in a big oak grove. Colored folkses had dey place in de gallery. Dey weren't allowed to join de church on Sunday, but dey had regular Saturday afternoons for de slaves to come and confess dey faith, and join de church. Us didn't know dey was no other church but de Baptist. All de baptizin' was done on Sunday by de white preacher. First he would baptize de white folkses in de pool back of de church and den he would baptize de slaves in the same pool.

My grandma was a powerful Christian woman, and she did love to sing and shout. Dat's how come Marse Billie had her locked up in de loom room when de Yankee mens come to our plantation. Grandma would get to shoutin' so loud and she would make so much fuss nobody in de church could hear de preacher and she would wander off from de gallery and go downstairs and try to go down to de white folkses aisles to get to de altar where de preacher was, and dey was always lockin' her up for disturbin' worship, but dey never could break her from dat shoutin' and wanderin' 'round de meetin' house, after she got old.

Dem Yankee soldiers rode up in de Big House yard and begun to ask me questions about where Marse Billy was, and where everything on de place was kept. But I was too scared to say nothin'. Everything was quiet and still as could be, 'cept for Grandma a-singin' and a-shoutin' up in de loom house all by herself. One of dem Yankees tried the door and he asked me how come it was locked. I told him it was 'cause Grandma had disturbed de Baptist meetin' with her shoutin'. Dem mens grabbed de ax from de woodpile and busted de door down. Dey went in and got Grandma. Dey asked her about how come she was locked up, and she told 'em de same thing I had told 'em. Dey asked her if she was hungry, and she said she was. Den dey took dat ax and busted down de smokehouse door and told her she was free now and to help herself to anything she wanted, 'cause everything on de plantation was to belong to de slaves dat had worked dere. Dey took Grandma to de kitchen and told Ma to give her some of de white folkses dinner. Ma said, "But de white folkses ain't et yet." "Go right on," de Yankees said, "and give it to her, de best in de pot, and if dey's anything left when she gets through, maybe us will let de white folkses have some of it."

Dem brash mens strutted on through de kitchen into de house and dey didn't see nobody else downstairs. Upstairs dey didn't even have de manners to knock at Mistess door. Dey just walked right on in where my sister, Lucy, was combin' Mistess' long pretty hair. They told Lucy she was free now and not to do no more work for Mistess. Den all of 'em grabbed dey big old rough hands into Mistess' hair, and dey made her walk downstairs and out in de yard, and all de time dey was a-pullin' and jerkin' at her long hair, tryin' to make her point out to 'em where Marse Billie had done had his horses and cattle hid out. Us chillens was a-cryin' and takin' on 'cause we loved Mistess and us didn't want nobody to bother her. Dey made out like dey was goin' to kill her if she didn't tell 'em what dey wanted to know, but after awhile dey let her alone.

After dey had told all de slaves dey could find on de place not to do no more work, and to go help deyselves to anything dey wanted in de smokehouse, and about de Big House and plantation, dey rode off, and us never seed no more of 'em.

After de Yankees was done gone off, Grandma begun to fuss: "Now, dem soldiers was tellin' us what ain't so, 'cause ain't nobody got no right to take what belongs to Marster and Mistess." And Ma joined in: "Sure it ain't no truth in what dem Yankees was a-sayin'," and us went right on livin' just like us always done till Marse Billie called us together and told us de War was over and us was free to go where us wanted to go and us could charge wages for our work.

When freedom come my pa wanted us to move off right away over to Mr. Smithies' place so our family could be together, but us stayed on with Marse Billie de rest of de year. Den Pa and Ma moved to Lexington, where Pa digged wells and ditches and made right good pay. Ma took all four of us chillen and run a good farm. Us got along fine.

Before de War, all work stopped on de plantation for de funeral of a slave. Grandma didn't think chillen ought to see funerals, so de first one I ever seed, was when Ma died two years after de War was done over. A jackleg colored preacher talked, but he didn't have sense 'nough to preach a sure 'nough sermon.

Us heard a heap about dem Ku Kluxers, but none of my folks never seed any of 'em. Dey was supposed to have done lots of beatin' of colored folks, but nobody knowed who dem Ku Kluxers was.

A long time after de War I got married to Traverse Colquitt. De weddin' took place at my sister's house, and us sure did have a big weddin' and a fine dinner afterwards. Den next day my husband carried me to where he was born, and his ma give us another big fine dinner. She had a table longer dan this room, and it was just loaded with all sorts of good things. De white folkses dat my husband had used to work for sent some of de good victuals.

Most of my life after de War was spent in Lexington.

CHENEY CROSS

Interviewed near Evergreen, Alabama
Interviewed by Annie D. Dean
Age when interviewed: 90+

ENDURIN' DE WAR I had done long past my thirteenth birthday. But if anybody in de world knowed my exact age, it was my young mistis. Her papa was Captain Purifoy. Back yonder he was de magistrate of our town, and he had all of dem lawin' books. I figgered dat my birthright would be down in one of dem books. I knowed dat my mistis still got dem books with her, 'cause dey ain't been no burnin's dat I done heard about.

I 'members Captain Purifoy just like a book. I does dat! Now, 'course, when he come in from de War he didn't 'zackly favor hisself den, 'cause when I seed him comin' round de house he look so ragged and ornery I took him for de old Bad Man hisself. I took out behind de smokehouse, and when I got a good look at him through a crack it look like I could recognize his favor, but I couldn't call his name to save my life. Lord, he's a sight! All growed over and bushy. You couldn't tell if he's man or beast. I kept on a-lookin' whilst he's comin' round de corner, and den I heard him say "Cheney, dat you?" I'se so happy, I just melt down.

You see, it's like dis. My parents, dey was bought. My mistis and my daddy's mistis, too, was Miss Mary Fields, and my daddy was Henry Fields. Den de Carters bought my daddy from Miss Mary Fields. Well, dey mix up and down like dat, till now my young mistis, what used to be little Frances Purifoy, she's married to Mr. Cunningham.

I was brung up right in de house with my white folks. I slept on de little trundler bed what pushed up under de big bed, during the day. I watched over dem chillen day and night. I washed 'em and fed 'em and played with 'em. One of de babies had to take goat's milk. When she cry, my mistis say, "Cheney, go on and get dat goat." Yes, Lord! And dat goat sure did talk sweet to dat baby. Just like it was her own. She look at it and wag her tail so fast and say: "Ma-a-a-a!" Den she lay down on de floor whilst us holds her feets and let de baby suck de milk. All de time de goat be's talkin', "Ma-a-a-a," till dat baby got satisfied.

When us chillen got took with any kind of sickness or diseases, us took asafetida and garlic. You know, garlic what smell like onions. Den we wore some round us necks.

Dese days it look like somethin' to eat don't taste like dat we cooked back yonder. De coffee us used had to be fresh ground every day. And when it commence to boil, I put dese knees down on de floor before de fire and stir dat coffee for de longest. Den my grandma, she hung dat pot up on dem pot hooks over de fire and washed de meat and drop it in. Time she done pick and overlook de greens and den rinsed 'em in spring water, de meat was boilin'. Den she take a great big mess of dem fresh turnip greens an' squash 'em down in dat pot. Dey must melt down and go to seasonin'.

Next thing I knowed, here come my mistis, and she say: "Now Cheney, I wants some pone bread for dinner." Dem hickory coals in dat fireplace was all time ready and hot. They wouldn't be no finger prints left on dat pone when Cheney got through pattin' it out, neither. Better not! Look like dem chillen just couldn't get 'nough of dat hard corn bread. Plenty of fancy coogin' went on round dat fireplace, but somehow de pot licker and pone bread 'longside with de fresh buttermilk stirs my memory worse than anything.

All dis good eatin' I'se speakin' about took place before de Yankees raided us. It was den, too, dat my mistis took me down to de spring back of de house. Down dere it was a hollow tree stump, taller'n you is. She tell me to climb up to de top of dat hollowtree, den she hand me a big heavy bundle, all wrapped up and tied tight. It sure was heavy! Den she say: "Drop it in, Cheney." I didn't know den what she's up to, but dat was de silver and jewelry she was hidin'.

I 'members de Yankee raid like it was just yesterday. I'se settin' dere in de loom room, and Mr. Thad Watts' little gal, Louise, she's standin' at the window. She say: "O-o-oh! Just look down yonder!" "Baby, what is dat?" I says. "Dem's de Yankees comin'!" "God help us!" I says, and before I can catch my breath, de place is covered. You couldn't stir 'em up with a stick. Feets sounded like mutterin' thunder. Dem bayonets stick up like dey just settin' on de mouth of dey guns. Dey swords hangin' on de sides singin' a tune while dey walk. A chicken better not pass by. If he do, off comes his head!

When dey pass on by me, dey pretty nigh shuck me outa my skin. "Where's de men's?" dey say and shake me up. "Where's de arms?" Dey shake me till my eyeballs loosen up. "Where's de silver?" Lord! Was my teeth droppin' out? Dey didn't give me time to catch my breath. All de time, Miss Mary just look 'em in de eye and say nothin'.

Dey took dem Enfield rifles, half as long as dat door, and bust in de smokehouse window. Dey jack me up off my feet and drag me up de ladder and say: "Get dat meat out." I kept on throwin' out Miss Mary's hams and sausages, till dey holler, "Stop!" I come backin' down dat ladder like a squirrel, and I ain't stop backin' till I reach Miss Mary.

Yes, Lord! Dem Yankees loaded up a wagon full of meat and took de whole barrel of 'lasses. Takin' dat 'lasses kilt us chillen. Our mainest 'musement was makin' 'lasses candy. Den us cakewalk 'round it. Now dat was all gone. Look like dem soldiers had to sharpen dey swords on everything in sight. De big crepe mullein bush by de parlor winder was bloomin' so pink and pretty, and dey just stood dere and whack off dem blooms like folks' heads droppin' on de ground.

I seed de sergeant when he run his bayonet clean through Miss Mary's best featherbed and rip it slam open! With dat, a wind blowed up and took dem feathers every which way for Sunday. You couldn't see where you's at. De sergeant, he just throwed his head back and laughed fit to kill hisself. Den first thing next, he done suck a feather down his wind-pipe! Lord, dat white man sure struggled. Den soldiers throwed water in his face. Dey shook him and beat him and rolled him over, and all de time he's gettin' limberer and bluerer. Den dey jack him up by his feets and stands him on his head. Den dey pump him up and down. Den they shook him till he spit. Den he come to. Dey didn't cut no more mattresses. And dey didn't cut nothin' much up in de parlor, 'cause dat's where de lieutenant and de sergeant slept. But when dey left de next day, de whole place was strewed with mutilation.

I 'members well back dere durin' de War how every once a month that come round, a big box, longer'n I is and wider too, was took to our soldier boys on de battlefield. You never seed de like of sausages dat went in dat box! With cake and chicken and pies, and, Lord, de butter all rolled up in corn shucks to keep it fresh. Everybody from everywhere come to fix dat box and help pile in de stuff. Den you hear 'em say: "Poor soldiers! Put it in here!" Den everything look sorta misty and dey heads droop over like. Den you see a mother's breast heave with her silent prayer.

Directly after de surrender, de Ku Kluxes sure was bad after de Yankees. Dey do all sorts of things to aggravate 'em. Dey's continually tying grapevines across de road, to get 'em tangled up and make 'em trip up and break dey own necks. Dat was bad, too, 'cause dem poor Yankees never suspicioned no better'n dat dem vines just blowed down or somethin'.

Long about den, too, seem like haunts and spirits was ridin' everything! Dey raided mostly round de graveyard. I ain't hankerin' after passin' by no graveyards. I 'members one night, way back dere, when I'se walkin' down de big road with Bud, and he say: "Look! Didn't you see me give dat road? Dat haunt done push me clean out of my place." Now let me tell you somethin'. Iffen you ain't never been dat close to a haunt, you don't know nothin'! I allowed he gwine follow me home. When I got dere I shook mustard seeds down on my floor. When you sprinkles 'em like dat he can't get out of dat room till he done count every last one of dem seeds. Look like he done counted hisself to a pulp.

After dat night, I puts a big sifter down at my door. You know haunts has to count every hole in dat sifter before dey can come through. Some folks puts de Bible down dere, too. Den de poor spirit has to read every word of dat book before he crosses over.

I reckon about de terriblest thing ever happen to me was dat big lookin' glass. De lookin' glass was laid out in de top of my trunk, waitin' for my weddin' day. One night I'se standin' by de trunk with it wide open. I seed somthin' black before my eyes and den a screech owl lit in my window and screech right in my face. I'se so scared I set right down in de middle of dat lookin' glass. It bust in a million pieces! Mamma threwed up her hands and holler, "Get up from dere, gal. You gonna have seven years of bad luck. Shoo dat hootin' owl away before you dies in your tracks!" Den I swoons off. I feels dem haunts gettin' ready to ride me clean down in my grave. About den somethin' kept sayin' to me, over and over, "Throw dem pieces of lookin' glass in runnin' water." Den it say: "Burn your mammy's old shoe and de screech owl leave." After I does dat my mind was at rest.

Soon as my daddy hear 'em firin' off for de surrender, he put out for de plantation where he first belong. He left me with my mistis at Pine Flat, but it wasn't long till he come back to get me and carry me home with him. I hates to leave my mistis, and she didn't want to part from me. She say: "Stay here with me, and I'll give you a school learnin'." She say to Captain Purifoy, "You go buy my little nigger a book. Get one of dem blue-black Websters," she say, "so I can educate her to spell." Den my daddy say: "Her mamma told me not to come home without her and she has to go with me."

I never forget ridin' behind my daddy on dat mule way in de night. Us left in such a hurry I didn't get none of my clothes hardly, and I ain't seed my mistis from dat day to dis!

KATIE DARLING
Interviewed near Marshall, Texas
Interviewer not identified
Age when interviewed: 88

YOU IS TALKIN' now to a nigger what nursed seven white chillen in them bullwhip days. Miss Stella, my young missy, got all our ages down in she Bible, and it say I'se born in 1849.

Massa Bill McCarty my massa and he live east and south of Marshall, close to the Louisiana line. Me and my three brothers, Peter and Adam and Willit, all lives to be growed and married, but Mammy die in slavery and Pappy run away while he and Massa Bill on their way to the battle of Mansfield. Massa say when he come back from the war, "That triflin' nigger run away and joins up with them damn Yankees."

Massa have six chillen when war come on and I nursed all of 'em. I stays in the house with 'em and slept on a pallet on the floor, and soon

I'se big 'nough to tote the milk pail they puts me to milkin', too. Massa have more'n one hundred cows and most of the time me and Violet do all the milkin'. We better be in that cow pen by five o'clock. One mornin' Massa cotched me lettin' one the calves do some milkin' and he let me off without whippin' that time, but that don't mean he always good, 'cause them cows have more feelin' for us than Massa and Missy.

We et peas and greens and collards and middlin's. Niggers had better let that ham alone! We have meal coffee. They parch meal in the oven and boil it and drink the liquor. Sometime we gets some of the Lincoln coffee and what was left from the next plantation.

When the niggers done anything Massa bullwhip them, but didn't skin them up very often. He'd whip the man for half doin' the plowin' or hoein' but if they done it right he'd find something else to whip them for.

At night the men had to shuck corn and the women card and spin. Us got two pieces of clothes for winter and two for summer, but us have no shoes. We had to work Saturday all day and if that grass was in the field we didn't get no Sunday, either.

They have dances and parties for the white folks' chillen, but Missy say, "Niggers was made to work for white folks," and on Christmas Miss Irene bakes two cakes for the nigger families but she doesn't let Missy know about it.

When a slave die, Massa make the coffin hisself and send a couple niggers to bury the body and say, "Don't be long," and no singin' or prayin' allowed, just put them in the ground and cover 'em up and hurry on back to that field.

Niggers didn't court then like they do now. Massa pick out a portly man and a portly gal and just put 'em together. What he want am the stock.

I 'member that fight at Mansfield like it yesterday. Massa's field am all tore up with cannon holes and every time a cannon fire, Missy go off in rage. One time when a cannon fire, she say to me, "You li'l black wench, you niggers ain't gwine be free. You's made to work for white folks." 'Bout that time she look up and see a Yankee soldier standin' in the door with a pistol. She say, "Katie, I didn't say nothing, did I?" I say, "I ain't tellin' no lie, you say niggers ain't gwine get free." That day you couldn't get 'round the place for the Yankees and they stays for weeks at a time.

When Massa come home from the War he wants let us loose, but Missy wouldn't do it. I stays on and works for them six years after the War and Missy whip me after the War just like she did before. She has a hundred lashes laid up for me now, and this how it am. My brudders done left Massa after the War and move next door to the Ware place, and one Saturday some niggers come and tell me my brudder Peter am comin' to get me away from old Missy Sunday night. That night the cows and calves got together and Missy say it my fault. She say, "I gwine give you one hun'erd lashes in the mornin', now go pen them calves."

I don't know whether them calves was ever penned or not, 'cause Peter was waitin' for me at the lot and takes me to live with him on the Ware place. I'se so happy to get away from that old devil Missy, I don't know what to do, and I stays there several years and works out here and there for money. Then I marries and moves here and me and my man farms and nothin' exciting done happened.

CHARLES DAVENPORT

Interviewed at Natchez, Mississippi
Interviewed by Edith Wyatt Moore
Age at interview: About 100

I WAS NAMED Charlie Davenport and accordin' to de way I figgers I ought to be nearly a hundred years old. Nobody knows my birthday, 'cause all my white folks is gone. I was born one night and de very next mornin' my poor little mammy died. Her name was Lucindy. My pa was William Davenport.

When I was a little mite dey turned me over to de granny nurse on de plantation. She was de one dat attended to de little pickaninnies. She got a woman to nurse me what had a young baby, so I didn't know no difference. Any woman what had a baby about my age would wet nurse me, so I growed up in de quarters and was as well and as happy as any other chile.

When I could tote 'taters dey'd let me pick 'em up in de field. Us always hid a pile away where us could get 'em an' roast 'em at night. Old Mammy nearly always made a heap o' dewberry an' persimmon wine. Us little tykes would gather black walnuts in de woods and store 'em under de cabins to dry.

At night when de work was all done and de candles was out us'd set 'round de fire and eat cracked nuts and 'taters. Us picked out de nuts with horseshoe nails and baked de 'taters in ashes. Den Mammy would pour herself and her old man a cup o' wine. Us never got none o' dat unless us be's sick. Den she'd mess it up with wild cherry bark. It was bad den, but us gulped it down, anyhow.

Old Grammy used to sing a song to us what went like dis:

> Kink head, wherefore you skeered?
> Old snake crawled off, 'cause he's a-feared.
> Pappy will smite on de back
> With a great big club—Ker whack! Ker whack!

Aventine, where I was born and bred, was across Second Creek. It was a big plantation with about a hundred head o' folks a-livin' on it. It was only one o' de marster's places, 'cause he was one o' de richest and highest quality gentlemen in de whole country. I'se tellin' you de truth, us didn't belong to no white trash. De marster was de Honorable Mister Gabriel Shields hisself. Everybody knowed about him. He married a Surget.

Dem Surgets was pretty devilish; for all dey was de richest family in de land. Dey was de out-fightin'est, outcussin'est, fastest ridin', hardest drinkin', out-spendin'est folks I ever seen. But Lord! Lord! Dey was gentlemen even in dey cups. De ladies was beautiful with big black eyes and soft white hands, but dey was high strung, too.

De marster had a town mansion what's pictured in a lot o' books. It was malled "Montebella." De big columns still stand at de end o' Shields Lane. It burnt about thirty years ago.

I'se part Injun. I ain't got no nigger nose and my hair is so long I has to keep it wrapped. I'se often heard my mammy was reddish-lookin' with long, straight, black hair. Her pa was a full blooded Choctaw and mighty nigh as young as she was. I'se been told dat nobody dare meddle with her. She didn't do much talkin', but she sure was a good worker. My pappy had Injun blood, too, but his hair was kinky.

De Choctaws lived all 'round Second Creek. Some of 'em had cabins like settled folks. I can 'member dey last chief. He was a tall powerful built man named Big Sam. What he said was de law, 'cause he was de boss o' de whole tribe. One rainy night he was kilt in a saloon down in "Natchez Under de Hill." De Injuns went wild with rage and grief. Dey sung and wailed and done a heap o' low mutterin'. De sheriff kept a steady watch on 'em, 'cause he was a-feared dey would do somethin' rash. After a long time he kinda let up in his vigilance. Den one night some o' de Choctaw mens slipped in town and stabbed de man dey believed had kilt Big Sam. I 'members dat well.

As I said before, I growed up in de quarters. De houses was clean and snug. Us was better fed den dan I is now, and warmer, too. Us had blankets and quilts filled with home raised wool and I just loved layin' in de big fat featherbed a-hearin' de rain patter on de roof.

All de little darkies helped bring in wood. Den us swept de yards with brush brooms. Den sometimes us played together in the street what run de length o' de quarters. Us throwed horseshoes, jumped poles, walked on stilts, and played marbles. Sometimes us made bows and arrows. Us could shoot 'em, too, jus'like de little Injuns.

A heap o' times old Granny would brush us hide with a peach tree limb, but us need it. Us stole eggs and roasted 'em. She sure wouldn't stand for no stealin' if she knowed it.

Us wore lowell-cloth shirts. It was a coarse towsackin'. In winter us had linsey-woolsey pants and heavy cowhide shoes. Dey was made in three sizes—big, little, and medium. 'Tweren't no right or left. Dey was sorta club-shaped so us could wear 'em on either foot.

I was a teasin', mischevious child and de overseer's little gal got it in for me. He was a big, hard fisted Dutchman bent on gettin' riches. He trained his pasty-faced gal to tattle on us niggers. She got a heap o' folks whipped. I knowed it, but I was hasty: One day she hit me with a stick and I throwed it back at her. About dat time up walked her pa. He seen what I done, but he didn't see what she done to me. But it wouldn't a-made no difference if he had.

He snatched me in de air and toted me to a stump and laid me across it. I didn't have but one thickness 'twixt me and daylight. He sure laid it on me with dat stick! I thought I'd die. All de time his mean little gal was a-gloatin' in my misery. I yelled and prayed to de Lord till he quit.

Den he say to me, "From now on you works in de field! I ain't gwine-a have no vicious boy like you round de lady folks." I was too little for field work, but de next mornin' I went to choppin' cotton. After dat I made a regular field hand. When I growed up I was a ploughman. I could sure lay off a pretty cotton row, too.

Us slaves was fed good plain grub. Before us went to de field us had a big breadfast o' hot bread, 'lasses, fried salt meat dipped in cornmeal, and fried 'taters. Sometimes us had fish and rabbit meat. When us was in de field, two women would come a dinner-time with baskets filled with hot pone, baked 'taters, corn roasted in de shucks, onion, fried squash, and boiled pork. Sometimes dey brought buckets o' cold buttermilk. It sure was good to a hungry man. At supper time us had hoocake and cold victuals. Sometimes dey was sweet milk and collards.

Most every slave had his own little garden patch and was allowed to cook out o' it. Most ever plantation kept a man busy huntin' and fishin' all de time. If dey shot a big buck, us had deer meat roasted on a spit. On Sundays us always had meat pie or fish or fresh game and roasted 'taters and coffee. On Christmas de marster would give us chicken and barrels o' apples and oranges. 'Course, every marster weren't as free handed as our'n was. He was sure 'nough quality. I'se heard dat a heap o' cullud people never had nothin' good t'eat.

I weren't learnt nothin' in no book. Don't think I'd a-took to it, nowhow. Dey learnt de house servants to read. Us field hands never knowed nothin' 'cept weather and dirt and to weigh cotton. Us was learnt to figger a little, but dat's all.

I reckon I was about fifteen when honest Abe Lincoln what called hisself a rail-splitter come here to talk with us. He went all through de country just a-rantin' an' a-preachin' about us being his black brothers. De marster didn't know nothin about it, cause it was sorta secret-like. It sure riled de niggers up and lots of 'em run away. I sure heard him, but I didn't pay him no mind.

When de War broke out dat old Yankee Dutch overseer o' our'n went back up North, where he belonged. Us was powerful glad and hoped he'd get his neck broke. After dat de Yankees come a-swoopin' down on us. My own pappy took off with 'em. He joined a company what fought at Vicksburg. I was plenty big 'nough to fight, but I didn't hanker to tote no gun. I stayed on de plantation and put in a crop. It was powerful uneasy times after dat. But what I care about freedom? Folks what was free was in misery first one way and den de other.

I was on the plantation closer to town, den. It was called "Fish Pond Plantation." De white folks come and told us we must burn all de cotton so de enemy couldn't get it. Us piled it high in de field like great mountains. It made my innards hurt to see fire attached to somethin' dat had cost us niggers so much labor and honest sweat. If I coulda hid some o' it in de barn I'd a-done it, but de boss searched everywhere. De little niggers thought it was fun. Dey laughed and brung out big armfuls from de cotton house. One little black gal clapped her hands and jumped in a big heap. She sunk down and down till she was buried deep. Den de wind picked up de flame and spread it like lightenin'. It spread so fast dat before us could bat de eye, she was in a mountain o' fire. She struggled up all covered with flames, a-screamin', "Lordy, help me!" Us snatched her out and rolled her on de ground, but 'tweren't no use. She died in a few minutes.

De marster's sons went to war. De one what us loved best never come back no more. Us mourned him a-plenty, 'cause he was so jolly and happy-like, and free with his change. Us all felt cheered when he come 'round.

Us niggers didn't know nothin' about what was gwine on in de outside world. All us knowed was dat a war was bein' fought. Personally, I believe in what Marse Jefferson Davis done. He done de only thing a gentleman coulda done. He told Marse Abe Lincoln to attend to his own business and he'd attend to his'n. But Marse Lincoln was a fightin' man and he come down here and tried to run other folks' plantations. Dat made Marse Davis so all fired mad dat he spit hard 'twixt his teeth and say, "I'll whip de socks off dem damn Yankees." Dat's how it all come about. My white folks lost money, cattle, slaves, and cotton in de War, but dey was still better off dan most folks.

Like all de fool niggers o' dat time I was right smart bit by de freedom bug for awhile. It sounded powerful nice to be told: "You don't have to chop cotton no more. You can throw dat hoe down and go fishin' when-soever de notion strikes you. And you can roam 'round at night and court gals just as late as you please. Ain't no marster gwine to say to you, "Charlie, you's got to be back when de clock strikes nine."

I was fool 'nough to believe all dat kind o' stuff. But to tell de honest truth, most o' us didn't know ourselfs no better off. Freedom meant us could leave where us'd been born and bred, but it meant, too, dat us had to scratch for us ownselfs. Dem what left de old plantation seemed so all fired glad to get back dat I made up my mind to stay put. I stayed right with my white folks as long as I could.

My white folks talked plain to me. Dey say real sadlike, "Charlie, you's been a dependence, but now you can go if you is so desirous. But if you wants to stay with us you can sharecrop. Dey's a house for you and wood to keep you warm and a mule to work. We ain't got much cash, but dey's de land and you can count on havin' plenty o' victuals. Do just as you please."

When I looked at my marster and knowed he needed me, I pleased to stay. My marster never forced me to do nary thing about it. Didn't nobody make me work after de War, but dem Yankees sure made my daddy work. Dey put a pick in his hand 'stead o' a gun. Dey made him dig a big ditch in front o' Vicksburg. He worked a heap harder fo his Uncle Sam dan he'd ever done for de marster.

I heard tell about some nigger soldiers a-plunderin' some houses. Out at Pine Ridge dey kilt a white man named Rogillio. But de head Yankee soldiers in Natchez tried 'em for somethin' or 'nother and hung 'em on a tree out near de Charity Hospital. Dey strung up de ones dat went to Mr. Sargent's door one night and shot him down, too. All dat hangin' seemed to squelch a heap o' lousy goin's-on.

Lord! Lord! I knows about de Kloo Kluxes. I knows a-plenty. Dey was sure 'nough devils a-walkin' de earth a-seekin' what dey could devour. Dey larruped de hide off de uppity niggers an' drove de white trash back where dey belonged.

Us niggers didn't have no secret meetin's. All us had was church meetin's in arbors out in de woods. De preachers would exhort us dat us was de chillen o' Israel in de wilderness an' de Lord done sent us to take dis land o' milk and honey. But how us gwine-a take land what's already been took?

I sure ain't never heard about no plantations bein' divided up, neither. I heard a lot o' yaller niggers spoutin' off how dey was gwine-a take over de white folks' land for back wages. Dem bucks just took all dey wages out in talk. 'Cause I ain't never seen no land divided up yet.

In dem days nobody but niggers and "shawl-strap" folks voted. Quality folks didn't have nothin' to do with such truck. If dey hada wanted to de Yankees wouldn'ta let 'em. My old marster didn't vote and if anybody knowed what was what he did. Sense didn't count in dem days. It was powerful ticklish times and I let votin' alone. De "shawl-strap" folks what come in to take over de country told us dat us had a right to go to all de balls, church meetin's, and entertainments de white folks give. But one night a bunch o' uppity niggers went to a entertainment in Memorial Hall. Dey dressed deyselfs fit to kill and walked down de aisle and took seats in de very front. But just about time dey got good set down, de curtain dropped and de white folks rose up without a-sayin' a word. Dey marched out de buildin' with dey chins up and left dem niggers a-sittin' in a empty hall.

Dat's de way it happen every time a nigger tried to get too uppity. Dat night after de breakin' up o' dat entertainment, de Kloo Kluxes rode through de land. I heard dey grabbed every nigger what walked down dat aisle ,but I ain't heard yet what dey done with 'em.

A heap o' niggers voted for a little while. Dey was a black man what had office. He was named Lynch. He cut a big figger up in Washington. Us had a sheriff named Winston. He was a ginger cake nigger and powerful mean when he got riled. Sheriff Winston was a slave and, if my memory ain't failed me, so was Lynch.

My granny told me about a slave uprisin' what took place when I was a little boy. None o' de marster's niggers would have nothin' to do with it. A nigger tried to get 'em to kill dey white folks and take dey land. But what us want to kill Old Marster and take de land when dey was de best friends us had? Dey caught de nigger and hung him to a limb.

D. DAVIS
Interviewed near Marvell, Arkansas
Interviewed by Watt McKinney
Age when interviewed: 85

I HAS BEEN in Phillips County for de past forty-five years and I is now past eighty-five. I was grown and settled man when I first come here and had chillen nigh about growed. I came here on account of one of my boys. Dis boy he come before I did and had done made one crop, and dat boy fooled me over here from Mississippi. You know how dese young bucks is, always driftin' round. And he had done drifted right down dere below Marvell on de Cypress Bayou, and was workin' for Mr. Fred Mayo when he wrote me de letter to come over here. Well, Mr. Fred Mayo is de man what my boy was with and after I come I joined up with Mr. Mayo and stayed with him for two years. I would of been with him for good, I reckon, if I hadn't wanted to buy me a place of my own, 'cause Mr. Fred Mayo was a natural good man and treated all he hands fair.

When I decided to get me a little place of my own, I went and got acquainted with Mr. Marve Carruth, 'cause he had a great name with de niggers. All de niggers in dem days went to Mr. Carruth for to get de advice, and Mr. Carruth, he helped me to get de place up de road what is mine yet. Dere never was no white man what was no better dan Mr. Marve Carruth.

You see, I was borned and raised in de hills of Mississippi, in Oktibbeha County not far from Starkville, and dat was a old country time. I had got grown and de land, it was gettin' powerful thin, and when I come to dis state and seen how much cotton de folks makin' on de ground, and how rich de land, I just went crazy over dis country and stayed right here and moved my fambly right off. Folkses had cotton piled up all round dey houses and I decided right off dat dis was gwine to be my home den.

My old Marster was Tom Davis and dere weren't never no finer man what ever lived dan Marse Tom. Marse Tom was loved by every nigger dat he had, and Marse Tom sure had a passel of 'em. He had better'n two hundred head and de last one crazy about Marse Tom Davis. He was rather old from my first recollection of him, and he never lived many years after de War. Marse Tom, he owned a great heap of land. His land stretch out for God knows how far and den, too, he had a big mill what runned with de water wheel where dey saw de lumber and grind de meal and de flour. Dey never bought no flour in dem days 'cause dey raised de wheat on de place and all de meat and nigh about everything what dey had need of. Marse Tom, he took de best kind of care of his slave people and he never believe in buyin' or sellin' no niggers. Dat he didn't. He never would sell a one, and he never did buy but three. Dat is a fact, and one of dem three what he bought was Henry, what was my own pappy, and he buyed Henry from Mr. Spence 'cause Henry had done got married to Malindy, what was my mammy. Dat is what my mammy and pappy both told me.

Marse Tom, he never join de army 'cause he too old when de War break out, but Marse Phil, he joined up. Marse Phil, he were Marse Tom's son, and de onliest boy dat Old Marster and Old Miss had, and dey just had one more child and dat was de girl, Miss Rachel. And after de War over Miss Rachel, she married Captain Dan Travis what come from Alabama. Old Marster, he never liked Captain Dan a bit, and he just bucked and rared about Miss Rachel gwine to get married to dat captain, but it never done him no good to cut up 'cause Old Miss, she sided with Miss Rachel, and den, too, Miss Rachel, she have a head of her own and she know her pa ain't gwine to stop her. Marse Tom, he didn't like Captain Dan 'cause de captain he big sport and mighty wild, and he love he whiskey too well and den he a gamblin' man besides dat, though he sure was a fine lookin' gentleman.

Whilst Marse Tom, he too old to join up with de army, he hired him a man to fight for him in his place just de same, and him and Old Miss dey never want Marse Phil to join up, and say dey gwine to hire a man for to take Marse Phil's place so he won't have to go, but Marse Phil, he say he gwine to do his own fightin'. And even though he ma and pa dey cut up right smart about Marse Phil goin' to de War, he up and join just de same. Marse Phil, he never was such a stout, healthy person, and he always sorta sickly, and it weren't long before he took down in de camp with some kind of bad spell or sickness and died. Dat was sure tough on Marse Tom and de Old Miss for dem to lose Marse Phil, 'cause dey put a heap of store by dat boy, him bein' de onliest son dat dey got, and dey so attached to him. It mighty nigh broke dem old peoples up.

I betcha dat dere weren't another slave-ownin' white man to be found dat was a finer man, or dat was more good to he niggers dan Marse Tom Davis. Now just take dis: dere was Uncle Joe, what was my grand-pappy, and he was just about de same age as Marse Tom, and dey growed up together. Dey told it dat Marse Tom's pappy get Uncle Joe when he was just a boy from de speculator for a red handkerchief, dats how cheap he get him, and dat right off he give him to Marse Tom. After Marse Tom get up and growed to be a man and he pappy died and left him all de land and slaves, and den after a lot more years pass, Uncle Joe done raise Marse Tom seven chillun. Den Marse Tom he up and set Uncle Joe free, and give him a home and forty acres and some stock 'cause Uncle Joe done been good and faithful all dem years and raise Marse Tom all dem seven chillen. One of dem seven was my own mammy.

De speculators was dem folkses what dealed in de niggers. Dat is, what brought 'em and sold 'em and dey would be gwine round through de country all de time with a great gang of peoples, both men and womens, a-tradin', and a-buyin' and a-sellin'. It was just like you might say dat dey would do with a gang of mules. Just before dese here speculators would get to a town or plantation where dey gwine to try to do some business like tradin' or such matter, dey stop de crowd alongside a creek or pond or water and make 'em wash up and clean up good like and comb 'em up right nice and make de womens wrap up dey heads with some nice red cloth so dey all look in good shape to de man what dey gwine try to do de business with. Dat's 'zackly de way dey do, just like curryin' and fixin' up mules for to sell, so dey look better'n dey actually is.

Whilst Marse Tom Davis had overseers hired to look after de farmin' of de land, he had his own way of doin' de business, 'cause he know dat all he niggers is good workers, and dat he can depend on 'em. So de first of every week he give each and every single man or family a task for to do dat week. After dat task is done den dey through work for dat week and can den tend de patches what he would give dem for to raise what dey want on. And what de slaves raise on dese patches dat he give 'em would be deres whatsoever it would be, cotton or 'taters or what, it would be dey own, and dey could sell it and have de money for demselves to buy what dey want.

Marse Tom, he would ride out over de place at least once a week and always on Saturday mornin', and generally he would pass de word out amongst de folkses for 'em all to come to de Big House on Saturday after-noon for a frolic. Every person on de place, from de littlest child to de oldest man or woman would clean deyselves up and put on dey best clothes for to "go before de King." Dat's what us called it. All would gather in back of de Big House under de big oak trees and Marse Tom, he would come out with he fiddle under he arm—you know Marse Tom was a great fiddler—and set hisself down in de chair what Uncle Joe done fetched for him. Den he tell Uncle Joe for to go get de barrel of whiskey and he would give 'em all a gill or two so's dey could all feel right good. Den Marse Tom, he start dat fiddle playin' right lively and all dem niggers would dance and have de best kind of frolic. Marse Tom, he get just as much fun outen de party as de niggers demselves. Dat's de kind of man what Marse Tom was.

My marster, he sure treated his slaves fair. Dey all draw a plenty rations once every week and iffen dey run out 'tween times dey could always get more, and Marse Tom tell 'em to get all de meal and flour at de mill any time dat dey need it. I sure tells dis for de truth, dat iffen all de slave owning white folks like Marse Tom Davis, den dere wouldn't been no use for freedom for de darkies. 'Cause Marse Tom's slaves, dey long ways better off with him in dey bondage dan dey was without him when dey set free and him dead and gone.

At Christmas time on Marse Tom's place dey would have de fun for a week or more, with no work gwin on at all. De candy pullin', and de dances would be gwine on nigh about constantly and everyone gets a present from de master.

All endurin' of de War times, Marse Tom, he never raised no cotton at all but instead he raised de wheat and de corn and hogs for de Confederates, and de baggage wagons would come from time to time for de loads of flour and meal and meat dat he would send to de army. De Yankees somehow dey missed us place and never did find it, and do de damage or burning and such dat I is heard dat dey done in places in other parts of de state. We all heard one time dat de Yankees was close around and was on de way to burn Marse Tom's mill but dey got on de wrong road and dey never did get to our place, and us sure was proud of dat, too. Yet and still after de War over, Marse Tom, he had about four hundred bales of cotton on hand at de barn and de Yankee government, dey sure took dat and didn't pay him a bit for dat cotton. I knows dat to be a fact.

I 'members de War real well, 'cause I was about twelve year old when it over. In de last two or three years of de trouble I was big enough to be doin' some work, so dey took me in de Big House for to be a waitin' boy 'round de house. I slept in dere too on a pallet on de floor. A lot of times de cavalry soldiers would stop at Marse Tom's and spend de night and I would be layin' on de pallet but wouldn't be sleep. I could hear dem talkin' to Marse Tom. Marster, he would ask dem how de fight comin' on, and iffen dey whippin' de Yankees, and de cavalry soldiers dey say dat dey whippin' de Yankees every day and killin' 'em out. And Marse Tom, he say, "You know you is just a big lie. How come you runnin' away iffen you whippin' dem Yankees? Dem Yankees is after you and you is running from 'em, dat's what you doin'. You know you ain't whippin' no Yankees, 'cause if you was you would be after dem right now 'stead dem after you." No, sir, dem cavalry soldiers couldn't fool Marse Tom.

Yessir, de slaves fared well with Marse Tom Davis, and dere wouldn't never been no war over de slavery question iffen everybody been like Marse Tom. All his peoples was satisfied and dey didn't even know what de Yankees and de Southern white folks was fightin' about, 'cause dey wasn't worried about no freedom. Yet and still, after de freedom come dey was glad to get it, but after dey get it dey don't know what to do with it. And after de bondage lifted, Marse Tom, he called 'em all up and tell 'em dat dey free as he is and dey can leave if dey want to, but dere wasn't nary nigger left de place. Dey every one stayed, and I 'spect dat a lot of dem Davis niggers is right dere yet on dat same land with whoever it belongs to.

When a slave man and woman got married in those days dere wasn't no such thing as a license for dem. All dey had to do was to get de permit from de marster and den to start in to livin' with each other. After de freedom, though, all of dem what was married and livin' with one another was given a slip to show dat dey married and to make dey marriage legal.

After de surrender Marse Tom, he had his whole place lined out by de surveyor and marked off in plots of ground, and he sell a plot of forty acres to every family dat he had, on de credit, too, and sell 'em de stock with de place so dey can all have a home. Dey all set in to buy de land from Marse Tom. But it weren't long after dat till Marse Tom and Old Miss both died. Dat was when Captain Dan Travis, Miss Rachel's husband, he taken charge of de business and broke all de contracts dat de darkies had made with Marse Tom. Dat was de last of de land buyin' on dat place and dat was de startin' of de niggers a-leavin' de Davis place, with Captain Dan Travis in charge and Marse Tom gone. But Captain Dan, he and Miss Rachel didn't keep dey place long after her pa dead, 'cause de captain he too wild and he soon fooled all de money and land off with he drinkin' and gamblin'.

After de War dey had de carpetbaggers and de Ku Klux before, and de white folks, dey didn't like de carpetbaggers tolerable well, dat dey didn't. I don't know who de carpetbaggers was but dey was powerful mean, so de white folks say. Some way or other de Yankees or de carpetbaggers or some of de crowd, dey put de niggers in de office at de courthouse and to makin' de laws at de statehouse in Jackson. Dat was de craziest business dat dey ever could have done, puttin' dem ignorant niggers what couldn't read or write in dem places. Dem what put dose niggers in de office must not had as much sense as de niggers, cause dey might know dat it wouldn't work and it sure didn't work long. Dey had de niggers messed up in some kind of clubs what dey persuaded dem to join and give 'em all a drum to beat and dey all go marchin' around a-beatin' de drums and going to de club meetin's. Dem ignorant niggers would sell out for a cigar or a stick of candy. It wasn't long, though, till de trouble broke out and de fight took place. De Ku Klux, dey was a-ridin' de country continually, and de niggers dey scared plumb sick by dem tall white lookin' haunts with dey hosses all white with de sheets. And some say dey just come outen dey graves and a-lookin' for niggers to take back with 'em when de daylight come.

All de time de niggers havin' dey club meetin's in a old loose house dere at Chapel Hill and de Klux a-gettin' more numerous all de time and de feelin' 'mongst de white and de black was a gettin' worse and worse. One night when de niggers havin' a great big meetin' and a-beatin' dey drums and a-carryin' on, here come de Ku Klux or somethin' a shootin' right and left a-pourin' de shots into dat old house and at every nigger dey see. De niggers dey start shootin' back, but not for long, 'cause most of 'em done lit out for de woods, dat's most all what ain't kilt, and dat was de very last of de club meetin's and de very last of de niggers a-holdin' de office in de courthouse. I heard about de fight de next mornin' 'cause Chapel Hill weren't far from where I lived at dat time. I seed Dr. Marris Gray on de road on he hoss, and he hoss was covered with mud from he tail to he head. Dr. Marris Grey, he pulled up and said, "Good mornin', D., is you heard about de fight what was had last night at Chapel Hill?" And I say, "No sir, Doctor. What fight was dat and what dey fightin' about?" De doctor say he didn't know what dey fightin' about less'n dey just tryin' to break up de club meetin'. And he went on to say dat a heap of niggers was kilt and also some white folks, too, and some more was shot what ain't dead yet, and dat he been tendin' to dem what is shot and still ain't dead.

Den I say, "Doctor Marris, was you dere when de fightin' goin' on?" And de doctor, he say, "Of course I weren't dere. You don't think I gwine be round where no shootin' takin' place, does you?" I say, "No sir," and de doctor he rode on down de road den. But I knowed in my own mind dat Dr. Marris was in dat fightin', 'cause he hoss so spattered up with mud; and I seed a long pistol barrel stickin' out from under he coat. Besides dat I is knowed de doctor ever since I was a child when Marse Tom used to have him to give de darkies de medicine when dey sick, and I seed him one night a-ridin' with de Ku Klux and heard him a-talkin' when I was hid in de bushes long side de road when I comin' home from catchin' me a possum in de thicket. Den Dr. Marris he with General Forest all through de War and he know what fightin' is and he sure wouldn't never go outen his way to miss no shootin'.

LUCINDA DAVIS
Interviewed at Tulsa, Oklahoma
Interviewer not identified
Age when interviewed: 85

What you gwine do when de meat give out?
What you gwine do when de meat give out?
   Set in de corner with my lips pooched out!
Lawsy!
What you gwine do when de meat come in?
What you gwine do when de meat come in?
   Set in de corner with a greasy chin!
Lawsy!

Dat's about de only little nigger song I know, less'n it be de one about:

Great big nigger, laying 'hind de log—
Finger on de trigger and eye on the hog!
Click go de trigger and bang go de gun!
Here come de owner and de buck nigger run!

And I think I learn both of dem long after I been grown, 'cause I belong to a full-blood Creek Indian and I didn't know nothing but Creek talk long after de Civil War. My mistress was part white and knowed English talk but she never did talk it because none of de people talked it. I heard it sometime, but it sound like whole lot of wild shoat in de cedar brake scared at something when I do hear it. Dat was when I was little girl in time of de War.

I don't know where I been born. Nobody never did tell me. But my mammy and pappy get me after de War and I know den whose child I is. De men at de Creek Agency help 'em get me, I reckon, maybe.

First thing I remember is when I was a little girl, and I belong to old Tuskayahiniha. He was big man in de Upper Creek, and we have a purty good size farm, just a little bit to de north of de wagon depot houses on de old road at Honey Springs. Dat place was about twenty-five mile south of Fort Gibson, but I don't know nothing about where de fort is when I was a little girl at dat time. I know de Elk River about two mile north of where we live, 'cause I been there many de time.

I don't know if Old Master have a white name. Lots de Upper Creek didn't have no white name. Maybe he have another Indian name, too, because Tuskayahiniha mean "head man warrior" in Creek, but dat what everybody call him and dat what de family call him too.

My Mistress' name was Nancy, and she was a Lott before she marry old man Tuskayahiniha. Her pappy name was Lott and he was purty near white. Maybe all white. Dey have two chillen, I think, but only one stayed on de place. She was named Luwina, and her husband was dead. His name was Walker, and Luwina bring Mr. Walker's little sister, Nancy, to live at de place too.

Luwina had a little baby boy and dat de reason Old Master buy me, to look after de little baby boy. He didn't have no name 'cause he wasn't big enough when I was with dem, but he get a name later on, I reckon. We all call him "Istidji." Dat mean "little man."

When I first remember, before de War, Old Master had about as many slaves as I got fingers, I reckon. I can think dem off on my fingers like dis, but I can't recollect de names.

Dey call all de slaves "Istilusti." Dat mean "black man."

Old man Tuskayahiniha was near about blind before de War, and about time of de War he go plumb blind and have to set on de long seat under de brush shelter of de house all de time. Sometime I lead him around de yard a little, but not very much. Dat about de time all de slaves begin to slip out and run off.

My own pappy was named Stephany. I think he take dat name 'cause when he little his mammy call him "Istifani." Dat mean a skeleton, and he was a skinny man. He belong to de Grayson family and I think his master's name was George, but I don't know. Dey big people in de Creek, and with de white folks too. My mammy name was Serena and she belong to some of de Gouge family. Dey was big people in de Upper Creek, and one de biggest men of the Gouge was name Hopoethleyoholo for his Creek name. He was a big man and went to de North in de War and died up in Kansas, I think. Dey say when he was a little boy he was called Hopoethli, which mean "good little boy," and when he get grown he make big speeches and dey stick on de "yoholo." Dat mean "loud whooper."

Dat de way de Creek made de name for young boys when I was a little girl. When de boy get old enough de big men in de town give him a name, and sometime later on when he get to going 'round with de grown men dey stick on some more name. If he a good talker dey sometime stick on "Yoholo," and if he make lots of jokes dey call him "Hadjo." If he is a good leader dey call him "Imala" and if he kind of mean dey sometime call him "Fixigo."

My mammy and pappy belong to two masters, but dey live together on a place. Dat de way de Creek slaves do lots of times. Dey work patches and give de masters most all dey make, but dey have some for demselves. Dey didn't have to stay on de master's place and work like I hear de slaves of de white people and de Cherokee and Choctaw people say dey had to do.

Maybe my pappy and mammy run off and get free, or maybeso dey buy demselves out, but anyway dey move away sometime and my mammy's master sell me to old man Tuskayahiniha when I was just a little gal. All I have to do is stay at de house and mind de baby.

Master had a good log house and a brush shelter out in front like all de houses had. Like a gallery, only it had de dirt for de floor and brush for de roof. Dey cook everything out in de yard in big pots, and dey eat out in de yard too. Dat was sure good stuff to eat, and it make you fat too! Roast de green corn on de ears in de ashes, and scrape off some and fry it! Grind de dry corn or pound it up and make ash cake. Den boil de greens — all kinds of greens from out in de woods — and chop up de pork and de deer meat, or de wild turkey meat. Maybe all of dem, in de big pot at de same time! Fish too, and de big turtle dat lay out on de bank!

Dey always have a pot full of sofki settin' right inside de house and anybody eat when dey feel hungry. Anybody come on a visit, always give 'em some of de sofki. If dey don't take none de old man get mad, too! When you make de sofki you pound up de corn real fine, den pour in de water and drain it off to get all de little skin from offen de grain. Den you let de grits soak and den boil it and let it stand. Sometime you put in some pounded hickory nuts meats. Dat make it real good.

I don't know where Old Master get de cloth for de clothes, lessen he buy it. Before I can remember I think he had some slaves dat weave de cloth, but when I was dere he get it at de wagon depot at Honey Springs,

I think. He go dere all de time to sell his corn, and he raise lots of corn, too.

Dat place was on de big road, what we called de road to Texas, but it go all de way up to de North, too. De traders stop at Honey Springs and Old Master trade corn for what he want. He get some purty checkedy cloth one time, and everybody get a dress or a shirt made offen it. I have dat dress till I get too big for it.

Everybody dress up fine when dey is a funeral. Dey take me along to mind de baby at two-three funerals, but I don't know who it is dat die. De Creek sure take on when somebody die! Long in de night you wake up and hear a gun go off, way off yonder, somewhere. Den it go again, and den again, just as fast as dey can ram de load in. Dat mean somebody dead. When somebody die de men go out in de yard and let de people know dat way. Den dey just go back in de house and let de fire go out, and don't even touch de dead person till somebody get dere what has de right to touch de dead. When somebody bad sick dey build a fire in de house, even in de summer, and don't let it die down till dat person get well or die. When dey die dey let de fire go out.

In de morning everybody dress up fine and go to de house where de dead is and stand around in de yard outside de house and don't go in. Pretty soon along come somebody what got a right to touch and handle de dead and dey go in. I don't know what give dem de right, but I think dey has to drink de red root and purge good before dey touch de body. When dey get de body ready dey come out and all go to de graveyard, mostly de family graveyard, right on de place or at some of the kinfolkses.

When dey get to de grave somebody shoots a gun at de north, den de west, den de south, and den de east. If dey had four guns dey used 'em. Den dey put de body down in de grave and put some extra clothes in with it and some food and a cup of coffee, maybe. Den dey takes strips of elm bark and lays over de body till it all covered up, and den throw in de dirt.

When de last dirt throwed on, everybody must clap dey hands and smile, but you sure hadn't better step on any of de new dirt around de grave, because it bring sickness right along with you back to your own house. Dat what dey said, anyways. Just soon as de grave filled up dey built a little shelter over it with poles like a pig pen and cover it over with elm bark to keep de rain from soaking down in de new dirt.

Den everybody go back to de house and de family go in and scatter some kind of medicine 'round de place and build a new fire. Sometime dey feed everybody before dey all leave for home.

Every time dey have a funeral dey always a lot of de people say, "Didn't you hear the stikini squalling in the night?" "I hear dat stikini all de night!" De stikini is de screech owl, and he supposed to tell when anybody going to die right soon. I hear lots of Creek people say dey hear de screech owl close to de house, and sure 'nough somebody in de family die soon.

When de big battle come at our place at Honey Springs dey just get through having de green corn "busk." De green corn was just ripened enough to eat. It must of been along in July. Dat busk was just a little busk. Dey wasn't enough men around to have a good one. But I seen lots of big ones. Ones where dey had all de different kinds of "banga." Dey call all de dances some kind of banga. De chicken dance is de "Tolosa-banga," and de "Istifanibanga" is de one where dey make like dey is skeletons and raw heads coming to get you. De "Hadjobanga" is de crazy dance, and dat is a funny one. Dey all dance crazy and make up funny songs to go with de dance. Everybody think up funny songs to sing and everybody whoop and laugh all de time.

But de worst one was de drunk dance. Dey just dance every which-a-way, de men and de women together, and dey wrassle and hug and carry on awful! De good people don't dance dat one. Everybody sing about going to somebody else's house and sleeping with dem, and shout, "We is all drunk and we don't know what we doing and we ain't doing wrong 'cause we is all drunk" and things like dat. Sometime de bad ones leave and go to the woods, too! Dat kind of doing make de good people mad, and sometime dey have killings about it. When a man catch one his women—maybeso his wife or one of his daughters—been to de woods, he catch her and beat her and cut off de rim of her ears! People think dat ain't so, but I know it is!

I was combing somebody's hair one time—I ain't going to tell who—and when I lift it up offen her ears I nearly drop dead! Dere de rims cut right offen 'em! But she was a married woman, and I think maybeso it happen when she was a young gal and got into it at one of dem drunk dances.

Dem Upper Creek took de marrying kind of light anyways. If de younguns wanted to be man and wife and de old ones didn't care dey just went ahead and dat was about all, 'cepting some presents maybe. But de Baptists changed dat a lot amongst de younguns.

I never forget de day dat battle of de Civil War happen at Honey Springs! Old Master just had de green corn all in, and us had been having a time getting it in, too. Just de women was all dat was left, 'cause de men slaves had all slipped off and left out. My uncle Abe done got up a bunch and gone to de North with dem to fight, but I didn't know den where he went. He was in dat same battle, and after de War dey called him Abe Colonel. Most all de slaves 'round dat place done gone off a long time before dat with dey masters when dey go with old man Gouge and a man named McDaniel.

We had a big tree in de yard, and a grapevine swing in it for de little baby "Istidji," and I was swinging him real early in de morning before de sun up. De house set in a little patch of woods with de field in de back, but all out on de north side was a little open space, like a kind of prairie. I was swinging de baby, and all at once I seen somebody riding dis way across dat prairie—just coming a-kiting and a-laying flat out on his hoss. When he see de house he begin to give de war whoop, "Eya-a-a-he-ah!" When he get close to de house he holler to get out de way 'cause dey gwine be a big fight, and Old Master start rapping with his cane and yelling to get some grub and blankets in de wagon right now!

We just leave everything setting right where it is, 'cepting putting out de fire and grabbing all de pots and kettles. Some de nigger women run to get de mules and de wagon and some start getting some meat and corn out of de place where we done hid it to keep de scouters from finding it before now. All de time we getting ready to travel we hear dat boy on dat horse going on down de big Texas road hollering, "Eya-a-a-a-he-he-hah!"

Den just as we starting to leave here come something across dat little prairie sure 'nough. We know dey is Indians de way dey is riding, and de way dey is all strung out. Dey had a flag, and it was all red and had a big criss-cross on it dat look like a sawhorse. De man carry it and rear back on it when de wind whip it, but it flap all round de horse's head and de horse pitch and rear like he know something going happen.

About dat time it turn kind of dark and begin to rain a little, and we get out to de big road and de rain come down hard. It rain so hard for a little while dat we just have to stop de wagon and set dere, and den 'long come more soldiers dan I ever seen before. Dey all white men, I think, and dey have on dat brown clothes dyed with walnut and butternut, and Old Master say dey de Confederate soldiers. Dey dragging some big guns on wheels and most de men slopping along in de rain on foot.

Den we hear de fighting up to de north along about where de river is, and de guns sound like hosses loping across a plank bridge way off some-where. De head men start hollering and some de hosses start rearing and de soldiers start trotting faster up de road. We can't get out on de road so we just strike off through de prairie and make for a creek dat got high banks and a place on it we call Rocky Cliff.

We get in a big cave in dat cliff, and spend de whole day and dat night in dere and listen to de battle going on. Dat place was about half a mile from de wagon depot at Honey Springs, and a little east of it. We can hear de guns going all day, and along in de evening here come de South side making for a getaway. Dey come riding and running by where we is, and it don't make no difference how much de head men hollers at 'em dey can't make dat bunch slow up and stop. After while here come de Yankees, right after 'em, and dey goes on into Honey Springs and pretty soon we see de blaze where dey is burning de wagon depot and de houses.

De next morning we goes back to de house and find de soldiers ain't hurt nothing much. De hogs is where dey is in de pen and de chickens come cackling round too. Dem soldiers going so fast dey didn't have no time to stop and take nothing, I reckon. Den long come lots of de Yankee soldiers going back to de North, and dey looks purty wore out, but dey is laughing and joshing and going on.

Old Master pack up de wagon with everything he can carry den, and we strike out down de big road to get out de way of any more war, is dey going be any. Dat old Texas road just crowded with wagons! Everybody doing de same thing we is, and de rains done made de road so muddy and de soldiers done tromp up de mud so bad dat de wagons get stuck all de time. De people all moving along in bunches, and every little while one bunch of wagons come up with another bunch all stuck in de mud, and dey put all de hosses and mules on together and pull 'em out, and den dey go on together awhile. At night dey camp, and de women and what few niggers dey is have to get de supper in de big pots, and de men so tired dey eat everything up from de women and de niggers, purty nigh.

After while we come to de Canadian town. Dat where old man Gouge been and took a whole lot de folks up North with him, and de South soldiers got in dere ahead of us and took up all de houses to sleep in.

Dey was some of de white soldiers camped dere, and dey was singing at de camp. I couldn't understand what dey sing, and I asked a Creek man what dey say and he tell me dey sing, "I wish I was in Dixie, look away—look away." I ask him where dat is, and he laugh and talk to de soldiers and dey all laugh, and make me mad.

De next morning we leave dat town and get to de big river. De rain make de river rise, and I never see so much water! Just look out dere and dere all dat water! Dey got some boats we put de stuff on, and float de wagons and swim de mules and finally get across, but it look like we gwine all drown.

Most de folks say dey going to Boggy Depot and around Fort Washita, but Old Master strike off by hisself and go way down in de bottom somewhere to live. I don't know where it was, but dey been some kind of fighting all around dere, 'cause we camp in houses and cabins all de time and nobody live in any of 'em. Look like de people all get away quick, 'cause all de stuff was in de houses, but you better scout up around de house before you go up to it. Liable to be some scouters already in it!

Dem Indian soldiers just quit de army and lots went scouting in little bunches and took everything dey find. If somebody try to stop dem dey get killed. Sometime we find graves in de yard where somebody just been buried fresh, and one house had some dead people in it when Old Mistress poke her head in it. We get away from dere, and no mistake!

By and by we find a little cabin and stop and stay all de time. I was de only slave by dat time. All de others done slip out and run off. We stay dere two year I reckon, 'cause we make two little crops of corn. For meat a man name Mr. Walker with us just went out in de woods and shoot de wild hogs. De woods was full of dem wild hogs, and lots of fish in de holes where he could sicken 'em with buck root and catch 'em with his hands, all we wanted.

I don't know when de War quit off, and when I get free, but I stayed with old man Tuskayahiniha long time after I was free, I reckon. I was just a little girl, and he didn't know where to send me to, anyways.

One day three men rid up and talk to de old man awhile in English talk. Den he called me and tell me to go with dem to find my own family. He just laugh and slap my behind and set me up on de hoss in front of one de men and dey take me off and leave my good checkedy dress at de house!

Before long we get to dat Canadian river again, and de men tie me on de hoss so I can't fall off. Dere was all dat water, and dey ain't no boat, and dey ain't no bridge, and we just swim de hosses. I knowed sure I was going to be gone dat time, but we get across. When we come to de Creek Agency dere is my pappy and mammy to claim me, and I live with dem in de Verdigris bottom above Fort Gibson till I was grown and dey is both dead. Den I marries Anderson Davis at Gibson Station, and we get our allotments on de Verdigris east of Tulsa—kind of south too, close to de Broken Arrow town.

WILLIAM DAVIS
Interviewed at Houston, Texas
Interviewer not identified
Age when interviewed: 92

I WAS BORN on de first day of April in 1845. De reason I knows was 'cause Miss Lizzie, our missy, told me so when we was set free. Mammy done told me I was born den, on de Tennessee River, near Kingston. I heared her say de turnpike what run past Massa John's house dere goes over de mountain to Bristol, over in Virginny. Mammy and Pappy and all us chillen belong to de Drapers, Massa Jonathan what us call Massa John and he wife, Miss Lizzie, and we is de only cullud folks what dey owns.

Massa John am de Baptist preacher, and while I'm sure glad to see my folks set free, I'll tell de truth and say Massa John and Miss Lizzie was mighty good to us. Dey have four chillen: Massa Milton, what am oldest and killed in de first battle; Massa Bob and Massa George and Massa Canero. Oh yes, dey have one gal, Missy Ann.

Course us didn't have no last names like now. Mammy named Sophie and Pappy named Billy. Sometimes de owners give de slaves last names according to what dey do, like Pappy was meat cook and Mammy cook pies and cakes and bread, so dey might have Cook for de last name.

We has a bigger family dan Massa John, 'cause dey eight of us chillen. I ain't seen none of dem since I left Virginny in 1869, but I 'member all de names. Dere was Jane and Lucy and Ellen and Bob and Solomon and Albert and John, and I'm de youngest de whole lot.

I heared Miss Lizzie tell some white folks dat my mammy and pappy give to her by her pappy in Alabama when she get married. Dat de custom with rich folks den, and Mammy belong to de Ames, what was Miss Lizzie's name before she marry. I heared her say when de stars falls,

I think she say in 1832. She was about eighteen, and dey think de world am endin'.

Pappy was a African. I knows dat. He come from Congo, over in Africa, and I heared him say a big storm drove de ship somewhere on de Ca'lina coast. I 'member he mighty 'spectful to Massa and Missy, but he proud, too, and walk straighter'n anybody I ever seen. He had scars on de right side he head and cheek what he say am tribe marks, but what dey means I don't know.

About de first I 'members real good am where we am in Virginny and Massa John runs de Washington College, in Washington County. I 'member all de pupils eats at Massa's house and dat de first job I ever had. 'Scuse me for laughin', but I don't reckon I thought of dat since de Lawd know when. Dat my first job. Dey has a string fasten to de wall on one side de room, with peafowl tail feathers strung along it, and it runs most de length de room, above de dinin' table, and round a pully-like piece in de ceilin' with one end de string hangin' down. When mealtime come, I am put where de string hang down and I pulls it easy like, and de feathers swishes back and forth sideways, and keeps de flies from lightin' while folks am eatin'. 'Ceptin' dat, all I does is play round with Massa George and Missy Ann.

Dey ain't no whippin' on our place and on Sunday us all go to church, and Massa John do de preachin'. Dey rides in de buggy and us follow in de wagon. De white folks sets in front de church and us in back.

I can't tell you how long us stay at de college, exactly, but us moves to Warm Springs, in Scott County, to take de baths and drink de water. Dat two, three years before de War, and Massa John run de hotel and preach on Sunday. I think dere am three springs, one sulphur water, and one lime water, and one a warm spring. I does a little bit of everything round de hotel, helps folks off de stage when it drove up, wait on table and such. When I hears de horn blow—you know, de stage driver blow it when dey top de hill about two miles away, to let you know dey comin'—I sure hustle round and get ready to meet it 'cause most times folks what I totes de grips for gives me something. Dat de first money I ever seen. Some de folks gives me de picayune—dat what us call a nickel, now, and some gives me two shillin's, what same as two-bits now. A penny was big den, just like a two-bit piece, now.

But when war begin between de Yankees and de South, it sure change everything up, 'cause folks quit comin' to de Springs and de soldiers takes over de place. Massa Milton go to join de South army and gets killed. Morgan and he men make de Springs headquarters most de War, till de Yankees come marchin' through toward de last part. I know Pappy say dem Yankees gwine win, 'cause dey always marchin' to de South, but none de South soldiers marches to de North. He didn't say dat to de white folks, but he sure say it to us. When de Yankees come marchin' through, de Morgan soldiers just hide out till dey gone. Dey never done no fightin' round Warm Springs. Lots of times dey goes way for couple weeks and den comes back and rests awhlie.

Den one mornin'—I 'members it just like it yesterday, it de Fourth of July in 1865—Miss Lizzie say to me, "William, I wants you to get you pappy and de rest de family and have dem come to de porch right away." I scurries round quick like and tells dem and she comes out of de house and says, "Now, de Yankees done set you free and you can do what you wants, but you gwine to see more carpetbaggers and liars dan you ever has seen, and you'll be worse off den you ever has been, if you has anythin' to do with dem." Den she opens de book and tells us all when us born and how old us am, so us have some record about ourselves. She tells me I'm just nineteen and one-fourth years old when I set free.

She tell Pappy Massa John want to see him in de house and when he come out he tells us Massa John done told him to take a couple wagons and de family and go to de farm about ten miles away on Possum Creek and work it and stay long as he wants. Massa has us load up one wagon with provisions. Pappy made de first crop with just hoes, 'cause us didn't have no hosses or mules to plow with. Us raise just corn and some wheat, but dey am fruit trees, peaches and apples and pears and cherries. Massa John pay Pappy one hundred and twenty dollars de year, besides us provisions, and us stays dere till Pappy dies in 1868.

Den I heared about de railroad what dey buildin' at Knoxville and leaves de folks and gets me de job totin' water. Dey asks my name and I say, William Davis, 'cause I knows Mr. Jefferson Davis am President of de South during de War, and I figgers it a good name. In 1869 I goes to Nashville and enlists in de army. I'm in de 24th Infantry, Company G, and us sent to Fort Stocton to guard de line of Texas, but all us do am build adobe houses. Colonel Wade was de commander de fort and Captain Johnson was captain of G Company. Out dere I votes for de first time, for General Grant, when Greely and him run for President. But I gets sick at de Fort and am muster out in 1870 and comes to Houston.

I gets me de deckhand job on de *Dinah*, de steamboat what haul freight and passengers between Galveston and Houston. Den I works on de *Lizzie*, what am a bigger boat. Course, Houston just a little bit of place to what it am now—dey wasn't no big buildin's like dey is now, and mud, I tell you de streets was just like de swamp when it rain.

Long about 1875 I gets marry to Mary Jones, but she died in 1883 and I gets marry again in 1885 to Arabelle Wilson and has four girls and one boy from her. She died about ten years back. 'Course, us cullud folks marry just like white folks do now, but I seen cullud folks marry before de War and Massa marry dem dis way: Dey goes in de parlor and each carry de broom. Dey lays de broom on de floor and de woman put her broom front de man and he put he broom front de woman. Dey face one another and step across de brooms at de same time to each other and takes hold of hands and dat marry dem. Dat's de way dey done, sure 'cause I seed my own sister marry dat way.

I has wished lots of time to go back and see my folks, but I never has been back and never seed dem since I left, and I guess dey am all gone along before now. I has jobbed at first one thing and another and, like Pappy tell me, I has trials and tribulations. And I has good chillen what ain't never got in trouble and what all helps take care deir old pappy so I guess I ain't got no complaint about things.

ELIGE DAVISON
Interviewed at Madisonville, Texas
Interviewer not identified
Age when interviewed: 86+

M Y BIRTH WAS in Richmond. That's over in Old Virginny, and George Davidson owned me and my pappy and mammy. I 'member one sister named Felina Tucker.

Massa and Missus were very good white folks and was good to the black folks. They had a great big rock house with pretty trees all round it, but the plantation was small, not more'n a hundred acres. Massa growed tobaccy on about thirty of them acres, and he had a big bunch of hogs. He waked us up about four in the mornin' to milk the cows and feed them hogs.

Our quarters was good, builded out of pine logs with a bed in one corner, no floors and windows. Us wore old lowell clothes and our shirt, it open all down the front. In winter Massa gave us woolen clothes to wear. Us didn't know what shoes was, though.

Massa, he look after us slaves when us sick, 'cause us worth too much money to let die just like you do a mule. He get doctor or nigger mammy. She make tea out of weeds, better'n quinine. She put string round our neck for chills and fever, with camphor on it. That sure keep off diseases.

Us work all day till just before dark. Sometimes us got whipping. We didn't mind so much. You know how stubborn a mule am, he have to be whipped. That the way slaves is.

When you gather a bunch of cattle to sell their calves, how the calves and cows will bawl, that the way the slaves was then. They didn't know nothin' about their kinfolks. Most chillen didn't know who their pappy was and some their mammy, 'cause they taken away from the mammy when she wean them. They sell or trade the chillen to someone else, so they wouldn't get attached to their mammy or pappy.

Massa learn us to read and us read the Bible. He learn us to write too. They a big church on he plantation and us go to church and learn to tell the truth.

I seed some few run away to the North and Massa sometime cotch 'em and put 'em in jail. Us couldn't go to nowhere without a pass. The patter-rollers would get us and they do plenty for nigger slaves. I'se went to my quarters and be so tired I just fall in the door, on the ground, and a patter-roller come by and hit me several licks with a cat-o-nine-tails, to see if I'se tired enough to not run away. Sometimes them patterrollers hit us just to hear us holler.

When a slave die, he just another dead nigger. Massa, he builded a wooden box and put the nigger in and carry him to the hole in the ground. Us march round the grave three times and that all.

I been marry once before freedom, with home weddin'. Massa, he bring some more women to see me. He wouldn't let me have just one woman. I have about fifteen and I don't know how many chillen. Some over a hundred, I'se sure.

I 'member plenty about the War, 'cause the Yankees they march on to Richmond. They kill everything what in the way. I heared them big guns and I'se scared. Everybody scared. I didn't see no fightin', 'cause I gets out the way and keeps out till it all over. But when they marches right on the town I'se tendin' horses for Massa. He have two hosses kilt right under him. Then the Yankees, they capture that town. Massa, he send me to get the buggy and hoss and carry Missus to the mountain, but them Yankees they capture me and say they gwine hang that nigger. But, glory be, Massa he saves me before they hangs me. He send he wife and my wife to another place then, 'cause they burn Massa's house and tear down all he fences.

When the War over Massa call me and tells me I'se free as he was, 'cause them Yankees win the War. He gives me five dollars and say he'll give me that much a month iffen I stays with him, but I starts to Texas. I heared I wouldn't have to work in Texas, 'cause everything growed on trees and the Texans wore animal hides for clothes. I didn't get no land or mule or cow. They warn't no plantations divided what I knowed about. Most niggers just got turn loose with a cuss, and not 'nough clothes to cover their bodies.

It about a year before I gets to Texas. I walks nearly all the way. Some-times I get a li'l ride with farmer. Sometimes I work for folks along the way and get fifty cents and start again. I got to Texas and try to work for white folks and try to farm. I couldn't make anything at any work. I made five dollars a month for I don't know how many years after the War. Iffen the woods wasn't full of wild game us niggers all starve to death them days.

I been marry three time. First wife Eve Shelton. She run off with another man. Then I marries Fay Elly. Us separate in a year. Then I marry Parlee Breyle. No, I done forgot. Before that I married Sue Wilford, and us have seven gals and six boys. They all in New York but one. He stays here. Then I marries Parlee and us have two gals. Parlee die three year ago.

The gov'ment give me a pension and I gets li'l odd jobs round, to get by. But times been hard and I ain't had much to eat the last few years. But I gets by somehow. I done the best I could, 'sidering I'se turned out with nothin' when I'se growed and didn't know much, neither. The young folks, they knows more, 'cause they got the chance for schoolin'.

ANTHONY DAWSON
Interviewed at Tulsa, Oklahoma
Interviewer not identified
Age when interviewed: 105

Run nigger, run,
De Patteroll get you!
Run nigger, run,
De Patteroll come!
Watch nigger, watch,
De Patteroll trick you!
Watch nigger, watch,
He got a big gun!

Dat one of the songs de slaves all knowed, and de children down on de "twenty acres" used to sing it when dey playing in de moonlight round de cabins in de quarters. Sometime I wonder iffen de white folks didn't make dat song up so us niggers would keep in line.

None of my old master's boys tried to get away 'cepting two, and dey met up with evil, both of 'em. One of dem niggers was fetching a bull-tongue from a piece of new ground way at de back of de plantation and bringing it to my pappy to get it sharped. My pappy was de blacksmith. Dis boy got out in de big road to walk in de soft sand, and 'long come a wagon with a white overseer and five, six, niggers going somewhere. Dey stopped and told dat boy to get in and ride. Dat was de last anybody seen him.

Dat overseer and another one was cotched after awhile and showed up to be underground railroaders. Dey would take a bunch of niggers into town for some excuse and on de way just pick up a extra nigger and show him where to go to get on de "railroad system." When de runaway niggers got to de North dey had to go in de army, and dat boy from our place got killed. He was a good boy, but dey just talked him into it. Dem railroaders was honest, and dey didn't take no presents, but de patrollers was low white trash! We all knowed dat if a patroller just rode right by and didn't say nothing dat he was doing his honest job, but iffen he stopped his hoss and talked to a nigger he was after some kind of trade.

Dat other black boy was hoeing cotton way in de back of de field and de patroller rid up and down de big road, saying nothing to nobody. De next day another white man was on de job, and 'long in de evening a man come by and axed de niggers about de fishing and hunting! Dat black boy seen he was de same man what was riding de day before and he knowed it was a underground trick. But he didn't see all de trick, bless God!

We found out afterwards dat he told his mammy about it. She worked at de Big House and she stole something for him to give dat low white trash I reckon, 'cause de next day he played sick along in de evening and de black overlooker—he was my uncle—sent him back to de quarters. He never did get there, but when dey started de hunt dey found him about a mile away in de woods with his head shot off, and Old Master sold his mammy to a trader right away. He never whipped his grown niggers.

Dat was de way it worked. Dey was all kinds of white folks just like dey is now. One man in Sesesh* clothes would shoot you if you tried to run away. Maybe another Sesesh would help slip you out to the underground and say "God bless you, poor black devil," and some of dem dat was poor would help you if you could bring 'em somethin' you stole, like a silver dish or spoons or a couple big hams. I couldn't blame them poor white folks, with the men in the War and the women and children hungry. The niggers didn't belong to them nohow, and they had to live somehow. But now and then they was a devil on earth, walking in the sight of God and spreading iniquity before him. He was de low-down Sesesh dat would take what a poor runaway nigger had to give for his chance to get away, and den give him 'structions dat would lead him right into de hands of de patrollers and get him caught or shot. Yes, dat's de way it was. Devils and good people walking in de road at de same time, and nobody could tell one from t'other.

I remember about de trickery so good 'cause I was "grown and out" at that time. When I was a little boy I was a house boy, 'cause my mammy was the house woman, but when the War broke I already been sent to the fields and Mammy was still at de house. I was born on July 25, 1832. I know, 'cause Old Master keep de book on his slaves just like on his own family. I was born on the plantation, soon after my pappy and mammy was brought to it. I don't remember whether they was bought or come from my mistress' father. He was mighty rich and had several hundred niggers. When she was married he give her forty niggers. One of them was my pappy's brother. His name was John, and he was my master's overlooker. We called a white man boss the "overseer," but a nigger was a overlooker. John could read and write and figger, and Old Master didn't have no white overseer.

Master was a good man, and Old Mistress was de best woman in de world! Master's name was Levi Dawson, and his plantation was eighteen miles east of Greenville, North Carolina. De plantation had more than five hundred acres and most was in cotton and tobacco. But we raised

* Secessionist or Confederate.

corn and oats, and lots of cattle and horses, and plenty of sheep for wool.
It was a beautiful place, with all the fences around the Big House and
along the front made out of barked poles, rider style, and all whitewashed.
The Big House set back from the big road about a quarter of a mile. It
was only one story, but it had lots of rooms. There was four rooms in a
bunch on one side and four in a bunch on the other, with a wide hall in
between. They was made of square adzed logs all weatherboarded on the
outside and planked up and plastered on the inside. Then they was a long
gallery clean across the front with big pillars made out of bricks and
plastered over. They called it the passage 'cause it didn't have no floor
excepting bricks, and a buggy could drive right under it. Mostly it was
used to set under and talk and play cards and drink the best whiskey Old
Master could buy. Back in behind the Big House was the kitchen, and the
smokehouse in another place made of plank, and all was whitewashed
and painted white all the time.

Old Mistress was named Miss Susie and she was born an Isley. She
brought forty niggers from her pappy as a present, and Master Levi just
had four or five, but he had got all his land from his pappy. She had the
niggers and he had the land. That's the way it was, and that's the way it
stayed! She never let him punish one of her niggers and he never asked
her about buying or selling land. Her pappy was richer than his pappy,
and she was sure quality!

My pappy's name was Anthony, and Mammy's name was Chanie. He
was the blacksmith and fixed the wagons, but he couldn't read and figger
like Uncle John. Mammy was the head house woman but didn't know any
letters either. They was both black like me. Old man Isley, where they
come from, had lots of niggers, but I don't think they was off the boat.

Master Levi had three sons and no daughters. The oldest son was
Simeon. He was in the Sesesh army. The other two boys was too young.
I can't remember their names. They was a lot younger and I was grown
and out before they got big.

Old Master was a fine Christian but he like his juleps anyways. He let
us niggers have preachings and prayers and would give us a parole to go
ten or fifteen miles to a camp meeting and stay two or three days with
nobody but Uncle John to stand for us. Mostly we had white preachers,
but when we had a black preacher that was heaven. We didn't have no
voodoo women nor conjure folks at our "twenty acres." We all knowed
about the Word and the unseen Son of God and we didn't put no stock
in conjure. 'Course we had luck charms and good and bad signs, but
everybody got dem things, even nowadays. My boy had a white officer in
the Big War and he tells me that man had a li'l old doll tied around his
wrist on a gold chain.

We used herbs and roots for common ailments, like sassafrass and
boneset and peach tree poultices and coon rot tea, but when a nigger got
bad sick Old Master sent for a white doctor. I remember that old doctor.
He lived in Greenville and he had to come eighteen miles in a buggy.
When he give some nigger medicine he would be afraid the nigger was

like lots of them that believed in conjure, and he would say, "If you don't take that medicine like I tell you and I have to come back here to see you I going to break your damn neck next time I come out here!" When it was bad weather sometime the black boy sent after him had to carry a lantern to show him the way back. If that nigger on his mule got too far ahead so old doctor couldn't see de light he sure catch de devil from that old doctor and from Old Master, too, lessen he was one of Old Missy's house niggers, and then Old Master just grumble to satisfy the doctor.

Down in the quarters we had the spinning house, where the old woman card the wool and run the loom. They made double weave for the winter time, and all the white folks and slaves had good clothes and good food.

Master made us all eat all we could hold. He would come to the smoke-house and look in and say, "You niggers ain't cutting down that smoke side and that souse like you ought to! You made dat meat and you got to help eat it up!"

Never no work on Sunday 'cepting the regular chores. The overlooker made everybody clean up and wash de children up, and after the praying we had games—antny over and marbles and "I Spy" and de likes of that. Sometimes de boys would go down in de woods and get a possum. I love possum and sweet 'taters, but de coon meat more delicate and de hair don't stink up de meat.

I wasn't at the quarters much as a boy. I was at the Big House with my mammy, and I had to swing the fly brush over my old mistress when she was sewing or eating or taking her nap. Sometime I would keep the flies offen Old Master, and when I would get tired and let the brush slap his neck he would kick at me and cuss me, but he never did reach me. He had a way of keeping us little niggers scared to death and never hurting nobody.

I was down in the field burning brush when I first heard the guns in the War. De fighting was de battle at Kingston, North Carolina, and it lasted four days and nights. After while bunches of Sesesh come riding by hauling wounded people in wagons, and then pretty soon big bunches of Yankees come by, but dey didn't act like dey was trying very hard to catch up.

Dey had de country in charge quite some time, and they had forages coming round all the time. By dat time Old Master done buried his money and all de silver and de big clock, but the Yankees didn't appear to search out dat kind of stuff. All day ask about was did anybody find a bottle of brandy!

When de War ended up most all de niggers stay with Old Master and work on de shares, until de land get divided up and sold off and the young niggers get scattered to town.

I never did have no truck with de Ku Kluckers, but I had to step mighty high to keep outen it! De sure 'nough Kluxes never did bother around us 'cause we minded our own business and never give no trouble. We wouldn't let no niggers come round our place talking about delegates and voting, and we just all stayed on the place. But dey was some low white trash and some devilish niggers made out like dey was Ku Klux ranging round de country stealing hosses and taking things. Old Master said dey wasn't sure 'nough, so I reckon he knowed who the regular ones was.

These bunches that come around robbing got into our neighborhood and Old Master told me I better not have my old horse at the house, 'cause if I had him they would know nobody had been there stealing and it wouldn't do no good to hide anything 'cause they would tear up the place hunting what I had and maybe whip or kill me. "Your old hoss ain't no good, Tony, and you better kill him to make them think you already been raided on," Old Master told me, so I led him out and knocked him in the head with an ax, and then we hid all our grub and waited for Kluckers to come most any night, but they never did come. I borried a hoss to use in the day and took him back home every night for about a year.

The niggers kept talking about being free, but they wasn't free then and they ain't now. Putting them free just like putting goat hair on a sheep. When it rain de goat come a-running and get in de shelter, 'cause his hair won't shed the rain and he get cold, but de sheep ain't got sense enough to get in the shelter but just stand out and let it rain on him all day. But the good Lord fix the sheep up with a woolly jacket that turn the water off, and he don't get cold, so he don't have to have no brains. De nigger during slavery was like de sheep. He couldn't take care of hisself but his Master looked out for him, and he didn't have to use his brains. De master's protection was like de woolly coat. But de 'mancipation come and take off de woolly coat and leave de nigger with no protection and he cain't take care of hisself either.

When de niggers was set free lots of them got mighty uppity, and everybody wanted to be a delegate to something or other. The Yankees told us we could go down and vote in the 'lections and our color was good enough to run for anything. Heaps of niggers believed them. You cain't fault them for that, 'cause they didn't have no better sense, but I knowed the black folks didn't have no business mixing in until they knowed more. It was a long time after the War before I went down to vote and everything quiet by that time, but I heard people talk about the fights at the schoolhouse when they had the first election.

I just stayed on around the old place a long time, and then I got on another piece of ground and farmed, not far from Greenville, until 1900. Then I moved to Hearn, Texas, and stayed with my son Ed until 1903 when we moved to Sapulpa in the Creek Nation. We come to Tulsa several years ago, and I been living with him ever since.

SARAH DEBRO

Interviewed at Durham, North Carolina
Interviewed by Travis Jordon
Age when interviewed: 85

I WAS BORN in Orange County way back sometime in de fifties. Mis'
Polly White Cain and Marse Doctor Cain was my white folks.
Marse Cain's plantation joined Mister Paul Cameron's land. Marse Cain
owned so many niggers dat he didn't know his own slaves when he met
dem in de road. Sometimes he would stop dem and say: "Whose niggers
am you?" Dey'd say, "We's Marse Cain's niggers." Den he would say,
"I'se Marse Cain," and drive on.

Marse Cain was good to his niggers. He didn't whip dem like some
owners did, but if dey done mean he sold 'em. Dey knew dis, so dey
minded him. One day Grandpappy sassed Mis' Polly White and she told
him dat if he didn't behave hisself dat she would put him in her pocket.
Grandpappy was a big man and I ask him how Mis' Polly could do dat.
He said she meant dat she would sell him, den put de money in her
pocket. He never did sass Mis' Polly no more.

I was kept at de Big House to wait on Mis' Polly, to tote her baskets of
keys and such as dat. Whenever she seed a child down in de quarters dat
she wanted to raise by hand, she took dem up to de Big House and
trained dem. I was to be a house maid. De day she took me my mammy
cried 'cause she knew I would never be allowed to live at de cabin with
her no more. Mis' Polly was big and fat and she made us niggers mind and
we had to keep clean. My dresses and aprons was starched stiff. I had a
clean apron every day. We had white sheets on de beds and we niggers
had plenty to eat too, even ham. When Mis' Polly went to ride she took
me in de carriage with her. De driver set way up high and me and Mis'
Polly set way down low. Dey was two hosses with shined harness. I toted
Mis' Polly's bags and bundles, and if she dropped her handkerchief I
picked it up. I loved Mis' Polly and loved stayin' at de Big House.

I was about waist high when de soldiers mustered. I went with Mis'
Polly down to de musterin' field where dey was marchin'. I can see dey
feets now when dey flung dem up and down, sayin', "Hep, hep, hep."
When dey was all ready to go and fight, de women folk fixed a big dinner.

Aunt Charity and Pete cooked two or three days for Mis' Polly. De table was piled with chicken, ham, shoat, barbecue, young lamb, and all sorts of pies, cakes and things, but nobody eat nothin' much. Mis' Polly and de ladies got to cryin'. De vittles got cold. I was so sad dat I got over in de corner and cried too. De man folks all had on dey new soldier clothes, and dey didn't eat nothin' neither. Young Marse Jim went up and put his arm round Mis' Polly, his mammy, but dat made her cry harder. Marse Jim was a cavalry. He rode a big hoss, and my Uncle Dave went with him to de field as his bodyguard. He had a hoss, too, so if Marse Jim's hoss got shot dere would be another one for him to ride. Mis' Polly had another son, but he was too drunk to hold a gun. He stayed drunk.

De first cannon I heard scared me near about to death. We could hear dem goin' boom, boom. I thought it was thunder, den Mis' Polly say, "Listen, Sarah, hear dem cannons? Dey's killin' our mens." Den she begun to cry.

I run in de kitchen where Aunt Charity was cookin' and told her Mis' Polly was cryin'. She said: "She ain't cryin' 'cause de Yankees killin' de mens; she's doin' all dat cryin' 'cause she scared we's goin' to be set free." Den I got mad and told her Mis' Polly wasn't like dat.

I 'members when Wheelers Cavalry come through. Dey was 'Federates but dey was mean as de Yankees. Dey stole everything dey could find and killed a pile of niggers. Dey come round checkin'. Dey ask de niggers if dey wanted to be free. If dey say yes, den dey shot dem down, but if dey said no, dey let dem alone. Dey took three of my uncles out in de woods and shot dey faces off.

I 'members de first time de Yankees come. Dey come gallopin' down de road, tromplin' down de rose bushes and messin' up de flower beds. Dey stomped all over de house, in de kitchen, pantries, smokehouse, and everywhere, but dey didn't find much, 'cause near about everything done been hid. I was settin' on de steps when a big Yankee come up. He had on a cap and his eyes was mean. "Where did dey hide de gold and silver, nigger?" he yells at me. I was scared and my hands was ashy, but I told him I didn't know nothin' about nothin'; dat if anybody hid things dey hid it while I was sleep.

"Go ask dat ole white headed devil," he said to me. I got mad 'cause he was talkin' about Mis' Polly, so I didn't say nothin.' I just set. Den he pushed me off de step and say if I didn't dance he gwine shoot my toes off. Scared as I was, I sure done some shufflin'. Den he give me five dollars and told me to go buy jim cracks, but dat piece of paper weren't no good. Twasn't nothin' but a shin plaster like all dat war money, you couldn't spend it.

Dat Yankee kept callin' Mis' Polly a white headed devil and said she done ram-shacked till dey wasn't nothin' left, but he made his mens tote off meat, flour, pigs, and chickens. After dat Mis' Polly got mighty stingy with de victuals and we didn't have no more ham.

When de War was over de Yankees was all round de place, tellin' de niggers what to do. Dey told dem dey was free, dat dey didn't have to slave for de white folks no more. My folks all left Marse Cain and went to live in houses dat de Yankees built. Dey was like poor white folks' houses, little shacks made out of sticks and mud with stick and mud chimneys. Dey wasn't like Marse Cain's cabins, planked up and warm. Dey was full of cracks, and dey wasn't no lamps and oil. All de light come from de lightwood knots burnin' in the fireplace.

One day my mammy come to de Big House after me. I didn't want to go; I wanted to stay with Mis' Polly. I begun to cry and Mammy caught hold of me. I grabbed Mis' Polly and held so tight dat I tore her skirt bindin' loose and her skirt fell down about her feets.

"Let her stay with me," Mis' Polly said to Mammy. But Mammy shook her head. "You took her away from me and didn't pay no mind to my cryin', so now I'se takin' her back home. We's free now, Mis' Polly, we ain't gwine be slaves no more to nobody." She dragged me away. I can see how Mis' Polly looked now. She didn't say nothin' but she looked hard at Mammy and her face was white.

Mammy took me to de stick and mud house de Yankees done give her. It was smoky and dark 'cause dey wasn't no windows. We didn't have no sheets and no towels, so when I cried and said I didn't want to live in no Yankee house, Mammy beat me and made me go to bed. I laid on de straw tick lookin' up through de cracks in de roof. I could see de stars, and de sky shinin' through de cracks looked like long blue splinters stretched 'cross de rafters. I ley dere and cried 'cause I wanted to go back to Mis' Polly.

I was never hungry till we was free and de Yankees fed us. We didn't have nothin' to eat 'cept hard tack and middlin' meat. I never saw such meat. It was thin and tough with a thick skin. You could boil it all day and all night and it wouldn't cook done. I wouldn't eat it. I thought 'twas mule meat; mules dat done been shot on de battlefield, den dried. I still believe 'twas mule meat.

One day me and my brother was lookin' for acorns in de woods. We found somethin' like a grave in de woods. I told Dave dey was somethin' buried in dat mound. We got de grubbin' hoe and dug. Dere was a box with eleven hams in dat grave. Somebody done hid it from de Yankees and forgot where dey buried it. We covered it back up 'cause if we took it home in de daytime de Yankees and niggers would take it away from us. So when night come we slipped out and toted dem hams to de house and hid dem in de loft.

Dem was bad days. I'd rather been a slave dan to been hired out like I was, 'cause I wasn't no field hand. I was a hand maid, trained to wait on de ladies. Den too, I was hungry most of de time and had to keep fightin' off dem Yankee mens. Dem Yankees was mean folks.

I looks back now and thinks. I ain't never forgot dem slavery days, and I ain't never forgot Mis' Polly an' my white starched aprons.

LUCY ANN DUNN

Interviewed at Raleigh, North Carolina
Interviewed by Mary Hicks
Age when interviewed: 90

MY PAPPY, Dempsey, my mammy, Rachel, and my brothers and sisters and me all belonged to Marse Peterson Dunn of Neuse, here in Wake County, North Carolina. Dere was five of us chillen, Allen, Charles, Corina, Madora, and me, all borned before de War. My mammy was de cook, and far back as I 'members almost, I was a house girl. I fanned flies offen de table and done a heap of little things for Mis' Betsy, Marse Peterson's wife. My pappy worked on de farm, which was bound to have been a big plantation with two hundert and more niggers to work it.

I 'members when word come dat war was declared, how Mis' Betsy cried and prayed and how Marse Peter quarreled and walked de floor cussin' de Yankees. De War comes on just de same and some of de men slaves was sent to Roanoke to help build de fort. De War comes to de Great House and to de slave cabins just alike.

De Great House was large and whitewashed, with green blinds and de slave cabins was made of slabs with plank floors. We had plenty to eat and enough to wear and we was happy. We had our fun and we had our troubles, like little whippin's, which weren't often.

After so long a time de rich folkses tried to hire, or make, de po' white trash go in dere places, but some of dem won't go. Dey am treated so bad dat some of dem decides to be Klu Kluxes and dey goes to de woods to live. When we starts to take up de eggs or starts from de spring house with de butter and milk dey grabs us and takes de food for theirselves.

Dis goes on for a long time and finally one day in de spring I sets on de porch and I hear a roar. I was 'sponsible for de goslin's dem days so I says to de missus, "I reckon dat I better get in de goslin's 'cause I hear it a-thunderin'."

"Dat ain't no thunder, nigger, dat am de canon," she says.

"What canon?" I asks.

"Why de canon what dey am fightin' with," she says.

Well, dat evenin' I is out gettin' up de goslin's when I hears music. I looks up de road and I sees flags, and about dat time de Yankees am

101

dere a-killin' as dey goes. Dey kills de geese, de ducks, de chickens, pigs, and everything. Dey goes to de house and dey takes all of de meat, de meal, and everything dey can get dere paws on. When dey goes to de kitchen where Mammy am cookin' she cuss dem out and run dem outen her kitchen. Dey shore am a rough lot.

I ain't never fergot how Mis' Betsy cried when de news of de surrender come. She ain't said nothin', but Marse Peter he makes a speech sayin' dat he ain't had to sell none of us, that he ain't whipped none of us bad, dat nobody has ever run away from him yet. Den he tells us dat all who wants to can stay right on for wages.

Well, we stayed two years, even though my pappy died de year after de surrender. Den we moves to Marse Peter's other place at Wake Forest. After dat we moves back to Neuse.

It was in de little Baptist church at Neuse where I first seed big black Jim Dunn and I fell in love with him den, I reckons. He said dat he loved me den too, but it was three Sundays before he asked to see me home.

We walked dat mile home in front of my mammy and I was so happy dat I ain't thought it a half a mile home. We et corn bread and turnips for dinner and it was night before he went home. Mammy wouldn't let me walk with him to de gate, I knowed, so I just set dere on de porch and says goodnight.

He come every Sunday for a year and finally he proposed. I had told Mammy dat I thought dat I ought to be allowed to walk to de gate with Jim and she said all right, iffen she was settin' dere on de porch lookin'.

Dat Sunday night I did walk with Jim to de gate and stood under de honeysuckles dat was a-smellin' so sweet. I heard de big ole bullfrogs a-croakin' by de river and de whippoorwills a-hollerin' in de woods. Dere was a big yellow moon, and I reckon Jim did love me. Anyhow he said so and asked me to marry him and he squeezed my hand. I told him I'd think it over and I did and de next Sunday I told him dat I'd have him.

He ain't kissed me yet but de next Sunday he asked my mammy for me. She says dat she'll have to have a talk to me and let him know. Well all dat week she talks to me, tellin' me how serious gettin' married is and dat it last a powerful long time. I tells her dat I knows it but dat I am ready to try it and dat I intends to make a go of it, anyhow.

On Sunday night Mammy tells Jim dat he can have me and you ought to seed dat black boy grin. He comes to me without a word and he picks me up out dat chair and dere in de moonlight he kisses me right before my mammy who am a-cryin'. De next Sunday we was married in de Baptist church at Neuse. I had a new white dress, though times was hard.

We lived together fifty-five years and we always loved each other. He ain't never whip nor cuss me and though we had our fusses and our troubles we trusted in de Lord and we got through. I loved him durin' life and I love him now, though he's been dead for twelve years. We had eight chillens, but only four of dem are livin'. De livin' are James, Sidney, Helen, and Florence who was named for Florence Nightingale.

I can't be here so much longer now 'cause I'se gettin' too old and feeble and I want to go to Jim anyhow. I thinks of him all de time, but seems like we're young again when I smell honeysuckles or see a yellow moon.

WILLIAM L. DUNWOODY

Interviewed at Little Rock, Arkansas
Interviewed by Samuel S. Taylor
Age when interviewed: 98

I WAS BORN IN CHARLESTON, South Carolina, in the year 1840. My father was killed in the Civil War when they taken South Carolina. His name was Charles Dunwoody. My mother's name was Mary Dunwoody. My father was a free man and my mother was a slave. When he courted and married her he took the name of Dunwoody.

Ain't you seen a house built in the country when they were clearing up and wanted to put up somethin' for the men to live in while they were working? They'd cut down a tree. They they'd line it—fasten a piece of twine to each end and whiten it and pull it up and let it fly down and mark the log. Then they'd score it with axes. Then the hewers would come along and hew the log. Sometimes they could hew it so straight you couldn't put a line on it and find any difference. Where they didn't take time with the logs, it would be where they were just putting up a little shack for the men to sleep in. Just like you box timber in the sawmill, the men would straighten out a log.

To make the log house, you would saw your blocks, set 'em up, then you put the sills on the blocks, then you put the sleepers. When you get them in, lay the planks to walk on. Then they put on the first log. You notch it. To make the roof, you would keep on cutting the logs in half, first one way and then the other until you got the blocks small enough for shingles. Then you would saw the shingles off. They had plenty of time.

The slaves ate just what the master ate. They ate the same on my master's place. All people didn't farm alike. Some just raised cotton and corn. Some raised peas, oats, rye, and a lot of different things. My old master raised corn, potatoes—Irish and sweet—goober peas, rye, and wheat, and I can't remember what else. He had hogs, goats, sheep, cows, chickens, turkeys, geese, ducks. That is all I can remember in the eating line. My old master's slaves et anything he raised.

He would send three or four wagons down to the mill at a time. One of them would carry sacks; all the rest would carry wheat. You know flour seconds, shorts, and brand come from the wheat. You get all that from the wheat. Buckwheat flour comes from a large grained wheat. The wagons came back loaded with flour, seconds, shorts, and brand. The old man had six wheat barns to keep the wheat in.

All the slaves ate together. They had a cook special for them. This cook would cook in a long house more than thirty feet long. Two or three women would work there and a man, just like the cooks would in a hotel now. All the working hands ate there and got whatever the cook gave them. It was one thing one time and another another. The cook gave the hands anything that was raised on the place. There was one woman in there cooking that was called "Mammy" and she seed to all the chillen.

After the old folks among the slaves had had their breakfast, the cook would blow a horn. That would be about nine o'clock or eight. All the children that were big enough would come to the cook shack. Some of them would bring small children that had been weaned but couldn't look after themselves. The cook would serve them whatever the old folks had for breakfast. They ate out of the same kind of dishes as the old folks.

Between ten and eleven o'clock, the cook would blow the horn again and the children would come in from play. There would be a large bowl and a large spoon for each group or larger children. There would be enough children in each group to get around the bowl comfortably. One would take a spoon of what was in the bowl and then pass the spoon to his neighbor. His neighbor would take a spoonful and then pass the spoon on, and so on until everyone would have a spoonful. Then they would begin again, and so on until the bowl was empty. If they did not have enough then, the cook would put some more in the bowl. Most of the time, bread and milk was in the bowl; sometimes mush and milk. There was a small spoon and a small bowl for the smaller children in the group that the big children would use for them and pass around just like they passed around the big spoon.

About two or three o'clock, the cook would blow the horn again. Time the children all got in there and et, it would be four or five o'clock. The old mammy would cut up greens real fine and cut up meat into little pieces and boil it with cornmeal dumplings. They'd call it pepper pot. Then she'd put some of the pepper pot into the bowls and we'd eat it. And it was good.

After the large children had et, they would go back to see after the babies. If they were awake, the large children would put on their clothes and clean them up. Then where there was a woman who had two or three small children and didn't have one large enough to do this, they'd give her a large one from some other family to look after her children. If she had any relatives, they would use their children for her. If she didn't then they would use anybody's children.

About eleven o'clock all the women who had little children that had not been weaned would come in to see after them and let them suck. When a woman had nursing children, she would nurse them before she went to work, again at around eleven o'clock, and again when she came from work in the evening. She would come in long before sundown. In between times, the old mammy and the other children would look after them.

I saw Jeff Davis once. He was one-eyed. He had a glass eye. My old mistiss had three girls. They got into the buggy and went to see Jeff Davis when he came through Auburn, Alabama. We were living in Auburn then. I drove them. Jeff Davis came through first, and then the Confederate Army, and then the Yankees. They didn't come on the same day but some days apart.

The way I happened to see the Yanks was like this. I went to carry some clothes to my young master. He was a doctor, and was out where they were drilling the men. I laid down on the carpet in his tent and I heard music playing "In Dixie Land I'll take my stand and live and die in Dixie." I got up and come out and looked up ever which way but I couldn't see nothing. I went back again and laid down again in the tent, and I heard it again. I run out and looked up and around again, and I still couldn't see nothin'. That time I looked and saw my master talking to another officer—I can't remember his name. My young master said, "What you looking for?"

I said, "I'm looking for them angels I hear playing. Don't you hear'em playing Dixie?" The other officer said, "Celas, you ought to whip that nigger." I went back into the tent. My young master said, "Whip him for what?" And he said, "For telling that lie." My young master said to him like this, "He don't tell lies. He heard something somewhere."

Then they got through talking and he come on in and I seed him and beckoned to him. He came to me and I said, "Lie down there." He laid down and I laid down with him, and he heard it. Then he said, "Look out there and tell him to come in."

I called the other officer and he come in. The doctor (that was my young master) said, "Lie down there." When he laid down by my young master, he heard it too. Then the doctor said to him, "You said William was telling a damn lie." He said, "I beg your pardon, doctor."

My young master got up and said, "Where is my spy glasses? Let me have a look." He went out and there was a mountain called the Blue Ridge Mountain. He looked but he didn't see nothin'. I went out and looked too. I said, "Look down the line beside those two big trees," and I handed the glasses back to him. He looked and then he hollered, "My God, look yonder," and handed the spy glasses to the other officer. He looked too. Then the doctor said, "What are we going to do?" He said, "I am goin' to put pickets way out." He told me to get to my mule. I got. He put one of his spurs on my foot and told me to go home, and tell "Ma" the Yanks were coming. You know what "Ma" he was talking about? That was his wife's mother, we all called her "Mother."

I carried the note. When I got to Mrs. Dobbins' house, I yelled, "The Yanks are coming—Yankees, Yankees, Yankees!" She had two boys. They runned out and said "What did you say?" I said, "Yankees, Yankees!" They said, "Hell, what could he see?"

I come on then and got against Miss Yancy's. She had a son, a man named Henry Yancy. He had a sore leg. He asked me what I said. I told him that the Yanks were coming. He called for Henry, a boy that stayed with him, and had him saddle his horse. Then he got on it and rode up town. When he got up there, he was questioned about how he know it. Did he see them? He said he didn't see them, that Celas Neal saw them and the doctor's mother's boy brought the message. Then he taken off.

Jeff Davis went on. The Confederates went on. They all went on. Then the Yanks passed through. The first fight they had there, they cleaned up the Sixty-ninth Alabama troops. My young master had been helping drill them. He went on and overtook the others.

I don't know whether all the whites did free their slaves or not. But I know this—when they quit fighting, I know the white children called we little children and all the grown people who worked around the house and said, "You all is just as free as we is. You ain't got no master and no mistress," and I don't know what they told them at the plantation.

I am not sure just what we did immediately after freedom. I don't know whether it was a year or whether it was a year and a half. I can just go by my mother. After freedom, we came from Auburn, Alabama, to Opelika, Alabama, and she went to cooking at a hotel till she got money enough for what she wanted to do. When she got fixed, she moved then to Columbus, Georgia. She rented a place from Ned Burns, a policeman. When that place gave out, she went to washing and ironing. Sterling Love rented a house from the same man. He had four children and they were going to school and they took me too. I fixed up and went to school with them. I didn't get no learning at all in slavery times.

Right after the War, my mother worked—washed—for an old white man. He took an interest in me and taught me. I did little things for him. When he died, I took up the teaching which he had been doing.

At first I taught in Columbus, Georgia. By and by, a white man came along looking for laborers for this part of the country. He said money grew on bushes out here. He cleaned out the place. All the children and all the grown folks followed him. Two of my boys came to me and told me they were coming. We hoboed on freights and walked to Chattanooga, Tennessee. We stayed there awhile. Then a white man came along getting laborers. I never kept the year nor nothin'. He brought us to Lonoke County, and I got work on the Bood Bar plantation. Squirrels, wild things, cotton, and corn, plenty of it. So you see, the man told the truth when he said money grew on bushes.

I taught and farmed all my life. Farming is the greatest occupation. It supports the teacher, preacher, the lawyer, the doctor. None of them can live without it.

ESTHER EASTER

Interviewed at Tulsa, Oklahoma
Interviewer not identified
Age when interviewed: 85

I WAS BORN NEAR MEMPHIS, Tennessee, on the old Ben Moore plantation, but I don't know anything about the Old South because Master Ben moves us all up into Missouri (about fourteen miles east of Westport, now Kansas City), long before they started fighting about slavery.

Mary Collier was my mother's name before she was a Moore. About my father, I don't know. Mammy was sickly most of the time when I was a baby, and she was so thin and poorly when they move to Missouri the white folks afraid she going to die on the way. But she fool 'em and she live two-three year after that. That's what good Old Master Ben tells me when I gets older.

I stay with Master Ben's married daughter, Mary, till the coming of the War. Times was good before the War, and I wasn't suffering none from slavery, except once in a while the mistress would fan me with the stick—bet I needed it, too.

When the War come along Master he say to leave Mistress Mary and get ready to go to Texas. Jim Moore, one of the meanest men I ever see, was the son of Master Ben; he's going take us there. Demon Jim, that's what I call him when he ain't around the place, but when he's home it was always Master Jim 'cause he was reckless with the wip. He was a Rebel officer fighting round the country and didn't take us slaves to Texas right away. So I stayed on at his place not far from Master Ben's plantation.

Master Jim's wife was a demon, just like her husband. Used the whip all the time, and every time Master Jim come home he whip me 'cause the mistress say I been mean.

One time I tell him, "You better put me in your pocket—sell me— Master Jim, else I'se going run away." He don't pay no mind, and I don't try to run away 'cause of the whips.

I done see one whipping and that enough. They wasn't no fooling about it. A runaway slave from the Henkin's plantation was brought back, and there was a public whipping, so's the slaves could see what happens when they tries to get away. The runaway was chained to the whipping post, and I was full of misery when I see the lash cutting deep into that boy's skin. He swell up like a deadhorse, but he gets over it, only he was never no 'count for work no more.

While Master Jim is out fighting the Yanks, the mistress is fiddling round with a neighbor man, Mister Headsmith. I is young then, but I knows enough that Master Jim's going be mighty mad when he hears about it. The mistress didn't know I knows her secret, and I'm fixing to even up for some of them whippings she put off on me. That's why I tell Master Jim next time he come home.

"See that crack in the wall?" Master Jim say, "Yes." And I say, "It's just like the open door when the eyes are close to the wall. He peek and see into the bedroom.

"That's how I find out about the mistress and Mister Headsmith," I tells him, and I see he's getting mad.

"What you mean?" And Master Jim grabs me hard by the arm like I was trying to get away.

"I see them in the bed."

That's all I say. The demon's got him and Master Jim tears out of the room looking for the mistress. Then I hears loud talking and pretty soon the mistress is screaming and calling for help, and if old Master Ben hadn't drop in just then and stop the fight, why, I guess she be beat almost to death, that how mad the master was.

Then Master Ben gets mad 'cause his boy Jim ain't got us down in Texas yet. Then we stay up all night packing for the trip. Master Jim takes us, but the mistress stay at home, and I wonder if Master Jim beat her again when he gets back.

We rides the wagons all the way, how many days, I don't know. The country was wild most of the way, and I know that we come through the same country where I lives now, only it was to the east. The trip was evidently made over the "Texas Road." And we keeps on riding and comes to the big river that's all brown and red looking* and the next thing I was sold to Mrs. Vaughn at Bonham, Texas, and there I stays till after the slaves is free.

The new mistress was a widow, no children round the place, and she treat me mighty good. She was good white folks—like old Master Ben— powerful good.

When the word get to us that the slaves is free, the mistress says I is free to go anywheres I want. And I tell her this talk about being free sounds like foolishness to me—anyway, where can I go? She just pat me on the shoulder and say I better stay right there with her, and that's what I do for a long time. Then I hears about how the white folks down at Dallas pays big money for house girls and there I goes.

That's all I ever do after that—work at the houses till I gets too old to hobble on these tired ole feets and legs. Then I just sits down. Just sits

---

* Red River.

down and wishes for old Master Ben to come and get me, and take care of this old woman like he used to do when she is just a little black child on the plantation in Missouri. God bless old Master Ben—he was good white folks!

ANNE ULRICH EVANS

Interviewed at St. Louis, Missouri
Interviewer not identified
Age when interviewed: 94

I WAS BORN MARCH 10, 1843, on Dolphin Street, Mobile, Alabama. My mother's name was Charlotte Ulrich and my father's was Peter Pedro Ulrich. I am the mother of eleven children and we has over one hundred grandchildren. Dere is so many great-grandchildren and great-great-grandchildren we just quit countin' when we comes to dem. I has four generations, and dey give me a party three years ago, and so many of my offspring come dere wasn't any room for half of 'em and even dat was not de beginning of de lot of 'em. I got a gang of 'em I never did see, and never will see, I don't reckon. Dey just write and tell us dey got 'em.

My father was owned by a rich old boss named Captain Bullmay. He owned a raft of boats, and my father was a cook on one of dem boats. Mamma only raised two of her children. De Ulriches sold me when I was a girl to Dr. Odem in de same county, and I worked in his field, spun thread to make cloth, pulled fodder, put de spinning in, and after a while, I don't know how long, he swapped me off for two boys. My new owner was Gilbert Faulkner. He was a railroad section man. I worked in de field for him until we was set free. I had some good times and some bad times both. De man I married worked on the railroad for him. His name was Moses Evans. Dat was in Helena, Arkansas. My husband's been dead more dan thirty years now. I got four daughters and three sons living and a host of grand and great-grand, and great-great-grandchildren living.

When freedom come I asked my old owner to please let me stay on with dem; I didn't have nowhere to go nohow. So he just up and said "Anne, you can stay here if you want to, but I ain't goin' to give you nothing but your victuals and clothes enough to cover your hide, not a penny in money, do no nigger get from me." So I up and said, "Why boss, dey tells me dat since freedom we get a little change," and he cursed me to all de low names he could think of and drove me out like a dog. I didn't know what to do, or where to go, so I sauntered off to a nearby plantation where a colored slave kept house for her bachelor slave owner and she let me stay with her, and her boss drove me off after two days because I kept company with a nigger who work for a man he didn't like. I was barefooted, so I asked Moses Evans to please buy me some shoes. My feet was so sore and I didn't have no money nor no home neither. So he said for me to wait till Saturday night and he'd buy me some shoes. Sure 'nough, when Saturday night come, he buyed me some shoes and handkerchiefs and a pretty string of beads and got an old man neighbor named Rochel to let me stay at his house. Den in a few weeks me and him got married, and I was mighty glad to marry him to get a place to stay. Yes, I was. 'Cause I had said, hard times as I was having if I seed a man walking with two sticks and he wanted me for a wife I'd marry him to get a place to stay. Yes, I did, and I meant just dat. In all my born days I never knowed of a white man giving a black man nothing, no I ain't.

I was always a heap more scared of dem Ku Klux dan I was of anything else. 'Cause de War was to help my folks. But dem old Ku Klux never did mean us no good. I used to make pallets on de floor after de War for my children, myself, and my husband to sleep on, 'cause dem Ku Klux just come all around our house at nighttime and shoot in de doors and windows. Dey never bothered nobody in de daytime. Den sometime dey come on in de house, tear up everything on de place, claim dey was looking for somebody, and tell us dey hungry 'cause dey ain't had nothin' to eat since de battle of Shiloh. Maybe twenty of 'em at a time make us cook up everything we got, and dey had false pockets made in deir shirt, and take up de skillet with de meat and hot grease piping hot and pour it every bit down de front of dem shirts inside de false pockets and drop de hot bread right down dere, behind de meat and go on.

One night dey come to our house after my husband to kill him, and my husband had a dream dey's coming to kill him. So he had a lot of colored men friends to be at our house with guns dat night, and time dey seed dem Ku Klux coming over de hill dey started shooting just up in de air and shout, and dem Ku Klux never did bother our house no more. I sure glad of dat. I'se so tired of dem devils. If it hadn't been for dat dey would have killed everyone of us dat night. I don't know how come dey was so mean to us colored folks. We never did do nothing to dem.

Dey go to some of dem niggers' house, and dey run up de chimney corner to hide and dem low down hounds shoot 'em and kill 'em in de chimney hole. Dey was terrible.

Den de next bad thing happened to us poor niggers after de war was dis. De white folks would pay niggers to lie to de rest of us niggers to get deir farming done for nothing. He'd tell us come on and go with me, a man wants a gang of niggers to do some work and he pay you like money growing on trees. Well we ain't had no money and ain't used to none, so we glad to hear dat good news. We just up and bundle up and go with this lying nigger. Dey carried us by de droves to different parts of Alabama, Arkansas, and Missouri.

After we got to dese places, dey put us to work all right on dem great big farms. We all light in and work like old horses, thinking now we making money and going to get some of it, but we never got a cent. We never did get out of debt. We always get through with fine big crops and owed de white man more dan we did when we started de crop, and got to stay to pay de debt. It was awful. All over was like dat. Dem lying niggers caused all dat. Yes dey did.

LORENZO EZELL
Interviewed at Beaumont, Texas
Interviewer not identified
Age when interviewed: 87

U S PLANTATION was just east from Pacolet Station on Thicketty Creek, Spartanburg County, in South Carolina. Dat near Little and Big Pacolet Rivers on de route to Limestone Springs, and it just a ordinary plantation with de main crops cotton and wheat.

I belong to de Lipscombs and my mamma, Maria Ezell, she belong to 'em too. Old Ned Lipscomb was amongst de oldest citizens of dat county. I'se born dere on July 29, in 1850, and I be eighty-seven year old dis year. Levi Ezell, he my daddy, and he belong to Landrum Ezell, a Baptist preacher. Dat young massa and de old massa, John Ezell, was de first Baptist preecher I ever heered of. He have three sons, Landrum, and Judson, and Bryson. Bryson have gift for business and was right smart of a orator.

Dey's fourteen niggers on de Lipscomb place. Dey's seven of us chillen, my mamma, three uncle, and three aunt, and one man what wasn't no kin to us. I was oldest of de chillen, and dey called Sallie and Carrie and Alice and Jabus and Coy and LaFate and Rufus and Nelson.

Old Ned Lipscomb was one de best massa in de whole county. You know dem old patterollers, dey call us "Old Ned's free niggers," and sure hate us. Dey cruel to us, 'cause dey think us have too good a massa. One time dey cotch my uncle and beat him most to death.

Us go to work at daylight, but us wasn't abused. Other massas used to blow de horn or ring de bell, but Massa, he never use de horn or

de whip. All de man folks was allowed raise a garden patch with tobaccy
or cotton for to sell in de market. Wasn't many massas what allowed
dere niggers have patches and some didn't even feed 'em enough. Dat's
why dey have to get out and hustle at night to get food for dem to eat.

De old massa, he insisted us go to church. De Baptist church have a
shed built behind de pulpit for cullud folks, with de dirt floor and split
log seat for de women folks, but most de men folks stands or kneels on
de floor. Dey used to call dat de coop. De white preacher back to us,
but iffen he want to he turn around and talk to us awhile. Us makes up
songs, 'cause us couldn't read or write. I 'member dis one:

> De rough, rocky road what Moses done travel,
> I'se bound to carry my soul to de Lord;
> It's a mighty rocky road but I must done travel,
> And I'se bound to carry my soul to de Lord.

Us sing "Sweet Chariot," but us didn't sing it like dese days. Us sing:

> Swing low, sweet chariot,
> Freely let me into rest,
> I don't want to stay here no longer;
> Swing low, sweet chariot,
> When Gabriel make he last alarm
> I wants to be rollin' in Jesus arm,
> 'Cause I don't want to stay here no longer.

Us sing another song what de Yankees take dat tune and make a hymn
out of it. Sherman army sung it, too. We have it like dis:

> Our bodies bound to morter and decay,
> Our bodies bound to morter and decay,
> Our bodies bound to morter and decay,
> But us souls go marchin' home.

Before de War I just big enough to drop corn and tote water. When
de little white chillen go to school about half mile, I wait till noon and
run all de way up to de school to run base when dey play at noon. Dey
several young Lipscombs, dere Smith and Bill and John and Nathan, and
de oldest son, Elias.

In dem days cullud people just like mules and hosses. Dey didn't have
no last name. My mamma call me after my daddy's massa, Ezell. Mamma
was de good woman and I 'member her more dan once rockin' de little
cradle and singin' to de baby. Dis what she sing:

> Milk in de dairy nine days old,
> Sing-song Kitty, can't you ki-me-o?
> Frogs and skeeters gittin' mighty bold
> Sing-song, Kitty, can't you ki-me-o?

(Chorus)

> Keemo, kimo, darro, wharro,
> With me hi, me ho;
> In come Sally singin'
> Sometime penny winkle,
> Lingtum nip cat,
> Sing-song, Kitty, can't you ki-me-o?
>
> Dere a frog live in a pool,
> Sing-song, Kitty, can't you ki-me-o?
> Sure he was de biggest fool,
> Sing-song, Kitty, can't you ki-me-o?
>
> For he could dance and he could sing
> Sing-song, Kitty, can't you ki-me-o?
> And make de woods around him ring
> Sing-song, Kitty, can't you ki-me-o?

Old massa didn't hold with de way some mean massas treat dey niggers. Dere a place on our plantation what us call "de old meadow." It was common for runaway niggers to have place along de way to hide and rest when dey run off from mean massa. Massa used to give 'em somethin' to eat when dey hide dere. I saw dat place operated, though it wasn't knowed by dat den, but long time after I finds out dey call it part of de "underground railroad." Dey was stops like dat all de way up to de North.

We have went down to Columbia when I about eleven year old and dat where de first gun fired. Us rush back home, but I could say I heered de first guns of de War shot, at Fort Sumter.

When General Sherman come across de Savannah River in South Carolina, some of he soldiers come right across us plantation. All de neighbors have brung dey cotton and stack it in de thicket on de Lipscomb place. Sherman's men find it and set it on fire. Dat cotton stack was big as a little courthouse and it took two months burnin'.

My old massa run off and stay in de woods a whole week when Sherman men come through. He didn't need to worry, 'cause us took care of everything. Dey a funny song us make up about him runnin' off in de woods. I know it was make up, 'cause my uncle have a hand in it. It went like dis:

> White folks, have you seed old massa
> Up de road, with he mustache on?
> He pick up he hat and he leave real sudden
> And I believe he's up and gone.
>
> Old massa run away
> And us darkies stay at home.
> It must be now dat Kingdom's comin'
> And de year of Jubilee.
>
> He look up de river and he seed dat smoke,
> where de Lincoln gunboats lay.

He big 'nough and he old 'nough and he orter know better,
But he gone and run away.

Now dat overseer want to give trouble
And trot us 'round a spell.
But we lock him up in de smokehouse cellar,
With de key done throwed in de well.

Right after dat I start to be boy what run mail from camp to camp for de soldiers. One time I was capture by a bunch of deserters what was hidin' in de woods along Pacolet River. Dey didn't hurt me, though, but dey most scare me to death. Dey parole me and turn me loose.

All four my young massas go to de War, all but Elias. He too old. Smith, he kilt at Manassas Junction. Nathan, he get he finger shot at de first round at Fort Sumter. But when Billy was wounded at Howard Gap in North Carolina and dey brung him home with he jaw split open, I so mad I could have kilt all de Yankees. I say I be happy iffen I could kill me just one Yankee. I hated dem 'cause dey hurt my white people. Billy was disfigure awful when he jaw split and he teeth all shine through he cheek.

After war was over, Old Massa call us up and told us we free but he advise not leave de place till de crop was through. Us all stay. Den us select us homes and move to it. Us folks move to Sam Littlejohn's, north of Thicketty Creek, where us stay two year. Den us move back to Billy Lipscomb, de young massa, and stay dere two more year. I'se right smart good banjo picker in dem day. I can 'member one dem songs just as good today as when I pick it. Dat was:

Early in de mornin'
Don't you head de dogs a-barkin'?
Bow, wow, wow!

Hush, hush, boys,
Don't make a noise,
Massa's fast a-sleepin'.
Run to de barnyard,
Wake up de boys,
Let's have banjo pickin'.

Early in de mornin'
Don't you hear dem roosters crowin'?
Cock-a-doodle-do.

I came in contact with de Klu Klux. Us left de plantation in '65 or '66 and by '68 us was havin' such a awful time with de Klu Klux. First time dey come to my mamma's house at midnight and claim dey soldiers done come back from de dead. Dey all dress up in sheets and make up like spirit. Dey groan around and say dey been kilt wrongly and come back for justice. One man, he look just like ordinary man, but he spring up about eighteen feet high all of a sudden. Another say he so thirsty he ain't have no water since he been kilt at Manassas Junction. He ask for water and he just kept pourin' it in. Us think he sure must be a spirit to drink dat much water. Course he not drinkin' it, he pourin' it in a bag under he sheet. My mamma never did take up no truck with spirits so she knowed it just a man. Dey tell us what dey gwine do iffen we don't all go back to us massas and us all agrees and den dey all disappear.

Den us move to New Prospect on de Pacolet River, on de Perry Clemmons place. Dat in de upper edge of de county and dat where de second swarm of de Klu Klux come out. Dey claim dey gwine kill everybody what am Republican. My daddy charge with bein' a leader amongst de niggers. He make speech and instruct de niggers how to vote for Grant's first election. De Klu Klux want to whip him and he have to sleep in a hollow log every night.

Dey's a old man name Uncle Bart what live about half mile from us. De Klu Klux come to us house one night, but my daddy done hid. Den I hear dem say dey gwine go kill old man Bart. I jump out de window and shortcut through dem wood and warn him. He get out de house in time and I save he life. De funny thing, I knowed all dem Klu Klux Spite dey sheets and things, I knowed dey voices and dey saddle hosses.

Dey one white man name Irving Ramsey. Us play fiddle together lots of time. When de white boys dance dey always wants me to go to play for dey party. One day I say to dat boy, "I done knowed you last night." He say, "What you mean?" I say, "You one dem Klu Klux." He want to know how I know. I say, "Member when you go under the chestnut tree and say, "Whoa, Sont, whoa, Sont, to your hoss?" He say, "Yes." And I laugh and say, "Well, I'se right up in dat tree." Dey all knowed I knowed dem den, but I never told on dem. When dey seed I ain't gwine to tell, dey never try whip my daddy or kill Uncle Bart no more.

I ain't never been to school but I just picked up readin'. With some my first money I ever earn I buy me a old blue-back Webster. I carry dat book wherever I goes. When I plows down a row I stop at de end to rest and den I overlook de lesson. I 'member one de very first lessons was, "Evil communications corrupts good morals." I knowed de words "evil" and "good" and a white man explain de others. I been done use dat lesson all my life.

After us left de Pacolet River us stay in Atlanta a little while and den I go on to Louisiana. I done left Spartanburg completely in '76 but I didn't git into Texas till 1882. I finally get to Brenham, Texas and marry Rachel Pinchbeck two year after. Us was marry in church and have seven chillen. Den us separate. I been batching about twenty year and I done lost track most dem chillen. My gal, Lula, live in Beaumont, and Will, he in Chicago.

Every time I tells dese niggers I'se from South Carolina dey all say, "Oh, he bound to make a heap." I could be a conjure doctor and make plenty money, but dat ain't good. In slavery time dey's men like dat regarded as bein' dangerous. Dey make charms and put bad mouth on you. De old folks wears de rabbit foot or coon foot and sometime a silver dime on a fishin' string to keep off de witches. Some dem old conjure people make lots of money for charm against ruin or cripplin' or dry up de blood. But I don't take up no truck with things like dat.

ROBERT FALLS
Interviewed at Knoxville, Tennessee
Interviewer not identified
Age when interviewed: 97

I F I HAD MY LIFE to live over again, I would die fighting rather than be a slave. I want no man's yoke on my shoulders no more. But in them days, us niggers didn't know no better. All we knowed was work, and hard work. We was learned to say, "Yes sir!" and scrape down and bow, and to do just exactly what we was told to do, make no difference if we wanted to or not. Old Master and Old Mistress would say, "Do this!" and we done it. And they say, "Come here!" and if we didn't come to them, they come to us. And they brought the bunch of switches with them.

They didn't half feed us, either. They fed the animals better. They gives the mules roughage and such, to chaw on all night. But they didn't give us nothing to chaw on. Learned us to steal, that's what they done. Why, we would take anything we could lay our hands on, when we was hungry. Then they'd whip us for lying when we say we don't know nothing about it. But it was easier to stand when the stomach was full.

Now, my father, he was a fighter. He was mean as a bear. He was so bad to fight and so troublesome he was sold four times to my knowing and maybe a heap more times. That's how come my name is Falls, even if some does call me Robert Goforth. Niggers would change to the name of their new marster every time they was sold. And my father had a lot of names but kept the one of his marster when he got a good home. That man was Harry Falls. He said he'd been trying to buy Father for a long time, because he was the best wagoner in all that country abouts. And the man what sold him to Falls, his name was Collins, he told my father, "You so mean, I got to sell you. You all time complaining about you don't like your white folks. Tell me now who you wants to live with. Just pick your man and I will go see him." Then my father tells Collins, "I want you to sell me to Marster Harry Falls." They made the trade. I disremember what the money was, but it was big. Good workers sold for one thousand and two thousand dollars. After that the white folks didn't have no more trouble with my father. But he'd still fight. That man would fight a she-bear and lick her every time.

My mother was sold three times before I was born. The last time when Old Goforth sold her, to the slave speculators—you know every time they needed money they would sell a slave—and they was taking them, driving them, just like a pack of mules, to the market from North Carolina into South Carolina, she begun to have fits. They got to the jail house where they was to stay that night, and she took on so, Jim Slade and Press Worthy—them was the slave speculators—couldn't do nothing with her. Next morning one of them took her back to Marse Goforth and told him, "Look here. We can't do nothing with this woman. You got to take her and give us back our money. And do it now," they says. And they mean it too. So Old Marse Goforth took my mother and give them back their money. After that none of us was ever separated. We all lived, a brother and my two sisters, and my mother, with the Goforths till freedom.

And you know, she never did get over having fits. She had them every change of the moon, or leastways every other moon change. But she kept on working. She was a hard worker. She had to be. Old Mistress see to that. She was meaner than Old Marster, she was. She would sit by the spinning wheel and count the turns the slave women made. And they couldn't fool her none neither. My mother worked until ten o'clock almost every night because her part was to spin so many cuts a day, and she couldn't get through no sooner. When I was a little shaver I used to sit on the floor with the other little fellows while our mothers worked, and sometimes the white folks girls would read us a Bible story. But most of the time we slept. Right there on the floor. Then later, when I was bigger, I had to work with the men at night shelling corn to take to town early mornings.

Marster Goforth counted himself a good old Baptist Christian. The one good deed he did, I will never forget, he made us all go to church every Sunday. That was the onliest place off the farm we ever went. Every time a slave went off the place, he had to have a pass, except we didn't for church. Everybody in that country knowed that the Goforth niggers didn't have to have a pass to go to church. But that didn't make no difference to the patterrollers. They'd hide in the bushes, or wait alongside of the road, and when the niggers come from meeting, the patterrollers say, "Where's your pass?" Us Goforth niggers used to start running soon as we was out of church. We never got caught. That is why I tell you I can't use my legs like I used to. If you was caught without a pass the patterrollers give you five licks. They was licks! You take a bunch of five to seven patterrollers each giving five licks and the blood flows.

Old Marster was too old to go to the War. He had one son was a soldier but he never come home again. I never seen a soldier till the

War was over and they begin to come back to the farms. We half-grown niggers had to work the farm because all the farmers had to give—I believe it was a tenth—of their crops to help feed the soldiers. So we didn't know nothing about what was going on, no more than a hog.

It was a long time before we knowed we was free. Then one night Old Marster come to our house and he say he wants to see us all before breakfast tomorrow morning and to come on over to his house. He got something to tell us.

Next morning we went over there. I was the monkey, always acting smart. But I believe they liked me better than all of the others. I just spoke sassy-like and say, "Old Marster, what you got to tell us?" My mother said, "Shut your mouth fool. He'll whip you." And Old Marster say, "No, I won't whip you. Never no more. Sit down there all of you and listen to what I got to tell you. I hates to do it but I must. You-all ain't my niggers no more. You is free. Just as free as I am. Here I have raised you all to work for me, and now you are going to leave me. I am an old man, and I can't get along without you. I don't know what I am going to do." Well sir, It killed him. He was dead in less than ten months.

Everybody left right now, but me and my brother and another fellow. Old Marster fooled us to believe we was duty bound to stay with him till we was all twenty-one. But my brother, that boy was stubborn. Soon he say he ain't going to stay there. And he left. In about a year, maybe less, he come back and he told me I didn't have to work for Old Goforth. I was free, sure enough free, and I went with him and he got me a job railroading. But the work was too hard for me. I couldn't stand it. So I left there and went to my mother. I had to walk. It was forty-five miles. I made it in a day. She got me work there where she worked.

I remember so well how the roads was full of folks walking and walking along when the niggers were freed. Didn't know where they was going. Just going to see about something else somewhere else. Meet a body in the road and they ask, "Where you going?" "Don't know." "What you going to do?" "Don't know."

And then sometimes we would meet a white man and he would say, "How you like to come work on my farm?" And we say, "I don't know." And then maybe he say, "If you come work for me on my farm, when the crops is in I give you five bushels of corn, five gallons of molasses, some ham-meat, and all your clothes and victuals while you works for me." Alright! That's what I do. And then something begins to work up in my head. I begins to think and to know things. And I knowed then I could make a living for my own self, and I never had to a slave no more.

Now, Old Marster Goforth had four sisters what owned slaves, and they wasn't mean to them like our Old Marster and Old Mistress. Some of the old slaves and their folks are still living on their places right to this day. But they never dispute none with their brother about how mean he treat his slaves. And him claiming to be such a Christian! Well, I reckon he's found out something about slave driving by now. The good Lord has to get his work in sometime. And he'll take care of them low down patterrollers and slave speculators and mean marsters and mistresses.

LINDSEY FAUCETTE
Interviewed at Durham, North Carolina
Interviewed by Daisey Whaley
Age when interviewed: 86

I WAS BORN IN 1851, de sixteenth of November, on de Occoneechee plantation, owned by Marse John Norwood and his good wife, Mis' Annie. And when I say "good" I mean just dat, for no better people ever lived den my Marse John and Mis' Annie.

One thing dat made our marse and mistis so good was de way dey brought up us niggers. We was called to de Big House and taught de Bible and dey was Bible readin's every day. We was taught to be good men and women and to be honest. Marse never sold any of us niggers. But when his boys and girls got married he would give dem some of us to take with dem.

Marse never allowed us to be whipped. One time we had a white overseer and he whipped a field hand called Sam Norwood, till de blood come. He beat him so bad dat de other niggers had to take him down to de river and wash de blood off. When Marse come and found dat out he sent dat white man off and wouldn't let him stay on de plantation overnight. He just wouldn' have him round de place no longer. He made Uncle Whitted de overseer 'cause he was one of de oldest slaves he had and a good nigger.

When any of us niggers got sick, Mis' Annie would come down to de cabin to see us. She brung de best wine, good chicken and chicken soup, and everything else she had at de Big House dat she thought we would like, and she done everything she could to get us well again.

Marse John never worked us after dark. We worked in de day and had de nights to play games and have singin's. We never cooked on a Sunday. Everything we ate on dat day was cooked on Saturday. Dey wasn't light in de cook stoves or fireplaces in de Big House or cabins neither. Everybody rested on Sunday. De tables was set and de food put on to eat, but nobody cut any wood and dey wasn't no other work done on dat day. Mammy Beckie was my grandmammy and she toted de keys to de pantry and smokehouse, and her word went with Marse John and Mis' Annie.

Marse John was a great lawyer and when he went to Pittsboro and other places to practice, if he was to stay all night, Mis' Annie had my mammy sleep right in bed with her, so she wouldn't be afraid.

Marse and Mistis had three sons and three daughters. De oldest son was not able to go to war. He had studied so hard dat it had affected his mind, so he stayed at home. De second son, named Albert, went to war and was brought back dead with a bullet hole through his head. Dat liked to have killed Marse John and Mis' Annie. Dey was three girls, named, Mis' Maggie, Mis' Ella Bella, and Mis' Rebena.

I was de cow tender. I took care of de cows and de calves. I would have to hold de calf up to de mother cow till de milk would come down and den I would have to hold it away till somebody done de milkin'. I tended de horses, too, and anything else dat I was told to do.

When de War started and de Yankees come, dey didn't do much harm to our place. Marse had all de silver and money and other things of value hid under a big rock by de river and de Yankees never did find anything dat we hid.

Our own soldiers did more harm on our plantation dan de Yankees. Dey camped in de woods and never did have 'nough to eat and took what dey wanted. And lice! I ain't never seed de like. It took fifteen years for us to get shed of de lice dat de soldiers left behind. You just couldn't get dem out of your clothes' less you burned dem up. Dey was hard to get shed of.

After de War was over Marse John let Pappy have eighteen acres of land for de use of two of his boys for a year. My pappy made a good crop of corn, wheat, and other food on his land. Dey was a time when you couldn't find a crust of bread or piece of meat in my mammy's pantry for us to eat, and when she did get a little meat or bread she would divide it between us chillen, so each could have a share and go without herself and never complained.

When Pappy was makin' his crop some of de others would ask him why he didn't take up some of his crop and get somethin' to eat. He would answer and say dat when he left dat place he intended to take his crop with him and he did. He took plenty of corn, wheat, potatoes, and other food; a cow, her calf, a mule and hogs, and he moved to a farm dat he bought.

Later on in years my pappy and mammy come here in Durham and bought a home. I worked for dem till I was thirty-two years old and give dem what money I earned. I worked for as little as twenty-five cents a day. Den I got a dray and hauled for fifteen cents a load from Durham depot to West Durham for fifteen years. Little did I think at dat time dat I would ever have big trucks and a payroll of six thousand dollars a year. De good Lord has blessed me all de way, and all I have is His'n, even to my own breath.

Den one day I went back home to see my old marse and I found him sittin' in a big chair on de porch and his health wasn't so good. He said, "Lindsey, why don' you stop runnin' round with de girls and stop you courtin'? You never will get nowhere makin' all de girls love you and den you walk away and make up with some other girl. Go get yourself a good girl and get married and raise a family and be somebody."

And I did. I quit all de girls and I found a fine girl and we was married. I sure got a good wife. I got one of de best women dat could be found and we lived together for over forty-five years. Den she died six years ago now, and I sure miss her for she was a real helpmate all through dese years. We raised five chillen and educated them to be school teachers and other trades.

M. S. FAYMAN

Interviewed at Baltimore, Maryland
Interviewed by —— Rogers
Age when interviewed: 87

I WAS BORN in St. Nazaire Parish in Louisiana, about sixty miles south of Baton Rouge, in 1850. My father and mother were Creoles; both of them were people of wealth and prestige in their days and considered very influential. My father's name was Henri de Sales and mother's maiden name was Marguerite Sanchez de Haryne. I had two brothers, Henri and Jackson, named after General Jackson, both of whom died quite young, leaving me the only living child. Both Mother and Father were born and reared in Louisiana. We lived in a large and spacious house surrounded by flowers and situated on a farm containing about seven hundred and fifty acres, on which we raised pelicans for sale in the market at New Orleans.

When I was about five years old I was sent to a private school in Baton Rouge, conducted by French Sisters, where I stayed until I was kidnapped in 1860. At that time I did not know how to speak English. French was the language spoken in my household and by people in the parish.

Baton Rouge, situated on the Mississippi, was a river port and stopping place for all large river boats, especially between New Orleans and large towns and cities north. We children were taken out by the Sisters after school and on Saturdays and holidays to walk. One of the places we went was the wharf. One day in June and a Saturday a large boat was at the wharf going north on the Mississippi River. We children were there. Somehow, I was separated from the other children. I was taken bodily up by a white man, carried on the boat, put in a cabin, and kept there until we got to Louisville, Kentucky, where I was taken off.

After I arrived in Louisville I was taken to a farm near Frankfort and installed there virtually a slave until 1864, when I escaped through the kindness of a delightful Episcopalian woman from Cincinnati, Ohio. As I could not speak English, my chores were to act as tutor and companion for the children of Pierce Buckran Haynes, a well known slave trader and plantation owner in Kentucky. Haynes wanted his children to speak French and it was my duty to teach them. I was the private companion of three girls and one small boy; each day I had to talk French and write French for them. They became very proficient in French and I in the rudiments of the English language.

I slept in the children's quarters with the Haynes' children, ate and played with them. I had all the privileges of the household accorded to me with the exception of one—I never was taken off nor permitted to leave the plantation. While on the plantation I wore good clothes, similar to those of the white children. Haynes was a merciless brutal tyrant with his slaves, punishing them severely and cruelly both by the lash and in the jail on the plantation.

The name of the plantation where I was held as a slave was called Beatrice Manor, after the wife of Haynes. It contained eight thousand acres, of which more than six thousand acres were under cultivation, and having three hundred and fifty colored slaves and five or six overseers, all of whom were white. The overseers were the overlords of the manor, as Haynes dealt extensively in tobacco and trading in slaves and he was away from the plantation nearly all the time. There was located on the top of the large tobacco warehouse a large bell, which was rung at sunup, twelve o'clock, and at sundown, the year round. On the farm the slaves were assigned a task to do each day, and in the event it was not finished they were severely whipped. While I never saw a slave whipped, I did see them afterwards. They were very badly marked and striped by the overseers who did the whipping.

I have been back to the farm on several occasions, the first time in 1872 when I took my father there to show him the farm. At that time it was owned by Colonel Hawkins, a Confederate Army officer. Let me describe the huts. These buildings were built of stone, each one about twenty feet high, fifty feet long, nine feet high in the rear, and about twelve feet high in front, with a slanting roof of chestnut boards and with a sliding door, two windows between each door back and front about two by four feet, at each end a door and window similar to those on the side. There were ten such buildings. Connected to each building there was another building twelve by fifteen feet, This was where the cooking was done. At each end of each building there was a fireplace, built and used for heating purposes. In front of each building there were barrels filled with water supplied by pipes from a large spring, situated about three hundred yards on the side of a hill which was very rocky, where the stones were quarried to build the buildings on the farm.

On the outside near each window and door there were iron rings firmly attached to the walls, through which an iron rod was inserted and locked each and every night, making it impossible for those inside to escape.

There was one building used as a jail, built of stone about twenty by forty feet with a hip roof about twenty-five feet high, two-story. On the ground in each end was a fireplace; in one end a small room where the whipping was done. To reach the second story there was built, on the outside, steps leading to a door, through which the female prisoners were taken to the room. All of the buildings had dirt floors.

I do not know much about the Negroes on the plantation who were there at the time. Slaves were brought and taken away always chained together, men walking and women in ox carts. I had heard of several escapes and many were captured. One of the overseers had a pack of six or eight trained bloodhounds which were used to trace escaping slaves.

Before I close let me give you a sketch of my family tree. My grandmother was a Haitian Negress, grandfather a Frenchman, father was a Creole. After returning home in 1864, I completed my high school education in New Orleans in 1870, graduated from Fisk University in 1874, taught French there until 1883, married Professor Fayman, teacher of history and English. Since then I have lived in Washington, New York, and Louisiana.

JOHN FINNELY

Interviewed at Fort Worth, Texas
Interviewer not identified
Age when interviewed: 86

ALABAMA AM DE STATE where I'se born and dat eighty-six year ago, in Jackson County, on Massa Martin Finnely's plantation, and him owns about seventy-five other slaves besides Mammy and me. My pappy am on dat plantation but I don't know him, 'cause Mammy never talks about him except to say, "He am here."

Massa run de cotton plantation but raises stock and feed and corn and cane and rations for de humans such as us. It am different when I's a youngun dan now. Den, it am needful for to raise everything you need 'cause dey couldn't depend on factory made goods. Dey could buy shoes and clothes and such, but we'uns could make dem so much cheaper. We'uns make shoes, and leather and clothes and cloth and grinds de meal. And we'uns cures de meat, preserves de fruit, and make 'lasses and brown sugar. All de harness for de mules and de hosses is made and de carts for haulin'. Massa make peach brandy and him have he own still.

De work am 'vided 'twist de cullud folks and us always have certain duties to do. I's am de field hand and before I's old enough for to do dat, dey has me help with de chores and errands.

Us have de cabins of logs with one room and one door and one window hole, and bunks for sleepin'. But no cookin' am done here. It am done in de cookhouse by de cooks for all us niggers and we'uns eats in de eatin 'shed. De rations am good, plain victuals, and dere plenty of it, and about twice a week dere somethin' for treat. Massa sure am particular about feedin', specially for de younguns in de nursery. You see, dere am de nursery for such what needs care while deir mammies am a-workin'.

Massa feed plenty and him demand plenty work. Dat cause heap of trouble on dat plantation, 'cause whippin's am given and hard ones, too. Lots of times at de end of de day I'se so tired I'se couldn't speak for to stop mule, I just have to lean back on de lines.

Dis nigger never gits whipped except for dis, before I'se a field hand. Massa use me for huntin' and use me for de gun rest. When him have de long shot I bends over and puts de hands on de knees and Massa puts his gun on my back for to get de good aim. What him kills I runs and fetches and carries de game for him. I turns de squirrels for him and dat disaway: de squirrel always go to other side from de hunter and I walks around de tree and de squirrel see me and go to Massa's side de tree and he gets shot.

All dat not so bad, but when he shoots de duck in de water and I has to fetch it out, dat give me de worryment. De first time he tells me to go in de pond I's skeert, powerful skeert. I takes off de shirt and pants but there I stands. I steps in de water, den back again, and again. Massa am gettin' mad. He say, "Swim in dere and get dat duck." "Yes, sir Massa," I says, but I won't go in dat water till Massa hit me some licks. I couldn't never get used to bein' de water dog for de ducks.

De worst whippin I seed was give to Clarinda. She hits Massa with de hoe 'cause he try 'fere with her and she try stop him. She am put on de log and give five-hundred lashes. She am over dat log all day and when dey takes her off, she am limp and act deadlike. For a week she am in de bunk. Dat whippin' cause plenty trouble and dere lots of arguments among de white folks round dere.

We has some joyments on de plantation, no parties or dancin' but we has de corn huskin' and de nigger fights. For de corn huskin' everybody come to one place and dey gives de prize for findin' de red ear. On Massa's place de prize am brandy or you am allowed to kiss de gal you calls for. While us huskin' us sing lots, but, I'se not gwine sing any dem songs, 'cause I'se forget and my voice sound like de bray of de mule.

De nigger fights am more for de white folks' joyment but de slaves am allowed to see it. De massas of plantations match deir niggers 'cording to size, and bet on dem. Massas Finnely have one nigger what weights about 150 pounds and him powerful good fighter and he like to fight. None lasts long with him. Den a new nigger comes to fight him.

Dat field am held at night by de pine torchlight. A ring am made by de folks standin' around in de circle. Deys allowed to do anything with dey hands and head and teeth. Nothin' barred except de knife and de club. Dem two niggers gets in de ring and Tom he starts quick, and dat new nigger he starts just as quick. Dat surprise Tom and when dey comes together it like two bulls—kersmash—it sounds like dat. Den it am hit and kick and bite and butt anywhere and any place for to best de other. De one on de bottom bites knees and anything him can do. Dat's de way it go for half de hour.

Findly dat new nigger gets Tom in de stomach with he knee and a lick side de jaw at the same time and down to Tom, and de other nigger jumps on him with both feets, den straddle him and hits with right, left, right, left, right, side Tom's head. Dere Tom lay, makin' no resistance. Everybody am sayin', "Tom have met he match, him am done." Both am bleedin' and am awful sight. Well, dat new nigger relaxes for to get he wind and den Tom, quick like de flash flips him off and jump to he feet and before dat new nigger could get to he feet, Tom kicks him in de stomach, again and again. Dat nigger's body start to quaver and he massa say, "Dat 'nough." Dat de closest Tom ever come to gettin' whipped what I'se know of.

I becomes a runaway nigger short time after dat fight. De War am started den for about a year, or somethin' like dat, and de Federals am north of us. I hears de niggers talk about it, and about runnin' away to freedom. I thinks and thinks about gettin' freedom, and I'se goin' run off. Den I thinks of de patterrollers and what happen if dey cotches me off de place without de pass. Den I thinks of some joyment such as de corn huskin' and de fights and de singin' and I don't know what to do. I tells you one singin' but I can't sing it:

> De moonlight, a shinin' star,
> De big owl hootin' in de tree;
> O, bye, my baby, ain't you gwineter sleep,
> A-rockin' on my knee?
>
> Bye, my honey baby,
> A-rockin' on my knee,
> Baby done gone to sleep,
> Owl hush hootin' in de tree.
>
> She gone to sleep, honey baby sleep,
> A-rockin' on my, a-rockin' on my knee.

Now, back to de freedom. One night about ten niggers run away. De next day we'uns hears nothin', so I says to myself, "De patterrollers don't catch dem." Den I makes up my mind to go and I leaves with de chunk of meat and corn bread and am on my way, half skeert to death I sure has de eyes open and de ears forward, watchin' for de patterrollers. I steps off de road in de night, at sight of anything, and in de day I takes to de woods. It takes me two days to make dat trip and just once de patters pass me by. I am in de thicket watchin' dem and I'se sure dey goin' search dat thicket, 'cause dey stops and am a-talkin' and lookin' my way. Dey stands dere for a li'l bit and den one comes my way. Lawd-a-mighty! dat sure look like de end, but dat man stop and den look and look. Den he pick up somethin' and goes back. It am a bottle and dey all takes de drink and rides on. I'se sure in de sweat and I don't tarry dere long.

De Yanks am camped near Bellfound and dere's where I get to. Imagine my 'sprise when I finds all de ten runaway niggers am dere too. Dat am on Sunday. And on de Monday de Yanks puts us on de freight train and we goes to Stevenson, in Alabama. Dere, us put to work buildin' breastworks. But after de few days, I gets sent to de headquarters at Nashville, in Tennessee.

I'se water toter dere for de army and dere am no fightin' at first but before long dey starts de battle. Dat battle am a experience for me. De noise am awful, just one steady roar of guns and de cannons. De window glass in Nashville am all shook out from de shakement of de cannons. Dere dead mens all over de ground and lots of wounded and some cussin' and some prayin'. Some am moanin' and dis and dat one cry for de water and, God-a-mighty I don't want any such again. Dere am men carryin' de dead off de field, but dey can't keep up with de cannons. I helps bury de dead and den I gets sent to Murfreesboro and dere it am just the same.

You knows when Abe Lincoln am shot? Well, I'se in Nashville den and it am near de end of de War and I am standin' on Broadway Street talkin' with de sergeant when a man walks up and him shakes hands with me and says, "I'se proud to meet a brave, young fellow like you." Dat man am Andrew Johnson and him come to be President after Abe's dead.

I stays in Nashville when de War am over and I marries Tennessee House in 1875. She died July 10, 1936. Dat make sixty-one year dat we'uns am together. Her old missy am now livin' in Arlington Heights, right here in Fort Worth and her name am Mallard and she come from Tennessee too.

I comes here from Tennessee fifty-one year ago and at first I farms and den I works for de packin' plants till dey lets me out, 'cause I'se, too old for to do 'enough work for dem.

I has eight boys and three girls, dat make eleven children, and dey makin' scatterment all over de country so I'se alone in my old age. I has dat seventeen dollars a month pension what I get from de state.

Dat am de end of de road.

DORA FRANKS

Interviewed at Aberdeen, Mississippi
Interviewed by Mrs. Richard Kolb
Age when interviewed: About 100

I WAS BORN in Chocktaw County, but I never knowed 'zackly how old I was, 'cause none o' my folks could read and write. I reckon I be's about a hundred, 'cause I was a big girl long time before surrender. I was old 'nough to marry two years after dat.

My mammy come from Virginny. Her name was Harriet Brewer. My daddy was my young Marster. His name was Marster George Brewer and my mammy always told me dat I was his'n. I knew dat dere was some difference 'tween me and de rest o' chillen, 'cause dey was all coal black, and I was even lighter dan I is now. Lord, it's been to my sorrow many a time, 'cause de chillen used to chase me round and holler at me, "Old yellow nigger." Dey didn't treat me good, neither.

I stayed in de house most o' de time with Miss Emmaline. Miss Emmaline's hair was *dat* white, den. I loved her 'cause she was so good to me. She taught me how to weave and spin. Before I was bigger'n a minute I could do things dat lots o' de old hands couldn't come nigh doin'. She and Marse Bill had about eight chillen, but most of 'em was grown when I come along. Dey was all mighty good to me and wouldn't allow nobody to hurt me.

I 'members one time when dey all went off and left me with a old black woman call Aunt Caroline what done de cookin' round de place some o' de time. When dey left de house I went in de kitchen and asked her for a piece o' white bread like de white folks eat. She haul off and slap me down and call me all kind o' names dat I didn't know what dey meant. My nose bled and ruint de nice dress I had on. When Mistis come back Marse George was with her. She asked me what on earth happen to me and I told her. Dey call Caroline in de room and asked her if what I say was de truth. She tell em it was, and dey sent her away. I hear tell dat dey whip her so hard dat she couldn't walk no more.

Us never had no big funerals or weddin's on de place. Didn't have no marryin' o' any kind. Folks in dem days just sorta hitched up together and call deyselves man and wife. All the cullud folks was buried on what dey called Platnum Hill. Dey didn't have no markers nor nothin' at de graves. Dey was just sunk in places. My brother Frank showed me once where my mammy was buried. Us didn't have no preachin', or nothin' neither. Us didn't even get to have meetin's on Sunday 'less us slip off and go to some other plantation. Course, I got to go with de white folks sometime and set in de back, or on de steps. Dat was when I was little.

Lots o' niggers would slip off from one plantation to de other to see some other niggers. Dey would always manage to get back before daybreak. De worst thing I ever heard about dat was once when my Uncle Alf run off to "jump de broom." Dat was what dey called goin' to see a woman. He didn't come back by daylight, so dey put de nigger hounds after him. Dey smelled his trail down in de swamp and found where he was hidin'.

Now, he was one o' de biggest niggers on de place and a powerful fast worker. But dey took and give him one hundred lashes with de cat-o'-ninety-nine-tails. His back was somethin' awful, but dey put him in de field to work while de blood was still a-runnin'. He work right hard till dey left. Den, when he got up to de end o' de row next to de swamp, he lit out again.

Dey never found time dat time. Dey say he found a cave and fix him up a room where he could live. At nights he would come out on de place and steal enough t'eat and cook it in his little dugout. When de War was over and de slaves was freed, he come out. When I saw him, he look like a hairy ape, without no clothes on and hair growin' all over his body.

Dem was pretty good days back in slavery times. My marster had a whole passel o' niggers on his place. When any of 'em would get sick dey would go to de woods and get herbs and roots and make tea for 'em to drink. Hogweed and May apples was de best things I knowed of. Sometimes old Mistis doctored 'em herself. One time a bunch o' us chillen was playin' in de woods and found some o' dem May apples. Us et a lot of 'em and got awful sick. Dey dosed us up on grease and Samson snakeroot to clean us out. And it sure done a good job. I'se been a-usin' dat snakeroot ever since.

De first thing dat I 'member hearin' about de War was one day when Marse George come in de house and tell Miss Emmaline dat dey's gwine have a bloody war. He say he feared all de slaves would be took away. She say if dat was true she feel like jumpin' in de well. I hate to hear her say dat, but from dat minute I started prayin' for freedom. All de rest o' de women done de same.

De War started pretty soon after dat and all de men folks went off and left de plantation for de women and de niggers to run. Us seen de soldiers pass by most every day. Once de Yankees come and stole a lot o' de horses and somethin' t'eat. Dey even took de trunk full o' Federate money dat was hid in de swamp. How dey found dat us never knowed. Marse George come home about two years after de War started and married Miss Martha Ann. Dey had always been sweethearts. Dey was promised before he left.

When de War was over, my brother Frank slipped in de house where I was still a-stayin'. He told me us was free and for me to come out with de rest. Before sundown dere weren't one nigger left on de place. I hear tell later dat Mistis and de gals had to get out and work in de fields to help gather in de crop.

Frank found us a place to work and put us all in de field. I never had worked in de field before. I'd faint away most every day about eleven o'clock. It was de heat. Some of 'em would have to tote me to de house. I'd soon come to. Den I had to go back to de field. Us was on Marse Davis Cox's place den.

Two years later I met Pete Franks and us married. De Cox's was good folks and give us a big weddin'. All de white folks and de niggers for miles round come to see us get married. De niggers had a big supper and had a peck t'eat. Us had eight chillen, but ain't but three of 'em livin. Me and Pete ain't been a-livin' together for de last twenty-three years. Us just couldn't get along together, so us quit.

I never will forget de Klu Klux Klan. Never will I forget de way dat horn sound at night when dey was a-goin' after some mean nigger. Us'd all run and hide. Us was livin' on de Troup place den, near old Hamilton, in one o' de brick houses back o' de house where dey used to keep de slaves. Marse Alec Troup was one o' de Klu Klux's and so was Marse Thad Willis dat lived close by. Dey'd make plans together sometime and I'd hear 'em. One time dey caught me listenin', but dey didn't do nothin' to me, 'cause dey knowed I weren't gwine tell. Us was all good niggers on his place.

Since I got religion it's de hardest thing in de world for me to 'member de songs us used to dance by. I do 'member a few like "Shoo, Fly," "Old Dan Tucker,' and "Run, Nigger, Run, de Paterroller Catch You." I don't 'member much o' de words. I does 'member a little o' "Old Dan Tucker.' It went dis way:

> Old Dan Tucker was a mighty mean man,
> He beat his wife with a fryin' pan.
> She hollered and she cried, "I'se gwine to go,
> Dey's plenty o' men won't beat me so."
>
> Get out o' de way, Old Dan Tucker,
> You come too late to get yo' supper.
>
> Old Dan Tucker, he got drunk,
> Fell in de fire, kicked up a chunk,
> Red hot coal got down his shoe
> Oh, Great Lord, how de ashes flew.
>
> Get out o' de way, Old Dan Tucker,
> You come too late to get yo' supper.

MITTIE FREEMAN

Interviewed at North Little Rock, Arkansas
Interviewed by Beulah Sherwood Hagg
Age when interviewed: 86

ORANGE COUNTY, Mississippi, was where I was borned at, but I been right here in Arkansas before such thing as war gonna be. In slavery, it was, when my white folks done come to Camden on the Quachita. It was long before the War when the doctor—I means Dr. Williams what owned my pappy and all us younguns—say he going to Arkansas. Theys rode in the fine carriage. Us slaves rode in ox wagons. Lord only knows how long it took a-coming. Every night we camped. I was just a little tyke then but I has a remembrance of everything. The biggest younguns had to walk till theys so tired theys couldn't hardly drag they feets; them what had been a-riding had to get out the ox wagon and walk a far piece; so it like this we go on.

Dr. Williams always wanted to keep his slaves together. He was sure a good man. He didn't work his slaves hard like some. My pappy was a king of a manager for Doctor. Doctor tended his business and Pappy runned the plantation where we lived at. Our good master died before freedom. He willed us slaves to his children, you know, parceled us out, some to this child, some to that. I went to his daughter, Miss Emma.

After Old Master died, poor old Pappy got sent to another plantation of the family. It had a overseer. He was a Northerner man and the meanest devil ever put foot on a plantation. My father was a gentleman; he was just that. He had been brung up that-a-way. Old Master teached us to never answer back to no white folks. But one day that overseer had my pappy whipped for somethin' he never done, and Pappy hit him.

So after that, he sent Pappy down to New Orleans to be sold. He said he would liked to kill Pappy, but he didn't dare 'cause he didn't own him. Pappy was old. Every auction sale, all the young niggers be sold; everybody pass old Pappy by. After a long time—oh, maybe five years— one day they ask Pappy—"Are you got some white folks in Arkansas?" He told them the Williams white folks in Camden on the Quachita. They's white. After while theys send Pappy home. Nobody ever seen such a homecoming. Old Miss and the young white folks gathered round hugged my old black pappy when he come home; they cry on his

130

shoulder, so glad to get him back. That's what them Williams folks thought of their slaves.

Old Miss was name Miss Eliza. She scared to stay by herself after Old Master died. I was took to be her companion. Every day she wanted me to brush her hair and bathe her feet in cool water. She said I was gentle and didn't never hurt her.

One day I was standing by the window and I seen smoke—blue smoke —a-rising beyond a woods. I heerd cannons a-booming and asked her what was it. She say: "Run, Mittie, and hide yourself. It's the Yanks. Theys coming at last, Oh lordy!" I was all excited and told her I didn't want to hide, I wanted to see 'em. "No," she says, right firm. "Ain't I always told you Yankees has horns on their heads? They'll get you. Go on now, do like I tells you."

So I runs out the room and went down by the big gate. A high wall was there and a tree put its branches right over the top. I climbed up and hid under the leaves. They was coming, all a-marching. The captain opened our big gate and marched them in. A soldier seen me and said, "Come on down here; I want to see you." I told him I would, if he would take off his hat and show me his horns.

The day freedom came, I was fishing with Pappy. My remembrance is sure good! All a-sudden cannons commence a-booming, it seem like everywhere. It was the fall of Richmond. Cannons was to roar every place when Richmond fell. Pappy jumps up, throws his pole and everything, and grabs my hand, and starts flying towards the house. "It's victory," he keep on saying. "It's freedom. Now we'se gwine be free." I didn't know what it all meant.

It seem like it took a long time for freedom to come. Everything just kept on like it was. We heard that lots of slaves was getting land and some mules to set up for theirselves. I never knowed any what got land or mules or nothing. We all stayed right on the place till the Yankees come through. They was looking for slaves what was staying on. Now we was free and had to get off de plantation. They packed us in their big ambulance, that is, covered army wagons, and took us to Little Rock. Well, right where the old penitentiary was is where the Yanks had a great big barracks. All chillens and growed womens was put there in tents. The first real free school in Little Rock was opened by the government for colored chillens and I went to it, right from the day we got there.

They took Pappy and put him to work in the big commissary. He got twelve dollars a month and all the grub we could eat. They was plenty of other refugees living in them barracks, and the government taking care of all of em.

I was a purty big sized girl by then and had to go to work to help Pappy. A man named Captain Hodge, a Northerner, got a plantation down the river. He wanted to raise cotton but didn't know how and had to get colored folks to help him. A lot of us niggers from the barracks was sent to pick. We got a dollar and twenty-five cents a hundred pounds.

I never seen that money hardly long enough to get it home. In them days chillens worked for their folks. I toted mine home to Pappy and he got us what we had to have. That's the way it was. We picked cotton all fall and winter and went to school after picking was over.

When I got nearly growed, we moved on this very ground. Pappy had a five year lease. I don't know—but anyhow, they told him he could have all the ground he could clear and work for five years and it wouldn't cost him nothing. He built a log house and put in a orchard. Next year he had a big garden and sold vegetables. Lord, them white ladies wouldn't buy from nobody but Pappy. They'd wait till he got there with his fresh beans and roasting ears. When he got more land broke out, he raised cotton and corn and made it right good. His name was Henry Williams. He was a stern man, and honest. He was named for his old master. When my brothers got growed they learned shoemaker's trade and had right good business in Little Rock. But when Pappy died, them boys give up that good business and took a farm so to make a home for Mammy and the little chillens.

I married Freeman. Onliest husband ever I had. He died last summer. He was a slave too. We used to talk over them days before we met. The K.K.K. never bothered us. They was gathered together to bother niggers and whites what made trouble. If you tended to your own business, they let you alone.

I never voted. My husband did. I can remember when they was colored men voted into office. Justice of peace, county clerks, and that fellow that comes running fast when somebody gets killed. What you call him? Coroner? Sure, that's him. I know that, 'cause I seen them a-setting in their offices.

We raised our family on a plantation. That's the bestest place for colored chillens. My five boys stayed with me till they was grown. They heard about the railroad shops and was bound they's going there to work. Ben—that was my man—and me couldn't make it by ourselfs, so we come on back to this little place where we come soon after the War. He was taken with a tumor on his brains last summer and died in two weeks. He didn't know nothing all that time. My onliest boy what stayed here died just two weeks after his pa. All them others went to Iowa after the big railroad strike here. They was out of work for many years. They didn't like no kind of work but railroad, after they been in the shops.

DELIA GARLIC

Interviewed in Fruiturst, Alabama
Interviewed by Margaret Fowler
Age when interviewed: 100

S LAVERY DAYS WAS HELL. I was growed up when de War come, and I was a mother before it closed. Babies was snatched from deir mother's breast and sold to speculators. Chillens was separated from sisters and brothers and never saw each other again. 'Course dey cry. You think they not cry when dey was sold like cattle? I could tell you about it all day, but even den you couldn't guess de awfulness of it.

It's bad to belong to folks dat own you soul and body, dat can tie you up to a tree, with yo' face to d' tree and yo' arms fastened tight around it, who take a long curlin' whip and cut de blood every lick. Folks a mile away could hear dem awful whippings. Dey was a terrible part of livin'.

I was born at Powhatan, Virginia, and was the youngest of thirteen chillen. I never seed none of my brothers and sisters 'cept brother William. Him and my mother and me was brought in a speculator's drove to Richmond and put in a warehouse with a drove of other niggers. Den we was all put on a block and sold to de highest bidder. I never seed brother William again.

Mammy and me was sold to a man by the name of Carter, who was de sheriff of de county. Dey wasn't no good times at his house. He was a widower and his daughter kept house for him. I nursed for her and one day I was playin' with de baby. It hurt its li'l hand and commenced to cry, and she whirl on me, pick up a hot iron and run it all down my arm and hand. It took off de flesh when she done it.

After awhile, Marster married again, but things weren't no better. I seed his wife blackin' her eyebrows with smut one day, so I thought I'd black mine just for fun. I rubbed some smut on my eyebrows and forgot to rub it off, and she cotched me. She was powerful mad and yelled: "You black devil, I'll show you how to mock your betters." Den she pick up a stick of stovewood and flails it against my head. I didn't know nothin' more till I come to, lyin' on de floor. I heard de mistis say to one of de girls: "I thought her thick skull and cap of wool could take it better than that."

I kept on stayin' dere, and one night de marster come in drunk and set at de table with his head lollin 'around. I was waitin' on de table, and he look up and see me. I was scared, and dat made him awful mad. He called an overseer and told him: "Take her out and beat some sense in her."

I begin to cry and run and run in de night, but finally I run back by de quarters and heard Mammy callin' me. I went in, and right away dey come for me. A horse was standin' in front of de house, and I was took dat very night to Richmond and sold to a speculator again. I never seed my mammy anymore.

I has thought many times through all dese years how Mammy looked dat night. She pressed my hand in both of hers and said: "Be good and trust in de Lord." Trustin' was de only hope of de poor black critters in dem days. Us just prayed for strength to endure it to de end. We didn't 'spect nothin' but to stay in bondage till we died.

I was sold by de speculator to a man in McDonough, Georgia. I don't recollect his name, but he was openin' a big hotel at McDonough and bought me to wait on tables. But when de time come around to pay for me, his hotel done fail. Den de Atlanta man dat bought de hotel bought me, too. Before long, though, I was sold to a man by de name of Garlic, down in Louisiana, and I stayed with him till I was freed. I was a regular field hand, plowin' and hoein' and choppin' cotton.

Us heard talk about de War, but us didn't pay no 'tention. Us never dreamed dat freedom would ever come.

Us didn't have no parties on our plantation; nothin' like dat. Us didn't have no clothes for goin' round. I never had a undershirt until just before my first child was borned. I never had nothin' but a shimmy and a slip for a dress, and it was made outen de cheapest cloth dat could be bought, unbleached cloth, coarse, but made to last.

Us didn't know nothin' 'cept to work. Us was up by three or four in de mornin' and everybody got dey somethin' to eat in de kitchen. Dey didn't give us no way to cook, nor nothin' to cook in our cabins. Soon as us dressed us went by de kitchen and got our piece of corn bread. Dey wasn't even no salt in dem last years. Dat piece of corn bread was all us had for breakfast, and for supper us had de same. For dinner us had boiled victuals; greens, peas, and sometimes beans. Us never knowed nothin' about coffee.

One mornin' I 'members I had started to de field, and on de way I lost my piece of bread. I didn't know what to do. I started back to try to find it, and it was too dark to see. But I walk right slow, and had a dog dat walked with me. He went on ahead, and after awhile I come on him lyin' dere guardin' dat piece of bread. He never touched it, so I gived him some of it.

Just before de War I married a man named Chatfield from another plantation; but he was took off to war and I never seed him again. After awhile I married a boy on de plantation named Miles Garlic.

Massa Garlic had two boys in de War. When dey went off de massa and missis cried, but it made us glad to see dem cry. Dey made us cry so much.

When we knowed we was free, everybody wanted to get out. De rule was dat if you stayed in yo' cabin you could keep it, but if you left, you lost it. Miles was workin' at Wetumpka, and he slipped in and out so us could keep on livin' on de cabin. My second baby soon come, and right den I made up my mind to go to Wetumpka where Miles was workin 'for de railroad. I went on down dere and us settled down.

After Miles died, I lived dere long as I could and den come to Montgomery to live with my son. I'se eatin' white bread now and havin' de best time of my life. But when de Lord say, "Delia, well done; come up higher," I'll be glad to go.

ROBERT GLENN

Interviewed at Raleigh, North Carolina
Interviewed by Pat Matthews
Age when interviewed: 87

I WAS A SLAVE before and during the Civil War. I am eighty-seven years old. I was born September 16, 1850. I was born in Orange County, North Carolina, near Hillsboro. At that time Durham was just a platform at the station and no house there whatever. The platform was lighted with a contraption shaped like a basket and burning coal that gave off a blaze. There were holes in this metal basket for the cinders to fall through.

I belonged to a man named Bob Hall; he was a widower. He had three sons, Thomas, Nelson, and Lambert. He died when I was eight years old and I was put on the block and sold in Nelson Hall's yard by the son of Bob Hall. I saw my brother and sister sold on this same plantation. My mother belonged to the Halls, and father belonged to the Glenns. They sold me away from my father and mother and I was carried to the state of Kentucky. I was bought by a Negro speculator by the name of Henry Long, who lived not far from Hurdles Mill in Person County. I was not allowed to tell my mother and father good-bye. I was bought and sold three times in one day.

My father's time was hired out and, as he knew a trade, he had by working overtime saved up a considerable amount of money. After the speculator, Henry Long, bought me, Mother went to Father and pled with him to buy me from him and let the white folks hire me out. No slave could own a slave. Father got the consent and help of his owners to buy me and they asked Long to put me on the block again. Long did so and named his price but when he learned who had bid me off, he backed down. Later in the day he put me on the block and named another price much higher than the price formerly set. He was asked by the white folks to name his price for his bargain and he did so. I was again put on the auction block and Father bought me in, putting up the cash. Long then flew into a rage and cursed my father saying, "You damn black son of a bitch, you think you are white do you? Now just to show you you are black, I will not let you have your son at any price."

Father knew it was all off. Mother was frantic, but there was nothing they could do about it. They had to stand and see the speculator put me on his horse behind him and ride away without allowing either of them to tell me good-bye. I figure I was sold three times in one day, as the price asked was offered in each instance. Mother was told under threat of a whipping not to make any outcry when I was carried away.

He took me to his home, but on the way he stopped for refreshments, at a plantation, and while he was eating and drinking, he put me into a room where two white women were spinning flax. I was given a seat across the room from where they were working. After I had sat there awhile wondering where I was going and thinking about Mother and home, I went to one of the women and asked, "Missus, when will I see my mother again?" She replied, "I don't know child. Go and sit down." I went back to my seat and as I did so both the women stopped spinning for a moment, looked at each other, and one of them remarked, "Almighty God, this slavery business is a horrible thing. Chances are this boy will never see his mother again." This remark nearly killed me, as I began to fully realize my situation.

Long, the Negro trader, soon came back, put me on his horse and finished the trip to his home. He kept me at his home awhile and then traded me to a man named William Moore who lived in Person County.

Moore at this time was planning to move to Kentucky, which he soon did, taking me with him. My mother found out by the "grapevine telegraph" that I was going to be carried to Kentucky. She got permission and came to see me before they carried me off. When she started home I was allowed to go part of the way with her, but they sent two Negro girls with us to insure my return. We were allowed to talk privately, but while we were doing so, the two girls stood a short distance away and watched, as the marster told them when they left that if I escaped they would be whipped every day until I was caught. When the time of parting came and I had to turn back, I burst out crying loud. I was so weak from sorrow I could not walk, and the two girls who were with me took me by each arm and led me along half carrying me.

This man Moore carried me and several other slaves to Kentucky. We traveled by train by way of Nashville, Tennessee. My thoughts are not familiar with the happenings of this trip but I remember that we walked a long distance at one place on the trip from one depot to another.

We finally reached Kentucky and Moore stopped at his brother's plantation until he could buy one; then we moved on it. My marster was named William Moore and my missus was named Martha Whitfield Moore. It was a big plantation and he hired a lot of help and had white tenants besides the land he worked with slaves. There were only six slaves used as regular field hands during his first year in Kentucky.

The food was generally common. Hog meat and corn bread most all the time. Slaves got biscuits only on Sunday morning. Our clothes were poor and I worked barefooted most of the time, winter and summer. No books, papers, or anything concerning education was allowed the slaves by his rules and the customs of these times.

Marster Moore had four children, among whom was one boy about my age. The girls were named Atona, Beulah, and Minnie, and the boy was named Crosby. He was mighty brilliant. We played together. He was the only white boy there, and he took a great liking to me, and we loved each other devotedly. Once in a undertone he asked me how I would like to have an education. I was overjoyed at the suggestion and he at once began to teach me secretly. I studied hard and he soon had me so I could read and write well. I continued studying and he continued teaching me. He furnished me books and slipped all the papers he could get to me and I was the best educated Negro in the community without anyone except the slaves knowing what was going on.

All the slaves on Marster's plantation lived the first year we spent in Kentucky in a one room house with one fireplace. There was a dozen or more who all lived in this one room house. Marster built himself a large house having seven rooms. He worked his slaves himself and never had any overseers. We worked from sun to sun in the fields and then worked at the house after getting in from the fields as long as we could see. I have never seen a patterroller, but when I left the plantation in slavery time I got a pass. I have never seen a jail for slaves, but I have seen slaves whipped and I was whipped myself. I was whipped particularly about a saddle I left in the night after using it during the day. My flesh was cut up so bad that the scars are on me to this day.

We were not allowed to have prayer meetings, but we went to the white folks' church to services sometimes. There were no looms, mills, or shops on the plantation at Marster Moore's. I kept the name of Glenn through all the years as Marster Moore did not change his slaves' names to his family name. My mother was named Martha Glenn and Father was named Bob Glenn.

I was in the field when I first heard of the Civil War. The woman who looked after Henry Hall and myself (both slaves) told me she heard Marster say old Abraham Lincoln was tryin to free the niggers. Marster finally pulled me up and went and joined the Confederate Army. Kentucky split and part joined the North and part the South. The war news

kept slipping through of success for first one side, then the other. Sometimes Marster would come home, spend a few days, and then go again to
the War. It seemed he influenced a lot of men to join the Southern army,
among them was a man named Enoch Moorehead. Moorehead was killed
in a few days after he joined the Southern army.

Marster Moore fell out with a lot of his associates in the army and
some of them who were from the same community became his bitter
enemies. Tom Foushee was one of them. Marster became so alarmed over
the threats on his life made by Foushee and others that he was afraid to
stay in his own home at night, and he built a little camp one and one-half
miles from his home and he and Missus spent their nights there on his
visits home. Foushee finally came to the Great House one night heavily
armed. Came right on into the house and inquired for Marster. We told
him Marster was away. Foushee lay down on the floor and waited a long
time for him. Marster was at the little camp but we would not tell where
he was.

Foushee left after spending most of the night at Marster's. As he went
out into the yard, when leaving, Marster's bulldog growled at him and
he shot him dead.

Marster went to Henderson, Kentucky, the county seat of Henderson
County, and surrendered to the Federal army and took the Oath of
Allegiance. Up to that time I had seen a few Yankees. They stopped now
and then at Marster's and got their breakfast. They always asked about
buttermilk, they seemed to be very fond of it. They were also fond of
ham. But we had the ham meat buried in the ground. This was about the
close of the War. A big army of Yankees came through a few months later
and soon we heard of the surrender. A few days after this, Marster told
me to catch two horses, that we had to go to Dickenson, which was the
county seat of Webster County. On the way to Dickenson he said to me,
"Bob, did you know you are free and Lincoln has freed you? You are as
free as I am." We went to the Freedman's Bureau and went into the office.
A Yankee officer looked me over and asked Marster my name, and
informed me I was free, and asked me whether or not I wanted to keep
living with Moore. I did not know what to do, so I told him yes. A fixed
price of seventy-five dollars and board was then set as the salary I should
receive per year for my work. The Yankee told me to let him know if I
was not paid as agreed.

I went back home and stayed a year. During the year I hunted a lot at
night and thoroughly enjoyed being free. I took my freedom by degrees
and remained obedient and respectful, but still wondering and thinking
of what the future held for me. After I retired at night I made plan after
plan and built air castles as to what I would do. At this time I formed a
great attachment for the white man, Mr. Atlas Chandler, with whom I
hunted. He bought my part of the game we caught and favored me in
other ways. Mr. Chandler had a friend, Mr. Dewitt Yarborough, who was
an adventurer and trader, and half brother to my ex-marster, Mr. Moore,
with whom I was then staying. He is responsible for me taking myself into

my own hands and getting out of feeling I was still under obligations to ask my marster or missus when I desired to leave the premises. Mr. Yarborough's son was off at school at a place called Kiloh, Kentucky, and he wanted to carry a horse to him and also take along some other animals for trading purposes. He offered me a new pair of pants to make the trip for him and I accepted the job. I delivered the horse to his son and started for home. On the way back I ran into Uncle Squire Yarborough who once belonged to Dewitt Yarborough. He persuaded me to go home with him to a wedding in Union County, Kentucky. The wedding was twenty miles away and we walked the entire distance. It was a double wedding, two couples were married. Georgianna Hawkins was married to George Ross and Steve Carter married a woman whose name I do not remember. This was in the winter during the Christmas holidays and I stayed in the community until about the first of January, then I went back home. I had been thinking for several days before I went back home as to just what I must tell Mr. Moore and as to how he felt about the matter, and what I would get when I got home. In my dilemma I almost forgot I was free.

.I got home at night and my mind and heart was full but I was surprised at the way he treated me. He acted kind and asked me if I was going to stay with him next year. I was pleased. I told him, "Yes sir!" and then I lay down and went to sleep. He had a boss man on his plantation then and next morning he called me, but I just couldn't wake. I seemed to be in a trance or something, I had recently lost so much sleep. He called me the second time and still I did not get up. Then he came in and spanked my head. I jumped up and went to work feeding the stock and splitting wood for the day's cooking and fires. I then went in and ate my breakfast. Mr. Moore told me to hitch a team of horses to a wagon and go to a neighbor's five miles away for a load of hogs. I refused to do so. They called me into the house and asked me what I was doing about it. I said I do not know. As I said that I stepped out of the door and left.

I went straight to the county seat and hired to Dr. George Rasby in Webster County for one hundred dollars per year. I stayed there one year. I got uneasy in Kentucky. The whites treated the blacks awful bad so I decided to go to Illinois, as I thought a Negro might have a better chance there, it being a Northern state. I was kindly treated and soon began to save money, but all through the years there was a thought that haunted me in my dreams and in my waking hours, and this thought was of my mother, whom I had not seen or heard of in many years.

Finally one cold morning in early December I made a vow that I was going to North Carolina and see my mother if she was still living. I had plenty of money for the trip. I wrote the postmaster in Roxboro, North Carolina, asking him to inform my mother I was still living, and telling him the circumstances, mailing a letter at the same time telling her I was still alive but saying nothing of my intended visit to her. I left Illinois bound for North Carolina on December fifteenth and in a few days I was at my mother's home. I tried to fool them. There were two men with me and they called me by a fictitious name, but when I shook my mother's hand I held it a little too long and she suspicioned something. Still she held herself until she was more sure. When she got a chance she came to me and said, "Ain't you my child?" Tell me ain't you my child whom I left on the road near Mr. Moore's before the War?"

I broke down and began to cry. Mother and Father did not know me, but Mother suspicioned I was her child. Father had a few days previously remarked that he did not want to die without seeing his son once more. I could not find language to express my feelings. I did not know before I came home whether my parents were dead or alive. This Christmas I spent in the county and state of my birth and childhood with Mother, Father, and freedom was the happiest period of my entire life, because those who were torn apart in bondage and sorrow several years previous were now united in freedom and happiness.

ANDREW GOODMAN
Interviewed at Dallas, Texas
Interviewer not identified
Age when interviewed: 97

I WAS BORN in slavery and I think them days was better for the niggers than the days we see now. One thing was, I never was cold and hungry when my old master lived, and I has been plenty hungry and cold a lot of times since he is gone. But sometimes I think Marse Goodman was the bestest man God made in a long time.

My mother, Martha Goodman, belonged to Marse Bob Goodman when she was born, but my paw come from Tennessee and Marse Bob heired* him was good to they niggers. Old Marse never 'lowed none of his nigger have been fine folks all-a-way round, 'cause my paw said them that raised him was good to they niggers. Old Marse never 'lowed none of his nigger families separated. He 'lowed he thought it right and fittin' that folks stay together, though I heard tell of some that didn't think so.

My missus was just as good as Marse Bob. My maw was a puny little woman that wasn't able to do work in the fields, and she puttered round the house for the Missus, doin' little odd jobs. I played round with little Miss Sallie and little Mr. Bob, and I ate with them and slept with them. I used to sweep off the steps and do things, and she'd brag on me. Many is the time I'd get to noddin' and go to sleep, and she'd pick me up and put me in bed with her chillen.

Marse Bob didn't put his little niggers in the fields till they's big 'nough

* Inherited.

to work, and the mammies was give time off from the fields to come back to the nursin' home to suck the babies. He didn't never put the niggers out in bad weather. He give us somethin' to do, in out of the weather, like shellin' corn, and the women could spin and knit. They made us plenty of good clothes. In summer we wore long shirts, split up the sides, made out of lowerings—that's same as cotton sacks was made out of. In winter we had good jeans and knitted sweaters and knitted socks.

My paw was a shoemaker. He'd take a calfhide and make shoes with the hairy sides turned in, and they was warm and kept your feet dry. My maw spent a lot of time cardin' and spinnin' wool, and I always had plenty things.

Life was purty fine with Marse Bob. He was a man of plenty. He had a lot of land and he built him a log house when he come to Texas. He had several hundred head of cattle and more than that many hogs. We raised cotton and grain and chickens and vegetables and most anything anybody could ask for.

Some places the masters give out a peck of meal and so many pounds of meat to a family for them a week's rations, and if they et it up that was all they got. But Marse Bob always give out plenty and said, "If you need more, you can have it, 'cause ain't any going to suffer on my place."

He built us a church, and a old man, Kenneth Lyons, who was a slave of the Lyons family nearby, used to get a pass every Sunday mornin' and come preach to us. He was a man of good learnin' and the best preacher I ever heard. He baptized in a little old mudhole down back of our place. Nearly all the boys and gals gets converted when they's about twelve or fifteen year old. Then on Sunday afternoon, Marse Bob learned us to read and write. He told us we oughta get all the learnin' we could.

Once a week the slaves could have any night they want for a dance or frolic. Mance McQueen was a slave belonging on the Dewberry place what could play a fiddle, and his master give him a pass to come play for us. Marse Bob give us chickens or kilt a fresh beef or let us make 'lasses candy. We could choose any night, 'cept in the fall of the year. Then we worked awful hard and didn't have the time. We had a gin run by horse-power and after sundown, when we left the fields, we used to gin a bale of cotton every night. Marse always give us from Christmas Eve through New Year's Day off, to make up for the hard work in the fall.

Christmas time everybody got a present and Marse Bob give a big hog to every four families. We had money to buy whiskey with. In spare time we'd make corn-shuck horse collars and all kinds of baskets, and Marse bought them off us. What he couldn't use, he sold for us. We'd take post oak and split it thin with drawin' knives and let it get tough in the sun, and then weave it into cotton baskets and fish baskets and little fancy baskets. The men spent they money on whiskey, 'cause everything else was furnished. We raised our own tobacco and hung it in the barn to season, and anybody could go get it when they wanted it. We always got Saturday afternoons off to fish and hunt. We used to have fish fries and plenty of game in dem days.

Course, we used to hear about other places where they had nigger drivers and beat the slaves. But I never did see or hear tell of one master's slaves gettin' a beatin'. We had a overseer, but didn't know what a nigger driver was. Marse Bob had some nigger dogs like other places and used to train them for fun. He'd get some of the boys to run for a hour or so and then put the dogs on the trail. He'd say, "If you hear them gettin' near, take to a tree." But Marse Bob never had no niggers to run off.

Old man Briscoll, who had a place next to ours, was vicious cruel. He was mean to his own blood, beatin' his chillen. His slaves was a-feared all the time and hated him. Old Charlie, a good old man who belonged to him, run away and stayed six months in the woods before Briscoll cotched him. The niggers used to help feed him, but one day a nigger 'trayed him and Briscoll put the dogs on him and cotched him. He made to Charlie like he wasn't goin' to hurt him none and got him to come peaceful. When he took him home, he tied him and beat him for a terrible long time. Then he took a big, pine torch and let burnin' pitch drop in spots all over him. Old Charlie was sick about four months and then he died.

Marse Bob knowed me better'n most the slaves, 'cause I was round the house more. One day he called all the slaves to the yard. He only had sixty-six then, 'cause he 'vided with his son and daughter when they married. He made a little speech. He said, "I'm going to a war, but I don't think I'll be gone long, and I'm turning the overseer off and leaving Andrew in charge of the place, and I wants everything to go on, just like I was here. Now, you all mind what Andrew says, 'cause if you don't, I'll make it rough on you when I come back home." He was joking, though, 'cause he wouldn't have done nothing to them.

Then he said to me, "Andrew, you is old 'nough to be a man and look after things. Take care of Missus and see that none the niggers wants, and try to keep the place going."

We didn't know what the War was about, but Master was gone four years. When Old Missus heard from him, she'd call all the slaves and tell us the news and read us his letters. Little parts of it she wouldn't read. We never heard of him getting hurt none, but if he had, Old Missus wouldn't tell us, 'cause the niggers used to cry and pray over him all the time. We never heard tell what the War was about.

When Marse Bob come home, he sent for all the slaves. He was sitting in a yard chair, all tuckered out, and shook hands all round, and said he's glad to see us. Then he said, "I got something to tell you. You is just as free as I is. You don't belong to nobody but yourselves. We went to the War and fought, but the Yankees done whip us, and they say the niggers is free. You can go where you wants to go, or you can stay here, just as you likes." He couldn't help but cry.

The niggers cry and don't know much what Marse Bob means. They is sorry about the freedom, 'cause they don't know where to go, and they's always 'pend on Old Marse to look after them. Three families went to get farms for theyselves, but the rest just stay on for hands on the old place.

The Federals has been coming by, even before Old Marse come home.

They all come by, carrying they little budgets and if they was walking they'd look in the stables for a horse or mule, and they just took what they wanted of corn or livestock. They done the same after Marse Bob come home. He just said, "Let them go they way, 'cause that's what they're going to do, anyway." We was scareder of them than we was of the devil. But they spoke right kindly of us colored folks. They said, "If you got a good master and want to stay, well, you can do that, but now you can go where you want to, 'cause ain't nobody going to stop you."

The niggers can't hardly get used to the idea. When they wants to leave the place, they still go up to the Big House for a pass. They just can't understand about the freedom. Old Marse or Missus say, "You don't need no pass. All you got to do is just take your foot in your hand and go."

It seem like the War just plumb broke Old Marse up. It wasn't long till he moved into Tyler and left my paw running the farm on a halfance with him and the nigger workers. He didn't live long, but I forgets just how long. But when Mr. Bob heired the old place, he 'lowed we'd just go 'long the way his paw has made the trade with my paw.

Young Mr. Bob apparently done the first rascality I ever heard of a Goodman doing. The first year we worked for him we raised lots of grain and other things and fifty-seven bales of cotton. Cotton was fifty-two cents a pound, and he shipped it all away, but all he ever gave us was a box of candy and a sack of store tobacco and a sack of sugar. He said the 'signment done got lost. Paw said to let it go, 'cause we had always lived by what the Goodmans had said.

I got married and lived on the old place till I was in my late fifties. I had seven chillen, but if I got any livin' now, I don't know where they is. My paw and maw got to own a little piece of land not far from the old place, and paw lived to be 102 and maw 106. I'm the last one of any of my folks.

MARY ELLA GRANDBERRY

Interviewed at Sheffield, Alabama
Interviewed by Levi D. Shelby, Jr.
Age when interviewed: 90

I DON'T KNOW just how old I is, but I knows dat I'm somewheres nigh ninety years old. I was borned in Barton, Alabama. My father and mother come from Richmond, Virginny. My mammy was name Margaret Keller and my pappy was Adam Keller. My five sisters was Martha, Sarah, Harriet, Emma, and Rosanna, and my three brothers was Peter, Adam, Jr., and William.

Us all live in a li'l two-room log cabin just off the Big House. Life weren't very much for us, 'cause we had to work and slave all de time. Massa Jim's house was a li'l old frame buildin' like a ordinary house is now. He was a single man and didn't have so terrible much, it seem. He had a whole lot, though, but just to look at him you'd think he was a poor white man. Dere was a lot o' cabins for de slaves, but dey wasn't fitten for nobody to live in. We just had to put up with 'em.

I don't 'member much about when I was a child. I disremembers ever playin' like chillens do today. Ever since I can 'member I had a water bucket on my arm totin' water to de hands. Iffen I weren't doin' dat, I was choppin' cotton. Chillens nowadays sees a good time to what we did den. Every mornin' just about hip of day de overseer was round to see dat we was ready to get to de fields. Plenty times us had to go withouten break-fast, 'cause we didn't get up in time to get it before de man done come to get us on de way to de field. Us worked till dinner time just de same before we got anything to eat.

De food we et was fixed just like it is now. My mammy fixed our grub at home. De only difference between den and now was us didn't get nothin' but common things den. Us didn't know what it was to get biscuits for breakfast every mornin'. It was corn bread till on Sundays, den us'd get four biscuits apiece. Us got fatback most every mornin'. Sometimes us might get chicken for dinner on a Sunday or some day like Christmas. It was mighty seldom us gets anything like dat, though. We liked possums and rabbits but dey didn't come till winter time when some of de men folks'd run cross one in de field. Dey never had no chance to get out and hunt none.

Dere was no such thing as havin' different clothes for winter and summer. Us wore de same thing in summertime as in de winter time. De same was true about shoes. Us wore brogans from one year to de other.

My old marse was a pretty good man but nothin' extra. One thing about him, he wouldn't allow none of de overseers to whip none of us, lessen he was dere to see it done. Good thing he was like dat, too, 'cause he saved de blacks a many a lick what dey'd got iffen he hadn't been dere. Massa Jim was a bachelor, and he ain't never had much truck with womenfolks. Iffen he had any chillens, I never knowed nothin' about 'em.

De overseers was terrible hard on us. Dey'd ride up and down de field and haste you so till you near about fell out. Sometimes and most gener-ally every time you behind de crowd you got a good lickin' with de bull-whip dat de driver had in de saddle with him. I heard Mammy say dat one day dey whipped poor Leah till she fall out like she was dead. Den dey rubbed salt and pepper on de blisters to make 'em burn real good. She was so sore till she couldn't lay on her back nights, and she just couldn't stand for no clothes to touch her back whatsoever.

Massa Jim had about one of de biggest plantations in dat section. I guess he had nigh onto a hundred blacks on de place. I never knowed 'zackly how many there was nor how big de place was.

De folks nowadays is always complainin' about how dey is havin' such hard times, but dey just don't know nothin'. Dey should have come up when I did and dey'd see now dey is livin' just like kings and queens. Dey don't have to get up before day when it's so dark you can just see your hands before your eyes. Dey don't know what it's like to have to keep up with de leader. You know dey was always somebody what could work faster dan de rest of de folks and dis fellow was always de leader, and everybody else was supposed to keep up with him or her whatsoever it was. Iffen you didn't keep up with de leader you got a good thrashin' when you gets home at night. It was always good dark when de hands got in from de field. 'Course, iffen dere was a lady what had a baby at home, she could leave just a little before de sun set.

Younguns nowadays don't know what it is to be punished; dey think iffen dey gets a li'l whippin' from dey mammy now dat dey is punish' terrible. Dey should of had to follow de leader for one day and see how dey'd be punish' iffen dey gets too far behind. De biggest thing dat us was punish' for was not keepin' up.

Dey'd whip us iffen we was caught talkin' about de free states, too. Iffen you weren't whipped, you was put in de "nigger box" and fed corn bread what was made withouten salt and with plain water. De box was just big 'nough for you to stand up in, but it had air holes in it to keep you from suffocatin'. Dere was plenty turnin' round room in it to allow you to change your position every once in a while. Iffen you had done a bigger 'nough thing you was kept in de "nigger box" for months at de time, and when you got out you was nothin' but skin and bones and scarcely able to walk.

Half de time a slave didn't know dat he was sold till de massa'd call him to de Big House and tell him he had a new massa from den on. Every time dat one was sold de rest of 'em'd say, "I hopes next time'll be me." Dey thought you'd get a chance to run away to de free states. I heard my mammy say dat when she come from Virginny she come on a boat built outen logs. She say she never was so sick in all her life. I seed a whole wagon load of slaves come through our farm one day what was on dere way to Arkansas. Dey was most I ever seed travel at de same time.

De white folks didn't allow us to even look at a book. Dey would scold and sometimes whip us iffen dey caught us with our head in a book. Dat is one thing I surely did want to do and dat was to learn to read and write. Massa Jim promised to teach us to read and write, but he never had de time.

Dere weren't but one church on de place what I lived on, and de colored and de white both went to it. You know we was never allowed to go to church withouten some of de white folks with us. We weren't even allowed to talk with nobody from another farm. Iffen you did, you got one of de worst whippin's of your life. After freedom Massa Jim told us dat dey was 'fraid we'd get together and try to run away to de North, and dat dat was why dey didn't want us gettin' together talkin'.

A few years before de War my pappy learnt to read de Bible. Whenever we would go to church he would read to us and we'd sing. About de most two popular songs dey sung was "Steal Away" and "I Wonder Where Good Old Daniel Was." "Steal Away" is such a popular song what everybody knows it. De other one is done mighty nigh played out, so I'll sing it for you. It goes like dis:

> I wonder where was good old Daniel,
> I wonder where was good old Daniel,
> I wonder where was thinkin' Peter,
> I wonder where was thinkin' Peter.
>
> (Chorus)
> I'm goin' away, goin' away.
> I'm goin' away, goin' away,
> I wonder where was weepin' Mary,
> I wonder where was weepin' Mary,
> I'm goin' away, I'm goin' away,
> I'm goin' away to live forever,
> I'll never turn back no more.

De slaves would get tired of de way dey was treated and try to run away to de North. I had a cousin to run away one time. Him and another fellow had got 'way up in Virginny before Massa Jim found out where dey was. Soon as Massa Jim found de whereabouts of George he went after him. When Massa Jim gets to George and 'em, George pretended like he didn't know Massa Jim. Massa Jim ask him, "George, don't you know me?" George he say, "I never seed you before in my life." Den dey ask George and 'em where did dey come from. George and dis other fellow look up in de sky and say, "I come from above, where all is love." Iffen dey had owned dey knowed Massa Jim he could have brung 'em back home. My pappy tried to get away de same time as George and dem did, but he couldn't see how to take all us chillen with him, so he had to stay with us. De blacks would slip off to de North and was caught and brung back. De paterrollers'd catch de colored folks and lock 'em up till de owner come after 'em.

Iffen a slave was cotched out after nine o'clock he was whipped. Dey didn't allow nobody out after it was dark, lessen he had a pass from de massa. One night, before George and dis fellow (I disremembers his name, but I think it was Ezra) runned away, George tried to get over to de bunk where he lived and one of de overseers seen him and dey put him in de "nigger box" for three weeks. Just as soon as he got out again, George and dis Ezra slipped off. Dey had a sign dat dey would give each other every night after sundown. George would hang de lantern in de window, and den he would take it outen de window and hang it right back in dere again. I couldn't never make no sense outen it. I asked him one day what he was a-doin' dat for. He say dat before long I'd know 'zackly what it all about. Dis was de sign of how long dey have to wait before dey try to get away.

After de day's work was over, de slaves didn't have nothin' to do but to go to bed. In fact, dey didn't feel like doin' nothin' else. On Saturday dey set up and washed so's dey could have some clean clothes to wear de comin' week. We worked all day, every day 'ceptin' some Saturdays, we had a half day off den. Us didn't get many and only when us asked for 'em. On Sundays us just laid round most all day. Us didn't get no pleasure outen goin' to church, 'cause we weren't allowed to say nothin'. Sometimes, even on Christmas, us didn't get no rest. I 'members on one Christmas us had to build a lime kiln. When us get a holiday us rested. Iffen dere was a weddin' or a funeral on our plantation us went. Otherways we don't go nowhere.

De War come when I was a big gal. I 'member dat my uncle and cousin joined in with de Yankees to help fight for de freedom. De Yankees come to our place and runned Massa Jim away and took de house for a hospital. Dey took all of Massa Jim's clothes and gived dem to some of deir friends. Dey burned up all de cotton, hay, peas, and everything dat was in de barns. Dey made de white folks cook for de colored and den serve 'em while dey et. De Yankees made 'em do for us like we done for dem. Dey showed de white folks what it was to work for somebody else. Dey stayed on our place for de longest. When dey did leave, dere weren't a mouthful to eat in de house. When de War was over, Massa Jim told us dat we had to find somewheres else to live. 'Course, some of my folks had already gone when he come home. Us left Massa Jim's and moved to another farm. We got pay for de work what we did on dis other place.

Right after de War de Ku Klux got after de colored folks. Dey would come to our houses and scare us most to death. Dey would take some of de niggers out and whip 'em and dose dat dey didn't whip dey tied up by deir fingers and toes. Dese Ku Klux would come to our windows at night and say: "Your time ain't long a-comin'." De Ku Klux got so bad dat dey would even get us in de daytime. Dey kept dis up till some folks from de North come down and put a stop to it.

I married Nelson Grandberry. De weddin' was private. I don't have no chillens, but my husband got four. I haven't heered from any of 'em in a long time now. I guess dey all dead.

ELIJAH GREEN
Interviewed at Charleston, South Carolina
Interviewed by Augustus Ladsen
Age when interviewed: 94

I WAS BORN in Charleston at 82 King Street, December 25, 1843. The house is still there. My ma and pa was Kate and John Green. My ma had seven chillen (boys), and I am the last of 'em. Their names was: Henry, Scipio, Ellis, Nathaniel, Robert, Michael, and myself.

From the southeast of Calhoun Street, which was then Boundary Street, to the Battery was the city limit and from the northwest of Boundary Street for several miles was nothin' but farm land. All my brothers was farm hands for our master, George W. Jones. I did all the house work till the War, when I was given to Mr. George W. Jones' son, William H. Jones, as his "daily give servant" whose duty was to clean his boots, shoes, sword, and make his coffee. He was First Lieutenant of the South Carolina Company Regiment. Being his servant, I wear all his cast-off clothes, which I was glad to have. My shoes was called brogans and had brass on the toe. When a slave had one of 'em you couldn't tell 'em he wasn't dressed to death!

As the "daily give servant" of Mr. William H. Jones I had to go to Virginia durin' the War. In the battle at Richmond General Lee had General Grant almost beaten. He drive him almost in the Potomac River and then take seven pieces of his artillery. When General Grant see how near defeat he was, he put up a white flag as a signal for time out to bury his deads. That flag stayed up for three weeks while General Grant was diggin' trenches. In the meantime he got the message to President Lincoln askin' him to send a reinforcement of soldiers. General Sherman was in charge of the regiment who send word to General Grant to hold his position till he had captured Columbia, Savannah, and burned out Charleston while on his way with the dispatch of 45,000 men. When General Sherman got to Virginia, the battle was renewed and continued for seven days at the end of which General Lee surrender to General Grant. Durin' the seven days fight the battle got so hot till Mr. William Jones made his escape, and it was two days before I know he was gone. One of the generals sent me home and I got here two days before Mr. William got home. He went up in the attic and stay there till the War was ended. I carry all his meals to him and tell him all the news. Master sure was a frightened man; I was sorry for him. That battle at Richmond, Virginia, was the worst in American history.

Mr. George W. Jones, my first master, ran a blockade. He had ships roamin' the sea to capture pirates' ships. He had a daughter, Ellen, who was always kind to the slaves. Master had a driver, William Jenkins, and an overseer, Henry Brown. Both was white. The driver see that the work was done by the supervision of the overseer. Master's farm amounted to twenty-five acres with about eighteen slaves. The overseer blow the horn, which was a conch shell, at six in the mornin' and every slave better answer when the roll was called at seven. The slaves didn't have to work on Saturday.

Mr. Ryan had a private jail on Queen Street near the Planters Hotel. He was very cruel; he'd lick his slaves to death. Very seldom one of his slaves survived a whippin'. He was the opposite to Governor Aiken, who lived on the northwest corner of Elizabeth and Judith Streets. He had several rice plantations; hundreds of his slaves he didn't know.

Not till John C. Calhoun's body was carried down Boundary Street was the name changed in his honor. He is buried in St. Phillip Church yard, across the street, with a laurel tree planted at his head. Four men and me dig his grave and I cleared the spot where his monument now stand. The monument was put up by Pat Collington, a Charleston mason. I never did like Calhoun 'cause he hated the Negro. No man was ever hated so much as him by a group of people.

The Work House (Sugar House) was on Magazine Street, built by Mr. Columbus C. Trumbone. On Charlmer Street is the slave market from which slaves was taken to Vangue Range and auctioned off. At the foot of Lawrence Street, opposite East Bay Street, on the other side of the trolley tracks, is where Mr. Alonzo White kept and sell slaves from his kitchen. He was a slave broker who had a house that extended almost to the train tracks, which is about three hundred yards goin' to the waterfront. No train or trolley tracks was there then 'cause there was only one railroad here, the Southern, and the depot was on Ann Street.

When slaves run away and their masters cotch them, to the stockade they go where they'd be whipped every other week for a number of months. And, for God's sake don't let a slave be cotch with pencil and paper. That was a major crime. You might as well had killed your master or missus.

One song I know I used to sing to the slaves when Master went away, but I wouldn't be so fool as to let him hear me. What I can 'member of it is:

> Master gone away
> But darkies stay at home,
> The year of jubilee is come
> And freedom will begun.

A group of white men was in Dr. Wilson's drugstore one day when I went to buy something. They commenced to ask me questions concerning some historical happenings and I answered them all. So Dr. Wilson bet me that I couldn't tell who fired the first shot on Fort Sumter. I tell him I did know and he offered a dollar if I was right. I tell him I wasn't goin' tell unless the dollar was given to one of the men. He did so and I told them it was Edward Ruffin who fired the first shot and the dollar was mine. Anderson was determined not to leave the fort, but when about four shells had hit it he was glad to be able to come out. When Sherman was comin' through Columbia, he fired and a shell lodged in the southeast end of the statehouse, which was forbidden to be fixed. He was comin' down Main Street when that happened.

The first two people that was hung in Charleston was Harry and Janie, husband and wife who was slaves of Mr. Christopher Black. Mr. Black had them whipped and they planned to kill the whole family. They poison the breakfast one morning and if two of the family hadn't oversleep, they too woulda been dead. The others died almost instantly. An investigation was made and the poison discovered and the two slaves hung on that big oak tree in the middle of Ashley Avenue.

When any in your owner's family was goin' to be married, the slaves was dressed in linen clothes to witness the ceremony. Only special slaves was chosen to be at the weddin'. Slaves was always asked how they liked the one who was comin' in the family. I didn't like that 'cause I had to lie on myself by sayin' nice things about the person and hated the person at the same time.

Henry McKinley, a Negro who ran as congressman from Charleston just after the War, lived on Calhoun Street. He was a mail carrier. He made an oath to Almighty God that if he was elected, he'd never betray his trust. In one of his speeches he said: "I hope God will paralyze me should I do as others have done." He was elected and never see the Congress. One white man from Orangeburg, Samuel Dibbin, bought him out. And three weeks later McKinley took a stroke that carry him to an early grave.

James Wright, a Negro judge of Charleston, in 1876, sold out for ten thousand dollars, a dime of which he hasn't received yet. He crossed the bridge and stayed in an old house and died there. The probate judge, A. Whipper, refused to give up the books of Judge Wright to the white man he sell out to. Judge Whipper went in Beaufort jail and died there 'cause he wouldn't give up the books. Wright kept such poor records that Judge Whipper was ashamed to have them exposed, and that's why he didn't give up the books.

After the War I did garden work. I was janitor at Benedict College in Columbia for two years and at Claflin in Orangeburg for twelve. The presidents under which I worked was: Allen Webster, grandson of the dictionary maker, J. C. Cook, and Dr. Dunton. Now all that is past and I'm livin' from hand to mouth. The banks took all my money and I can't work. I do the collectin' for my landlord and he give me a room free. If it wasn't for that I don't know what I'd do.

SARAH GUDGER

Interviewed in Asheville, North Carolina
Interviewed by Marjorie Jones
Age when interviewed: 121

I WAS BORN about two miles from Old Fort on de Old Morgantown Road. I sure has had a hard life. Just work and work and work. I never know nothin' but work. My boss he was Ole Man Andy Hemphill. He had a large plantation in de valley. Plenty of everythin'. All kind of stock: hogs, cows, mules, and hosses. When Marse Andy die I got live with he son, William Hemphill. I never forget when Marse Andy die. He was a good ole man, and de Missie she was good, too. She used to read de Bible to us chillen afore she pass away.

My pappy, he live with Joe Gudger. He old and feeble, I 'members. He depend on my pappy to see after everythin' for him. He always trust my pappy. One mornin' he follow Pappy to de field. Pappy he stop his work and Ole Marse Joe, he say: "Well, Smart (Pappy, he name Smart), I'se tired, worried, and troubled. All dese years I work for my chillen. Dey never do de right thing. Dey worries me, Smart. I tell, you, Smart, I'se a good mind to put myself away. I'se a good mind to drown myself right here. I terrible worried, Smart."

Pappy, he take hold Old Marse Joe and lead him to de house. "Now Marse Joe, I wouldn't talk such talk iffen I'se you. You been good to you family. Just you content yo'self and rest." But a few days after dat, Ole Marse Joe was found a-hangin' in de barn by de bridle. Ole Marse had put heself away.

I never knowed what it was to rest. I just work all de time from mornin' till late at night. I had to do everythin' dey was to do on de outside. Work in de field, chop wood, hoe corn, till sometime I feels like my back surely break. I done everythin' 'cept split rails. You know, dey split rails back in dem days. Well, I never did split no rails.

Ole Marse strop us good if we did anythin' he didn't like. Sometime he get his dander up and den we dassent look round at him, else he tie you hands afore you body and whip you, just like you a mule. Lordy, I'se took a thousand lashin's in my day. Sometimes my poor old body be sore for a week.

Ole Boss he send us niggers out in any kind of weather, rain or snow, it never matter. We had to go to de mountains, cut wood and drag it down to de house. Many de time we come in with our clothes stuck to our poor old cold bodies, but 'twarn't no use to try to get 'em dry. If de Ole Boss or de Ole Missie see us dey yell: "Get on out of here, you black thing, and get you work out of de way!" And we knowed to get, else we get de lash. Dey didn't care how old or how young you were, you never too big to get de lash.

De rich white folks never did no work; dey had darkies to do it for dem. In de summer we had to work outdoors, in de winter in de house. I had to card and spin till ten o'clock. Never get much rest, had to get up at four de next mornin' and start again. Didn't get much to eat, neither, just a li'l corn bread and 'lasses. Lordy, you cain't know what a time I had. All cold and hungry. I ain't tellin' no lies. It de gospel truth. It sure is.

I 'member well how I used to lie awake till all de folks was sleepin', den creep out of de door and walk barefoot in de snow, about two miles to my ole auntie's house. I knowed when I get dere she fixe hot corn pone with slice o' meat and some milk for me to eat. Auntie was good to us darkies.

I never sleep on a bedstead till after freedom. Just an old pile o' rags in de corner. Hardly 'nough to keep us from freezin'. Law, nobody knows how mean darkies was treated. Why, dey was better to de animals dan to us. My first Ole Marse was a good ole man, but de last one, he was rapid — he sure was rapid.

Weren't none o' de slaves offen our plantation ever sold, but de ones on de other plantation of Marse William were. Oh, dat was a terrible time! All de slaves be in de field, plowin', hoein', and singin' in de boilin' sun. Ole Marse, he come through de field with a man call de speculator. Dey walked round just lookin', just lookin'. All de darkies know what dis mean. Dey didn't dare look up, just work right on. Den de speculator he see who he want. He talk to Ole Marse, den dey slaps de handcuffs on him and take him away to de cotton country.

Oh, dem was awful times! When de speculator was ready to go with de slaves, if dere was anyone who didn't want to go, he thrash 'em, den tie 'em behind de wagon and make 'em run till dey fall on de ground, den he thrash 'em till dey say dey go without no trouble. Sometime some of dem run away and come back to de plantation, den it was harder on dem dan before. When de darkies went to dinner de ole nigger mammy she ask where am such and such. None of de others want to tell her. But when she see dem look down to de ground she just say: "De speculator, de speculator." Den de tears roll down her cheeks, cause maybe it her son or husband and she know she never see 'em again. Maybe dey leaves babies to home, maybe just pappy and mammy. Oh, my lordy, my ole boss was mean, but he never sent us to de cotton country.

Dey was very few schools back in dat day and time, very few. We darkies didn't dare look at no book, not even to pick it up. Ole Missie, dat is, my first ole missie, she was a good ole woman. She read to de niggers and to de white chillun. She come from 'cross de water. She weren't like de smart white folks livin' here now. When she come over here she brung darky boy with her. He was her personal servant. 'Course, dey got different names for dem now, but in dat day dey calls 'em "Guinea niggers." She was good ole woman, not like other white folks. Niggers like Ole Missie.

When de darkies get sick, dey were put in a li'l ole house close to de Big House, and one of de other darkies waited on 'em. Dere were very few doctors den. Only three in de whole section. When dey wanted medicine dey went to de woods and gathered horehound, slippery elm for poultices, and all kinds bark for teas. All dese herbs bring you round.

I 'members when my ole mammy die. She lived on Reems Creek with other Hemphills. She sick long time. One day white man come to see me. He say: "Sarah, did you know you mammy was dead?" "No," I say, "but I wants to see my mother afore dey puts her away." I went to de house and say to Ole Missie: "My mother she die today. I wants to see my mother afore dey puts her away," but she look at me mean and say: "Get on out of here, and get back to you work afore I wallop you good." So I went back to my work, with the tears streamin' down my face, just a-ringin' my hands, I wanted to see my mammy so. About two weeks later, Ole Missie she get terrible sick. She just linger along for long time, but she never gets up no more. Weren't long afore dey puts her away, too, just like my mammy.

I 'members de time when my mammy was alive, I was a small child, afore dey took her to Reems Creek. All us chillens was playin' in de yard one night. Just a-runnin' and a-playin' like chillen will. All of a sudden Mammy come to de door all 'cited. "Come in here dis minute," she say. "Just look up at what is a-happenin'." And, bless you life, de stars were fallin' just like rain. Mammy was terrible scared, but we chillen weren't afraid, no we weren't afraid. But Mammy, she say every time a star fall, somebody gonna die. Look like a lot of folks gonna die from de looks of dem stars. Everythin' was just as bright as day. You could of pick a pin up. You know de stars don't shine as bright as dey did back den. Weren't long afore dey took my mammy away, and I was left alone.

On de plantation was an ole woman what de boss bought from a drover up in Virginny. De boss he bought her from one of de speculators. She laugh and tell us: "Some of dese days yo'all gwine be free, just like de white folks," but we all laugh at her. No, we just slaves, we always have to work and never be free. Den when freedom come, she say: "I told yo'all, now you got no learnin', you got nothin', got no home; what you gwine do? Didn't I tell you?"

I was gettin' along smartly in years when de War come. I 'member just like yesterday just afore de War. Marse William was a-talkin' to his brother. I was standin' off a piece. Marse's brother, he say: "William, how old Aunt Sarah now?" Marse William look at me and he say: "She gettin' nigh on to fifty." Dat was just a li'l while afore de War.

Dat was awful time. Us darkies didn't know what it was all about. Only one of de boys from de plantation go. He Alexander, he about twenty-five den. Many de time we get word de Yankees comin'. We take our food and stock and hide it till we sure dey's gone. We weren't bothered much. One day, I never forget, we look out and see soldiers marchin'; look like de whole valley full of dem. I thought: "Poor helpless critters, just goin' away to get kilt." De drums were beatin' and de fifes a-playin'. Dey were de foot company. Oh, glory, it was a sight! Sometime dey come home on furlough. Sometime dey get kilt afore dey gets through. Alexander, he come home a few times afore freedom.

When de War was over, Marse William he say: "Did yo'all know yo'all's free. You free now." I chuckle, 'memberin' what de ole woman tell us about freedom, and no learnin'. Lots o' men want me to go to foreign land, but I tell 'em I go live with my pappy, long as he live. I stay with de white folks about twelve months, den I stay with my pappy long as he live.

FIL HANCOCK

Interviewed at Rolla, Missouri
Interviewer not identified
Age when interviewed: 86

I WAS BORN in 1851, de twenty-eighth day of February. My granny come here to Missouri with her missus — Hancock — when dey brung de Cherokee Indian tribe here from middlin' Tennessee, de time dey moved de Missouri Indians back to Oklahoma, what dey called Indian Territory way back about a hundred thirty-five or a hundred forty years ago. Our old missus' maiden name was Riggs. My old master was Scotch-Irish, a big, red faced man with sandy hair, mostly bald-headed. Us little niggers was scairt of him and run and hid when we see him coming. He weren't allowed to whip us, 'cause he didn't own us. Our old missus had eleven of us and he had twenty-one niggers of his own. And our old missus wouldn't let him touch us.

We had to mind him, though. But she done de whipping. My own mammy whipped us good and proper — she used a razor strap, and sure poured it on us. She was puny and sick most all de time. Dey said she had consumption, nowdays dey calls it T.B. But it was plain old consumption in dem days. I 'member she were so sick dat she were not able to hold us and whip us, and she made one of us little niggers push de other one up to her bed while she whipped us. We took our turns in gittin' a whipping 'ceptin' we needed it. Old Granny, my mammy's mother and Old Missus whipped us a little, and only with buckbrush, just a little round de ankles. All us little niggers was just like stair-steps, one after de other. I got whipped plenty, but I needed it.

My old missus Hancock named me herself — called me Filmore Taylor Hancock, after two presidents who took deir seats in 1850. Old Colonel Hancock was our master and he was de richest man in Green County, Missouri, and owned more slaves than any man in Missouri. His wife, Old Missus, was born in 1804. My own granny on my mammy's side was born in 1805. My granny was given to Missus as her own de day she was born. 'Course Old Missus was only a year old den. Dere was thirty-two of us slaves on our old missus place, and eleven of us sprung from old Granny.

We had five young misses. My young misses' names were Winnie, Elizabeth, Lucinda, Luella, and Tennessee. Dey was so rich and proud dey

154

wouldn't look at anybody to marry. Only two of 'em ever married. Dey was fine ladies, but dey sure had me plumb spilt.* Some of dem whipped me three or four times, but I 'member how dey just brushed me a little round de legs, and turn away and laugh a little. I can see now I needed more'n I got. If I told a lie I got whipped for it, and Old Missus poured it on if we lied.

When our mammy died, Old Missus took us — I and de other two gals, my sisters, and a brother of mine — down to her house, away from our cabin, so she could look after us. Our old granny was de white folks' cook. She helped look after us. We got to eat what de white folk did. Up to de cabins, where de other niggers was, dey had salt meat, cabbage, 'taters, and shortnin' bread three times a day. We had all plenty vegetables we raised ourselves. Every Sunday mornin' our missus sent us up a big tray about three feet long — made of sycamore — and it full of flour. Once a week we had hot biscuits. But me and Squire, my brother, and sisses Mary and Margot, had it a little better. We had what our old missus had.

I was ten years and six months old when de War come up. In '61, I see General Lyons, when he passed right by our house. All de Union soldiers had to pass by our house time of de War. We lived on the main wagon road from Rolla to Springfield.

It was a sight to see him with them "purties!" And we asked Old Missus what dat was, them "purties" he had on his shoulders. She says to us chillen: "He is de general. All dem other men got to mind him." He was killed in dat battle of Wilson Creek. Dey kept him in an icehouse in a spring, owned by a man named Phelps. He lived west of Springfield. Dey keep General Lyon two weeks before they brung him down dis-a-way. Dey shipped him out of Rolla to Connecticut — dat's what I hear de old folks says. Dat man Phelps was our neighbor and later he got to be governor of Missouri in 1876. Crittenden was first de Democratic governor in '73.

Old Missus called us little darkies all up — and carried us down to de wagon, dat General Lyon's body was in, when dey was bringin' him back here. And we looked at him and asked what was de matter. Old Missus said; "He was killed." He was packed in ice in de wagon and de wagon had four mules hitched to it. I wanted to know if he was de man who had dem "purties" on his shoulders. She said, "Yes."

I said, "Did Marse Bill and Marse George and Marse Jeff Hancock help kill him?" She said: "Yes." Marse Bill, Marse George and Marse Jeff was my young bosses, my old master's sons. Old Missus didn't seem glad or anything, just looked kinda sad. We asked her would he ever fight again. She said, "No." I won't ever forget how General Lyon looked. He rode a kinda gray-white horse when I first see him and looked so tall and proud like.

De Rebels held Springfield from 1861 to 1862, when General Frémont come in and took it. Marmaduke and Price had de biggest armies of de Southerners, Frémont come sneaking in, wrapped his wagon wheels

* Spoiled.

with old blankets so dey wouldn't hear him coming, and he had a body-guard of three hundred. Marmaduke and Price was den in Springfield. Frémont come about daybreak, and started shooting de town up. He got de town and held it.

Marmaduke and Price drifted round de southeast part of de state and went into Arkansas. Later dey had a three hour scrimmage at Pea Ridge, Arkansas. Either '62 or '63, I cain't 'member much. I was too little and scared to know, being only ten or eleven years old. Dey was a man named Finis McCraw, a Rebel in de Marmaduke and Price army, in de infantry. He took sick some place in Arkansas. Dey brung him to us, we being Rebels, and keep him two weeks in our upstairs, not letting anyone know he was dere. We kept him till he got better and he went back into de army and fought some more.

I seen Marmaduke in person when he was making his campaign for governor, down in Cuba, Missouri. All de Union soldiers stopped at our house to get water. We had a runnin' stream that never did go dry. They filled their canteens there. All us chillen fussed about 'em takin' our milk and butter out of de spring house. Old Missus keep all her milk and butter and cheese in dere to keep it cool. When de Union soldiers come by our house to Rolla dey took so much of de water to fill dere canteens it nearly took our spring dry. Took everything we had in de spring house—milk, butter—everything.

I don't 'member how dey was dressed, but dey all had on somethin' blue. Uniforms, I guess. Me and four more little darkies was one-half off of de big road when dey passed, and got scared and run back to Old Missus' house and hid in de old barn loft all dat night. Old Missus asked us what we did for somethin' to eat. We told her we bent de rye down in de field and rubbed de grain out with our hands and eat dat. She took us to de house and give us somethin' to eat. De soldiers was still passing de house den.

In time of de Civil War we wouldn't come to Rolla; we went south to do our trading. We wasn't Union and Rolla was Union Headquarters. Old Master was getting old den. He had been a colonel in some army or other' way before de Civil War.

Lincoln issued "greenbacks" along about '61 or '62, after Stephen A. Douglas goes up to Washington to tell Lincoln, after he got de nomination, dat if he didn't get Jeff Davis and some of de leaders and prosecute 'em, he was going to have war on his hands. Lincoln tells Douglas to go back and tell Jeff Davis to lay dem guns down, dat in ninety days he would allow dem so much a head for deir niggers. Dat if dey would free dem dey could be paid for so much a head, by taxation. But Lincoln told dem dey would all have to come back together again same as before like dey was. You see dese folks in de South had done got eight million dollars, and all dat ammunition and guns and things from England. Jeff Davis and dem leaders wouldn't give it up. De first issue of greenbacks was 175,000,000 dollars and de next issue was 250,000,000 dollars. We had been told all dis and I ask Old Missus if she reckon we could whip dem "blue bellied Yankees." I says: "Dey ain't got no money." We called de Union soldiers "Yankees," and our side was called de Gray or de Rebels. It's seventy-five years, the tenth day of August, 1937, that General Lyon was killed.

My boss—Hancock—was de biggest slaveholder in Missouri when de War first come up. He settled four miles east of Springfield, Missouri. He owned close to twelve hundred or fifteen hundred acres of ground. From Springfield to Strafford—east. We had 375 acres in cultivation—corn, oats, wheat, rye, and clover was our main crops.

My daddy belonged to a man named Lou Langston. There is a railroad station named for this same Langston. What was known as the "Gulf Road."

I took my mammy's white folk's name. They were as fine and good as anybody. The first child Old Missus had was a boy, Bill Hancock. The first child my old granny had (on my mammy's side) was a boy, named Joe. Old Missus gave Granny's boy Joe to her boy Bill, as a slave. You see my old missus and my old granny was born a year apart demselves like I said.

One time my old master Hancock got mad at my uncle, who was a growed up nigger. Old Marse wanted to whip him. He tried to make my uncle put his head twixt his (Old Master's) knees. My uncle didn't offer to fight him, but twisted him round and round trying to get his head out. He gave one twist dat throwed Old Marse down to de ground. My uncle jumped and run and jumped over de fence. My uncle did not belong to Old Marse but to his son, Bill. But Old Marse sure got mad when my uncle run. So he sold him to a man named Dokes, a nigger trader of dat neighborhood. Dokes bought niggers and sold dem on de block in St. Louis. When Dokes took my uncle away, one of our neighbors by de name of Fisher—up near Strafford—gets on his horse and goes to Springfield and tells my young boss, Bill, dat old man Hancock had sold Joe and Jane. Jane belonged to Marse Hancock. Mister Fisher had only one colored man, and he told my young boss, Bill, dat if he would buy both them niggers back, dat he would buy Jane for his (Fisher's) colored man. He didn't have no woman for him.

Old Doke was on his way den to St. Louis with 'em. Bill and Fisher started out, rode and caught up with dem near what is now known as Knob View, Missouri. When dey come in sight of Dokes, Bill stopped and dropped back. Fisher goes up to de wagon, stopped Dokes and asked him what he would take for Joe and Jane. They was settin' up in the wagon handcuffed together. I think it was a thousand dollars or fifteen hundred dollars he asked for both. Den Fisher beckoned to Bill Hancock to come on. Bill come up and paid Dokes what he asked. Dokes was to take 'em back, hisself, to deir own neighborhood.

When Marse Bill rode up, my uncle said, "Take these handcuffs off me." Mr. Dokes took them off. My uncle jumped out of de wagon and run up to de big mule my young boss was settin' on he reached up and took Bill, his marster, off dat mule so quick and lay him down on de ground. He commenced to love and kiss him on side of his head. He picked him up and sat Marse Bill on his mule again and said, "I know Marse Bill wasn't goin' to let me be sold." He takes him off his mule again and lay him down two times more and keep lovin' and kissin' him, he was dat happy.

But Old Marse Hancock, just wouldn't let Joe live on his place again, no more. He was dat mad. It made him so mad to think Joe had turn him over when he had his head 'twixt his knees. But young Marse Bill took Joe to Springfield and hired him out to a blacksmith by de name of Lehr. He got forty dollars a month for him. Joe stayed dere till de Civil War. Old Marster let Joe come to de house to see his mother, my old granny, once in a while, but never to live.

Old man Fisher bought de colored woman from Marse Bill, for his colored man, and paid him as he could. Our white folks had plenty of money to get anything they wanted.

When I was young, we didn't know nothin' about churches. Us kids never got to go no place unless de old niggers took us. And dey wouldn't take us. De older ones had church out in de brush, under de shade trees. I can 'member one of my cousins carryin' me pickaback, one time, three miles to church. Dey only had church in de summertime, or meeting dey called it. It was always in de woods.

We dare not be catched with a book to read or to try to be educated. 'Course everyone wasn't treated dat-a-way. Sometimes de niggers would have dancin', if de bosses or masters gave dem passes. De passes read sumpin' like dis: "Let my nigger file pass and repass to such and such a place."

In dem days boys had cotton shirts and de gals had cotton dresses. No nigger got boots till he was big and able to work for 'em. I was Old Missus' pet and she plumb spoilt me. I always got more'n de other niggers got. I 'member once, my missus bought me a pair of high top red boots. My, I was proud! In dem days, we went barefoot most all year around. But my missus tried to make us happy on Christmas. I put dem boots on and I pranced around and round just to hear dem squeak. I done thought dat was de purtiest noise I ever heard. I asked Old Missus, could I go to old Massey's house. He were our neighbor, about half mile—but it were dark. Old Missus said, "Hain't you scared to go?" I say, "No." I went up de road, my boots squeaking and squeaking. Didn't have time to be scared— listenin' to dem boots.

Aunt Rachel, my own aunt, lived at Massey's house. You see Masseys was deir name and dey was white folks but we say Massey's house. I wanted my old aunt to see my new boots. When I got dere I called my aunt to come see my boots. She come and say, "Hain't you scared to come here all alone." I say, "No." I twisted and turn round and round so she could hear 'em squeak. But when it come time to go home, I got plumb scared. Aunt Rachel had to take me. She took me where I could see our house. My! Old Missus laughed when she found I had to be brung home. She say, "I told you, you be scared to come alone."

You know its a funny thing, de white folks took everything from us niggers, even try to take our old songs and have dem on de radio. We niggers say de white folks take everything, dis, dat, and 'tother, but what we got is just natural borned to us.

I first come to Rolla in 1869 and stayed till 1870. Then dere was only one brick house in Rolla, standin' where the Edwin Long Hotel now stands. Den I left and went to Cuba and stayed dere and at Salem till 1882. I come back to Rolla when de Crandel House was built, where de Rolla Hospital now is located. I started a barber shop here under the Crandel House basement. I have been here and at Salem ever since 1882. Rolla is my headquarters.

ABRAM HARRIS
Interviewed near Marvell, Arkansas
Interviewed by Watt McKinney
Age when interviewed: 93

MY NAME IS Abram Harris and I is just past ninety-three years old. I was borned and raised in South Carolina not far from Greenville and my old master what I belonged to was Marse Hodges Brown and my young Marster, he was Marse Hampton. Me and Marse Hampton was sure born in de same month and de same year. De month, it was October, and dat's 'zacktly what Old Marster told me and Marse Hampton said dat same thing. Us was boys together, me and Marse Hampton, and was just about de same size and Marse Hampton, he claimed me, and I gwine to be his property when both us grown. Dat is iffen de War not come on and Marse Hampton hadn't-a got kilt in de battle.

When de War first break out, Marse Hampton he too young den to join de troops; howsoever he want to join up den when he older brother, Marse Thad, join up. But Old Miss she wouldn't hear to Marse Hampton gwine off den, 'cause he not old enough, and den, he Old Miss' baby child. Marse Thad, he about two or three year older dan Marse Hampton and he join de troops at de first muster and went off to de War and fit de Yankees nigh about two years when de ball shot him in de shoulder. He wounded den and have to come back home for to get well again. Marse Thad come home and stay for a month or such time for he wound to heal up. Den he ready to go back to de company and Marse Hampton gwine to be eighteen year old pretty soon den, so dey persuade Old Miss to let Marse Hampton go with Marse Thad back to de War. Old

Miss and Old Marster, dey give in and Marse Hampton left with Marse Thad to join up with him in de same company what he in when de ball hit him.

Now dat was in de spring when Marse Hampton join up with de troops, and him and me gwine to be eighteen dat fall in October. But tweren't so awful long before Marse Hampton got kilt in de big battle, and Marse Thad, too. Dey was both kilt in de charge, right dere on de breastworks, with de guns in dey hands, dem two young masters of mine, right dere in dat Gettysburg battle. Dat's what Old Marster and Old Miss both told me many a time. And I was eighteen in dat October after dat big fight what Marse Thad and Marse Hampton got kilt in. Marse Hodges writ it down for me on a paper and every October since den I gets somebody what can figger to tell me how old I is so's I can know and tell folks when dey ask me. Just last month, my gal Hannah figgered it out again and she say dat I is now ninety-three past, so dat is de way dat I gets at it.

My white folks was sure good to all dey niggers. Dere was nigh about no whippin' at all, least Old Master never did whip his slaves to do no good. He most generally told us mammies and pappies to do de whippin' of de chillen and de older boys and gals. He have whip me, though, and he whip Marse Hampton, too, when us was boys. Old Master start in with dat hickory and make out like he gwine to frail us out. But after he done landed a few licks on us, and den us commence hollerin' like he hurtin' bad, den he quit whippin'. Dat de way Old Marster was. He never want to hurt nobody.

My pa was named Jake and my mammy was named Fanny. Old Marster bought dem from somewhere, but I was borned right dere, me and Delia and all de rest of de chillen. Delia and me was sure stole. De speculators stole us away from Old Marster when us was chillen, about twelve or thirteen year old. It happened in de night when dere weren't nobody dere in de quarters but de women. Old Marster and all de men was down on de river dat night a-floatin' logs or cuttin' timber or some such work as dat, when dese here folks come a-stealin' chillen. Delia and me was de first ones dat dey grab and de onliest ones dat dey get from Old Marster, but dey sure got us.

I 'members dat stealin' good. Dem folks took us off to de woods where dey tied us up to a tree for a whole night and day and tell us dat iffen we cry or holler dat dey gwine to kill us sure. Den dey come and took us away and ganged us up with a lot more nigger boys and gals what dey done stole somewheres else. Dey yoked us together and walked us clean to Georgia where dey sold us. Dey sure pushed dem chillen hard over de rocks and de hard places till our feets would bleed from de sores where de rocks and de thorns scratch.

Dey sold me and Delia to a young white man and he wife what ain't been married long and ain't got no start or niggers yet. Us stayed dere for more dan a year, I reckon, and dem was good white folks and was good to us. De miss teach Delia to be a house gal and de marster teach me to handle stock and plow with him every day. Us was scared to tell dem white folks what bought us where us home was and who us marsters used to be, 'cause we scared dat de speculators might come back and steal us some more and take us away some more. I don't know how it was dat Old Marster Hodges Brown come to find out where we was, but he sure learnt about it some such a way, and one mornin' early here come Old Marster Hodges Brown with two white mens comin' after me and Delia. After dey through identifyin' us, Old Marster took us on back home with him and we sure was glad to go.

My pappy, Jake, was de wagoner for Marster till he died. Then Marster took me and trained me for de wagoner after den. My marster weren't no big, rich man like a heap of de white folks in dem slavery times, yet and still, he sure had plenty of everything and best of all, he fed he niggers good and was always good to dem. Marster used to peddle a heap in Columbia and Greenville both after I got to be de wagoner for him. Us would take big loads of 'taters and truck to dem towns where Marster would sell 'em to de folks dere. Sometimes he would take about twenty beefs to one of dem towns and rent him a yard where he would butcher about one beef every day and peddle out de meat. Marster never had many niggers like lots de white folks. He just had about a dozen in all. He say dat all he want or got any use for.

Marster had a big fruit orchard. Just all kinds of fruit would be in dat orchard. When dey ripe, Marster send loads dem apples and peaches down to de still where he had dem made up into brandy and put in de kegs and barrels and brought back home when it was done. Heap of times dat I 'members he call de folks up to de back gallery and say, "Come on up here, folks, and get you all a dram." Dat's what he say.

Whilst our marster was good to all he niggers, dere was heap of de marsters in dem slavery times what was mean and dat what make de niggers run off and hide in de woods. Dat's when dey get de nigger hounds on 'em and track 'em down just like you de a coon. My pappy, Jake, he owned by a mean white man before Old Marster bought him in. I 'members about him tellin' us chillen dat he used to run off and hide in de cane thickets for days and days 'cause he marster so mean and beat him up so bad. Den he get so hungry dat he slip back in close to de house in de night and some de womens slip him some meat and bread. He say dat he used to sleep with de dogs under de crib so de dogs could keep him warm.

Dere weren't none of de white folks in dem slavery times what would let dey niggers have any learnin'. You sure better not be cotch a-tryin' to learn no readin' or writin'. Our marster even never allowed dat. Iffen a nigger was to be found what could write, den right straight dey would chop his forefinger offen dat hand what he write with. Dere weren't no such a thing as no schools for de niggers till after de surrender.

Endurin' of de War, dere weren't no fightin' took place round where us lived, and de onliest Yankees dat I ever seed was in Greenville after de surrender. I sure was surprised when I seed dem Yankees 'cause I never knowed what sort of lookin' thing dat a Yankee was. I never knowed dat a Yankee was a man just like my white folks till I seed dem in Greenville. A Yankee looks just like all white mens, only he do talk funny and fast, more so dan de kind of white folks dat I is always been around.

Dere weren't nary one of Old Marster's niggers what left him even when dey set free, dat is, dey didn't leave him for two or three years anyway. But after den some of 'em started to driftin' around and hirin' around about. When de surrender come, Old Marster told 'em all dat dey free and can go iffen dey want to go and iffen dey want to go dat he give 'em some grub to go on. Marster was a good man and iffen he was living today, I would sure quit dis place and go on with him, wheresoever he want me to go.

De niggers didn't know what de War was gwine on for, and didn't know dat dey free till deir marsters told 'em, whilst dey was wantin' to be free all right. After us was free, de white folks have to teach us just like you teach a child.

Dem Ku Klux what dey brought on after de surrender was sure poison. Dey was white mens. Dat's what dey was, and all dressed up in dem long white garments with a red cross on 'em and ridin' a big hoss. Dey was after dem niggers what dey claim is mean and deserted dey marsters and went and took up with de Yankees. When dem Ku Klux first come in operation de niggers think dat dey is haunts or spirits, till dey find out dat dey weren't nothin' but white mens with dem garments on 'em. Dem Klux would cotch a nigger dat dey want and pin he head down to de ground with a forked stick and one would hold him whilst de others whip him with a strap or a lash. Dem Ku Klux sure did dis-encourage de niggers a heap.

Plenty of de white mens what was mustered into de War would take a nigger with 'em to wait on 'em and to tend to de hosses and do such ever what dey want done, I sure did want to go with Marse Hampton, and maybe I could take care of him. Marse Hampton want me to go with him, too, and try to persuade Old Marster to let me go. But Old Marster say dat he have to have me dere at home to help make de crops so's dat he can send corn and meat to de soldiers. De day dat Marse Hampton leave, he come down to de quarters for to tell all de niggers good-bye, and he say to me, "Abe (he called me Abe), I gwine off to dat war and kill out dat whole crowd of Yankees. Den I'se comin' back and gwine to Georgia and buy me a farm where I can get rich makin' cotton and tobacco. You know you is my nigger, and you gwine to Georgia with me, when I goes." It sure did hurt me when Marse Hampton got kilt, 'cause I loved dat white man. He was sure good to me.

In my dreams at night I can yet see Marse Hampton, and a heap of times in de day when I is by myself or hoein' de cotton he talks to me plain so's I can understand. He ask me iffen I is yet and still a good nigger and he tell me to not be dis-encouraged. De Bible is right when it say dat "de young mens dream dreams and de old ones see de visions."

TEMPIE HERNDON

Interviewed at Durham, North Carolina
Interviewed by Travis Jordon
Age when interviewed: 103

I WAS THIRTY-ONE years old when de surrender come. Dat makes me sure 'nough old. Near about a hundred and three years done passed over dis here white head of mine. 'Spects I'se de oldest nigger in Durham. I'se been here so long dat I done forgot near about as much as dese here new generation niggers knows or ever gwine know.

My white folks lived in Chatham County. Dey was Marse George and Mis' Betsy Herndon. Mis' Betsy was a Snipes before she married Marse George. Dey had a big plantation and raised corn, wheat, cotton, and tobacca. I don't know how many field niggers Marse George had, but he had a mess of dem, and he had hosses too, and cows, hogs, and sheeps. He raised sheeps and sold de wool, and dey used de wool at de Big House too. Dey was a big weavin' room where de blankets was wove, and dey wove de cloth for de winter clothes. Linda Herndon and Milla Edwards was de head weavers; dey looked after de weavin' of de fancy blankets. Mis' Betsy was a good weaver too. She weave de same as de niggers. She say she love de clackin' sound of de loom and de way de shuttles run in and out carryin' a long tail of bright colored thread. Some days she set at de loom all de mornin' peddlin' with her feets and her white hands flittin' over de bobbins.

De cardin' and spinnin' room was full of niggers. I can hear dem spinnin' wheels now turnin' round and sayin' hum-m-m-m, hum-m-m-m, and hear de slaves singin' while dey spin. Mammy Rachel stayed in de dyein' room. Dey wasn't nothin' she didn't know about dyein'. She knew every kind of root, bark, leaf, and berry dat made red, blue, green, or whatever color she wanted. Dey had a big shelter where de dye pots set over de coals. Mammy Rachel would fill de pots with water, den she put in de roots, bark, and stuff and boil de juice out. Den she strain it and put in de salt and vinegar to set de color. After de wool and cotton done been carded and spun to thread, Mammy take de hanks and drop dem in de pot of boilin' dye. She stir dem round and lift dem up and down with a stick, and when she hang dem up on de line in de sun, dey was every color of de rainbow. When dey dripped dry dey was sent to de weavin' room where dey was wove in blankets and things.

When I growed up I married Exter Durham. He belonged to Marse Snipes Durham who had de plantation 'cross de county line in Orange County. We had a big weddin'. We was married on de front porch of de Big House. Marse George killed a shoat and Mis' Betsy had Georgianna, de cook, to bake a big weddin' cake all iced up white as snow with a bride and groom standin' in de middle holdin' hands. De table was set out in de yard under de trees, and you ain't never seed de like of eats. All de niggers come to de feast and Marse George had a dram for everybody. Dat was some weddin'. I had on a white dress, white shoes, and long white gloves dat come to my elbow, and Mis' Betsy done made me a weddin' veil out of a white net window curtain. When she played de weddin march on de piano, me and Exter marched down de walk and up on de porch to de altar Mis' Betsy done fixed. Dat de prettiest altar I ever seed. Back 'against de rose vine dat was full or red roses, Mis' Betsy done put tables filled with flowers and white candles. She done spread down a bed sheet, a sure 'nough linen sheet, for us to stand on, and dey was a white pillow to kneel down on. Exter done made me a weddin' ring. He made it out of a big red button with his pocket knife. He done cut it so round and polished it so smooth dat it looked like a red satin ribbon tied round my finger. Dat sure was a pretty ring. I wore it about fifty years. Den it got so thin dat I lost it one day in de wash tub when I was washin' clothes.

Uncle Edmond Kirby married us. He was de nigger preacher dat preached at de plantation church. After Uncle Edmond said de last words over me and Exter, Marse George got to have his little fun. He say, "Come on, Exter, you and Tempie got to jump over de broom stick backwards. You got to do dat to see which one gwine be boss of your household." Everybody come stand round to watch. Marse George hold de broom about a foot high off de floor. De one dat jump over it backwards, and never touch handle, gwine boss de house. If both of dem jump over without touchin' it, dey won't gwine be no bossin', dey just gwine be congenial. I jumped first, and you ought to seed me. I sailed right over dat broom stick same as a cricket. But when Exter jump he done had a big dram and his feets was so big and clumsy dat dey got all tangled up in dat broom and he fell headlong. Marse George he laugh and laugh, and told Exter he gwine be bossed 'twell he scared to speak lessen I told him to speak. After de weddin' we went down to de cabin Mis' Betsy done all dressed up, but Exter couldn't stay no longer den dat night 'cause he belonged to Marse Snipes Durham and he had to go back home. He left de next day for his plantation, but he come back every Saturday night and stay 'twell Sunday night.

We had eleven chillen. Nine was born before surrender and two after we was set free. So I had two chillen dat wasn't born in bondage. I was worth a heap to Marse George 'cause I had so many chillen. De more chillen a slave had de more day was worth. Lucy Carter was de only nigger on de plantation dat had more chillen den I had. She had twelve, but her chillen was sickly and mine was muley strong and healthy. Dey never was sick.

When de War come, Marse George was too old to go, but Young Marse Bill went. He went and took my brother Sim with him. Marse Bill took Sim along to look after his hoss and everything. Dey didn't neither one get shot, but Mis' Betsy was scared near about to death all de time, scared dey was gwine be brung home shot all to pieces like some of de soldiers was.

De Yankees wasn't so bad. De most dey wanted was sumpin' to eat. Dey was all de time hungry, de first thing dey ask for when dey come was sumpin' to put in dey stomach. And chicken! I ain't never seed even a preacher eat chicken like dem Yankees. I believes to my soul dey ain't never seed no chicken 'twell dey come down here. And hot biscuit too. I seed a passel of dem eat up a whole sack of flour one night for supper. Georgianna sift flour 'twell she look white and dusty as a miller. Dem soldiers didn't turn down no ham neither. Dat de onliest thing dey took from Marse George. Dey went in de smokehouse and toted off de hams and shoulders. Marse George say he come off mighty slight if dat all dey want. Besides he got plenty of shoats anyhow.

We had all de eats we wanted while de War was shootin' dem guns, 'cause Marse George was home and he kept de niggers workin'. We had chickens, gooses, meat, peas, flour, meal, potatoes, and things like dat all de time, and milk and butter too. But we didn't have no sugar and coffee. We used ground parched corn for coffee and cane 'lasses for sweetnin'. Dat wasn't so bad with a heap of thick cream. Anyhow, we had enough to eat to divide with de neighbors dat didn't have none when surrender come.

I was glad when de War stopped 'cause den me and Exter could be together all de time 'stead of Saturday and Sunday. After we was free we lived right on at Marse George's plantation a long time. We rented de land for a fourth of what we made, den after while we bought a farm. We paid three hundred dollars we done saved. We had a hoss, a steer, a cow, and two pigs, besides some chickens and four geese. Mis' Betsy went up in de attic and give us a bed and bed tick. She give us enough goose feathers to make two pillows. Den she give us a table and some chairs. She give us some dishes too. Marse George give Exter a bushel of seed corn and some seed wheat, den he told him to go down to de barn and get a bag of cotton seed. We got all dis. Den we hitched up de wagon and throwed in de passel of chillen and moved to our new farm, and de chillun was put to work in de field. Dey growed up in de field 'cause dey was put to work time dey could walk good.

MARRIAH HINES
Interviewed near Norfolk, Virginia
Interviewed by David Hoggard
Age when interviewed: 102

I LIVED WITH good people. My white folks treated us good. There was plenty of 'em that didn't fare as we did. Some of the poor folks almost starved to death. Why, the way their masters treated them was scandalous, treated them like cats and dogs. We always had plenty of food, never knowed what it was to want food bad enough to have to steal it like a whole lot of 'em. Master would always give us plenty when he give us our rations. Of course we slaves were given food and clothing and just enough to keep us goin' good. Why, master would buy cloth by the loads and heaps, shoes by the big boxful; den he'd call us to the house and give each of us our share. Plenty to keep us comfortable. Course it weren't silk nor satin, no ways the best there was, but 'twas plenty good 'nough for us, and we was plenty glad to get it. When we would look and see how the slaves on the joining farm was farming, 'twould almost make us shed tears. It made us feel like we was getting along most fine. Dat's why we loved and respected Master, 'cause he was so good to us. 'Cause Master was good and kind to us, some of the other white folks used to call him "nigger lover." He didn't pay dat no mind, though. He was a true Christian man, and I mean he sure lived up to it. He never did force any of us to go to church if we didn't want to. Dat was left to us to decide. If you wanted to you could; if you didn't you didn't have to. But he'd always tell us, you ought to go.

Not only was Master good but his whole family was, too. When the weather was good we worked in the fields and on other little odd jobs that was needed done. We slaves would eat our breakfast, and go to the fields; dere weren't no hurry-scurry. Lots o' times when we got in the fields the other slaves had been in the field a long time. Dere was times, though, we had to get to it early, too. 'Specially if it had been rainy weather and the work had been held up for a day or so. Master didn't make us work at all in bad weather, neither when it got real cold. The men might have to get in firewood or somethin' of that sort but no all day work in the cold—just little odd jobs. We didn't even have to work on Sundays, not even in the "house." The master and the preacher both said dat was the Lord's day and you weren't supposed to work on that day. So we didn't. We'd cook the white folks victuals on Saturday and lots o' times dey eat cold victuals on Sundays.

Master would sometimes ask the preacher home to dinner. "You plenty welcome to go home with me for dinner, but you'll have to eat cold victuals 'cause there ain't no cooking on Sundays at my house." Lots of times we slaves would take turns on helping 'em serve Sunday meals just 'cause we liked them so much. We hated to see Missie fumbling round in the kitchen all out o' her place. We didn't have to do it; we just did it on our own free will. Master sometimes gives us a little money for it, too, which made it all the better. Master and Missus was so good to us we didn't mind working a little on Sunday, in the house.

Master had prayer with the whole family every night, prayed for us slaves too. Any of the slaves that wanted to join him could. Or if they wanted to pray by demselves they could. Sundays we went to church and stayed the biggest portion of the day. Nobody had to rush home.

On our plantation we had general prayer meeting every Wednesday night at church. 'Cause some of the masters didn't like the way we slaves carried on we would turn pots down and tubs to keep the sound from going out. Den we would have a good time, shouting, singing, and praying just like we pleased. The patterrollers didn't pay us much attention 'cause they knew how Master let us do. Dey would say nasty things about Master 'cause he let us do like we did.

We had plenty time to ourselves. Most of the time we spent singing and praying 'cause Master was such a good Christian and most of us had confessed religion. Evenings we would spin on the old spinning wheel, quilt, make clothes, talk, tell jokes, and a few had learned to weave a little bit from Missus. We would have candy pulls from cooked molasses and sing in the moonilght by the tune of an old banjo picker. Chillen was mostly seen, not heard, different from younguns of today talking backward and forward cross their mammies and pappies. Chillen dat did dat would get de breath slapped out on 'em. Your mammies didn't have to do it, either; any old person would and send you home to get another lickin'.

We slaves had two hours off for dinner, when we could go home and eat before we finished work about sundown. We ain't had no colored overseers to whip us nor no white ones. We just went along so and did what we had to, without nobody watching over us. Everybody was just plumb crazy about Master. During the day you could see him strutting down the field like a big turkey gobbler to see how the work was going on. Always had a smile and a joke with you. He always tell us we was doing fine, even sometimes when we weren't. We'd always catch up our work, so he wouldn't have to fuss. We loved Missus and the chillen so much we wouldn't even let 'em eat hardly, Missus didn't have to do nothing, hardly. Dere was always some of us round the house.

About a year before we heard about freedom, Master took sick and the slaves wouldn't a-looked sadder if one of their own younguns had been sick. Dey 'spected him to die, and he kept calling for some cabbage.

Misses finally let me cook him some cabbage and let him have some "pot likker" (the water the cabbage was cooked in). He didn't die den, but a few years later he did die. Dat was the first and the last time any cooking ever was done in that house on Sunday.

When Master told us we was free it didn't take much effect on us. Told us we could go where we pleased and come when we pleased, that we didn't have to work for him any more 'less we wanted to. Most of us slaves stayed right there and raised our own crops. Master helped us much as he could. Some of us he gave a cow or a mule or anything he could spare to help us. Some of us worked on the same plantation and bought our own little farms and little log cabins, and lived right there till Master dies and the family moved away. Some of us lived there right on. Master married me to one of the best colored men in the world, Benjamin F. Hines. I had five chillen by him, four girls and one boy; two of the girls and the boy are dead. Dey died about 1932 or '33. I stay with one a while, den I go and stay a while with the other one.

BILL HOMER
Interviewed at Fort Worth, Texas
Interviewer not identified
Age when interviewed: 87

I IS EIGHTY-SEVEN years old, 'cause I is born on June 17, in 1850, and that's according to de statement my missy give me. I was born on Massa Jack Homer's plantation, close to Shreveport. Him owned my mammy and my pappy and about one hundred other slaves. Him's plantation was a big one. I don't know how many acres him have, but it was miles long. Dere was so many buildings and shed on dat place it was a small town. De massa's house was a big two-story building and dere was de spinnin' house, de smokehouse, de blacksmith shop, and a nursery for de cullud chillens, and a lot of sheds and such. In de nigger quarters dere was fifty one-room cabins and dey was ten in a row and dere was five rows.

De cabins was built of logs and had dirt floors and a hole where a window should be and a stone fireplace for de cookin' and de heat. Dere was a cookhouse for de Big House and all de cookin' for de white folks was 'tended to by four cooks. We has lots of food, too—cornmeal and vegetables and milk and 'lasses and meat. For most de meat dey catched hogs in de Mississippi River bottoms. Once a week, we have white flour biscuit.

Some work was hard and some easy, but Massa don't believe in over-workin' his slaves. Saturday afternoon and Sunday, dere was no work. Some whippin' done, but most reasonable. If de nigger stubborn, dey whips 'nough for to change his mind. If de nigger runs off, dat calls de good whippin's. If any of de cullud folks has de misery, dey lets him rest in bed and if de misery bad de massa call de doctor.

I learned to be coachman and drive for Massa's family. But in de year of 1860, Missy Mary gets married to Bill Johnson and at dat weddin' Massa Homer gives me and forty-nine other niggers to her for de weddin' present. Massa Johnson's father gives him fifty niggers too. Dey has a grand weddin'. I helps take care of de hosses and dey just kept a-comin'. I expected dere was more'n one hundred peoples dere and dey have lots of music and dancin' and eats and, I expects, drinks, 'cause we'uns made peach brandy. You see, de massa had his own still.

After de weddin' was over, dey gives de couple de infare. Dere's where dis nigger comes in. I and de other niggers was lined up, all with de clean clothes on and den de massa say, "For to give my lovin' daughter de start, I gives you dese fifty niggers." Massa Bill's father done de same for his son, and dere we'uns was, one hundred niggers with a new massa.

Dey loads fifteen or twenty wagons and starts for Texas. We travels from daylight to dark, with most de niggers walkin'. Of course, it was hard, but we enjoys de trip. Dere was one nigger called Monk and him knows a song and learned it to us, like this:

> Walk, walk, you nigger, walk!
> De road am dusty, de road am tough,
> Dust in de eye, dust in de tuft;
> Dust in de mouth, yous can't talk—
> Walk, you niggers, don't you balk.
>
> Walk, walk, you nigger walk!
> De road am dusty, de road am rough—
> Walk till we reach dere, walk or bust—
> De road am long, we be dere by and by.

Now we'uns was a-follerin' behind de wagons and we'uns sings it to de slow steps of de ox. We'uns don't sing it many times till de missy come and sit in de back of de wagon, facin' we'uns and she begin to beat de slow time and sing with we'uns. Dat please Missy Mary to sing with us and she laugh and laugh.

After about two weeks we comes to de place near Caldwell, in Texas, and dere was buildin's and land cleared, so we's soon settled. Massa plants mostly cotton and corn and clears more land. I learned to be a coachman, but on dat place I de ox driver or uses de hoe.

Yous never drive de ox, did yous? De mule ain't stubborn side of de ox, de ox am stubborn and den some more. One time I'se haulin' fence rails and de oxen starts to turn gee when I wants dem to go ahead. I calls for haw, but dey pays dis nigger no mind and keeps goin' gee. Den dey starts to run and de overseer hollers and asks me, "Where you goin'?" I hollers back, "I'se not goin', I'se bein' took." Dem oxen takes me to de well for de water, 'cause if dey gets dry and is near water, dey goes in spite of de devil.

De treatment from new massa am good, 'cause of Missy Mary. She says to Massa Bill, "If you must abuse de nigger, abuse yous own." We has music and parties. We plays de quill, make from willow stalk when de sap am up. Yous takes de stick and pounds de bark loose and slips it off, den split de wood in one end and down one side, puts holes in de bark and put it back on de stick. De quill plays like de flute.

I never goes out without de pass, so I never has trouble with de patterrollers. Nigger Monk, him have de experience with 'em. Dey catched him twice and dey sure makes him hump and holler. After dat he gets pass or stays to home.

De War make no difference with us, except de soldiers comes and takes de rations. But we'uns never goes hungry, 'cause de massa puts some niggers hustlin' for wild hogs. After surrender, Missy reads de paper and tells dat we'uns is free, but dat we'uns kin stay till we is adjusted to de change.

De second year after de War, de massa sells de plantation and goes back to Louisiana and den we'uns all left. I goes to Laredo for seven year and works on a stock ranch, den I goes to farmin'. I gets married in 1879 to Mary Robinson and we'uns has fourteen chilluns. Four of dem lives here. I works hard all my life till 1935 and den I'se too old. My wife and I lives on de pensions we gets.

WILLIAM HUTSON

Interviewed at Tulsa, Oklahoma
Interviewer not identified
Age when interviewed: 98

WHEN A FELLER gets as old as me it's a heap easier to forget things than it is to remember, but I ain't never forgot that old plantation where good old Doctor Allison lived back there in Georgia long before the War that brought us slaves the freedom. I hear the slaves talking about mean masters when I was a boy. They wasn't talking about Master Allison, though, 'cause he was a good man and took the part for the slaves when any trouble come up with the overseer. The Mistress' name was Louisa, the same name as the gal I was married to later after the War, and she was just about as mean as was the old master good. I was the house boy when I gets old enough to understand what the master wants done and I does it just like he says, so I reckon that's why we always get along together.

The master helped my mammy to raise me. When I was born he says to her (my mammy tells me when I gets older): "Cheney," the old master say, "that boy is going be different from these other children. I aims to see that he is. He's going to be in the house all the time, he ain't going work in the fields; he's going to stay right with me all the time." They was about twenty slaves on the plantation but I was the one master called for when he wanted something special for himself. I was the one he took with him on the trips to town. I was the one who fetch him the cooling drink after he look about the fields and sometimes I carry the little black bag when he goes a-doctoring folks with the misery away off some other farm.

The master hear about there going to be an auction one day and he figgered maybe he needed some more slaves if they was good ones, so he took me and started out early in the morning. It wasn't very far and we got there early before the auction started. Reckon that was the first time I ever see any slaves sold.

They was a long platform made of heavy planks and all the slaves was lined up on the platform, and they was stripped to the waist, men, women, and children. One or two of the womenfolks was bare naked. They wasn't young women neither, just middle age ones, but they was built good. Some of them was well greased and that grease covered up many a scar they'd earned for some foolishment or other.

The master don't buy none and pretty soon we starts home. The Master was riding horseback—he didn't ever use no buggy 'cause he said that was the way for folks to travel who was too feeble to sit in the saddle— and I rode back of him on another horse, but that horse I rides is just horse while the master's was a real thoroughbred like maybe you see on race tracks down in the South.

That auction kept bothering me all the way back to the plantation. I keep seeing them little children standing on the platform, their mammy and pappy crying hard 'cause their younguns is being sold. They was a lot of heartaches even they was slaves and it gets me worried. I asked the master is he going to have an auction and he just laugh. "I ain't never sold no slaves yet and I ain't going to," he says. And I gets easier right then. I kind of hates to think about standing up on one of them platforms, kinder sorry to leave my old mammy and the master, so I was easy in the heart when he talked like that.

The plantation house was a big frame and the yard was shaded with trees all around. The master's children—four boys and two girls— would play in the yard with me just like I was one of the family. And we'd go hunting and fishing. There was a creek not far away and they was good fishing in the stream and squirrels in the trees. Mighty lot of fun to catch them fishes but more fun when they is all fried brown and ready for to eat with a piece of hot pone. Ain't no fish ever taste that good since!

One thing I sort of ponders about. The old master don't let us have no religion meetings and reading and writing is something I learn after the War. Some of the slaves talk about meetings round the country and wants to have preaching on the plantation. Master says, "NO". No preacher around here to tell about the Bible and religion will be just a puzzlement, the master say, and we let it go at that. I reckon that was the only thing he was set against.

That and the Yankees. The master went to the War and stayed till it was most over. He was a mighty sick man when he come back to the old plantation, but I was there waiting for him just like always. All the time he was away I take care around the house. That's what he say for me to do when he rides away to fight the Yankees. Lot's of talk about the War but the slaves goes right on working just the same, raising cotton and tobacco. The slaves talk a heap about Lincoln and some tries to run away to the North.

The day of freedom come around just like any other day, except the master say for me to bring up the horses, we is going to town. That's when he hears about the slaves being free. We gets to the town and the master goes into the store. It's pretty early but the streets was filled with folks talking and I wonder what makes the master in such a hurry when he comes out of the store.

He gets on his horse and tells me to follow fast. When we gets back to the plantation he sounds the horn calling the slaves. They come in from the fields and meet round back of the kitchen building that stood separate from the master's house. They all keeps quiet while the master talks. "You-all is free now, and all the rest of the slaves is free too. Nobody owns you now and nobody going to own you anymore!" That was good news, I reckon, but nobody knew what to do about it.

The crops was mostly in and the master wants the folks to stay till the crop is finished. They talk about it the rest of that day. They wasn't no celebration round the place, but they wasn't much work after the master tells us we is free. Nobody leave the place, though. Not till in the fall when the work is through. Then some of us go into the town and gets work 'cause everybody knows the Allison slaves was the right kind of folks to have around. That was the first money I earn and then I have to learn how to spend it. That was the hardest part 'cause the prices was high and the wages was low.

Then I moves on and meets the gal that maybe I been looking for, Louisa Baker, and right away she takes to me and we is married. Ain't been no other woman but her and she's waiting for me wherever the dead waits for the living. I reckon she won't have so long to wait now, even if I is feeling pretty spry and got good use of the feets and hands. Ninety-eight years brings a heap of wear and some of these days the old body'll need a long time rest and then I'll join her for all the time. I is ready for the New Day a-coming!

MARTIN JACKSON

Interviewed at San Antonio, Texas
Interviewer not identified
Age when interviewed: 90

I HAVE ABOUT eighty-five years of good memory to call on. I'm ninety, and so I'm not counting my first five years of life. I'll try to give you as clear a picture as I can. If you want to give me a copy of what you are going to write, I'll appreciate it. Maybe some of my children would like to have it.

I was here in Texas when the Civil War was first talked about. I was here when the War started and followed my young master into it with the First Texas Cavalry. I was here during Reconstruction, after the War. I was here during the European World War and the second week after the United States declared war on Germany I enlisted as cook at Camp Leon Springs.

This sounds as if I liked the war racket. But, as a matter of fact, I never wore a uniform—grey coat or khaki coat—or carried a gun, unless it happened to be one worth saving after some Confederate soldier got shot. I was official lugger-in of men that got wounded, and might have been called a Red Cross worker if we had had such a corps connected with our company. My father was head cook for the battalion and between times I helped him out with the mess. There was some difference in the food served to soldiers in 1861 and 1917!

Just what my feelings was about the War, I have never been able to figure out myself. I knew the Yanks were going to win, from the beginning. I wanted them to win and lick us Southerners, but I hoped they was going to do it without wiping out our company. I'll come back to that in a minute, As I said, our company was the First Texas Cavalry. Colonel Buchell was our commander. He was a full-blooded German and as fine a man and a soldier as you ever saw. He was killed at the Battle of Marshall and died in my arms. You may also be interested to know that my old master, Alvy Fitzpatrick, was the grandfather of Governor Jim Ferguson.

Lots of old slaves closes the door before they tell the truth about their days of slavery. When the door is open, they tell how kind their masters was and how rosy it all was. You can't blame them for this, because they had plenty of early discipline, making them cautious about saying anything uncomplimentary about their masters. I, myself, was in a little different position than most slaves and, as a consequence, have no grudges or resentment. However, I can tell you the life of the average slave was not rosy. They were dealt out plenty of cruel suffering.

Even with my good treatment, I spent most of my time planning and thinking of running away. I could have done it easy, but my old father used to say, "No use running from bad to worse, hunting better." Lots of colored boys did escape and joined the Union army, and there are plenty of them drawing pension today. My father was always counseling me. He said, "Every man has to serve God under his own vine and fig tree." He kept pointing out that the War wasn't going to last forever, but that our forever was going to be spent living among the Southerners, after they got licked. He'd cite examples of how the whites would stand flat-footed and fight for the blacks the same as for members of their own family. I knew that all was true, but still I rebelled, from inside of me. I think I really was afraid to run away, because I thought my conscience would haunt me. My father knew I felt this way and he'd rub my fears in deeper. One of his remarks still rings in my ears: "A clear conscience opens bowels, and when you have a guilty soul it ties you up and death will not for long desert you."

I haven't had any education. I should have had one, though. My old missus was sorry, after the War, that she didn't teach me. Her name, before she married my old master, was Mrs. Long. She lived in New York City and had three sons. When my old master's wife died, he wrote up to a friend of his in New York, a very prominent merchant named C. C. Stewart. He told this friend he wanted a wife and gave him specifications for one. Well, Mrs. Long, whose husband had died, fitted the bill and she was sent down to Texas. She became Mrs. Fitzpatrick. She wasn't the grandmother of Governor Ferguson. Old Fitzpatrick had two wives that preceded Mrs. Long. One of the wives had a daughter named Fanny Fitzpatrick and it was her that was the Texas governor's mother. I seem to have the complicated family tree of my old master more clear than I've got my own, although mine can be put in a nutshell! I married only once and was blessed in it with forty-five years of devotion. I had thirteen children and a big crop of grandchildren.

My earliest recollection is the day my old boss presented me to his son, Joe, as his property. I was about five years old and my new master was only two.

It was in the Battle of Marshall, in Louisiana, that Colonel Buchell got shot. I was about three miles from the front, where I had pitched up a kind of first-aid station. I was all alone there. I watched the whole thing. I could hear the shooting and see the firing. I remember standing there and thinking the South didn't have a chance. All of a sudden I heard someone call. It was a soldier, who was half carrying Colonel Buchell in. I didn't do nothing for the Colonel. He was too far gone. I just held him comfortable, and that was the position he was in when he stopped breathing. That was the worst hurt I got when anybody died. He was a friend of mine. He had had a lot of soldiering before and fought in the Indian War.

Well, the Battle of Marshall broke the back of the Texas Cavalry. We began straggling back towards New Orleans, and by that time the War was over. The soldiers began to scatter. They was a sorry-lookin' bunch of lost sheep. They didn't know where to go, but most of 'em ended up pretty close to the towns they started from. They was like homing pigeons, with only the instinct to go home and, yet, most of them had no homes to go to.

I never went into books. I used to handle a big dictionary three times a day, but it was only to put it on a chair so my young master could sit up higher at the table. I never went to school. I learned to talk pretty good by associating with my masters in their Big House.

We lived on a ranch of about one thousand acres close to the Jackson County line in Victoria County, about 125 miles from San Antonio. Just before the War ended they sold the ranch, slaves and all, and the family, not away fighting, moved to Galveston. Of course, my father and me wasn't sold with the other blacks because we was away at war.

My mother was drowned years before when I was a little boy. I only remember her after she was dead. I can take you to the spot in the river today where she was drowned. She drowned herself. I never knew the reason behind it, but it was said she started to lose her mind and pre-ferred death to that.

The master's name was usually adopted by a slave after he was set free. This was done more because it was the logical thing to do and the easiest way to be identified than it was through affection for the master. Also, the government seemed to be in a almighty hurry to have us get names. We had to register as someone, so we could be citizens. Well, I got to thinking about all us slaves that was going to take the name Fitzpatrick. I made up my mind I'd find me a different one. One of my grandfathers in Africa was called Jeaceo, and so I decided to be Jackson.

SILAS JACKSON
Interviewed at Baltimore, Maryland
Interviewed by —— Rogers
Age when interviewed: 90

I WAS BORN at or near Ashbie's Gap in Virginia, either in the year 1846 or '47. I do not know which, but I will say I am ninety years of age. My father's name was Sling and mother's Sarah Louis. They were purchased by my master from a slave trader in Richmond, Virginia. My father was a man of large stature and my mother was tall and stately.

They originally came from the eastern shore of Maryland, I think from the Legg estate; beyond that I do not know. I had three brothers and two sisters. My brothers were older than I, and my sisters younger. Their names were Silas, Carter, Rap or Raymond, I do not remember; my sisters were Jane and Susie, both of whom are living in Virginia now. Only one I have ever seen and he came North with General Sherman. He died in 1925. He was a Baptist minister like myself.

The only thing I know about my grandparents were: My grandfather ran away through the aid of Harriet Tubman and went to Philadelphia and saved three hundred and fifty dollars, and purchased my grandmother through the aid of a Quaker or an Episcopal minister, I do not know. I have on several occasions tried to trace this part of my family's past history, but without success.

I was a large boy for my age. When I was nine years of age my tasks began and continued until 1864. In Virginia where I was, they raised tobacco, wheat, corn, and farm products. I have had a taste of all the work on the farm, besides digging and clearing up new ground to increase the acreage to the farm. We all had task work to do—men, women, and boys. We began work on Monday and worked until Saturday. That day we were allowed to work for ourselves and to garden or to do extra work. When we could get work, or work on someone else's place, we got a pass from the overseer to go off the plantation, but to be back by nine o'clock on Saturday night or when cabin inspection was made. Sometimes we could earn as much as fifty cents a day, which we used to buy cakes, candies, or clothes.

On Saturday each slave was given ten pounds cornmeal, a quart of black strap, six pounds of fatback, three pounds of flour and vegetables, all of which were raised on the farm. All of the slaves hunted, or those who wanted to, hunted rabbits, opossums, or fished. These were our choice food as we did not get anything special from the overseer. Our food was cooked by our mothers or sisters and, for those who were not married, by the old women and men assigned for that work. Each family was given three acres to raise their chickens or vegetables, and if a man raised his own food he was given ten dollars at Christmas time extra, besides his presents.

In the summer or when warm weather came each slave was given something: the women, linsey goods or gingham clothes; the men overalls, muslin shirts, top and underclothes, two pair of shoes, and a straw hat to work in. In the cold weather, we wore woolen clothes, all made at the sewing cabin.

My master was named Tom Ashbie, a meaner man was never born in Virginia—brutal, wicked, and hard. He always carried a cowhide with him. If he saw anyone doing something that did not suit his taste, he would have the slave tied to a tree, man or woman, and then would cowhide the victim until he got tired, or sometimes, the slave would faint.

Mrs. Ashbie was kind and lovely to her slaves when Mr. Ashbie was out. The Ashbies did not have any children of their own, but they had boys and girls of his own sister and they were much like him. They had maids or private waiters for the young men if they wanted them.

I have heard it said by people in authority, Tom Ashbie owned nine thousand acres of farm land besides wood land. He was a large slave owner, having more than a hundred slaves on his farm. They were awakened by blowing of the horn before sunrise by the overseer, started work at sunrise and worked all day to sundown, with no time to go to the cabin for dinner. You carried your dinner with you. The slaves were driven at top speed and whipped at the snap of the finger by the overseers. We had four overseers on the farm, all hired white men. I have seen men beaten until they dropped in their tracks; or knocked over by clubs; women stripped down to their waist and cowhided.

I have heard it said that Tom Ashbie's father went to one of the cabins late at night. The slaves was having a secret prayer meeting. He heard one slave ask God to change the heart of his master and deliver him from slavery so that he may enjoy freedom. Before the next day the man disappeared, no one ever seeing him again. But after that down in the swamp, at certain times of the moon, you could hear the man who prayed in the cabin praying. When old man Ashbie died, just before he died, he told the white Baptist minister that he had killed Zeek for praying and that he was going to hell.

The Ashbie's home was a large stone mansion, with a porch on three sides, wide halls in the center up and downstairs, numerous rooms and a stone kitchen built on the back connected with the dining room. There was a stone building on the farm. It is there today. I saw it this summer while visiting in Virginia. The old jail, it is now used as a garage. Downstairs there were two rooms, one where some of the whipping was done, and the other used by the overseer. Upstairs was used for women and girls. The iron bars have corroded, but you can see where they were. I have never seen slaves sold on the farm, but I have seen them taken away and brought there. Several times I have seen slaves chained taken away and chained when they came.

No one on the place was taught to read or write. On Sunday the slaves who wanted to worship would gather at one of the large cabins with one of the overseers present and have their church, after which the overseer would talk. When communion was given the overseer was paid for staying there with half of the collection taken up, sometimes he would get twenty-five cents. No one could read the Bible. Sandy Jasper, Mr. Ashbie's coachman, was the preacher. He would go to the white Baptist church on Sunday with family and would be better informed because he heard the white preacher.

Twice each year, after harvest and after New Year's, the slaves would have their protracted meeting, or their revival, and after each closing they would baptize in the creek. Sometimes in the winter they would break the ice singing "Going to the Water" or some other hymn of that nature. And at each funeral, the Ashbies would attend the service conducted in the cabin where the deceased was, from there taking him to the slave graveyard. A lot dedicated for that purpose was situated about three-fourths of a mile from cabins, near a hill.

There were a number of slaves on our plantation who ran away. Some were captured and sold to a Georgia trader, others who were never captured. To intimidate the slaves, the overseers were connected with the patrollers, not only to watch our slaves, but sometimes for the rewards for other slaves who had run away from other plantations. This feature caused a great deal of trouble between the whites and blacks. In 1858, two white men were murdered near Warrenton on the road, by colored people. It was never known whether by free people or slaves.

When work was done the slaves retired to their cabins. Some played games, others cooked or rested or did what they wanted. We did not work on Saturdays unless in harvest times, then Saturdays were days of work. At other times, on Saturdays you were at leisure to do what you wanted. On Christmas day, Mr. Ashbie would call all the slaves together, give them presents, money, after which they spent the day as they liked. On New Year's day, we all were scared—that was the time for selling, buying, and trading slaves. We did not know who was to go or come.

BENJAMIN JOHNSON
Interviewed in Georgia
Interviewed by Edwin Driskell
Age when interviewed: About 85

ON OUR PLANTATION de white folks been feedin' de slaves off rat meat, jowls and heads and jaws. Dey kept all de meat out in de smokehouse in de back yard. In dis house dey kept de hams all hangin' up high and above dem dey kept sausages and den above dem dey kept de finest hams all trimmed and everything. De slaves eat dat fat meat and thought dat dey was eatin' pound cake. Come down to chicken—if you got it you stole it when de white folks was sleep at night and den you had to be careful and bury all de feathers in de ground 'cause if you burned 'em de white folks would smell 'em. We boys in de field used to be so hungry till we didn't know what to do. De overseers would be settin' down under a tree and he would holler, "Keep goin'!" De sweat would be just runnin' off you and sometimes you could smell one another.

Dere was a spring nearby and when we would get to it we would fall down and drink from de branch. De women would be plowin' and hoein' grain and de Spanish needles and cockle burrs would be stickin' to dere dresses from dere knees to dere feet. Further down dere would be a man diggin' a ditch. Every now and den white folks would walk over to de ditch and see if it was de same width all de way.

You go off to see somebody at night—just like you and me want to laugh and talk—and if dey catch you and you ain't got no pass dey gwine to whip you. You be glad to get away too, 'cause when dey hit you, you was hit.

I was hit. I was down to old John Brady's place one night talkin' to a lady and old man Brady slipped up behind me and caught me in de collar and he say: "What you doin' over here? I'm goin' to give you twenty-five lashes." And den he say to me: "Come here." He was just about as tall as I am and when I got to him he say, "Turn 'round." And I say to him dat I ain't doin' nothin', and den he say: "Dat's what I'm goin' to whip you for, 'cause you ought to be home doin' somethin'." About dat time when I stopped over to take off my coat I caught him in his pants and throwed him in a puddle o' water and den I lit out for home. If you get home, den dey couldn't do nothin' to you. He tried to chase me, but he didn't know de way through de woods like I did and fell in a gully and hurt his arm.

De next mornin' when I was hitchin' up de boss man's horse I seed him comin' and I told de boss dat he tried to whip me de night before and den de boss man say, "Did he have you?" I told him dat he did but I got away. And den de boss say: "He had you and he didn't have you—is dat right?" Den he say, "Don't worry about dat. I can get you out of dat. If he had you he shoulda whipped you and dat woulda been his game, but he let you get away, and so dat was yo' game."

About dat time old man Brady had done got dere and he told de marster I was on his place de night before and dat I got away when he tried to whip me. De marster say to him: "Dat was his game. If you had him, you shoulda whipped him. Dat's de law. If you had whipped him, dat woulda been you' game, but you let him get away and so dat was his game." Old man Brady's face turned so red dat it looked like he was gonna bust.

We worked in de field every day and way in de night we shucked and shelled corn. De cooks done all de cookin'. When all of de marster's seventy-five slaves was in de field dey had two cooks to feed 'em. At twelve o'clock de cooks would blow a horn at de stump in de yard back o' de house. Even de hosses and de mules knowed dat horn and dey wouldn't go a step further.

You had to take de mule out of de harness and take him to de spring and water him and den take him to de house where a colored man up dere named Sam Johnson had all de feed ready for de hosses. When you get dere all de hosses go to dere own stalls where dere was ten ears o' corn and one bundle o' fodder for each hoss. While dem hosses is eatin' you better be out dere eatin' you' own. Sarah and Annie, de cooks, had a big wooden tray with de greens and de meat all cut up on it and you pass by with you' tin pan and dey put you' meat all cut up on it along with de greens and den you could eat anywhere you wanted to—on de stump or in big road if you wanted to. Sometimes some of 'ems meat would give out or deir bread would give out and den dey would say: "I'll give give you a piece of my bread for some of you' bread." Some of 'em would have a big old ash cake and some of 'em would have just plain corn bread. Dere was usually a big skillet o' potatoes at de cook house and when you eat and drink your water den you is ready to go back to work. Dey was goin' to let you lay down in de shade for about a hour but you would make de time up by workin' till dark. Some of 'em worked so till dey back was gone. Dey couldn't even stand up straight.

Sometimes Old Missus would come along and she would be mad with some of de women and she would want to go to whippin' on 'em. Sometimes de women wouldn't take it and would run away and hide in de woods. Sometimes dey would come back after a short stay and den again dey would have to put de hounds on deir trail to bring dem back home.

As a general rule dere wasn't much whippin' on our plantation. 'Course, if you didn't do what dey told you to do dey would take you out and put your hands round a pole and tie you so your feet touch de ground and den dey would go to work on you with a cowhide. Every time dey hit you de blood would fly with de whip.

De clothes den wasn't but old plain white cloth. Most of 'em was patched from de legs to de waist. Some was patched so till dey looked like a quilt. Some of de women wore dese long striped cotton dresses. De only shoes dat you got was red brogans. If you got anything better it was some dat marster give you for brushing off his shoes at de house. You was proud whenever dey give you a pair o' shoes or a old straw hat dat dey was through with at de house dat you went back and showed it to everybody and you was mighty proud, too. I used to drive my marster's hoss and buggy for him and so I used to get a lotsa stuff like dat.

Old Marster was a judge and his name was Luke Johnson. His wife was named Betsy and his sons was named Jim, Tom, Will, and Dorn. His daughters was Janie, Mary, Catherine, and Lissie. He had three hundred acres of land and seventy-five slaves.

All de houses on de plantation 'cept Old Marster's was built out o' logs. Old Marster lived in a fine house. Sometimes when one o' de slaves had a chance to go inside his house all de rest of de slaves would be waitin' outside for you to come out. When you did come out dey would say: "You been in de marster's house—how did it look in dere? What did you see?" Dey would tell 'em: "You ought to go in dere. It's pretty!" Whenever you got a chance to go in dere you had done pulled off your hat long before you got to de door.

On Sunday we would take soot out of de chimney and wet it and den go and borrow marster's shoes brush and go and brush our shoes. We was gettin' ready to go to church. At church all de white folks would sit in de front and de slaves would sit in de back. De preacher would preach and say: "Obey your master and your missus and you will always do right. If you see eggs in de yard take 'em to your marster or your missus and put 'em at her feet. If you don't do dis she will needle you well or break bark over your head and de bad man will get you."

Sometimes dey would give us a dollar at Christmas time and if somebody didn't take it from us we would have it de next Christmas 'cause we didn't have nothin' to spend it for.

When de War broke out Old Marster enlisted and he took me 'long to wait on him and to keep his clothes clean. I had plenty o' fun 'cause dere wasn't so very much work to do. I 'members seein' him fightin' in Richmond and Danville, Virginia. I had a good time just watchin' de soldiers fightin'. I didn't have to fight any at all. I used to stand in de door of de tent and watch 'em fight. It was terrible—you could hear de guns firin' and see de soldiers fallin' right and left. All you could see was men gettin' all shot up. One day I seed one soldier get his head shot off from his body. Others got arms and legs shot off. And all de time all you could hear was de guns goin'—bam, bam, bam! It was terrible to see and hear. One mornin' as I was standin' in de door of de tent I had a dose of it. I was leanin' against de side of de tent with my hand stretched out and a load o' grape shot from de guns hit me in de hand and de blood flew everywhere. I just hollered. It come pretty near scaring me to death. After de doctor got it patched up it was as good as it every was.

After de War was over Old Marster was all shot up and I had to take him on back home. When we got dere all de slaves crowded round me and wanted to know if dey was gonna be freed or not and when I told 'em dat de War was over and dat dey was free dey was all very glad. After de War a whole lots of 'em stayed on de plantation and a whole lots of 'em left as soon as dey could get away.

HENRY JOHNSON
Interviewed at St. Louis, Missouri
Interviewed by Grace E. White
Age when interviewed: 90+

MY NAME IS Henry Johnson. I was born in Patrick County, Virginia, and was raised all over de state. I was only sold twice. My father's name was Bill Alexander and my mother's name was Fannie, but I didn't know nothin' about my parents till I was past eighteen years old or about that. I never knowed my real age. My owner's name was

Billy Johnson in Patrick County so I always carried his name. When I was a little bit a fellow, I used to pack water to twenty-five and thirty men in one field, den go back to de house and bring enough water for breakfast de next morning. When I got a little bigger, I had to take a little hoe and dig weeds out of de crop. If our white boss see a little grass we overlooked he would handcuff our feet to a whipping post, den chain de slave around de stomach to de post and strap de chin over de top of de post and place your hands in front of you.

Slaves have been stripped naked and lashed, often to death. Dey would be left strapped after from twenty-five to fifty lashes every two or three hours to stand dere all night. De next day, de overseer would be back with a heavy paddle full of holes dat had been dipped in boiling water and beat until de whole body was full of blisters. Den he'd take a cat-and-nine-tails dipped in hot salt water to draw out de bruised blood and would open every one of dem blisters with dat. If de slave did not die from dat torture, he would be unfastened from de whipping post, and made to go to de field just as he was. Oftentimes he would die shortly after. Dey did the women de same.

I never knowed what a shirt was until I was past twenty.

When my young master went three miles to school, he rode on a horse. I had to walk alongside de horse to carry his books, den go home and fetch him a hot dinner for noon and go back after him at night to carry dem books.

My boss had eleven children. He had one hundred and twenty-five slaves on one of de plantations, two hundred on another. Of all his plantations he owned better'n fifteen hundred slaves. He was one of de richest landowners in de state of Virginia. He often told me I was born just one hour before his youngest son. I stayed with dat family until way after de War was fought.

Dey would take a great string of slaves in de road on Sunday and make us walk to church. Buggies with de white folks in would be in front of us, in de midst of us, and all betwixt and behind us. When we got dat four or five miles we had to sit on a log in de broiling sun, while a white man preached to us. All dey ever would say would be: "Niggers, obey your masters and mistress and don't steal from 'em." And, lo and behold, de masters would make us slaves steal from each of the slave owners. Our master would make us surround a herd of his neighbor's cattle, round dem up at night, and make us slaves stay up all night long and kill and skin every one of dem critters, salt the skins down in layers in de master's cellar, and put de cattle piled ceilin' high in de smokehouse so nobody could identify skinned cattle.

Den when de sheriff would come around lookin' for all dem stolen critters, our boss would say, "Sheriff, just go right on down to dem niggers' cabins and search dem good. I know my niggers don't steal." 'Course de sheriff come to our cabins and search. Sure we didn't have nothin' didn't belong to us, but de boss had plenty. After de sheriff's search, we had to salt and smoke all dat stolen meat and hang it in Old Marse's smokehouse for him. Den dey tell us, don't steal.

Dey raised turkeys in de five-hundred lots and never did give us one. So we wanted one so bad once, I put corn underneath de cabin and a turkey, a great big one, would come under our cabin to eat dat corn, and him and me went round and round under dat old cabin house. He was de biggest, strongest bird I ever see. I was only a boy but finally I beat. I twisted his neck till he died. Den I took out up to de Big House, fast as anything, to tell my old miss one of our finest turkeys dead. She said, "Stop crying, Henry, and throw him under de hill."

I was satisfied. I run back, picked dat old bird, taken all his feathers to de river and throwed dem in. Dat night we cooked him. And didn't we eat somethin' good! I had to tell her about dat missin' bird cause when dey check up it all had to tally, so dat fixed dat.

When de War was being fought and the Yankees was on de way coming through Franklin County, Virginia, my old master say: "My little nigger, do you know how old you is?" I said: "No sir, boss." He said, "You are seventeen years old."

I never even saw my mother and father until I was in my twenties. A white man taken me to Danville, Virginia, to drive his carriage for him. After I was dere a spell a colored man kept watching me so much I got plumb scared. Dis was after de War was over. Den one day, lo and behold, he jumped at me and he grabbed me and asked me where was I staying. I did not know whether to tell him or not, I was scared. Den he said, "I am your father and I am goin' to take you to your mother and sisters and brothers down in Greenhill, Virginia. When he got me dere, I found two sisters and four brothers. Dey was all so glad to see me dey shouted and cried and carried on so I was so scared I tried to run away, 'cause I didn't know nothin' about none of them. And I thought dat white man what brought me down dere ought to have saved me from all dis. I just thought a white man was my God, I didn't know no better.

Well, when my folks finally stopped rejoicin', my mother killed and cooked two chickens for me.

My father and brothers would go to work every day and leave me at home with my mother for over a year. They wouldn't trust me to work, feared I would run off 'cause I didn't know nothin' about them. Hadn't even heard of a mother and father. My brother and father would work all day and only get one peck of corn or one pound of meat or one quart of molasses for a whole day's work from sunup till sundown. We had to grind dat corn for our flour, and got biscuits once a year at Christmas and den only one biscuit apiece.

After a little bettern' a year after I come, the white man told my father to bring him family and move from Greenhill, Virginia, to Patrick County, Virginia, to his big farm, and farm dere for him and he would give him one-half of all he raised for his share. We went and did we raise a big crop! He kept his word all right and we stayed dere till de white man died five years later. Den we went to another farm. We had cleared enough in the five years to buy us a fine pair of oxen and had money besides. So we went to another farm and went to work, giving the owner of the farm one-third of the crop and kept two-thirds ourselves. We stayed there two years. Then father sold de oxen and went to Sweetville, Virginia, and bought two hundred dollars worth of land and stayed about five years.

We made our crop with a hoe and made good. Den I left home and run about all over, learned how to play a violin, and made my livin' with it for a long time.

I quit dat and railroaded about eight years working on sections and new grading. Den I went to Decatur, Alabama, and worked with a land company putting down pipings about three months. I quit dat and married Anna Johnson and come to Jiles County, Tennessee. We had one son.

I came to St. Louis from Tennessee more dan forty years ago. I got work right away at Cycle and Harris Stell Plant on eighteenth street and worked dere about six months, when I got scalded almost to death on the job. I got a new nose and a new ear from dat accident. All de flesh of my right arm was off to de bone. I was in de hospital eight months from it and I got five-hundred dollars out of de damage suit. I bought me a horse and wagon out of it and done light hauling, and moved out here in Lincoln Terrace and been out here ever since. I landscaped out here for sixteen years until I was disable to work hard anymore. I got a garden but I can't make any money from it, 'cause all de other folks out here got gardens too.

I only went to school three days in my whole life but a colored friend taught me how to spell out of a blue-back spelling book. His name was Charlie Snowball. I was learning fine until I got burned. Den my eyesight was poor for a long time, but I see now very good. I only need glasses for to read what little I can read. I can't write at all.

NELLIE JOHNSON

Interviewed in Oklahoma
Interviewer not identfied
Age when interviewed: 88

I DON'T KNOW how old I is, but I is a great big half grown gal when the time of the War come, and I can remember how everything look at that time and what all the people do, too. I'm pretty nigh to blind right now, and all I can do is set on this little old front porch and maybe try to keep the things picked up behind my grandchild and his wife, because she has to work and he is out selling wood most of the time.

But I didn't have to live in any such a house during the time I was young like they is, because I belonged to Old Chief Rolley McIntosh, and pappy and mammy have a big, nice, clean log house to live in, and everything round it look better than most renters got these days.

We never did call Old Master anything but the Chief or the General, for that's what everybody called him in them days, and he never did act towards us like we was slaves, much anyways. He was the mikko of the Kawita town long before the War and long before I was borned, and he was the chief of the Lower Creeks even before he got to be the chief of all the Creeks.

But just at the time of the War the Lower Creeks stayed with him and the Upper Creeks, at least them that lived along to the south of where we live, all go off after that old man Gouge, and he take most of the Seminoles too. I hear of old Tuskenugge, the big man with the Seminoles, but I never did see him, nor mighty few of the Seminoles.

My mammy tells me old General ain't been living in that Kawita town very many years when I was borned. He come up there from down in the fork of the river where the Arkansas and the Verdigris run together a little while after all the last of the Creeks come out to the Territory. His brother, old Chili McIntosh, live down in that forks of the rivers too, but I don't think he ever move up into that Kawita town. It was in the narrow stretch where the Verdigris come close to the Arkansas. They got a pretty good sized white folks town there now they call Coweta, but the old Creek town was different from that. The folks lived all around in that stretch between the rivers, and my old Master was the boss of all of them.

For a long time after the Civil War they had a court at the new town called Coweta court, and a schoolhouse too, but before I was born they had a mission school down the Kawita Creek from where the town is now.

Earliest I can remember about my master was when he come to the slave settlement where we live and get out of the buggy and show a preacher all around the place. That preacher named Mr. Loughridge, and he was the man had the mission down on Kawita Creek before I was born, but at that time he had a school off at some other place. He get down out the buggy and talk to all us children and ask us how we getting along. I didn't even know at that time that Old Chief was my master, until my pappy tell me after he was gone. I think all the time he was another preacher.

My pappy's name was Jackson McIntosh, and my mammy's name was Hagar. I think Old Chief bring them out to the Territory when he come out with his brother Chili and the rest of the Creek people. My pappy tell me that Old Master's pappy was killed by the Creeks because he signed up a treaty to bring his folks out here, and Old Master always hated that bunch of Creeks that done that.

I think old man Gouge was one of the big men in that bunch, and he fit in the War on the government side, after he done holler and go on so about the government making him come out here.

Old Master have lots of land took up all around that Kawita place, and I don't know how much, but a lot more than anybody else. He have it all fenced in with good rail fence, and all the Negroes have all the horses and mules and tools they need to work it with. They all live in good log houses they built themselves, and everything they need.

Old Master's land wasn't all in one big field, but a lot of little fields scattered all over the place. He just take up land what already was a kind of prairie, and the niggers don't have to clear up much woods. We all live around on them little farms, and we didn't have to be under any overseer like the Cherokee Negroes had lots of times. We didn't have to work if they wasn't no work to do that day. Everybody could have a little patch of his own, too, and work it between times, on Saturdays and Sundays if he wanted to. What he made on that patch belong to him, and the old chief never bothered the slaves about anything.

Every slave can fix up his own cabin any way he want to, and pick out a good place with a spring if he can find one. Mostly the slave houses had just one big room with a stick-and-mud chimney, just like the poor people among the Creeks had. Then they had a brush shelter built out of four poles with a room made out of brush, set out to one side of the house where they do the cooking and eating, and sometimes the sleeping too. They set there when they is done working, and lay around on corn shuck beds, because they never did use the log house much, only in cold and rainy weather. Old Chief just treat all the Negroes like they was just hired hands, and I was a big girl before I knowed very much about belonging to him.

I was one of the youngest children in my family; only Sammy and

Millie was younger than I was. My big brothers was Adam, August, and Nero, and my big sisters was Flora, Nancy, and Rhoda. We could work a mighty big patch for our own selves when we was all at home together, and put in all the work we had to for the old master too, but after the War the big children all get married off and took up land of they own.

Old Chief lived in a big log house made double with a hall in between, and a lot of white folks was always coming there to see him about something. He was gone off somewhere a lot of the time, too, and he just trusted the Negroes to look after his farms and stuff. We would just go on out in the fields and work the crops just like they was our own, and he never come around excepting when we had harvest time, or to tell us what he wanted planted.

Sometimes he would send a Negro to tell us to gather up some chickens or turkeys or shoats he wanted to sell off, and sometimes he would send after loads of corn and wheat to sell. I hear my pappy say Old Chief and Mr. Chili McIntosh was the first ones to have any wheat in the Territory, but I don't know about that.

Along during the War the Negro men got pretty lazy and shiftless, but my pappy and big brothers just go right on and work like they always did. My pappy always said we better off to stay on the place and work good and behave ourselves because Old Master take care of us that way. But on lots of other places the men slipped off.

I never did see many soldiers during the War, and there wasn't any fighting close to where we live. It was kind of down in the bottoms, not far from the Verdigris and that Gar Creek, and the soldiers would have bad crossings if they come by our place. We did see some whackers riding around sometimes, in little bunches of about a dozen, but they never did bother us and never did stop. Some of the Negro girls that I knowed of mixed up with the poor Creeks and Seminoles, and some got married to them after the War, but none of my family ever did mix up with them that I knows of.

Along toward the last of the War I never did see Old Chief come around any more, and somebody say he went down into Texas. He never did come back that I knows of, and I think he died down there.

One day my pappy come home and tell us all that the Creek done sign up to quit the War, and that Old Master send word that we all free now and can take up some land for our own selves or just stay where we is if we want to. Pappy stayed on the place where he was at until he died.

I got to be a big girl and went down to work for a Creek family close to where they got that Checotah town now. At that time it was just all a scattered settlement of Creeks and they call it Eufaula town. After a while I marry a man name Joe Johnson, at a little settlement they call Rentesville. He have his freedmen's allotment close to that place, but mine is up on the Verdigris, and we move up there to live. We just had one child, named Louisa, and she married Tom Amstrong. They had three-four children, and one was named Tom, and it is him I live with now. My husband's been dead a long, long time now.

PRINCE JOHNSON

Interviewed at Clarksdale, Mississippi
Interviewed by Carrie Campbell
Age when interviewed: About 85

I SURE CAN TELL all about slavery 'cause I was dere when it all happened. My grandpa, Peter, grandma, Millie, my pa, John, and my ma, Frances, all come from Alabama to Yazoo County to live in de Love family. Dey names was Dennis when de come but, after de custom o' dem days, dey took de name o' Love from dey new owner. Me and all o' my brothers and sisters was born right dere. Dey was eleven head o' us. I was de oldest. Den come Harry, John, William, Henry, Phillis, Polly, Nellie, Virginny, Millie, and de baby, Ella.

Us all lived in de quarters and de beds was homemade. Dey had wooden legs with canvas stretched across 'em. I can't 'member so much about de quarters 'cause about dat time de young miss married Colonel Johnson and moved to dis place in Carroll County. She carried with her over one hundred head o' darkies.

Den us names was changed from Love to Johnson. My new marster was sure a fine gentleman. He lived in a big two-story white house dat had big white posts in front. De flowers all round it just set it off.

Marster took me for de house boy. Den I sure carried my head high. He'd say to me, "Prince, does you know who you is named for?" And I'd say to him, "Yes sir. Prince Albert." And den he'd say to me, "Well, always carry yourself like he did." To dis good day I holds myself like Marster said.

On certain days o' de week one o' de old men on de place took us house servants to de field to learn us to work. Us was brought up to know how to do anything dat come to hand. Marster would let us work at odd times for outsiders and us could use de money for anything us pleased. My grandma sold 'nough corn to buy her two featherbeds.

Us always had plenty to eat. De ole folks done de cookin' for all de field hands, 'cept on Sunday when every family cooked for dey ownselfs. Old Miss would come over every Sunday mornin' with sugar and white flour. Us would most generally have fish, rabbits, possums, or coons. Lord, dem possums was good eatin'. I can taste 'em now. Folks dese days don't know nothin' about good eatin'. My marster had a great big garden for everybody and I ain't never seen such 'taters as growed in dat garden.

Dey was so sweet de sugar would bust right through de peelin' when you roasted 'em in de ashes. Old Aunt Emily cooked for all de chillen on de place. Half an hour by de sun, dey was all called in to supper. Dey had pot likker and ash cake and such things as would make 'em grow.

Chillen den didn't know nothin' about all de fancy ailments what chillen have now. Dey run and played all day in dey shirt tails in de summertime. When winter come dey had good warm clothes same as us older ones.

One day Marster's chillen and de cullud chillen slipped off to de orchard. Dey was just a-eatin' green apples fast as dey could when along come de master, hisself. He lined 'em all up, black and white alike, and cut a keen switch. 'Twan't a one in dat line dat didn't get a few licks. Den he called de old doctor woman and made her give 'em every one a dose o' medicine. Dey didn't a one of 'em get sick.

Marster and Old Miss had five chillen. Dey is all dead and gone now, and I'se still here. One o' his sons was a Supreme Judge before he died. My folks was sure quality. Marster bought all de little places round us so he wouldn't have no poor white trash neighbors. Yes sir! He owned about thirty-five hundred acres and at least a hundred and fifty slaves.

Every mornin' about four 'clock us could hear dat horn blow for us to get up and go to de field. Us always quit work before de sun went down and never worked at night. De overseer was a white man. His name was Josh Neighbors, but de driver was a cullud man, "Old Man Henry." He wasn't allowed to mistreat nobody. If he got too uppity dey'd call his hand, right now. De rule was, if a nigger wouldn't work he must be sold. Another rule on dat place was dat if a man got dissatisfied, he was to go to de marster and ask him to "put him in his pocket." Dat meant he wanted to be sold and de money he brought put in de marster's pocket. I ain't never known o' but two askin' to be "put in de pocket." Both of 'em was sold.

Dey had jails in dem days, but dey was built for white folks. No cullud person was ever put in one of 'em till after de War. Us didn't know nothin' about dem things. Course, Old Miss knowed about 'em, 'cause she knowed everything. I recollect she told me one day dat she had learnin' in five different languages.

None o' us didn't have no learnin' at all. Dat is us didn't have no book learnin'. 'Twan't no teachers or anything like dat, but us sure was taught to be Christians. Everything on dat place was a blue stockin' Presbyterian. When Sunday come us dressed all clean and nice and went to church. Us went to de white folks' church and set in de gallery.

Us had a fine preacher. His name was Gober. He could sure give out de words o' wisdom. Us didn't have big baptisms like was had on a heap o' places, 'cause Presbyterians don't go down under de water like de Baptists do. If one o' de slaves died de was sure give a grand Christian funeral. All o' us mourners was on hand. Services was conducted by de white preacher.

Old Miss wouldn't stand for no such things as voodoo and haunts. When she inspected us once a week, you better not have no charm round your neck, neither. She wouldn't even allow us wear a bag o' asfittidy. Most folks believed dat would keep off sickness. She called such as dat superstition. She say us was enlightened Christian Presbyterians, and as such us must conduct ourselfs.

Nobody worked after dinner on Saturday. Us took dat time go scrub up and clean de houses so as to be ready for inspection Sunday mornin'. Some Saturday nights us had dances. De same old fiddler played for us dat played for de white folks. And he sure could play. When he got dat old fiddle out you couldn't keep your foots still.

Christmas was de time o' all times on dat old plantation. Dey don't have no such as dat now. Every child brought a stockin' up to de Big House to be filled. Dey all wanted one o' de mistis' stockin's, 'cause now she weighed nigh on to three hundred pounds. Candy and presents was put in piles for everyone. When de names was called dey walked up and got it. Us didn't work on New Year's Day. Us could go to town or anywhere us wanted to.

De most fun was de corn shuckin'. Dey was two captains and each one picked de ones he wanted on his side. Den de shuckin' started. You can't make mention o' nothin' good dat us didn't have to eat after de shuckin'. I still studies about dem days now. Dey was big parties at de white folks' house, me, all dressed up with tallow on my face to make it shine, a-servin' de guests.

One time, just when ever'thing was a-goin' fine, a sad thing happened. My young mistis, de one named for her ma, ups and runs off with de son o' de Irish ditch digger and marries him. She wouldn't a-done it if dey'd a-let her marry de man she wanted. Dey didn't think he was good 'nough for her. So just to spite 'em, she married de ditch digger's son. Old Miss wouldn't have nothin' more to do with her, same as if she weren't her own child. But I'd go over to see her and carry milk and things out o' de garden.

It was pitiful to see my little miss poor. When I couldn't stand it no longer I walks right up to Old Miss and I says, "Old Miss, does you know Miss Farrell ain't got no cow." She just act like she ain't heard me, and put her lips together dat tight. I couldn't do nothin' but walk off and leave her. Pretty soon she called, "Prince!" I says, "Yes, ma'am." She says, "Seein' you is so concerned about Miss Farrell not havin' no cow, you better take one to her." I found de rope and carried de best cow in de lot to Miss Farrell.

Shortly after dat I left with Old Marster to go to North Carolina. Just before de War come on, my marster called me to him and told me he was a-goin' to take me to North Carolina to his brother for safe keepin'. Right den I knowed somethin' was wrong. I was a-wishin' from de bottom o' my heart dat de Yankees would stay out o' us business and not get us all disturbed in de mind.

Things went on at his brother's place about like dey done at home. I stayed dere all four years o' de War. I coudn't leave 'cause de men folks all went to de War and I had to stay and protect de womenfolks.

De day peace was declared wagon loads o' people rode all through de place a-tellin' us about bein' free. De old colonel was killed in battle and his wife had died. De young marster called us in and said it was all true, dat us was free as he was, and us could leave whenever us got ready. He said his money weren't no good anymore and he didn't have no other to pay us with. I can't recollect if he got new money and paid us or not.

I never left dat place till my young marster, Mr. Jim Johnson, de one dat was de Supreme Judge, come for me. We was a-livin' in South Carolina den. He took us all home with him. Us got dere in time to vote for Govenor Wade Hampton. Us put him in office, too. De first thing I done was join de Democrat Club and helped 'em run all o' de scalawags away from de place. My young marster had always told me to live for my country and I had seen 'nough o' dat war to know just what was a-goin' on.

I'se seen many a patrol in my lifetime; but dey dassent come on us place. Now de Kloo Kluxes was different. I rid with 'em many a time. 'Twas de only way in dem days to keep order.

When I was about twenty-two year old, I married Clara Breaden. I had two chillen by her, Diana and Davis. My second wife's name was Annie Bet Woods. I had six chillen by her: Mary, Ella, John D., Claud William, and Prince, Jr. Three boys and two gals is still livin'. I lives with my daughter, Claud, what is farmin' a place about five miles from Clarksdale. I has about fifteen head o' grandchillen and every last one of 'em's farmers.

RICHARD JONES
Interviewed at Union, South Carolina
Interviewed by Caldwell Sims
Age when interviewed: 125?

E VERYBODY DAT knows me knows dat I was born on de Jim Gist plantation, and it used to join Mr. Winsmith's and de Glenn Peak plantations. Mr. Winsmith was a doctor. Marse Jim sure was a good man to his darkies. My father was named Ned Jones and he belonged to Marse Berry Jones. His plantation was across de forest, next to West Springs. Mother was Lucy Gist, belonging to Marse Jim. My parents had de following chillens: Esther, Bella, Ephriam, Griggs, John, Penfield, me and Richard. Dey married and so we was all Jones.

De slaves in de Gist quarter lived well. All nigger chillens in dat quarter had very small tasks until dey was seventeen or eighteen years old. De quarter had nine houses. Dere was seventeen hundred acres in our plantation; or dat is, de part where we lived and worked. We lived in one-room log cabins dat had to be well kept all of de time.

All de chillens in de quarter was well fed, clothed, housed, and doctored until dey was strong and well developed younguns. Den dey was give tasks and learnt to do what de master and de mistress thought dey would do well at.

In de houses we had comfortable homemade beds and chairs. We had nice tables and plenty to eat. Our clothes was kept mended by a seamstress, and dese things was looked after by one of de mammies on de plantation dat was too old to work.

Well does I 'member my Granny from Africa, and straight from dere, too; Judith Gist, dey named her. Dat old lady could not work when she died, for she was a hundred and ten years old. Dey had in de paper dat I was 125. It gives me notice to say dat I is de oldest man in Union County. Can't 'member any of my grandfathers. Millie Gist was my mother and Aunt Judith was her mother.

Granny Judith said dat in Africa dey had very few pretty things, and dat dey had no red colors in cloth. In fact, dey had no cloth at all. Some strangers with pale faces come one day and dropped a small piece of red flannel down on de ground. All de black folks grabbed for it. Den a larger piece was dropped a little further on, and on, until de river was reached. Den a large piece was dropped in de river and on de other side. Dey was led on, each one trying to get a piece as it was dropped. Finally, when de ship was reached, dey dropped large pieces on de plank and up into de ship till dey got as many blacks on board as dey wanted. Den de gate was chained up and dey could not get back. Dat is de way Granny Judith say dey got her to America. Of course she did not even know dat de pieces was red flannel, or dat she was being enticed away. Dey just dropped red flannel to dem like us drops corn to chickens to get dem on de roost at night.

When dey got on board de ship dey were tied until de ship got to sea. Den dey was let loose to walk about 'cause dey couldn't jump overboard. On de ship dey had many strange things to eat, and dey liked dat. Dey was give enough red flannel to wrap around demselves. She liked it on de boat. Granny Judith born Millie, and Millie born me.

Uncle Tom come along with Granny Judith. Two womenfolks come with dem, Aunt Chany and Daphne. Aunt Chany and Aunt Daphne was bought by de Frees dat had a plantation near Jonesville. Uncle Tom and Granny was bought by Marse Jim Gist, but deir marsters always allowed dem to visit on July Fourth and Christmas. When dey talk, nobody didn't know what dey was talking about. My granny never could speak good like I can. She talk half African, and all African when she get bothered. I can't talk no African.

After I was seventeen I did all kinds of hoeing and plowing and other farm work for my marster. He said dat by dis time, his little niggers' bones had done got hard enough for dem to work. We had a "driver," a older person, dat showed us how to do everything right. Marse never let him overwork or hurry us. We liked him—"Uncle July Gist" we called him, and dat was his real name too. His wife, Aunty Sara, was good to us. Dey both buried at Woodson's Chapel Baptist Church.

For my first task I had one-quarter of an acre in 'taters, tobacco, and watermelons de first year. Some of de boys had 'pinders, cantaloupes, and tomatoes in dere task of a quarter acre.

De next year, we made corn and sold it to our master for whatever he give us for it. All de use we had for money was to buy fishhooks, barlows, jew's harps, and marbles. Boys did not use tobacco den until dey got twenty-one or over. Marse always carried a roll of money as big as my arm. He would come to de quarter on Christmas, July Fourth, and Thanksgiving, and get up on a stump and call all the chillens out. Den he would throw money to 'em. De chillens get dimes, nickels, quarters, half-dollars, and dollars. At Christmas he would throw ten dollar bills. De parents would take de five and ten dollars bills in change, but Marse made dem let de chillens keep de small change. I ain't never seed so much money since my marster been gone. He buried at Fairforest Presbyterian Cemetery as white folks calls it, but we calls it Cedar Grove.

When he died, he had sixteen plantations, you can see dat at de courthouse in Union. All his darkies went in a drove of wagons to his burying. He was killed by dem Yankees in Virginny. Uncle Wylie Smith, his bodyguard, come back with his body and told us dat Marse was kilt by a Yankee. Marse Jim was a sentinel, and dat Yankee shot him in his nose, but strange to say, it never tore his face up none. Miss Sara buried him in his uniform and she wrapped a Confederate flag over de top of de coffin. Uncle Wylie put Master's watch around Miss Sara's neck like he had done told him to do when he got home. Miss Sara cried and us cried, too. Jim never married and day's why Miss Sara had to do everything, 'cause she was his sister what lived with him.

I run on Broad River for over twenty-four years as boatman carrying Marse Jim's cotton to Columbia for him. Us had de excitement on dem trips. Lots times water was deeper dan a tree is high. Sometimes I was throwed and fell in da water. I rise up every time, though, and float and swim back to de boat and get on again. If de weather be hot, I never think of changing no clothes, but just keep on what I got wet. Five niggers always went on Marse's boat. One man steer de boat and of course he was de steerman, and dat what he went by. I recollects two steermans, Bradley Kennedy and Andy McCluny. Charlie Gilliam was de second steerman, by dat I means he de young nigger dat Bradley and Andy had to break in.

Sometimes Marster have three flatboats a-gwine down at one time, and I had recollections of as many as five a-gwine from our plantation. Dat was not so often, though. Us had long poles to steer de boats with. Den dere was some paddles, and some of de niggers was called privates dat handled de cotton and used de paddles when dey had to be used. Bateaus was what dey always used de paddles with. Privates did de shoving and other heavy work. De seconds and de privates always shoved with de poles when de water was rough, and de steerman give orders. I was always a boatman.

Charlie Gilliam acted as boatman, some; and den de other boatmen was: Bill Hughes, Warren Worthy, Green Stokes, and John Glenn. Dey made de poles to suit de job. Some of de poles was longer dan others was. Some of dem was broad and flat at de end; others was blunt, and others was made sharp. When de Broad River rose, sometimes de waves got higher dan my house dere. Den it was a real job to handle one of Marse's boats. Fact is, it was five men's jobs. With water a-roaring and a-foaming and a-gwine round you like a mad tiger a-blowing his breath, so dat you was scared dat all your marster's cotton gwine to be spilt, you had to be up and a-doing something real fast. Sometimes dat river take your boat round and round like a merry-go-round, till you get so swimmy-headed dat you have to puke up all de victuals dat you done eat. Den it swing from dat whirl into a swift stream dat take you a mile a minute, yes sir, a mile a minute for I don't know how far.

Den you see a tree a-coming right straight to you. If de boat hit dat tree, you knowed dat you be busted into a million pieces. You had to get your poles and somebody had to let a pole hit dat tree ahead of de boat. Of course dat change de boat's course from de tree and you went sailing on by. Once in a freshet us raced twenty-five miles in twenty-five minutes. Marse Jim was with us dat time, and he told us so by his watch. De water a-jumping real high and dat boat a-jumping still worse made me so scared dat I just shake in my knees and all de way up and down my legs.

On dis trip we had went plumb up in North Carolina. Us never had been dat far up before. I ain't never seed North Carolina before; neither is I seed it since. Broad River was real narrow when we went up and she look like a lamb. But when we come down it had done and took and rained and dem banks was vanished. Dat water sure did rare up dere to get back in its regular channel. De rocks up dere was more scary looking dan dey is where it run through Union to Columbia. Dat night we run into a nine-mile shoal. Couldn't none de niggers keep dat boat offen dat shoal it was so powerful. Dat is, de water just took dat boat plumb smack outen our hands. But it throwed our boat in shallow water and of course dat made it drag. Good dat it never drug over no sharp rocks—and dey was setting all around us—but it happened dat it hit sand. We camped dere for de night. By morning we had done gone a quarter mile from de channel.

When we et, we worked de boat out into de main channel again. Den we staked her to a tree and took a look around before we started down stream for Union. Dat seemed far off right den. Finally de master boatman give de order, "Shove off, boys!" We shoved and we fell into a clear open channel and our boat went a-skeeting downstream. We never had to hit a lick, but she went so fast dat we was all scared to take a long breath. Finally Marster said, "Boys, see dem willow trees down yonder; well, steer her to run over dem so dat she will slack her speed." Us did, but it never deadened our speed a mite, dat us could see. Marster shake his head and allow, "Bound fer hell, maybe, boys."

Got to Cherokee Falls with water so high couldn't tell no falls dere. Marster say, "Lay her to de right, we can't wreck dis boat without putting up a honest man's fight." Den he say, "If us does, us'll sure go to hell." We tried to swing her by grabbing to a big willow, and we broke a lot of limbs in trying, but we did swing her and she run a hundred yards without steering, and de boat landed on a little mountain of land. Marse allow, "Ain't never seed such a ocean of water since I was eighteen years old, damned if I have." He looked at me and say, "Don't know whether Dick scared or not, but he sure is a brave man." I was a-setting my feets on land den, and I look at him and allow, "No sir, I ain't scared, why I could come over dat little place in my bateau." Truth is, dat I was so scared dat I wasn't scared. We lay over a day and a half. De water had done receded back some, and we come twenty-seven miles down to Lockhart Shoals in dat one day. De water was still so high dat we run over de shoals without a tremor. Come sailing on down to Fish Dam and went over de Fish Dam and never knowed dat it was dere. Den we landed at de road with everybody safe but still scared.

Dere was two Charlie Gilmores; one was killed right below Fish Dam. He was hit in de head by a private. When de private was cutting de boat, Charlie got in de way of de pole and it hit him in one of his temples and he fell over in de water dead. When dey got him, wasn't nary drap of water in his lungs, dat's how come us knowed dat he was kilt straight out. Some says dat he was hit in de ear, but anyway it was on a tender spot and de lick sure done him up. Nothing wasn't done to de private, 'cause it was all accidental and Marse and everybody felt sorry for him.

On river trips, we took rations such as meat, bread, and cabbage, and us catch all de fish dat we wanted and had coffee. We each took day in and day out to cook, dat is, all dem dat could halfway cook did dat.

SAM KILGORE
Interviewed at Fort Worth, Texas
Interviewer not identified
Age when interviewed: 92

You asks me when I'se born and was I born a slave. Well, I'se born on July 17, 1845, so I'se a slave for twenty years, and had three massas. I'se born in Williamson County, near Memphis, in Tennessee. Massa John Peacock owned de plantation and am it de big one! Dere am a thousand acres and about a thousand slaves.

De slave cabins am in rows, twenty in de first row, and eighteen in de second, and sixteen in de third. Den dere am house servants' quarters near de Big House. De cabins am logs and not much in dem but homemade tables and benches and bunks beside de wall. Each family has deir own cabin and sometimes dere am ten or more in de family, so it am kind of crowded. But Massa am good and let dem have de family life, and once each week de rations am measure out by a old darky what have charge de commissary, and dere am always plenty to eat.

But dem eats ain't like nowadays. It am home-cured meat and mostly cornmeal, but plenty veg'tables and 'lasses and brown sugar. Massa raised lots of hogs, what am Berkshires and razorbacks. Razorback meat am considered de best and sweetest.

De work stock am eighty head of mules and fifty head of hosses and fifteen yoke of oxen. It took plenty feed for all dem and Massa have de big field of corn, far as we could see. De plantation am run on system and everything clean and in order, not like lots of plantations with tools scattered around and dirt piles here and there. De chief overseer am white and de second overseers am black. Stein was nigger overseer in de shoemakin' and harness, and Aunty Darkins am overseer of de spinnin' and weavin'.

Dat place am so well manage dat whippin' am not necessary. Massa have he own way of keepin' de niggers in line. If dey bad he say, "I expect dat nigger driver comin' round tomorrow and I'se gwine sell you." Now, when a nigger get in de hands of de nigger driver it am de big chance he'll get sold to de cruel massa, and dat make de niggers powerful skeert, so dey behaves. On de next plantation we'd hear de niggers pleadin' when dey's whipped, "Massa, have mercy!" and such. Our massa always say, "Boys, you hears dat misery and we don't want no such on dis place and it am up to you." So us all behaves ourselves.

When I'se four years old I'se took to de Big House by young Massa Frank, old Massa's son. He have me for de errand boy and, I guess, for de plaything. When I gits bigger I'se his valet and he like me and I sure like him. He am kind and smart, too, and am choosed from nineteen other boys to go to England and study at de military academy. I'se about eight when we starts for Liverpool. We goes from Memphis to Newport and takes de boat, *Bessie*. It am a sailboat and den de fun starts for sure. It am summer and not much wind and sometimes we just stand still day after day in de fog so thick we can't see from one end de boat to de other.

I'll never forget dat trip. When we gets far out on de water, I'se dead sure we'll never get back to land again. First I takes de seasick and dat am something. If there am anything worser it can't be stood! It ain't possible to explain it, but I wants to die, and if dey's anything worser dan dat seasick misery, I says de Lord have mercy on dem. I can't believe dere am so much stuff in one person, but plenty come out of me. I almost raised de ocean! When dat am over I gets homesick and so do Massa Frank. I cries and he tries to console me and den he gets tears in he eyes. We am weeks on dat water, and good old Tennessee am allus on our mind.

When we gets to England it am all right, but often we goes down to de warf and looks over de cotton bales for dat Memphis gin mark. Couple times Massa Frank finds some and he say, "Here a bale from home, Sam," with he voice full of joy like a kid what find some candy. We stands round dat bale and wonders if it am raised on de plantation.

But we has de good time after we gets acquainted and I seed lots and gets to know some West India niggers. But we's ready to come home and when we gets dere it am plenty war. Massa Frank joins de 'Federate Army and course I'se his valet and goes with him, right over to Camp Carpenter, at Mobile. He am de lieutenant under General Gordon and before long dey pushes him higher. Finally he gets notice he am to be a colonel and dat separates us, 'cause he has to go to Floridy. "I'se gwine with you," I says, for I thinks I belongs to him and he belongs to me and can't nothing part us. But he say, "You can't go with me this time. Dey's gwine put you in de army." Den I cries and he cries.

I'se seventeen years old when I puts my hand on de Book and am a soldier. I talks to my captain about Massa Frank and wants to go to see him. But it wasn't more'n two weeks after he leaves dat him was kilt. Dat am de awful shock to me and it am a long time before I gets over it. I always feels if I'd been with him maybe I could save his life.

My company am moved to Birmingham and builds breastworks. Dey say General Lee am comin' for a battle but he didn't ever come and when I been back to see dem breastworks, dey never been used. We marches north to Lexington in Kentuck' but am gone before de battle to Louisville. We comes back to Salem, in Georgia, but I'se never in no big battle, only some skirmishes now and den. We always fixes for de battles and builds bridges and doesn't fight much.

I goes back after de War to Memphis. My mammy am on de Kilgore place and Massa Kilgore takes her and my pappy and two hundred other slaves and comes to Texas. Dat how I gets here. He settles at de place called Kilgore, and it was named after him, but in 1867 he moves to Cleburne.

Before we moved to Texas de Klu Kluxers done burn my mammy's house and she lost everything. Dey was about a hundred dollars in green-backs in dat house and a three hundred pound hog in de pen, what die from de heat. We done run to Massa Rodger's house. De riders gets so bad dey come most any time and run cullud folks off for no cause, just to be ornery and plunder de home. But one day I seed Massa Rogers take a dozen guns out his wagon and he and some men digs a ditch round de cotton field close to de road. Couple nights after dat de riders come and when dey gets near dat ditch a volley am fired and lots of dem draps off dey hosses. Dat ended de Klux trouble in dat section.

After I been in Texas a year I joins de Federal army for de Indian war. I'se in de transportation division and drives oxen and mules, haulin' supplies to de forts. We goes to Fort Griffin and Dodge City and Laramie, in Wyoming. Dere am always two or three hundred soldiers with us, to watch for Indian attacks. Dey travels on hosses, ahead, beside, and behind de wagon. One day de sentinel reports Indians am round so we gets hid in de trees and brush. On a high ledge off to de west we sees de Indians travelin' north, two abreast. De lieutenant say he counted about seven hundred but dey sure missed us, or maybe I'd not be here today.

I stays in de service for seven years and den goes back to Johnson County, farmin' on de Rodgers place, and stays till I comes to Fort Worth in 1889. Den I gets into another war, de Spanish 'Merican War. But I'se in de commissary work so don't see much fightin'. In all dem wars I sees almost no fightin', 'cause I always works with de supplies.

After dat war I goes to work laborin' for buildin' contractors. I works for several, den gets with Mr. Bardon and learns de cement work with him. He am awful good man to work for, dat John Bardon. Finally I starts my own cement business and am still runnin' it. My health am good and I'se always on de job, 'cause dis home I owns has to be kept up. It cost several thousand dollars and I can't afford to neglect it.

I'se married twice. I marries Mattie Norman in 1901 and separates in 1904. She could spend more money den two niggers could shovel it in. Den I marries Lottie Young in 1909, but dere am no chillens. I'se never dat lucky.

I'se voted every election and believes it de duty for every citizen to vote.

Now, I'se told you everything from Genesis to Rev'lations, and it de truth, as I 'members it.

SILVIA KING

Interviewed at Marlin, Texas
Interviewer not identified
Age when interviewed: 100

I KNOW I WAS borned in Morocco, in Africa, and was married and had three chillen before I was stoled from my husband. I don't know who it was stole me, but dey took me to France, to place called Bordeaux, and drugs me with some coffee, and when I knows anything about it, I'se in de bottom of a boat with a whole lot of other niggers. It seem like we was in dat boat forever, but we comes to land, and I'se put on de block and sold. I finds out afterwards from my white folks it was in New Orleans where dat block was, but I didn't know it den.

We was all chained and dey strips all our clothes off and de folks what gwine buys us comes round and feels us all over. Iffen any de niggers don't want to take dere clothes off, de man gets a long, black whip and cuts dem up hard. I'se sold to a planter what had a big plantation in

Fayette County, right here in Texas, don't know no name 'cept Marse Jones.

Marse Jones, he am awful good, but de overseer was de meanest man I ever knowed, a white man name Smith, what boasts about how many niggers he done kilt. When Marse Jones seed me on de block, he say, "Dat's a whale of a woman." I'se scairt and can't say nothin', 'cause I can't speak English. He buys some more slaves and dey chains us together and marches us up near La Grange, in Texas. Marse Jones done gone on ahead and de overseer marches us. Dat was a awful time, 'cause us am all chained up and whatever one does us all has to do. If one drinks out of de stream we all drinks, and when one gets tired or sick, de rest has to drag and carry him. When us get to Texas, Marse Jones raise de devil with dat white man what had us on de march. He get de doctor man and tell de cook to feed us and lets us rest up.

After while, Marse Jones say to me, "Silvia, am you married?" I tells him I got a man and three chillen back in de old country, but he don't understand my talk and I has a man give to me. I don't bother with dat nigger's name much, he just Bob to me. But I fit him good and plenty till de overseer shakes a blacksnake whip over me.

Marse Jones and Old Miss finds out about my cookin' and takes me to de Big House to cook for dem. De dishes and things was awful queer to me, to what I been brung up to use in France. I mostly cooks after dat, but I'se de powerful big woman when I'se young and when dey gets in a tight spot I helps out.

Before long Marse Jones 'cides to move. He always say he goin' get where he can't hear de neighbor's cow horn, and he do. Dere ain't nothin' but woods and grass land, no houses, no roads, no bridges, no neighbors, nothin' but woods and wild animals. But he builds a mighty fine house with a stone chimney six foot square at de bottom. De sill was a foot square and de house am made of logs, but dey splits out two inch plank and puts it outside de logs, from ground clean up to de eaves. Dere wasn't no nails, but dey whittles out pegs. Dere was a well out de back and a well on de back porch by de kitchen door. It had a wheel and a rope. Dere was another well by de barns and one or two around de quarters, but dey am fixed with a long pole sweep. In de kitchen was de big fireplace and de big back logs am haul to de house. De oxen pull dem dat far and some men takes poles and rolls dem in de fireplace. Marse Jones never allow dat fire go out from October till May, and in de fall Marse or one he sons lights de fire with a flint rock and some powder.

De stores was a long way off and de white folks loans seed and things to each other. If we has de toothache, de blacksmith pulls it. My husband manages de ox teams. I cooks and works in Old Miss' garden and de orchard. It am big and fine and in fruit time all de women works from light to dark dryin' and 'servin' and de like.

Old Marse goin' feed you and see you quarters am dry and warm or knew de reason why. Most every night he goes round de quarters to see if dere any sickness or trouble. Everybody work hard but have plenty to eat. Sometimes de preacher tell us how to get to heaven and see de ring lights dere.

De smokehouse am full of bacon sides and cure hams and barrels lard and 'lasses. When a nigger want to eat, he just ask and get he passel. Old Miss always depend on me to spice de ham when it cure. I larnt dat back in de old country, in France.

Dere was spinnin' and weavin' cabins, long with a chimney in each end. Us women spins all de thread and weaves cloth for everybody, de white folks, too. I'se de cook, but times I hit de spinnin' loom and wheel fairly good. Us bleach de cloth and dyes it with barks.

Dere always de big woodpile in de yard, and de big caboose kettle for renderin' hog fat and beef tallow candles and makin' soap. Marse always have de niggers take some apples and make cider, and he make beer, too. Most all us had cider and beer when we want it, but nobody get drunk. Marse sure cut up if we do.

Old Miss have de floors sanded, dat where you sprinkles fine, white sand over de floor and sweeps it round in all kinds purty figgers. Us make a corn shuck broom.

Marse sure a fool about he hounds and have a mighty fine pack. De boys hunts wolves and panthers and wild game like dat. Dere was lots of wild turkey and droves of wild prairie chickens. Dere was rabbits and squirrels and Indian pudden', make of cornmeal. It am real tasty. I cooks goose and pork and mutton and bear meat and beef and deer meat, den makes de fritters and pies and dumplin's. Sure wish us had dat food now.

On de cold winter night I'se sat many a time spinnin' with two threads, one in each hand and one my feets on de wheel and de baby sleepin' on my lap. De boys and old men was always whittlin' and it wasn't just foolishment. Dey whittles traps and wooden spoons and needles to make seine nets and checkers and sleds. We all sits workin' and singin' and smokin' pipes. I likes my pipe right now, and has two clay pipes and keeps dem under de pillow. I don't aim for dem pipes to get out my sight. I been smokin' close to a hundred years now and it takes two cans tobaccy de week to keep me goin'.

Dere wasn't many doctors dem days, but always de closet full of samples* and most all de old women could get medicine out de woods. Every spring, Old Miss line up all de chillen and give dem a dose of garlic and rum.

De chillen all played together, black and white. De young ones purty handy trappin' quail and partridges and such. Dey didn't shoot if dey could catch it some other way, 'cause powder and lead am scarce. Dey catch de deer by makin' de salt lick, and uses a spring pole to cotch pigeons and birds.

De black folks gets off down in de bottom and shouts and sings and prays. Dey gets in de ring dance. It am just a kind of shuffle, den it get faster and faster and dey gets warmed up and moans and shouts and claps and dances. Some gets exhausted and drops out and de ring gets

* Home remedies.

closer. Sometimes dey sings and shouts all night, but come break of day
de nigger got to get to he cabin. Old Marse got to tell dem de tasks of de
day.

Old black Tom have a li'l bottle and have spell roots and water in it
and sulphur. He sure could find out if a nigger goin' get whipped. He have
a string tie round it and say, "By sum Peter, by sum Paul, by de God dat
make us all, Jack don't you tell me no lie, if Marse goin' whip Mary, tell
me." Sure's you born, if dat jack turn to de left, de nigger get de whippin',
but if Marse ain't make up he mind to whip, dat jack stand and quiver.

White folks just go through de woods and don't know nothin'. You digs
out splinters from de north side a old pine tree what been struck by
lightnin', and gets dem hot in a iron skillet and burns dem to ashes; den
you puts dem in a brown paper sack. Iffen de officers gets you and you
goin' have it before de judge, you gets de sack and goes outdoors at
midnight and hold de bag of ashes in you hand and look up at de moon—
but don't you open you mouth. Next mornin' get up early and go to de
courthouse and sprinkle dem ashes in de doorway and dat law trouble, it
goin' get tore up just like de lightnin' done tore up dat tree.

De shoestring root am powerful strong. Iffen you chews on it and spits
a ring round de person what you wants somethin' from, you goin' get it.
You can get more money or a job or most anythin' dat way. I had a black
cat bone, too, but it got away from me.

I'se got a big frame and used to weigh two hundred pounds, but dey
tells me I only weighs a hundred now. I lives with de youngest son of my
grandson, who was de son of my youngest daughter. My Marse he
knowed General Houston and I seed him many a time. I lost what teeth
I had a long time ago and in 1920 two more new teeth come through.
Dem teeth sure did worry me and I'se glad when dey went, too.

GEORGE KYE
Interviewed at Fort Gibson, Oklahoma
Interviewer not identified
Age when interviewed: 110

I WAS BORN in Arkansas under Mr. Abraham Stover, on a big farm
about twenty miles north of Van Buren. I was plumb grown when
the Civil War come along, but I can remember back when the Cherokee
Indians was in all that part of the country.

Joe Kye was my pappy's name what he was born under back in Garrison
County, Virginia, and I took that name when I was freed, but I don't

know whether he took it or not because he was sold off by old Master Stover when I was a child. I never have seen him since. I think he wouldn't mind good, leastways that what my mammy say.

My mammy was named Jennie and I don't think I had any brothers or sisters, but they was a whole lot of children at the quarters that I played and lived with. I didn't live with Mammy because she worked all the time, and us children all stayed in one house. It was a little one room log cabin, chinked and daubed, and you couldn't stir us with a stick. When we went to eat we had a big pan and all ate out of it. One what ate the fastest got the most.

Us children wore homespun shirts and britches and little slips, and nobody but the big boys wore any britches. I wore just a shirt until I was about twelve years old, but it had a long tail down to my calves. Four or five of us boys slept in one bed, and it was made of hewed logs with rope laced across it and a shuck mattress. We had stew made out of pork and potatoes, and sometimes greens and pot liquor, and we had ash cake mostly, but biscuits about once a month. In the winter time I had brass toed shoes made on the place, and a cloth cap with ear flaps.

The work I done was hoeing and plowing, and I rid a horse a lot for Old Master because I was a good rider. He would send me to run chores for him, like going to the mill. He never beat his Negroes, but he talked mighty cross and glared at us until he would nearly scare us to death sometimes.

He told us the rules and we lived by them and didn't make trouble, but they was a neighbor that had some mean Negroes and he nearly beat them to death. We could hear them hollering in the field sometimes. They would sleep in the cotton rows and run off, and then they would catch the cat-o-nine-tails sure 'nough. He would chain them up too, and keep them tied out to trees, and when they went to the field they would be chained together in bunches sometimes after they had been cutting up.

We didn't have no place to go to church, but Old Master didn't care if we had singing and praying, and we would tie our shoes on our backs and go down the road close to the white church and all set down and put our shoes on and go up close and listen to the service. Old Master was baptized almost every Sunday and cussed us all out on Monday. I didn't join the church until after freedom, and I always was a scoundrel for dancing. My favorite preacher was old Pete Conway. He was the only ordained colored preacher we had after freedom, and he married me.

Old Master wouldn't let us take herb medicine, and he got all our medicine in Van Buren when we was sick. But I wore a buckeye on my neck just the same.

When the War came along I was a grown man, and I went off to serve because Old Master was too old to go, but he had to send somebody anyways. I served as George Stover, but every time the sergeant would call out "Abe Stover," I would answer, "Here."

They had me driving a mule team wagon that Old Master furnished, and I went with the Sesesh soldiers from Van Buren to Texarkana and back a dozen times or more. I was in the War two years, right up to the day of freedom. We had a battle close to Texarkana and another big one near Van Buren, but I never left Arkansas and never got a scratch. One time in the Texarkana battle I was behind some pine trees and the bullets cut the limbs down all over me. I dug a big hole with my bare hands before I hardly knowed how I done it.

One time two white soldiers named Levy and Briggs come to the wagon train and said they was hunting slaves for some purpose. Some of us black boys got scared because we heard they was going to Squire Mack and get a reward for catching runaways, so me and two more lit out of there. They took out after us and we got to a big mound in the woods and hid. Somebody shot at me and I rolled into some bushes. He rid up and got down to look for me but I was on t'other side of his horse and he never did see me. When they was gone we went back to the wagons just as the regiment was pulling out and the officer didn't say nothing.

They was eleven Negro boys served in my regiment for their masters. The first year was mighty hard because we couldn't get enough to eat. Some ate poke greens without no grease and took down and died.

How I knowed I was free, we was bad licked, I reckon. Anyways, we quit fighting and a Federal soldier come up to my wagon and say: "Whose mules?" "Abe Stover's mules," I says, and he tells me then, "Let me tell you, black boy, you are as free now as old Abe Stover his own self!" When he said that I jumped on top of one of them mule's back before I knowed anything!

I married Sarah Richardson, February 10, 1870, and had only eleven children. One son is a deacon and one grandson is a preacher. I am a good Baptist. Before I was married I said to the gal's old man, "I'll go to the mourners bench if you'll let me have Sal," and sure 'nough I joined up just a month after I got her. I am head of the Sunday school and deacon in the St. Paul Baptist church in Muskogee now. I lived about five miles from Van Buren until about twelve years ago when they found oil and then they run all the Negroes out and leased up the land. They never did treat the Negroes good around there anyways.

HENRY LEWIS

Interviewed at Beaumont, Texas
Interviewer not identified
Age when interviewed: 102

OLD BOB CADE, he my massa, and Annie Cade, she my missus. Dey had a big plantation over in Louisiana and another in Jefferson County, out at Pine Island. I'se born a hundred and one year ago, on Christmas day, out at Pine Island. If I lives to see next Christmas day again, I'll be a hundred two year old.

My mammy she come from Mississippi and she named Judy Lewis. Washington Lewis, one de slaves on Massa Bob's Louisiana plantation, he my daddy. I can't 'member nobody else 'cept my great-gramma, Patsy. She's 130 when she die. She look awful, but den she my folks. My own dear mammy was 112 year old when she die. She have ten chillen and de biggest portion of dem born in slavery time. Dey two sisters older'n me, Mandy and Louise. I named after my daddy's brother Henry Lewis.

My white folks have a plantation in Louisiana, at Caginly, and stay over dere most de time. I 'member when Old Massa Bob used to come to Pine Island to stay a month or two, all us li'l chillen gather round him and he used to throw out two bitses and big one cent pieces 'mongst us, just to see us scramble for dem. When Christmas time come round dey give us a Christmas gift and a whole week for holiday.

I never been no nearer east dan Lake Charles and dat been lately, so I ain't never seen de old plantation. At Pine Island us have de big woods place with a hundred workin' hands, without de underlin's. All he niggers say Cade de good man. He hire he overseers and say, "You can correct dem for dey own good and make dem work right, but you ain't better cut dey hide or draw no blood." He get a-hold some mean overseers but dey didn't tarry long. He find out dey beatin' the niggers and den he beat dem and say, "How dat suit you?" Old Massa he a big, stocky Irishman with sandy hair, and he ain't had no beard or mustache. When he grow old he have de gout and he put de long mattress out on de gallery and lay down on it. He say, "Come here, my li'l niggers," and den he make us rub he foots so he can get to sleep.

Dey used to have old slavery-day judge and jury of white folks and dey hear de case and 'cide how many lashes to give de darky. Dey put de lash on dem, but dey never put no jail on dem. I seed some slaves in

204

chains and I heared of one massa what had de place in de fence with de hole cut out for de nigger's neck. Dey hoist up de board and de nigger put he head through de hole and den dey beat him with a lash with holes bored in it and every hole raise de blister. Den he bust dem blisters with de handsaw and dey put salt and pepper in de bucket water and annoint dem blisters with de mop dipped in de water. Dey do dat when dey in particular bad humor, iffen de nigger ain't chop 'nough cotton or corn. Sometime a overseer kilt a nigger, and dey don't do nothin' to him 'cept make him pay for de nigger. But our massa good.

Old Massa allow us praise God, but lots of massas didn't allow dem to get on dey knees. Us have church house and de white folks go in de mornin' and us go after dinner. Us used to sing:

> My knee-bones achin',
> My body's rackin' with pain,
> I calls myself de child of God,
> Heaven am my aim.
> If you don't believe I'se a child of God,
> Just meet me on dat other shore,
> Heaven is my home.
> I calls myself a child of God,
> I'se a long time on my way,
> But heaven am my home.

Old Massa have de house made out of hand-sawed planks in slavery times. It put together with homemade nails, dem spikes, square nails dey make deyselfs. It have de long gallery on it. De slaves have li'l log cabin house with mud-cut chimney on de side, and de furniture mostly Georgia hosses for beds and mattress made out of two sacks. Dey no floor in dem houses, 'cept what God put in dem.

When I six or seven year old dey 'cides I'se big 'nough to start ridin' hosses. Dey have de big cattle ranch and I ride all over dis territory. I'se too li'l to get on de hoss and dey lift me up, and dey have de real saddle for me, too. I couldn't get up, but I sure could stay up when I get dere. I'se just like a hoss-fly.

Beaumont was just a briarpatch in dem times, just one li'l store and one blacksmith shop, and Massa John Herring he own dat. Dat de way I first see my wife, ridin' de range. De Cade brand was a lazy RC dat done registered before I'se born. Us brand from de first of March to de fifteenth of December.

Old Massa have de big field divided in tracts and each slave could have a part and raise what he want. Us have good clothes, too, wool for winter and cotton for summer. Us have six suits de year, underwear and all. Dey a trunk like in de cabin for Sunday clothes and de rest hang on a peg.

Us have plenty food to eat, too. Beef and hogs and bacon and syrup and sugar and flour was plenty. All de possums and rabbits and fish and such was just dat much more. He give us de barrel of whiskey every year, too.

Dey allow de li'l chillen lots of playtime and no hard tasks. Us play stick hoss and seven-up marble game with marbles us make and de "well-game." De gal or boy set in de chair and lean way back and pretend like dey in de well. Dey say dey so many feet down and say, "Who you want pull you out?" And de one you want pull you out, dey s'posed to kiss you.

Dey used to be nigger traders what come through de country with de herd of niggers, just like cattlemen with de herd of cattle. Dey fix camp and den have a pen on de ridge of town and people what want to buy more slaves go dere. Dey have a block and make de slaves get up on dat. Maybe one man say, "I give you, two hundred dollars," and when dey's through de slave sold to de highest bidder. Old Massa warn us look out and not let de trader cotch us, 'cause a trader just as soon steal a nigger and sell him.

De patterrollers come round before de War to see if de massas treat dere slaves good. My wife's gramma say dey come round to her massa's place, but before dey get dere he take a meat skin and make dem rub it round dey mouth and get dey face all greasy so it look like dey have plenty to eat, and he tell dem dey better tell de patterrollers dey gettin' plenty to eat. But dere one big nigger say, "Please take me with you, 'cause if you don't Massa gwine to kill me when you get gone."

Old Massa he die before de War and den he son, John Cade, take over de place, and he brothers help. Dey named Overton and Taylor and Bob, Junior. Us all want to get free and talk about it in de quarters amongst ourselfs, but we ain't say nothin' where de white folks heared us.

When de War come on I seed soldiers every day. Dey have de camp in Liberty and I watches dem. I heared de guns, too, maybe at Sabine Pass, but I didn't see no actual fightin'. Dat a long year to wait, de last year of de War. Dey sent de papers down on March fifth, I done heared, but dey didn't turn us loose den. Dis de last state to turn de slaves free. When dey didn't let dem go in March, de Yankee soldiers come in June and make dem let us go. Next mornin' after de soldiers come, de overseer reads de papers out and say we's free as he is and we can go. Some stay on de old place a long time and some go off. You know, dey just slaves and wasn't civilized. Some ain't never got civilized yet. Old Massa never give us nothin', but he told us we could stay on iffen we want, but I left.

I goes down to Anahuac and builds a li'l log cabin at Monroe City, and dat's where dey puttin' in oil wells now. Washington Lewis, dat my daddy, he have 129 acres dere. De white folks say to sign de paper to let dem put de well on it and dey give us fifty dollars and us sign dat paper and dey have de land.

I marries in slavery time, when I'se about twenty-two year old. My first wife named Rachel and she live on Double Bayou. She belong to de Mayes place. I see her when I ridin' de range for Massa Bob. I tells Massa I wants to get marry and he make me ask Massa Mayes and us have de big weddin'. She dress all in white. I have de nice hat and suit of black clothes and Daddy a shoemaker and make me de good pair of shoes to get marry in. Us stand front of Massa Mayes and he read out de Bible. Us had a real big supper and some de white folks give us money.

De first money I makes am workin' for de government in Galveston. After de War de government hire folks to clean up de trash what de fightin' make and I am hired. Dey lots of wood and stones and brick and trees and such dem big guns knock down.

I goes back to ridin' de prairie and rides till I'se ninety-four year old. When I quits I'se out workin', tendin' Mr. Langham's chickens and I forgets it Christmas and my birthday till Mr. Langham comes ridin' out with my money. Dat's de last work I done and dat in 1931 and I'se ninety-four year old, like I say. I bet dese 1900 niggers ain't gwine live dat long.

MARY LINDSAY

Interviewed at Tulsa, Oklahoma
Interviewer not identified
Age when interviewed: 91

MY SLAVERY DAYS wasn't like most people tell you about, 'cause I was give to my young mistress and sent away to Texas when I was just a little girl, and I didn't live on a big plantation a very long time.

I got an old family Bible what say I was born on September 20, 1846, but I don't know who put de writing in it unless it was my mammy's mistress. My mammy had de book when she die.

My mammy come out to the Indian country from Mississippi two years before I was born. She was the slave of a Chickasaw part-breed named Sobe Love. He was the kinfolks of Mr. Benjamin Love, and Mr. Henry Love what bring two big bunches of the Chickasaws out from Mississippi to the Choctaw country when the Chickasaws sign up de treaty to leave Mississippi, and the whole Love family settle round on the Red River below Fort Washita. There is where I was born.

My mammy say dey have a terrible hard time against the sickness when they first come out into that country, because it was low and swampy and all full of cane brakes, and everybody have the smallpox and the malaria and fever all the time. Lots of the Chickasaw families nearly died off.

Old Sobe Love marry Mammy off to a slave named William, what belong to a full-blood Chickasaw man name Chick-a-lathe, and I was one of de children. De children belong to the owner of the mother, and me and my brother, Franklin, what we called "Bruner," was born under the name of Love and then old Master Sobe bought my pappy

William, and we was all Love slaves then. My mammy had two more girls, name Hetty and Rena.

My mammy name was Mary, and I was named after her. Old Mistress' name was Lottie, and they had a daughter name Mary. 'Cause my name was Mary, and so was my mammy's and my young Mistress' too, Old Master Sobe called me Mary-Ka-Chubbe to show which Mary he was talking about.

Old Master Sobe was powerful rich, and he had about a hundred slaves and four or five big pieces of that bottom land broke out for farms. He had niggers on all the places, but didn't have no overseers, just hisself, and he went around and seen that everybody behave and do they work right.

Old Master Sobe was a mighty big man in the tribe, and so was all his kinfolks, and they went to Fort Washita and to Boggy Depot and the time on business, and leave the Negroes to look after Old Mistress and the young daughter. She was almost grown along about that time, when I can first remember about things.

Miss Mary have a black woman name Vici what wait on her all the time and do the carding and spinning and cooking around the house, and Vici belong to Miss Mary. I never did go around the Big House, but just stayed in the quarters with my mammy and pappy and helped in the field a little.

Then one day Miss Mary run off with a man and married him, and Old Master Sobe nearly went crazy! The man was name Bill Merrick, and he was a poor blacksmith and didn't have two pair of britches to his name, and Old Master Sobe said he just stole Miss Mary 'cause she was rich, and no other reason. 'Cause he was a white man and she was mostly Chickasaw Indian. Old Master wouldn't even speak to Mr. Bill, and wouldn't let him set foot on the place. He just reared and pitched around, and threatened to shoot him if he set eyes on him, and Mr. Bill took Miss Mary and let out for Texas. He set up a blacksmith shop on the big road between Bonham and Honey Grove, and lived there until he died.

Miss Mary done took Vici along with her, and pretty soon she come back home and stay awhile, and Old Master Sobe kind of soften up a little bit and give her some money to get started on, and he give her me, too.

Dat just nearly broke my old mammy's and pappy's heart, to have me took away off from them, but they couldn't say nothing, and I had to go along with Miss Mary back to Texas. When we got away from the Big House I just cried and cried until I couldn't hardly see, my eyes was so swole up, but Miss Mary said she gwine to be good to me.

I ask her how come Master Sobe didn't give her some of the grown boys and she say she reckon it because he didn't want to help her husband out none, but just wanted to help her. If he give her a man her husband have him working in the blacksmith shop, she reckon.

Master Bill Merrick was a hard worker, and he was more sober than most the men in them days, and he never told me to do nothing. He just let Miss Mary tell me what to do. They have a log house close to the shop and a little patch of a field at first, but after awhile he got more land, and then Miss Mary tell me and Vici we got to help in the field too.

That sure was hard living then! I have to get up at three o'clock sometimes so I have time to water the hosses and slop the hogs and feed the chickens and milk the cows, and then get back to the house and get the breakfast. That was during the times when Miss Mary was having and nursing her two children, and old Vici had to stay with her all the time. Master Bill never did do none of that kind of work, but he had to be in the shop sometimes until way late in the night, and sometimes before daylight, to shoe people's hosses and oxen, and fix wagons. He never did tell me to do that work, but he never done it his own self and I had to do it if anybody do it.

He was the slowest one white man I ever did see. He just move round like de dead lice falling offen him all the time, and every time he go to say anything he talk so slow that when he say one word you could walk from here to way over there before he say de next word. He don't look sick, and he was powerful strong in his arms, but he act like he don't feel good just the same.

I remember when the War come. Mostly by the people passing along the big road, we heard about it. First they was a lot of wagons hauling farm stuff into town to sell, and then purty soon they was soldiers on the wagons, and they was coming out into the country to get the stuff and buying it right at the place they find it.

Then purty soon they commence to be little bunches of mens in soldier clothes riding up and down the road going somewhere. They seem like they was mostly young boys like, and they just laughing and jollying and going on like they was on a picnic.

Then the soldiers come round and got a lot of the white men and took them off to the War even if they didn't want to go. Master Bill never did want to go, 'cause he had his wife and two little children, and anyways he was getting all the work he could do fixing wagons and shoeing hosses, with all the traffic on de road at that time. Master Bill had just two hosses, for him and his wife to ride and to work the buggy, and he had one old yoke of oxen and some more cattle. He got some kind of paper in town and he kept it with him all the time, and when the soldiers would come to get his hosses or his cattle he would just draw that paper on 'em and they let 'em alone.

By and by the people got so thick on the big road that they was somebody in sight all the time. They just keep a dust kicked up all day and all night 'cepting when it rain, and they get all bogged down and be strung all up and down the road camping. They kept Master Bill in the shop all the time, fixing the things they bust trying to get the wagons outen the mud. They was whole families of them with they children and they slaves along, and they was coming in from every place because the Yankees was getting in their part of the country, they say.

We all get mighty scared about the Yankees coming but I don't reckon they ever got there, 'cause I never seen none, and we was right on the big road and we would of seen them. They was a whole lot more soldiers in them brown looking jeans, roundabout jackets and cotton britches a-faunching up and down the road on their hosses, though. Them hoss soldiers would come boiling by, going east, all day and night, and then two-three days later on dey would all come tearing by going west! Dey acted like dey didn't know where dey gwine, but I reckon dey did.

Den Master Bill get sick. I reckon he more wore out and worried than anything else, but he go down with de fever one day and it raining so hard Mistress and me and Vici can't neither one go nowhere to get no help. We puts peach tree poultices on his head and wash him off all the time, until it quit raining so Mistress can go out on de road, and then a doctor man come from one of the bunches of soldiers and see Master Bill. He say he going be all right and just keep him quiet and go on.

Mistress have to tend de children and Vici have to take care of Master Bill and look after the house, and dat leave me all by myself with all the rest of everything around the place. I got to feed all the stock and milk the cows and work in the field, too. Dat the first time I ever try to plow, and I nearly got killed! I got me a young yoke of oxens I broke to pull the wagon, 'cause Vici have to use the old oxens to work the field. I had to take the wagon and go about ten miles west to a patch of woods Master Bill owned to get firewood, 'cause we lived right on a flat patch of prairie, and I had to chop and haul the wood by myself. I had to get post oak to burn in the kitchen fireplace and willow for Master Bill to make charcoal out of to burn in his blacksmith fire.

Well, I hitched up them young oxen to the plow and they won't follow the row, and so I go get the old oxens. One of them old oxens didn't know me and took in after me, and I couldn't hitch 'em up. And then it begins to rain again.

After the rain was quit I get the bucket and go milk the cows, and it is time to water the hosses too, so I started to the house with the milk and leading one of the hosses. When I gets to the gate I draws the halter across my arm and hooks the bucket of milk on my arm, too, and starts to open the gate. The wind blow the gate wide open, and it slap the hoss on the flank. That was when I nearly got killed! Out the hoss go through the gate to the yard, and down the big road and my arm all tangled up in the halter rope and me dragging on the ground! The first jump knock the wind out of me and I can't get loose, and that hoss drag me down the road on the run until he meet up with a passel of soldiers and they stop him. The next thing I knowed I was laying on the back kitchen gallery, and some soldiers was pouring water on me with a bucket. My arm was broke, and I was stove up so bad that I have to lay down for a whole week, and Mistress and Vici have to do all the work.

Just as I getting able to walk round here come some soldiers and say they come to get Master Bill for the War. He still in the bed sick, and so they leave a parole paper for him to stay until he get well, and then he got to go into Bonham and go with the soldiers to blacksmith for them that got the cannons, the man said.

Mistress take on and cry and hold onto the man's coat and beg, but it don't do no good. She say they don't belong in Texas but they belong in the Chickasaw Nation, but he say that don't do no good, 'cause they living in Texas now. Master Bill just stew and fret so, one night his fever get way up and he go off into a kind of a sleep and about morning he died.

My broke arm begin to swell up and hurt me, and I got sick with it again, and Mistress got another doctor to come look at it. He say I got bad blood from it, how come I get so sick, and he got out his knife outen his satchel and bleed me in the other arm. The next day he come back and bleed me again two times, and the next day one more time, and then I got so sick I puke and he quit bleeding me.

While I still sick Mistress pick up and go off to the Territory to her pappy and leave the children there for Vici and me to look after. After while she come home for a day or two and go off again somewhere else. Then the next time she come home she say they been having big battles in the Territory and her pappy moved all his stuff down on the river, and she home to stay now.

We get along the best we can for a whole, winter, but we nearly starve to death, and then the next spring when we getting a little patch planted, Mistress go into Bonham and come back and say we all free and the War over. She say, "You and Vici just as free as I am, and a lot freer, I reckon, and they say I got to pay you if you work for me, but I ain't got no money to pay you. If you stay on with me and help me I will feed and home you and I can weave you some good dresses if you card and spin the cotton and wool."

Well, I stayed on, 'cause I didn't have no place to go, and I carded and spinned the cotton and wool and she make me just one dress. Vici didn't do nothing but just wait on the children and Mistress.

Mistress go off again about a week, and when she come back I see she got some money, but she didn't give us any of it. After while I asked her ain't she got some money for me, and she say, no, ain't she giving me a good home? Den I starts to feeling like I ain't treated right. Every evening I get done with the work and go out in the back yard and just stand and look off to the west towards Bonham, and wish I was at that place or some other place.

Den along come a nigger boy and say he working for a family in Bonham and he get a dollar every week. He say Mistress got some kinfolks in Bonham and some of Master Sobe Love's niggers living close to there. So one night I just put that new dress in a bundle and set foot right down the big road a-walking west, and don't say nothing to nobody! It's ten miles into Bonham, and I gets in town about daylight. I keeps on being afraid, 'cause I can't get it outen my mind I still belong to Mistress.

Purty soon some niggers tells me a nigger name Bruner Love living down west of Greenville, and I know that my brother Franklin, 'cause we all called him Bruner. I don't remember how all I gets down to Greenville, but I know I walks most the way, and I finds Bruner. Him and his wife working on a farm, and they say my sister Hetty and my sister Rena what was little is living with my mammy way back up on the Red River. My pappy done died in time of the War and I didn't know it.

Bruner taken me in a wagon and we went to my mammy, and I lived with her until she died and Hetty was married. Then I married a boy name Henry Lindsay. His people was from Georgia, and he live with them way west at Cedar Mills, Texas. That was right close to Gordon-ville, on the Red River. We live at Cedar Mills until my children was born and then we come to the Creek Nation in 1887. My last one was born there. My oldest is named Georgia on account of her pappy. He was born in Georgia and that was in 1838, so his white folks got a book that say. My next child was Henry. We called him William Henry, after my pappy and his pappy. Then come Donnie, and after we come here we had Madison, my youngest boy.

I lives with Henry here on this little place we got in Tulsa. When we first come here we got some land for fifteen dollars an acre from the Creek Nation, but our papers said we can only stay as long as it is the Creek Nation. Then in 1901 comes the allotments, and we found out our land belong to a Creek Indian, and we have to pay him to let us stay on it. After while he makes us move off and we lose out all around.

KIZIAH LOVE
Interviewed at Colbert, Oklahoma
Interviewer not identified
Age when interviewed: 93

LORD HELP US, I sure remembers all about slavery times, for I was a grown woman, married and had one baby when de War done broke out. That was a sorry time for some poor black folks but I guess Master Frank Colbert's niggers was about as well off as the best of 'em. I can recollect things that happened way back better than I can things that happen now.

Frank Colbert, a full blood Choctaw Indian, was my owner. He owned my mother but I don't remember much about my father. He died when I was a little youngun. My Mistress' name was Julie Colbert. She and Master Frank was de best folks that ever lived. All the niggers loved Master Frank and knowed just what he wanted done and they tried their best to do it, too.

I married Isom Love, a slave of Sam Love, another full-blood Indian that lived on a joining farm. We lived on Master Frank's farm and Isom went back and forth to work for his master and I worked ever day for mine. I don't 'spect we could of done that way if we hadn't of had Indian masters. They let us do a lot like we pleased just so we got our work done and didn't run off.

Old Master Frank never worked us hard and we had plenty of good food to eat. He never did like to put us under white overseers and never tried it but once. A white man come through here and stopped overnight. He looked round the farm and told Master Frank that he wasn't getting half what he ought to out of his rich land. He said he could take his bunch of hands and double his amout of corn and cotton. Master Frank told him that he never used white overseers, that he had one nigger that bossed around some when he didn't do it hisself. He also told the white man that he had one nigger named Bill that was kind of bad, that he was a good worker but he didn't like to be bothered as he liked to do his own work his own way. The white boss told him he wouldn't have any trouble and that he could handle him all right.

Old Master hired him and things went very well for a few days. He hadn't said anything to Bill and they had got along fine. I guess the new boss got to thinking it was time for him to take Bill in hand so one morning he told him to hitch up another team before he caught his own team to go to work.

Uncle Bill told him that he didn't have time, that he had a lot of plowing to get done that morning and besides it was customary for every man to catch his own team. Of course this made the overseer mad and he grabbed a stick and started cussing and run at Uncle Bill. Old Bill grabbed a single-tree and went meeting him. Dat white man all on a sudden turned round and run for dear life and I tell you, he fairly bust old Red River wide open getting away from there and nobody never did see hide nor hair of him round to this day.

Master Colbert run a stage stand and a ferry on Red River and he didn't have much time to look after his farm and his niggers. He had lots of land and lots of slaves. His house was a big log house, three rooms on one side and three on the other, and there was a big open hall between them. There was a big gallery clean across the front of the house. Behind the house was the kitchen and the smokehouse. The smokehouse was always filled with plenty of good meat and lard. They would kill the polecat and dress it and take a sharp stick and run it up their back jest under the flesh. They would also run one up each leg and then turn him on his back and put him on top of the house and let him freeze all night. The next morning they'd pull the sticks out and all the scent would be on them sticks and the cat wouldn't smell at all. They'd cook it like they did possum, bake it with 'taters or make dumplings.

We had plenty of salt. We got that from Grand Saline. Our coffee was make from parched meal or wheat bran. We make it from dried sweet potatoes that had been parched, too.

One of our choicest dishes was "Tom Pashofa," an Indian dish. We'd take corn and beat it in a mortar with a pestle. They took out the husks with a riddle and a fanner. The riddle was a kind of a sifter. When it was beat fine enough to go through the riddle we'd put it in a pot and cook it with fresh pork or beef. We cooked our bread in a Dutch oven or in the ashes.

When we got sick we would take butterfly root and life-everlasting and boil it and made a syrup and take it for colds. Balmony and queen's delight boiled and mixed would make good blood medicine.

The slaves lived in log cabins scattered back of the house. He wasn't afraid they'd run off. They didn't know as much as the slaves in the states, I reckon. But Master Frank had a half brother that was as mean as he was good. I believe he was the meanest man the sun ever shined on. His name was Buck Colbert and he claimed he was a patroller. He was sure bad to whip niggers. He'd stop a nigger and ask him if he had a pass and even if they did he'd read it and tell them they had stayed overtime and he'd beat 'em most to death. He'd say they didn't have any business off the farm and to get back there and stay there.

One time he got mad at his baby's nurse because she couldn't get the baby to stop crying and he hit her on the head with some fire tongs and she died. His wife got sick and she sent for me to come and take care of her baby. I sure didn't want to go and I begged so hard for them not to make me that they sent an older woman who had a baby of her own so she could nurse the baby, if necessary.

In the night the baby woke up and got to crying and Master Buck called the woman and told her to get him quiet. She was sleepy and was sort of slow and this make Buck mad and he made her strip her clothes off to her waist and he began to whip her. His wife tried to get him to quit and he told her he'd beat her if she didn't shut up. Sick as she was she slipped off and went to Master Frank's and woke him up and got him to go and make Buck quit whipping her. He had beat her so that she was cut up so bad she couldn't nurse her own baby any more.

Master Buck kept on being bad till one day he got mad at one of his own brothers and killed him. This made another one of his brothers mad and he went to his house and killed him. Everybody was glad that Buck was dead.

We had lots of visitors. They'd stop at the stage inn that we kept. One morning I was cleaning the rooms and I found a piece of money in the bed where two men had slept. I thought it was a dime and I showed it to my mammy and she told me it was a five dollar piece. I sure was happy, for I had been wanting some hoops for my skirts like Mistress had so Mammy said she would keep my money till I could send for the hoops. My brother got my money from my mammy and I didn't get my hoops for a long time. Miss Julie give me some later.

When me and my husband got married we built us a log cabin about halfway from Master Frank's house and Master Sam Love's house. I would go to work at Master Frank's and Isom would go to work at Master Sam's. One day I was at home with just my baby and a runner come by and said the Yankee soldiers was coming. I looked round and I knowed they would get my chickens. I had 'em in a pen right close to the house to keep the varmits from getting 'em, so I decided to take up the boards in the floor and put 'em in there as the wall logs come to the ground and they couldn't get out. By the time I got my chickens under the floor and the house locked tight the soldiers had got so close I could hear their bugles blowing so I just flew over to Old Master's house. Them Yankees clumb down the chimbley and got every one of my chickens and they killed about fifteen of Master Frank's hogs. He went down to their camp and told the captain about it and he paid him for his hogs and sent me some money for my chickens.

We went to church all the time. We had both white and colored preachers. Master Frank wasn't a Christian but he would help build brush arbors for us to have church under and we sure would have big meetings. One day Master Frank was going through the woods close to where niggers was having church. All on a sudden he started running and beating hisself and hollering and the niggers all went to shouting and saying "Thank the Lord, Master Frank has done come through!" Master Frank after a minute say, "Yes, through the worst of 'em." He had run into a yellow jacket's nest.

One night my old man's master sent him to Sherman, Texas. He aimed to come back that night, so I stayed at home with just my baby. It went to sleep so I set down on the steps to wait and every minute I thought I could hear Isom coming through the woods. All a sudden I heard a scream that fairly made my hair stand up. My dog that was laying out in the yard give a low growl and come and set down right by me. He kept growling real low. Directly, right close to the house I heard that scream again. It sounded like a woman in mortal misery. I run into the house and made the dog stay outside. I locked the door and then thought what must I do. Supposing Isom did come home now and should meet that awful thing? I heard it again. It wasn't more'n a hundred yards from the house. The dog scratched on the door but I dassent open it to let him in. I knowed by this time that it was a panther screaming. I turned my table over and put it against the opening of the fireplace. I didn't aim for that thing to come down the chimbley and get us.

Purty soon I heard it again a little mite further away—it was going on by. I heard a gun fire. Thank God, I said, somebody else heard it and was shooting at it. I set there on the side of my bed for the rest of the night with my baby in my arms and praying that Isom wouldn't come home. He didn't come till about nine o'clock the next morning and I was that glad to see him that I just cried and cried.

I ain't never seen many spirits but I've seen a few. One day I was laying on my bed here by myself. My son Ed was cutting wood. I'd been awful sick and I was powerful weak. I heard somebody walking real light like they was barefooted. I said, "Who's dat?"

He catch hold of my hand and he has the littlest hand I ever seen, and he say, "You been mighty sick and I want you to come and go with me to Sherman to see a doctor."

I say, "I ain't got nobody at Sherman what knows me."

He say, "You'd better come and go with me anyway."

I just lay there for a minute and didn't say nothing and purty soon he say, "Have you got any water?"

I told him the water was on the porch and he got up and went outside and I set in to calling Ed. He come hurrying and I asked him why he didn't lock the door when he went out and I told him to go see if he could see the little man and find out what he wanted. He went out and looked everywhere but he couldn't find him nor he couldn't even find his tracks.

I always keep a butcher knife near me but it was between the mattress and the featherbed and I couldn't get to it. I don't guess it would have done any good, though, for I guess it was just a spirit.

The funniest thing that ever happened to me was when I was a real young gal. Master and Miss Julie was going to see one of his sisters that was sick. I went along to take care of the baby for Miss Julie. The baby was about a year old. I had a bag of clothes and the baby to carry. I was riding a pacing mule and it was plumb gentle. I was riding along behind Master Frank and Miss Julie and I went to sleep. I lost the bag of clothes and never missed it. Purty soon I let the baby slip out of my lap and I don't know how far I went before I fell off myself and just think how I felt when I missed that baby! I turned around and went back and found the baby setting in the trail sort of crying. He wasn't hurt a mite, as he fell in the grass. I got off the mule and picked him up and had to look for a log so I could get back on again. Just as I got back on Master Frank rode up. He had missed me and come back to see what was wrong. I told him that I had lost the bag of clothes but I didn't say anything about losing the baby. We never did find the clothes and I sure kept awake the rest of the way. I wasn't going to risk losing that precious baby again! I guess the reason he didn't cry much was because he was an Indian baby. He was sure a sweet baby, though.

Just before the War people would come through the Territory stealing niggers and selling 'em in the states. Us women dassent get far from the house. We wouldn't even go to the spring if we happened to see a strange wagon or horsebacker. One of Master Sam Love's woman was stole and sold down in Texas. After freedom she made her way back to her family. Master Frank sent one of my brothers to Sherman on an errand. After several days the mule come back but we never did see my brother again. We didn't know whether he run off or was stole and sold.

I was glad to be free. I just clapped my hands together and said, "Thank God Almighty, I'se free at last!" I live on the forty acres that the government give me. I have been blind for nine years and don't get off my bed much. I live here with my son Ed. Isom has been dead for over forty years. I had fifteen children, but only ten of them are living.

JAMES LUCAS
Interviewed at Natchez, Mississippi
Interviewer not identified
Age at interview: 104

I WAS BORN on October 11, 1833. My young Marster give me my age when he heired de property of his uncle, Marse W. B. Withers. He was a-goin' through de papers and a-burnin' some of 'em when he found de one about me. Den he says, "Jim, dis one's about you. It gives you birthday."

I recollect a heap about slavery times, but I'se all by myself now. All o' my friends has left me. Even Marse Fleming has passed on. He was a little boy when I was a grown man.

I was born in a cotton field in cotton pickin' time, and de womens fixed my mammy up so she didn't hardly lose no time at all. My mammy sure was healthy. Her name was Silvey and her mammy come over to dis country in a big ship. Somebody give her de name o' Betty, but 'tweren't her right name. Folks couldn't understand a word she say. It was some sort o' gibberish dey called "gulluh-talk," and it sound *dat* funny. My pappy was Bill Lucas.

When I was a little chap I used to wear coarse lowell-cloth shirts on de week-a-days. Dey was long and had big collars. When de seams ripped de hide would show through. When I got big enough to wait round at de Big House and got to town, I wore clean rough clothes. De pants was white linsey-woolsey and de shirts was rough white cotton what was wove at de plantation. In de winter de sewin' womens made us heavy clothes and knit wool socks for us. De womens wore linsey-woolsey dresses and long leggin's like de soldiers wear. Dis was a long narrow wool cloth and it wrapped round and round dey legs and fasten at de top with a string.

At Christmas de marster give de slaves a heap o' fresh meat and whiskey for treats. But you better not get drunk. No-sir-ree! Den on Christmas Eve dey was a big dance and de white folks would come and see de one what dance de best. Marster and Mistis laugh fit to kill at de capers us cut. Den sometimes dey had big weddin's and de young white ladies dressed de brides up like dey was white. Sometimes dey sent to New Orleans for a big cake. De preacher married 'em with de same testimony dey use now. Den everybody'd have a little drink and some cake. It sure was larrupin'. Den everybody'd get right. Us could dance near about all night. De old-time fiddlers played fast music and us all clapped hands and tromped and swayed in time to de music. Us sure made de rafters ring.

Us slaves didn't pay no attention to who owned us, leastways de young ones didn't. I was raised by a marster what owned a heap o' lands. Lemme see, dey is called Artonish, Lockdale, and Lockleaven. Dey is plantations along together.

I'se sure my first marster was Marse Jim Stamps and his wife was Miss Lucindy. She was nice and soft-goin'. Us was glad when she stayed on de plantation.

Next thing I knowed us all belonged to Marse Withers. He was from de North and he didn't have no wife. Marsters without wives was de devil. I knows a-plenty what I oughtn't tell to ladies. 'Tweren't de marsters what was so mean. 'Twas dem poor white trash overseers and agents. Dey was mean; dey was meaner dan bulldogs.

Wives made a big difference. Dey was kind and went about amongst de slaves a-lookin' after 'em. Dey give out food and clothes and shoes. Dey doctored de little babies. When things went wrong de womens was all de time puttin' me up to tellin' de Mistis. Marse D. D. Withers was my young marster. He was a little man, but everybody stepped when he come round.

De best I 'member my next marster was President Jefferson Davis hisself. Only he weren't no president den. He was just a tall quiet gentleman with a pretty young wife what he married in Natchez. Her name was Miss Varina Howell, and he sure let her have her way. I 'spect I'se de only one livin' whose eyes ever seed 'em both. I talked with her when dey come in de big steamboat. Before us got to de Big House, I told her all about de goins'-on on de plantations. She was a fine lady. When I was a boy about thirteen years old dey took me up de country toward Vicksburg to a place call Briarsfield. It must-a been named for her old home in Natchez what was called "de Briars." I didn't belong to Marse Jeff no great while, but I ain't never forget de look of him. He was always calm like and savin' on his words. His wife was just de other way. She talked more dan a-plenty.

I b'lieves a bank sold us next to Marse L. Q. Chambers. I 'members him well. I was a house servant and de overseer dassent hit me a lick.

Marster done lay de law down. Most planters lived on dey plantations just a part o' de year. Dey would go off to Saratoga and places up North. Sometimes Marse L. Q. would come down to de place with a big wagon filled with a thousand pair o' shoes at one time. He had a nice wife. One day whilst I was a-waitin' on de table I see Old Marse lay his knife down just like he tired. Den he lean back in his chair, kinda still like. Den I say, "What de matter with Marse L. Q.?" Den dey all jump and scream and, bless de Lord, if he weren't plumb dead.

Slaves didn't know what to 'spect from freedom, but a lot of dem hoped dey would be fed and kept by de government. Dey all had different ways o' thinkin' about it. Mostly, though, dey was just like me, dey didn't know just 'zackly what it meant. It was just somethin' dat de white folks and slaves all de time talk about. Dat's all. Folks dat ain't never been free don't rightly know de *feel* of bein' free. Dey don't know de meanin' of it. Slaves like us, what was owned by quality folks, was satisfied and didn't sing none of dem freedom songs. I recollect one song dat us could sing. It went like dis:

> Drinkin' o' de wine, drinkin' o' de wine,
> Ought-a been in heaven three-thousan' years
> A-drinkin' o' dat wine, a-drinkin' o' dat wine.

Us could shout dat one.

I was a grown-up man with a wife and two chillen when de War broke out. You see, I stayed with de folks till along come de Yanks. Dey took me off and put me in de War. First, dey shipped me on a gunboat and, next, dey made me help dig canal at Vicksburg. I was on de gunboat when it shelled de town. It was terrible, seein' folks a-tryin' to blow each other up. Whilst us was bulldoggin' Vicksburg in front, a Yankee army slipped in behind de Rebels and penned 'em up. I fit at Fort Pillow and Harrisburg and Pleasant Hill and before I was half through with it I was in Baltimore and Virginny.

I was on hand when General Lee handed his sword to General Grant. You see, dey had him all hemmed in and he just naturally had to give up. I seen him stick his sword up in de ground. It sure was terrible times! Dese old eyes o' mine seen more people crippled and dead. I'se even seen 'em saw off legs with hacksaws. I tell you it ain't right what I seen. It ain't right at all.

Den I was put to buryin' Yankee soldiers. When nobody was lookin' I stripped de dead of dey money. Sometimes dey had it in a belt around dey bodies. Soon I got a big roll o' foldin' money. Den I come a-trampin' back home. My folks didn't have no money but dat worth-less kind. It was all dey knowed about. When I grabbed some of it and throwed it in de blazin' fire, dey thought I was crazy, till I told 'em, "Dat ain't money; it's no 'count!" Den I give my daddy a greenback and told him what it was.

After de War was over de slaves was worse off dan when dey had marsters. Some of 'em was put in stockades at Angola, Louisiana, and some in de terrible corral at Natchez. Dey weren't used to de stuff de Yankees fed 'em. Dey fed 'em wasp-nest bread, 'stead o' corn pone and hoecake, and all such like. Dey caught diseases and died by de hundreds, just like flies. Dey had been fooled into thinkin' it would be good times, but it was de worst times dey ever seen. 'Tweren't no place for 'em to go, no bed to sleep on, and no roof over dey heads. Dem what could get back home set out with dey minds made up to stay on de land. Most of dey marsters took 'em back so dey worked de land again. I means dem what lived to get back to dey folks was more'n glad to work! Dey done had a sad lesson. Some of 'em was worse'n slaves after de War.

Dem Ku Kluxes was de devil. De niggers sure was scared of 'em, but dey was more after dem carpetbaggers dan de niggers. I lived right in amongst 'em, but I wouldn't tell. I knowed 'em, but I dasn't talk! Sometimes dey would go right in de fields and take folks out and kill 'em. Ain't none of 'em left now. Dey is all dead and gone, but dey sure was rabid den. I never got in no trouble with 'em, 'cause I tended my business and kept out o' dey way. I'd-a been kilt if I'd-a run round and done any big talkin'.

I never knowed Marse Lincoln, but I heard he was a powerful good man. I 'members plain as yesterday when he got kilt and how all de flags hung at half mast. De North nearly went wild with worryin' and blamed everybody else. Some of 'em even tried to blame de killin' on Marse Davis. I fit with de Yankees, but I thought a mighty heap o' Marse Davis. He was quality.

I guess slavery was wrong, but I 'members us had some mighty good times. Some marsters was mean and hard but I was treated good all time. One thing I does know is dat a heap of slaves was worse off after de War. Dey suffered 'cause dey was too triflin' to work without a boss. Now dey is got to work or die. In dem days you worked and rested and knowed you'd be fed. In de middle of de day us rested and waited for de horn to blow to go back to de field. Slaves didn't have nothin' terrible to worry about if dey acted right. Dey was mean slaves de same as dey was mean marsters.

When my white folks told us us was free, I waited. When de soldiers come dey turned us loose like animals with nothin'. Dey had no business to set us free like dat. Dey gimmie 160 acres of land, but 'tweren't no 'count. It was in Mt. Bayou, Arkansas, and was low and swampy. 'Tweren't you land to keep lessen you lived on it. You had to clear it, drain it, and put a house on it. How I gwine-a drain and clear a lot o' land with nothin' to do it with? Reckon somebody livin' on my land now. One of de rights of bein' free was dat us could move round and change bosses. But I never cared nothin' about dat.

I'se raised a big family. Dem what ain't dead, some'em looks as old as I does. I got one grandchild I loves just like my own chillen. I don't rightly 'member dis minute how many chillen I had, but I ain't had but two wives. De first one died long about seventeen years ago, and I done what de Good Book say. It say, "When you goes to de graveyard to bury you first wife, look over de crowd and pick out de next one." Dat's just what I done. I picked Janie McCoy, 'cause she ain't never been married before. She's a good cook, even if she does smoke a pipe, and don't know much about nothin'.

I sure don't live by no rules. I just takes a little dram whenever I wants it, and I smokes a pipe 'ceptin when the mistis give me a cigar. I can't chew tobacco on 'count my teeth is gone. I ain't been sick in bed but once in seventy years. De longer I lives de plainer I see dat it ain't right to want more dan you can use. De Lord put a-plenty here for everybody, but shucks! Us don't pay no mind to his teachin'. Sometimes I gets lonesome for de friends I used to know, 'cause ain't nobody left but me. I'se sure been left a far piece behind. De white folks say, "Old Jim is de last leaf on de tree," and I 'spect dey's about right.

ANDY MARION
Interviewed in South Carolina
Interviewed by W. W. Dixon
Age when interviewed: 92

I WAS BORN before de War 'tween de white folks on account of us niggers. They was powerful concerned about it and we was not. My mammy always said she found me a babe in de chinkapin bushes. The way I comed into de world in 1844. I sure was a good plowhand when de first gun was fired at some place down near Charleston; I think it was at Sumter. They say I was born where Marster Eugene Mobley lives now, but it belonged to Marster William Brice, when I was born in 1844, bless God! My father named Aleck and my mother Mary. Us colored folks didn't get names till after de War. I took my name when I went up to de 'lection box first time to vote for General Grant for President. My father was from old Virginia, my mother from South Carolina.

Our plantation had seventy-two slaves living about here and yon in log houses with dirt floors. They bored auger holes in de sides of de room, stuck end of poles in dese holes. De pole reach out into room and rested on wooden blocks sort of hollowed out on top; then some slats of pine finish up de contraption bed. Quilts was spread on dis, which was all de bed we had.

I been married four times since de War and I'm here to tell you dat a nigger had a hell of a time gettin' a wife durin' slavery. If you didn't see one on de place to suit you, and chances was you didn't suit them, why what could you do? Couldn't spring up, grab a mule and ride to de next plantation without a written pass. S'pose you gets your marster's consent to go? Look here, de gal's marster got to consent, de gal got to consent, de gal's daddy got to consent, de gal's mammy got to consent. It was a hell of a way! I helped my marster among de bullets out along de Mississippi River, but I'se glad we didn't whip them 'cause I'se had four wives.

In slavery I was de carriage driver. Us had a fine carriage and two high-steppin' horses, Frank and Charlie. I used to hear lots of things from behind me, while drivin' de folks and sayin' nothin'. We had no use for money. Kind words from de white folks was money 'nough for me. We just worked hard, eat more and slept well. We got meat, hominy, and cornmeal on Mondays and wheat bread, lard and 'lasses on Saturdays. No time for fishin' 'or huntin'. Married slaves was encouraged to have their own gardens. Our clothes was of wool in de winter from our own sheep, and cotton in de summer from our own fields. Had many spinnin' wheels and cards. Miss Mary, de mistress, saw to dis part.

Our white folks was psalm-singin' old style Presbyterians. You daren't whistle a hymn on Sunday, which they called Sabbath. Just as soon as I got free, I joined de Baptist church, hard shell. My marster, William Brice, his wife, Miss Mary, his son, Christie, and his daughters, Miss Lizzie, Miss Kitty, and Miss Mary, was de ones I drove de carriage to Hopewell church on Sunday for. Dat church is flourishin' now. De pastor of dat church, Reverend John White, before he died I waited on him sixteen years, and in his will, he give me dis house and forty acres around it for my life. Dat's what I calls religion. My mistress was an angel, good, and big hearted. I lay my head in her lap many a time.

Marster had a overseer twice. They was poor white trash, not as de niggers. Miss Mary run them both off and told Marster what she couldn't see to when he was away, she'd pick out one of de slaves to see after. All de overseer done was to wake us up, see to feeding stock, and act biggity. Us slaves worked from sunup to sundown.

Sometime before de War, my marster sold out and bought a big place in Mississippi. On de way dere, de grown slaves was chained together. Yes sir, de chain was round de necks. We went by wagons and steamboats sometimes. We stayed in Mississippi till durin' de War we refugeed back to South Carolina. Dat's when de Yankees got possession of de river. We settled near New Hope church. It was in dis church dat I saw sprinkling with a kind of brush when baptizin' de chillen. Over at Hopewell, you had to have a brass trinket—(token)—to show before you could take Communion of de Saints. We was always compelled to go to church.

Boss like for de slaves to sing while workin'. We had a jackleg slave preacher who'd hist de tunes. Some was spirituals. Nothing stopped for slave funerals. De truth is, I can't remember any dyin' on our places. None of our slaves ever run away.

A pass was like dis: On it was your name, what house you goin' to, and de hour expected back. If you was cotched at any other house, patterroller whip you sure. Always give us Christmas Day. Dere was a number of dances dis time of de year. Got passes to different plantations. Dere would be corn shuckin' different places. Not much games or playin' in our set. Sickness of slaves was quickly 'tended to by de doctor. I remember gallopin' for old Doctor Douglas many a time.

I went to de War from Mississippi as bodyguard for my Marster. I was close to de fightin' and see it. If it was hell then, it must be tarnation now with all dese airplanes flyin' round droppin' booms on old people like me.

I was free three years before I knowed it. Worked along just de same. One day we was in de field on Mr. Chris Brice's place. Man come along on big, black horse, tail platted and tied with a red ribbon. Stopped, waved his hands and shouted, "You is free, all of you. Go anywhere you wants to." Us quit right then and acted de fool. We ought to have gone to de white folks about it. When the Yankees come they tied me up by my two thumbs, try to make me tell where I hided de money and gold watch and silver, but I swore I didn't know. I hid it, but so good it was two years before I could find it again. I put everything in a keg, went into de woods, spaded the dirt by a pine stump, put de keg in, covered it up with leaves and left it. Sometimes after we looked for it, but couldn't find. Two years later I had a mule and cart in de woods. De mule's feet sunk down into de old stump hole and dere was de keg, de silver, and de watch. Marster was mighty glad dat I was a faithful servant and not a liar and a thief like he thought I was. My marster was not a Ku Klux. They killed some obstreppary niggers in them times.

I first married Sara Halsey in 1875; she had three chillen. She died. Ten months after, I took Harriet Daniels; she had three chillen, then she died. Eight months after, I married Millie Gladden, no chillen. She lived seventeen years, died, and ten years ago I fooled dat good-lookin' Jane a settin' over dere. She was a widow then, she was a widow Arthur. She was a Caldwell, when she was born. We have no chillen but she is still lookin' for a blessin'.

SUSAN MERRITT

Interviewed near Marshall, Texas
Interviewer not identified
Age when interviewed: 87

I COULDN'T TELL how old I is, but does you think I'se ever forget them slave days? I believe I'se about eighty-seven or more, 'cause I'se a good size gal spinnin' all the thread for the white folks when they lets us loose after surrender.

I'se born right down in Rusk County, not a long way from Henderson, and Massa Andrew Watt am my owner. My pappy, Hob Rollins, he come from North Carolina and belonged to Dave Blakely and Mammy come from Mississippi. Mammy have eleven of us chillen, but four dies when they babies. Albert, Hob, John, Emma, Anna, Lula, and me lives to be growed and married.

Massa Watt lived in a big log house what set on a hill so you could see it round for miles, and us lived over in the field in little log huts, all huddled along together. They have homemade beds nailed to the wall and baling sack mattresses, and us call them bunks. Us never had no money but plenty clothes and grub, and wear the same clothes all the year round. Massa Watt made our shoes for winter hisself. He made furniture and saddles and harness, and run a grist mill and a whiskey still there on the place. That man had everything.

The hands was woke with the big bell and when Massa pulls that bell rope the niggers falls out them bunks like rain fallin'. They was in that field before day and stay till dusk dark. They work up till Saturday night and then washes their clothes, and sometimes they gets through and has time for the party and plays ring plays.

When the hands come in from the field at dusk dark, they has to tote water from the spring and cook and eat; and be in bed when that old bell rings at nine o'clock. About dusk they calls the chillen and gives 'em a piece of corn pone about size my hand and a tin cup milk and puts them to bed. But the growed folks et fat pork and greens and beans and such like and have plenty milk. Every Sunday Massa give 'em some flour and butter and a chicken. Lots of niggers caught a good cow-hiding for slippin' round and stealin' a chicken before Sunday.

Massa Watt didn't have no overseer, but he have a nigger driver what am just as bad. He carry a long whip round the neck and I'se seed him tie niggers to a tree and cowhide 'em till the blood run down onto the ground. Sometimes the women gets slothful and not able to do their part but they makes 'em do it anyway. They digs a hole, about body deep, and makes them women lie face down in it and beats 'em nearly to death. That nigger driver beat the chillen for not keepin' their cotton row up with the lead man. Sometimes he made niggers drag long chains while they works in the field and some of 'em run off, but they oughtn't to have done it, 'cause they chase 'em with hounds and nearly kilt 'em.

Lots of times Massa Watt give us a pass to go over to George Petro's place or Dick Gregg's place. Massa Petro run a slave market and he have big, high scaffold with steps where he sells slaves. They was stripped off to the waist to show their strength.

Our white folks have a church and a place for us in the back. Sometimes at night us gather round the fireplace and pray and sing and cry, but us daren't allow our white folks know it. Thank the Lord us can worship where us wants nowadays. I 'member one song we always sing:

> I heard the voice of Jesus callin'
> Come unto me and live.
> Lie, lie down, weepin' one,
> Rest thy head on my breast.
> I come to Jesus as I was,
> Weary and lone and tired and sad,
> I finds in him a restin' place,
> And he has made me glad.

Us have two white doctors call Dr. Dan and Dr. Gill Shaw, what wait on us when we real sick. Us wore asafetida bags round the neck and it kept off sickness.

I stay most the time in the Big House and Massa good but Missy am the devil. I couldn't tell you how I treated. Lots of times she tie me to a stob in the yard and cowhide me till she give out, then she go and rest and come back and beat me some more. You see, I'se Massa nigger and she have her own niggers what come on her side and she never did like me. She stomp and beat me nearly to death and they have to grease my back where she cowhide me and I'se sick with fever for a week. If I have a dollar for every cowhidin' I get, I'se never have to work no more.

Young Missy Betty like me and try to learn me readin' and writin' and she slip to my room and have me doin' right good. I learn the alphabet. But one day Missy Jane cotch her schoolin' me and she say, "Niggers don't need to know anything," and the lams me over the head with the butt of a cowhide whip. That white woman so rough—one day us makin' soap and some little chickens gets in the fire round the pot and she say I let 'em do it and make me walk barefoot through that bed of coals several times.

I hears about freedom in September and they's pickin' cotton and a white man rides up to Massa's house on a big, white hoss and the house-

boy tell Massa a man want see him and he hollers, "Light,* stranger."
It a government man. He have the big book and a bunch papers and
say why ain't Massa turn the niggers loose. Massa say he tryin' get the
crop out, and he tell Massa have the slaves in. Uncle Steven blows the
cow horn what they use to call to eat and all the niggers come runnin',
'cause that horn mean, "Come to the Big House, quick." That man reads
the paper tellin' us we's free, but Massa make us work several months
after that. He say we get twenty acres land and a mule but we didn't
get it.

Lots of niggers was kilt after freedom, 'cause the slaves in Harrison
County turn loose right at freedom and them in Rusk County wasn't.
But they hears about it and runs away to freedom in Harrison County
and they owners have 'em bushwacked, that shot down. You could see
lots of niggers hangin' to trees in Sabine bottom right after freedom,
'cause they catch 'em swimmin' 'cross Sabine River and shoot 'em. They
sure am goin' be lots of soul cry against 'em in Judgment!

FANNIE MOORE
Interviewed at Asheville, North Carolina
Interviewed by Marjorie Jones
Age when interviewed: 88

Nowadays when I hear folks a-growlin' and a-grumblin' about
not havin' this and that I just think what would they done if
they be brought up on de Moore Plantation. De Moore plantation
belong to Marse Jim Moore, in Moore, South Carolina. De Moores had
owned de same plantation and de same niggers and dey children for
years back. When Marse Jim's pappy die he leave de whole thing to
Marse Jim, if he take care of his mammy. She sure was a rip-jack. She
say niggers didn't need nothin' to eat. Dey just like animals, not like
other folks. She whip me, many time with a cowhide, till I was black
and blue.

Marse Jim's wife was Mary Anderson. She was the sweetest woman
I ever saw. She was always good to every nigger on de plantation. Her
mother was Harriet Anderson and she visit de missus for long time on
de farm. All de little niggers like to work for her. She never talk mean.
Just smile dat sweet smile and talk in de softest tone. An when she
laugh, she sound just like de little stream back of de spring house

* Alight.

gurglin' past de rocks. And her hair all white and curly, I can 'member her always.

Marse Jim own de biggest plantation in de whole country. Just thousands acres of land. And de old Tiger River a-runnin' right through de middle of de plantation. On one side of de river stood de Big House, where de white folks live, and on the other side stood de quarters. De Big House was a purty thing all painted white, a-standin' in a patch of oak trees. I can't remember how many rooms in dat house but powerful many. O'course it was built when de Moores had such large families.

Marse Jim, he only had five children, not twelve like his mammy had. Dey was Andrew, and Tom, den Harriet, Nan, and Nettie Sue. Harriet was just like her Granny Anderson. She was good to everybody. She get de little niggers down and teach 'em dey Sunday school lesson. If old Marse Jim's mammy catch her she sure raise torment. She make life just as hard for de niggers as she can.

De quarters just long row of cabins daubed with dirt. Everyone in de family live in one big room. In one end was a big fireplace. Dis had to heat de cabin and do de cookin' too. We cooked in a big pot hung on a rod over de fire and bake de corn pone in de ashes, or else put it in de skillet and cover de lid with coals. We always have plenty wood to keep us warm. Dat is if we have time to get it out of de woods.

My granny she cook for us chillens while our mammy away in de field. Dey wasn't much cookin' to do. Just make corn pone and bring in de milk. She have a big wooden bowl with enough wooden spoons to go round. She put de milk in de bowl and break it up. Den she put de bowl in de middle of de floor and all de chillen grab a spoon.

My mammy she work in de field all day and piece and quilt all night. Den she have to spin enough thread to make four cuts for de white folks every night. Why sometime I never go to bed. Have to hold de light for her to see by. She have to piece quilts for de white folks too. Why, dey is a scar on my arm yet where my brother let de pine drip on me. Rich pine was all de light we ever had. My brother was a-holdin' de pine so's I can help mammy tack the quilt and he go to sleep and let it drop.

I never see how my mammy stand such hard work. She stand up for her chillen though. De old overseer he hate my mammy, 'cause she fight him for beatin' her chillen. Why she get more whippin' for dat dan anythin' else. She have twelve chillen. I 'member I see de three oldest stand in de snow up to dey knees to split rails, while de overseer stand off and grin.

My mammy she trouble in her heart about de way they treated. Every night she pray for de Lord to get her and her chillen out of de place. One day she plowin' in de cotton field. All sudden like she let out big yell. Den she start singin' and a-shoutin' and a-whoopin' and a-hollerin'. Den it seems she plow all de harder.

When she come home, Marse Jim's mammy say: "What all dat goin' on in de field? You think we send you out there just to whoop and yell?

No siree, we put you out there to work and you sure better work, else we get de overseer to cowhide you old black back."

My mammy just grin all over her black wrinkled face and say: "I'se saved. De Lord done tell me I'se saved. Now I know de Lord will show me de way, I ain't gwine to grieve no more. No matter how much you all done beat me and my chillen de Lord will show me de way. And some day we never be slaves." Old Granny Moore grab de cowhide and slash Mammy cross de back but Mammy never yell. She just go back to de field a singin'.

My mammy grieve lots over brother George, who die with de fever. Granny she doctor him as best she could, every time she get ways from de white folks' kitchen. My mammy never get chance to see him, 'cept when she get home in de evenin'. George, he just lie. One day I look at him and he had such a peaceful look on his face, I think he sleep and just let him alone. 'Long in the evenin' I think I try to wake him. I touch him on de face, but he was dead. Mammy never know till she come at night. Poor Mammy she kneel by de bed and cry her heart out. Old Uncle Allen, he make pine box for him and carry him to de graveyard over de hill. My mammy just plow and cry as she watch 'em put George in de ground.

My pappy he was a blacksmith. He shoe all de horses on de plantation. He work so hard he have no time to go to de field. His name was Stephen Moore. Marse Jim call him Stephen Andrew. He was sold to de Moores, and his mammy too. She was brought over from Africa. She never could speak plain. All her life she been a slave. White folks never recognize 'em any more dan if dey was a dog.

It was a terrible sight to see de speculators come to de plantation. Dey would go through de fields and buy de slaves dey wanted. Marse Jim never sell Pappy or Mammy or any of dey chillen. He always like Pappy. When de speculator come all de slaves start a-shakin'. No one know who is a-goin'.

Den sometimes dey take 'em and sell 'em on de block. De "breed woman" always bring more money den de rest, even de men. When dey put her on de block dey put all her chillen around her to show folks how fast she can have chillen. When she sold, her family never see her again. She never know how many chillen she have. Sometime she have colored chillen and sometimes white. 'Tain't no use to say anything, 'cause if she do she just get whipped.

Why, on de Moore plantation Aunt Cheney—everybody call her Aunt Cheney—have two chillen by de overseer. De overseer name was Hill. He was as mean as de devil. When Aunt Cheney not do what he ask he tell Granny Moore. Old Granny call Aunt Cheney to de kitchen and make her take her clothes off, den she beat her till she just black and blue. Many boys and girls marry dey own brothers and sisters and never know de difference lest they get to talkin' about dey parents and where dey used to live.

De niggers always have to get pass to go anywhere off de plantation.

Dey get de pass from de massa or de missus. Den when de patterrollers come dey had to show de pass to dem. If you had no pass dey strip you and beat you.

I remember one time dey was a dance at one of de houses in de quarters. All de niggers was a-laughin and a-pattin' dey feet and a-singin', but dey was a few dat didn't. De patterollers shove de door open and start grabbin' us. Uncle Joe's son he decide dey was one time to die and he start to fight. He say he tired standin' so many beatin's, he just can't stand no more. De patterrollers start beatin' him and he start fightin'. Oh lordy, it was terrible. Dey whip him with a cowhide for a long time, den one of dem take a stick and hit him over de head, and just bust his head wide open. De poor boy fell on de floor just a-moanin' and a-groanin. De patterrollers just whip about half dozen other niggers and send 'em home and leave us with de dead boy.

None of the niggers have any learnin', weren't never allowed to as much as pick up a piece of paper. My daddy slip and get a Webster book and den he take it out in de field and he learn to read. De white folks afraid to let de chillen learn anythin'. They afraid dey get too smart and be harder to manage. Dey never let 'em know anythin' about anythin'.

Never have any church. If you go, you set in de back of de white folks' church. But de niggers slip off and pray and hold prayer-meetin' in de woods, den dey turn down a big wash pot and prop it up with a stick to drown out de sound of de singin'. I 'member some of de songs we used to sing. One of dem went somethin' like dis:

> Hark from de tomb a doleful sound,
> My ears hear a tender cry,
> A livin' man come through the ground
> Where we may shortly lie.
> Here in dis clay may be your bed,
> In spite of all your toil,
> Let all de wise bow reverent head
> Must lie as low as ours.

Back in those times dey wasn't no way to put away fruit and things for winter like dey is today. In de fall of de year it certainly was a busy time. We peel bushels of appels and peaches to dry. Dey put up lots of brandied peaches too. De way dey done, dey peel de peaches and cut em up. Then dey put a layer of peaches in a crock, den a layer of sugar, den another layer of peaches until de crock was full. Den dey seal de jar by puttin' a cloth over de top, then a layer of paste, then another cloth, then another layer of paste. Dey keep dey meat about de same way folks do today 'cept dey had to smoke it more, since salt was so scarce back in dat day. Dey can most of de other fruit and put it in de same kind of jars dat dey put de peaches in. Dey string up long strings of beans and let 'em dry and cook 'em with fatback in de winter.

Folks back den never hear tell of all de ailments de folks have now.

Dey were no doctors. Just use roots and bark for teas of all kinds. My old granny used to make tea out of dogwood bark and give it to us chillen when we have a cold, else she make a tea out of wild cherry bark, pennyroyal, or horehound. My goodness but dey was bitter. We do most anything to get out of takin' de tea, but 'twarn't no use. Granny just get you by de collar, hold your nose, and you just swallow it or get strangled. When de baby have de colic she get rats vein and make a syrup and put a little sugar in it and boil it. Den soon as it cold she give it to de baby. For stomachache she give use snake root. Sometime she make tea, other time she just cut it up in little piece and make you eat one or two of dem. When you have fever she wrap you up in cabbage leaves or ginseng leaves. Dis make de fever go. When de fever got too bad, she take the hoofs off de hog dat had been killed and parch 'em in de ashes and den she beat 'em up and make a tea. Dis was de most terrible of all.

De year before de War started Marse Jim died. He was out in de pasture pickin 'up cow loads, a-throwin' 'em in de garden. And he just drop over. I hate to see Marse Jim go, he not such a bad man. After he die his boys, Tom and Andrew, take charge of de plantation. Dey think dey run things different from dey daddy, but dey just get started when de War come. Marse Tom and Marse Andrew both have to go. My pappy he go along with dem to do dere cookin'. My pappy he say dat some day he run four or five miles with de Yankees behind him before he can stop to do any cookin'. Den when he stop he cook with de bullets a fallin' all round de kettles. He say he walk on dead men just like he walkin' on de ground. Some of de men be dead, some moanin' and some a-groanin', but nobody pay no attention, 'cause de Yankees keep a-comin'.

One day de Yankees come awful close. Marse Andrew have de Confederate flag in his hand. He raise it high in de air. Pappy say he yell for him to put de flag down 'cause de Yankees was a-comin' closer and was a-goin' to capture him anyway. But Marse Andrew just hold de flag up and run behind a tree. De Yankee soldiers just take one shot at him and dat was de last of him. My pappy bring him home. De family put him in alcohol. One day I went to see him and there he was a-swimmin' round in de water. Most of his hair done come off, though. He buried at Nazareth. I could go right back to de graveyard if I was there.

Den my pappy go back to stay with Marse Tom. Marse Tom was just wounded. If he hadn't had a Bible in his pocket de bullet go clear though his heart. But you all know no bullet ain't goin' through de Bible. No, you can't shoot through God's word. Pappy he bring Marse Tom home and take care of him till he well. Marse Tom give Pappy a horse and wagon 'cause he say he save his life.

Many time de soldiers come through de plantation and dey load up dey wagons with everything dey find, 'lasses, hams, chickens. Sometime dey give part of it to de niggers but de white folks take it away when dey get gone. De white folks hide all de silverware from de soldiers.

Dey afraid dey take it when dey come. Sometimes dey make us tell if dey think we know.

After de War Pappy go back to work on de plantation. He make his own crop on de plantation. But de money was no good den. I played with many a Confederate dollar. He sure was happy dat he was free. Mammy, she shout for joy and say her prayers were answered. Pappy get pretty feeble, but he work till just before he die. He made patch of cotton with a hoe. Dey was enough cotton in de patch to make a bale. Pappy die when he 104 years old. Mammy she lived to be 105.

After de War de Ku Klux broke out. Oh, dey was mean! In dey long white robes dey scare de niggers to death. Dey keep close watch on dem, afraid dey try to do somethin'. Dey have long horns and big eyes and mouth. Dey never go round much in de day. Just night. Dey take de poor niggers away in de woods and beat 'em and hang 'em. De niggers was afraid to move, much less try to do anything. Dey never know what to do, dey have no learnin'. Have no money. All dey can do was stay on de same plantation till dey can do better. We live on de same plantation till de chillen all grown and Mammy and Pappy both die. Then we leave. I don't know where any of my people are now. I knows I was born in 1849. I was eighty-eight years old de first of September.

ANDREW MOSS
Interviewed at Knoxville, Tennessee
Interviewer not identified
Age when interviewed: 85

ONE THING dat's all wrong with dis world today is dat dey ain't no "prayer grounds." Down in Georgia where I was born— dat way back in 1852—us colored folks had prayer grounds. My mammy's was a old twisted thick-rooted muscadine bush. She'd go in dere and pray for deliverance of de slaves. Some colored folks cleaned out knee-spots in de canebrakes. Cane, you know, grows high and thick, and colored folks could hide demselves dere and nobody could see and pester dem.

You see it was just like dis. Durin' de War, and before de War too, white folks make a heap o' fun of de colored folks for all time prayin'. Sometime, say, you was a slave and you get down to pray in de field or by de side of de road and Marster come along and see a slave on his knees. He say, "What you prayin' about?" And you say, "Oh, Marster,

I'se just prayin' to Jesus 'cause I wants to go to Heaven when I dies."
And Marster says, "You's my Negro. I get ye to Heaven. Get up offen
your knees." De white folks what owned slaves thought that when dey
go to Heaven de colored folks would be dere to wait on 'em.

And if it was a Yank come along, he say too, "What you prayin' about?"
You gives de same response. And he say, "We's gwine save you. We
goin' to set you free. You wants to be free, don't you?" "Yes sir, Boss!"
"Well den," Yank say, "come go along with me." Ain't no use keep
sayin', "Please, sir, Boss. I'll have to ask my marster." Yank say, "What
you mean, Marster? You ain't got no marster. We's settin' you free."

Sometimes dey takes and tie a rope round you, and they starts ridin'
off, but dey don't go too fast so you walk behind. Sometimes along
comes another Yank on a horse and he ask, "Boy, ain't you tired?" "Yes
sir, Boss!" "Well, you get up here behind me and ride some." Den he
wrap de rope all round de saddle horn. Wraps and wraps, but leaves
some slack. But he keeps you tied, so's you won't jump down and run
away. And many's de time a prayin' Negro got took off like dat and
weren't never seen no more.

Course, if you goes with 'em, you 'member your trainin' and before
you leaves de field, you stacks your hoe nice, like you was quittin'
de days work. Dey learned de little 'uns to do dat, soon's dey begins to
work in de fields. Dey had little hoes, handles about de size of my arm,
for de little fellers. I've walked many a mile, when I was a little feller,
up and down de rows, followin' de grown folks, and chopping with
de hoe round de corners where de earth was soft so de little 'uns could
hoe easy.

Whoopee! Let dat dinner horn blow, and everybody stacks dey hoes,
nice, neat stack standin' up, and starts to run. Some eats in dey own
cabins, but dem what eats at de Big House sets down at a long table
and gets good grub too. Every night our marster give us every one a
glass o' whiskey. Dat's to keep off disease. Mornin's we had to all drink
tar water for de same purpose. Dat wasn't so tasty.

My marster's name was George Hopper. Dat man paid taxes on more'n
two thousand acres of land in two counties. I lived in dem two counties,
was born in Wilkes and raised in Lincoln county, Georgia. We called
it de middle south. My marster he never did marry. Lots of folks
didn't; dey just took up with one another. Marster Hopper had five
children by my grandmother. She was his house woman; dat's what
he call her. And when he died he willed her and all dem chillens a
house, some land, and a little money. He'd of left 'em a heap more
money and he'd been one of the richest men in the county, if de War
hadn't broke out.

When it was over he had a barrel full of 'Federate greenbacks. But
'tweren't no count. He done broke den. One day my uncle—he was the
colored overseer—he went to Danbury, six miles from where we lived
at, and he paid five dollars a pound for coffee. Dat was before de North

whipped de South, and dey hadn't killed down de money value for de South.

Talk about hard times! We seed 'em in dem days, durin' de War and most 'specially after de surrender. Folks dese days don't know what trouble looks like. We was glad to eat ash cakes and drink parched corn and rye 'stead o' coffee. I'se seed my grandmother go to de smokehouse and scrape up de dirt where de meat had dropped off and take it to de house for seasonin'. You see, both armies fed off de white folks, and dey cleaned out dey barns and cellars and smokehouses when dey come. One time when de Yanks was on de way to Augusta, I was picking up chips to make the supper fire, when I seed 'em comin'. I hit it out from dere and hide behind two little hills down by de big spring. After awhile my brother find me and he tell me to come on back to the house and see dem white mens dance. De Yanks kept comin' 'and dey eat all night. By daylight dey was through marchin' past.

And den come de Rebels. When dey come we had five thousand bushel of corn, one-hundred head o' hogs, three-hundred and fifty gallons o' syrup and such. When dey left, dey took and set fire to everything, to keep it away from the Yanks, aimin' to starve 'em out o' dat country. Dat's what dey done. Some of dem Rebels was mean as the Yanks. And dat was bein' mean! Some called de Yanks, "de Hornets," 'cause dey fight so. Take a Yank and he'd fight across a buzz saw and it circlin' fifty mile a minute.

Dat time when the Yanks was goin' to Augusta, and I went to black my marster's boot—he'd give us a two-cent piece, big as a quarter, for boot blackin'—I say, "Marster, who is dem soldiers?" And he say to me, "Dey is de Yankees come to try to take you away from me." And I say, "Looks like to me, Marster, if dey wants to take us dey'd ask you for us." Marster laughed and say, "Boy! Dem fellers don't ask with words. Dey does all they talkin' with cannons."

Did you know that a white woman shot de first cannon dat was ever fired in de state of Georgia? She was a Yankee colonel's wife, dey say, named Miss Anna. I dunno the rest of her name. She wants to be de first to fire a cannon, she say, to set de Negroes free. Dat was before de War begin. De roar of dat cannon was in folk's ears for more'n five days and nights.

How I come to Knoxville—I was a young man when I started off from Georgia, aimin' to go over de mountains to Kentucky where I heard dey pay good wages. I stopped in Campbell County, Tennessee, with another feller, and I seed a pretty gal workin' in de field, And I says, 'I'm goin' to marry dat gal." Sure 'nough me and her was married in less dan six months. Her marster built us a log house and we lived there till we come to Knoxville, Tennessee. Now all of my boys is dead. Every one of 'em worked for Mr. Peters, of Peters and Bradley Flour Mills, and dey all died workin' for him. So Mister Willie, he say he gwine let me live here, in de company house, the rest o 'my days.

WYLIE NEALY

Interviewed at Biscoe, Arkansas
Interviewed by Irene Robertson
Age at interview: 85

I WAS BORN IN 1852. I am eighty-five years old. I was born in Gordon County. The closest town was Calhoun, South Carolina. My sister died in '59. That's the first dead person I ever saw. One of my sisters was give away and another one was sold before the Civil War started. Sister Mariah was give to the young mistress, Miss Ella Conley. I didn't see her sold. I never seed nobody sold but I heard 'em talking about it. I had five sisters and one brother. My father was a free man always. He was a Chocktaw Indian. Mother was part Cherokee Indian. My mother's mistress was Mrs. Martha Christian. He died and she married Tom Nealy, the one they call me for, Wylie Nealy.

We had a pretty hard time before freedom. My mother was a field woman. When they didn't need her to work they hired her out and they got the pay. The master mated the colored people. I got fed from the white folks' table whenever I curried the horses. I was sorta raised up with Mr. Nealy's children. They didn't mistreat me.

On Saturday the mistress would blow a conch shell and they knowed to go and get the rations. We got plenty to eat. They had chickens and ducks and geese and plenty of milk. They did have hogs. They had seven or eight guineas and a lot of peafowls. I never heard a farm bell till I come to Arkansas. The children et from pewter bowls or earthenware. Sometimes they et greens or milk from the same bowl, all just dip in.

Liberty and freedom was all I ever heard any colored folks say dey expected to get out of de War, and mighty proud of dat. Nobody knowed they was goin' to have a war till it was done broke out and they was fightin' about it. Didn't nobody want land, they just wanted freedom. I remembers when Lincoln was made the President both times and when he was killed. I recollects all that like yesterday.

The army had been through and swept out everything. There wasn't a chicken or hog nowhere to be had, took the stock and cattle and all the provisions. So de slaves just had to scatter out and leave right now. And after de army come through I was goin' back down to the old place and some soldiers passed ridin' along and one said, "Boy, where you goin'?"

234

Said, "Nothing up there." I says, "I knows it." Then he say, "Come on here; walk along back there," and I followed him. I was twelve years old. He was Captain McClendon. Then when I got to the camp with him he say, "You help around here." I got sick and they let me go back home then to Resacca, Georgia. And my mother died.

When I went back they sent me to Chattanooga with Captain Story. I was in a colored regiment nine months. I saw my father several times while I was at Chattanooga. We went down through Marietta and Atlanta and through Kingston. We was in Sherman's army till it went past Atlanta. They burned up the city. Two of my masters come out of the War alive and two dead. I was mustered out in August, 1865.

I stayed in camp till my sisters found a cabin to move in. Everybody got rations issued out. It was a hard time. The Yankees promised a lot and wasn't as good as the old masters. All dey wanted was to be waited on, too. The colored folks was freed when the Yankees took all the stock and cattle and rations. Everybody had to leave and let the government issue them rations. Everybody was proud to be free. They shouted and sung.

They all did pretty well till the War was about to end, then they was told to scatter and nowheres to go. Cabins all tore down or burned. No work to do. There was no money to pay. I got hungry lots of times. No plantations was divided and the masters didn't have no more than the slaves had when the War was done. I never went back or seen any more of Old Master or Missus. Everybody left and a heap of the colored folks went where rations could be issued to them and some followed on in the armies.

After I was mustered out I stayed around the camps and went to my sister's cabin till we left there. Made anything we could pick up. Men came in there getting people to go work for them. Some folks went to Chicago. A heap of the slaves went to the Northern cities. Colonel Stocker, a officer in the Yankee army, got us to come to a farm in Arkansas. We wanted to stay together is why we all went on the farm. May, 1866, when we come to Arkansas is the first farmin' I had seen done since I left Tom Nealy's place.

Colonel Stocker is mighty well known in St. Francis County. He brought lots of families, brought me and my brother, my two brothers and a nephew. We come on the train. It took four or five days. When we got to Memphis we come to Linden on a boat, *Molly Hamilton*, they called it. I heard it was sunk at Madison long time after that. Colonel Stocker promised to pay six dollars a month and feed us. When Christmas come he said all I was due was twelve dollars and forty-five cents. We made a good crop. That wasn't it. Been there since May. Had to stay till got all the train and boat fare paid. There wasn't no difference in that and slavery 'cept they couldn't sell us.

The first votin' I ever heard of was in Grant's election. Both black and white voted. I voted Republican for Grant. Lots of the Southern soldiers was franchised and couldn't vote. Just the private soldiers could vote at all. I don't know why it was. I was a slave for thirteen years from birth.

Every slave could vote after freedom. Some colored folks held office. I knew several magistrates and sheriffs. There was one at Helena and one at Marianna. He was a high sheriff. I voted some after that, but I never voted in the last president election. I heard 'em say it wasn't no use, this man would be elected anyhow. I sorta quit off long time ago.

In 1874 and 1875 I worked for halves and made 'nough to buy a farm in St. Francis County. It cost nine hundred and twenty-five dollars. I bought it in 1887. Eighty acres to be cleared down in the bottoms. My family helped and when my help got shallow, the children leaving me, I sold it for two thousand dollars in 1904. I was married just once and had eight children; five livin' and three dead. Me and the old woman went to Oklahoma. We went in January and come back to Biscoe in September. It wasn't no place for farming. I bought forty acres from Mr. Aydelott and paid him five hundred dollars. I sold it and come to Mr. Joe Perry's place, paid five hundred dollars for forty acres of timber land. We cleared it and I got way in debt and lost it. Clear lost it! I'se been working anywhere I could make a little since then. My wife died and I been doing little jobs and stays about with my children. The welfare gives me a little check and some supplies now and then.

I can't read much. I was not learnt. I could figure a little before my eyes got bad. The white folks did send their children to pay schools but we colored children had to stay around the house and about in the field to work. I never got no schoolin'. I went with Old Missus to camp meeting down in Georgia one time and got to go to white church sometimes. At the camp meeting there was a big tent and all around it there was brush harbors and tents where people stayed to attend the meetin's. They had four meetin's a day. Lots of folk got converted and shouted. They had a lot of singing. They had a lots to eat and a big time.

I don't recollect of any slave uprisin's. I never heard of any. We didn't know they was going to have a war till they was fighting. They heard Lincoln was going to set 'em free, but they didn't know how he was going to do it. Everybody wanted freedom. Mr. Hammond ask me not long ago if I didn't think it best to bring us from Africa and be slaves than like wild animals in Africa. He said we was taught about God and the Gospel over here if we was slaves. I told him I thought dat freedom was de best anywhere.

HENRI NECAISE

Interviewed in Mississippi
Interviewed by C. E. Wells
Age when interviewed: 105

I WAS BORN in Harrison County, nineteen miles from Pass Christian, along de ridge road from de swamp near Wolf River. My marster was Ursan Ladnier. De Mistis' name was Popone. Us was all French. My father was a white man, Anatole Necaise. I knowed he was my father, 'cause he used to call me to him and tell me I was his oldest son.

I never knowed my mother. I was a slave and my mother was sold from me and her other chillens. Dey told me when dey sold her my sister was a-holdin' me in her arms. She was standin' behind de Big House peekin' round de corner and seen de last of her mother. I seen her go, too. Dey tell me I used to go to de gate a-huntin' for my mammy. I used to sleep with my sister after dat.

De Big House was about sixty feet long, built of hewed logs, in two parts. De floors was made of clay; dey didn't have lumber for floors den. Us lived right close to de Big House in a cabin. To tell de truth, de fact of de business is, my marster took care of me better'n I can take care of myself now.

When us was slaves Marster tell us what to do. He say, "Henri, do dis, do dat." And us done it. Den us didn't have to think where de next meal comin' from, or de next pair of shoes or pants. De grub and clothes give us was better'n I ever gets now.

Let me think and count. My marster didn't have a lot of slaves. Dere was one, two, three, four, yes, just four of us slaves. I was de stockholder. I tended de sheep and cows and such like. My marster didn't raise no big crops, just corn and garden stuff. He had a heap of cattle. Dey could run out in de big woods den, and so could de sheeps. He sold cattle to New Orleans and Mobile, where he could get de best price. Dat's de way folks does now, ain't it? Dey sells wherever dey can get de most money.

Dey didn't give me money but, you see, I was a slave. Dey sure give me everything else I need, clothes and shoes. I always had a-plenty to eat, better'n I can get now. I was better off when I was a slave dan I is now, 'cause I had everything furnished me den. Now I got to do it all by myself.

My marster was a Catholic. One thing I can thank dem godly white folks for, dey raise me right. Dey taught me out of God's word, "Our Father, Which are in Heaven," Everybody ought-a know dat prayer.

I was raise a Catholic, but when I come here 'twern't no church and I joined de Baptist and was baptized. Now de white folks let me go to dey church. Dey ain't no cullud church near 'nough so's I can go. I 'spect it's all right. I figures dat God is everywhere.

My mistis knowed how to read and write. I don't know about de marster. He could keep store anyway. Us all spoke French in dem days. I near about forget all de songs us used to sing. Dey was all in French anyway, and when you don't speak no French for about sixty years, you just forget it.

I'se knowed slaves to run away, and I'se seen 'em whipped. I seen good marsters and mean ones. Dey was good slaves and mean ones. But to tell de truth, if dey told a slave to do anything, den he just better do it.

I was big 'nough in de Civil War to drive five yoke of steers to Mobile and get grub to feed de womens and chillens. Some of de mens was a-fightin' and some was a-runnin' and hidin'. I was a slave and I had to do what dey told me. I carried grub into de swamp to men, but I never knowed what dey was a-hidin' from. My old marster had four sons, and de youngest one went to de War and was killed.

De Yankees come to Pass Christian. I was dere, and seen 'em. Dey come up de river and tore up things as dey went along.

I was thirty-one years old when I was set free. My marster didn't tell us about bein' free. De way I found it out, he started to whip me once and de young marster up and says, "You ain't got no right to whip him now; he's free." Den Marster turn me loose.

It was dem carpetbaggers dey destroyed de country. Dey went and turned us loose, just like a passel of cattle, and didn't show us nothin' or give us nothin'. Dey was acres and acres of land not in use, and lots of timber in dis country. Dey should-a give each one of us a little farm and let us get out timber and build houses. Dey ought to put a white marster over us, to show us and make us work, only let us be free 'stead of slaves. I think dat would-a been better'n turnin' us loose like dey done.

I left my marster and went over to de Jordon River, and dere I stayed and worked. I saved my money and dat give me a start. I never touched it till de year was winded up. To tell de truth, de facts of de matter is, it was my marster's kinfolks I was workin' for. I bought me a schooner with dat money and carried charcoal to New Orleans. I done dis for about two years and den I lost my schooner in a storm off of Bay St. Louis.

After I lost my schooner, I come here and got married. Dis was in 1875 and I was forty-three years old. Dat was my first time to marry. I'se got dat same wife today. She was born a slave, too. I didn't have no chillen, but my wife did. She had one gal-child who is de mammy of ten chillen. She done better'n us done. I'se got a lot o' grandchillen, and great-grandchillen.

I never did look for to get nothin' after I was free. I had dat in my head to get me eighty acres of land and homestead it. As for de government making me a present of anything, I never thought about it. But just now I needs it.

I did get me dis little farm, forty acres, but I bought it and paid for it myself. I got de money by workin' for it. When I come to dis country I dug wells and built chimneys and houses. Once I dug a well twenty-seven feet and come to a coal bed. I went through de coal and found water. Dat was on de Jordon River. Dat clay chimney and dis here house has been built fifty-two years. I'se still livin' in 'em. Dey's mine. One acre, I give to de Lord for a graveyard and a churchhouse. I wants to be buried dere myself.

I'se gettin' mighty old now, but I used to be pretty spry. I used to go sixty miles out on de Gulf o 'Mexico, as interpreter on dem big ships dat come from France. Dat was 'fore I done forgot my French talk what I was raised to speak.

DELICIA PATTERSON

Interviewed at St. Louis, Missouri
Interviewer not identified
Age when interviewed: 92

I WAS BORN in Boonville, Missouri, January 2, 1845. My mother's name was Maria and my father's was Jack Wiley. Mother had five children but raised only two of us. I was owned by Charles Mitchell until I was fifteen years old. They were fairly nice to all of their slaves and they had several of us.

I only got whipped once in the whole fifteen years there, and that was because I was working in the garden with one of my owner's daughters and I pulled up something that she did not want pulled up, so she up and slapped me for it. I got so mad at her. I taken up a hoe and run her all the way in the Big House, and of course I got whipped for that.

I did not even have to sleep in the cabins. I slept on a pallet in the bedrooms with Old Marse's children. I was a pet anywhere I worked, because I was always very neat and clean, and a good worker.

When I was fifteen years old, I was brought to the courthouse, put up on the auction block to be sold. Old Judge Miller from my county was there. I knew him well because he was one of the wealthiest slave owners in the county, and the meanest one. He was so cruel all the slaves and many owners hated him because of it. He saw me on the block for sale, and he knew I was a good worker. So, when he bid for me, I spoke right out on the auction block and told him: "Old Judge Miller don't you bid for me, 'cause if you do, I would not live on your plantation. I will take a knife and cut my own throat from ear to ear before I would be owned by you."

So he stepped back and let someone else bid for me. My own father knew I was to be for sale, so he brought his owner to the sale for him to buy me, so we could be together. But when father's owner heard what I said to Judge Miller, he told my father he would not buy me, because I was sassy, and he never owned a sassy nigger and did not want one that was sassy. That broke my father's heart, but I couldn't help that. Another nigger trader standing right beside my father's owner said, "I wouldn't own a nigger that didn't have some spunk." So I was sold to a Southern Englishman named Thomas Steele for fifteen hundred dollars. He had an old slave he had in his home for years as their housekeeper, and his wife did not like her, and he had to sell her to keep peace at home. So he put me in his buggy and taken me home to his wife and told her, "I bought you another girl, Susianna, but I don't want you to lay the weight of your finger on her when she disobeys. Let me know and I will punish her myself."

I lived in that family until after the Civil War was over. Mr. Steele's wife's people had a big family and they visited the Steeles a great deal. Mr. Tom didn't like them because they were Yankees and the Steeles were Confederates. So one time Mr. Tom was going away on a trip and he knew, when he was gone, his wife would have all of her folks in the home visiting, and that was against his wishes. He told me to keep tab on every time her relatives come to the house and how long they stayed, and tell him when he come back home, and that he would leave orders in the home to let me work in the field, so I would not have to bother with that great big family. When he left, all his wife's folks come right down on our plantation, so I had to work in the house for them so hard. I did not have time to even look at the field.

When my old boss come home I told him I had not worked in the field and why. Him and his wife had a big fight about that, and she hated me for a long time, and said the idea of her husband taking a nigger's word to hers and mistreat her on account of it. But he did not let her bother me about nothing, so I stayed on with them until one day, while I had a fly brush in my hand fanning flies while they ate, she told him something I done she didn't like. Just to please her, he taken the fly brush out of my hand and just tapped me with it. It didn't hurt me a bit, but it made me so mad I just went straight to the kitchen, left all the dishes, put on my sunbonnet and run away.

I stayed two weeks. He sent everybody he thought knew where I was after me, nad told them to tell me if I would only come on back home, no one would ever bother me anymore. I hid in the woods two weeks and was not afraid. I would be afraid out in those woods now, but I wasn't then. At night I would come up to some of the slave cabins who were my friends and eat and stay all night. So I went back home after my two weeks off as a runaway nigger and no one ever bothered me any more either. I came to St. Louis with them, during the Civil War.

When freedom was declared Mr. Steele told me that I was as free as he was. He said I could leave them if I please or could stay, that they wanted me and would be glad to have me if I would stay, and his wife said, " 'Course she is our nigger. She is as much our nigger now as she was the day you bought her two years ago and paid fifteen hundred dollars for her."

That made me mad so I left right then. Since she was so smart. Her husband told her, "Now, Sue, you might as well face it. There are no more slaves and won't ever be any more, regardless of how much we paid for them. So just quiet yourself down. She don't have to stay here if she don't want to." Till this day some of their children come to visit me, but they never give me anything ever.

I hired myself out to a family named Miller at three dollars a week, and lived on the place. I had a baby about three years old. I married before the War and when my baby was two weeks old they taken my husband in the army. He died in the army. I worked for the Millers about eleven months. One day Mrs. Miller misplaced her silver thimble and she accused me of stealing it. She did not tell me that but she told the white nurse girl, and the nurse told me. I got so mad at her for that 'cause I never stole anything in my whole life and never been accused of stealing, so I quit. They begged me to stay and offered to raise my salary, but I told them I would not work for anyone who felt I would steal. The very next day she found her thimble in the nursery where she remembered she put it herself, but forgot about it at the time. She thought it was lost.

I don't know what the ex-slaves expected, but I do know they didn't get anything. After the War we just wandered from place to place, working for food and a place to stay. Now and then we got a little money, but a very little. I only voted once in my life and that was when working for Mr. Gerhart. He was a real estate dealer and he taken me to the polls and showed me how to vote for a Republican president. It has been so long ago I don't even remember who the President was, but I do know he got elected. I think the time will soon be when people won't be looked on as regards to whether you are black or white, but all on the same equality. I may not live to see it but it is on the way. Many don't believe it, but I know it.

JOHN PETTY

Interviewed at Gaffney, South Carolina
Interviewed by Caldwell Sims
Age when interviewed: 87

I WAS BORN on the Jim Petty place in what was then Spartanburg County. Marse raised all his darkies to ride young. I no more 'members when I learned to ride than I 'members when I come into the world. Marse had his stables built three logs high from the outside of the lot. When the horse step down into the lot, then I jump on his back from the third log. I was so little that I never could have got on no other way without help. The horse what I rid had a broad fat back and he trot so fast that sometimes I fall off, but I hang on to the mane and swing back on his back and he never break his gait. Then again if I didn't swing right back up he take and stop till I get landed on his back once more.

One horse called Butler, the farm horse named Tom, the mule called Jack, the slave horse called Stoneman, then one called Cheny, one Jane, one Thicketty, and the studhorse named Max. I always play with him, but my folks was ignorant to that fact. I lay down and he jump straight up over me. I get corn and he eat it from my hand. There was apples and salt that he loved to eat from my palm. He throw his forelegs plumb over my head, and never touch me at all.

All this gwine on in Max's stable. It big enough for a dozen or more horses, 'cause it hardly ever been that Max get out, and his stable had to be big so as he could exercise in it. So I slip in there and we play unbeknownst to the old folks, white or black. The door slided open. When I get tired and ready to go out, then I slide the door open. Maxie knowed that I was gwine and he had the most sense. He watch till I get the door slid open and if he could he run by me and jump out. I never could get him back in and he race round that lot till the hands come in from the field at dark. He have a good time and get all sweaty.

When he jump over me out the sliding door, then I hide under the feed house till Mammy holler, "Lordy, for the living! Yonder is Max a-ripping hisself plumb to his death in that lot." Then they send for some of the mens to get him back. After they done that, then I crawl out, climb the lot fence, and run through the field home. When I sets down Maw allows, "Does you know it's real curious thing how that old studhorse get his door open and come out that stable. It must be haunts creeping about right

242

here in the broad open daylight." At that I draw up real near the fire and say, "Maw, does you reckon that the haunts is gwine to come and open our door some time?"

On t'other hand, if I be real quick a-getting out of the stable door before Max turn and see me, why then he couldn't get out. None of them never knowed about the good times that me and Max used to have. And it appears real strange to me now that he never did hit me with his foots nor nothing. That horse sure 'nough did love me and that's just all what it is to that. I also used to slip in the extra feed house and fetch him oats and the like 'twixt and 'tween times. He stay that fat and slick. But there wasn't nary lil' darky would go near that studhorse but me. They's all skeered to death when he get in the lot and when they seed him in there they would run and get in the house and slam the door plumb shut.

When I done come up nigh eighteen or something like that, the big freedom come round. Marse Jim say us could all go and see the world as we was free niggers. Us jump up and shout, "Glory!" and sing, but us never sassed our white folks like it appears to be the knowledge up North. I've done been there and they thinks us turned our backs on our white folks, but I never seed nothing but scalawag niggers and poor white trash a-doing that, that I ain't.

One nigger went from the plantation to the North, as they called it. When he had done stayed there for five years, then he come back and hired out to Marse Jim. He looked real lanky, but I never paid that no mind then. He was older than I was and he always allowing, "John, up in Winston all the niggers makes five dollar a day; how come you don't go up there and get rich like I is?" Some of the older ones laugh when he talk to me like that and he lean to my ear and say real low, "They's ignorant."

One day when the crops done laid by I told Marse Jim, as I always call him, that, I allows, "Marse, dis fall I gwine North to get rich, but I sure is gwine to bring you folks something when I comes South again." So Marse give me my money and I set out for the North. I got to Winston-Salem and got me a job. But it was that hard, a-cleaning and a-washing all the time, 'cause I never knowed nothing about no tobacco and there wasn't nothing that I could turn off real quick that would bring me no big money. It got cold and I never had no big oak logs to burn in my fireplace and I set and shivered till I lay down. Then it wasn't no cover like I had at Marse Jim's. Up there they never had 'nough wood to keep no fire all night.

Next thing I knowed I was down with the grippe and it took all the money dat I had and then I borrowed some to pay the doctor. So I up and come back home. It took me a long time to reach Spartanburg and from there I struck up with the first home niggers I seed since I left in the fall. That make me more better than I feel since the first day what I arrive at Winston. Long before I arrive at home, I knowed that I done been a fool to ever leave the plantation.

When I get home all the darkies that glad to offer me the "glad hands."

I ask where that nigger what enticed me off to the North and they all allow that he done took the consumption and died soon after I done gone from home. I never had no consumption, but it took me long time to get over the grippe. I goes to Old Marse and hires myself out and I never left him no more till the Lord took him away.

DOC QUINN
Interviewed at Texarkana, Arkansas
Interviewed by Cecil Copeland
Age at interview: 94

I WAS BORN March 15, 1843, in Monroe County, Mississippi, near Aberdeen. My master was Colonel Ogburn, one of de biggest planters in de state of Mississippi. Many's de time he raised so much cotton dat dem big steamers just couldn't carry it all down to New Orleans in one year. But den along came de Civil War and we didn't raise nothin' for several years. Why? Because most of us joined the Confederate Army in Colonel Ogburn's regiment as servants and bodyguards. And let me tell you somethin'. Dere never was a war like dis war. Why, I 'member dat after de battle of Corinth, Mississippi, a five acre field was so thickly covered with de dead and wounded dat you couldn't touch de ground in walkin' across it. And de onliest way to bury dem was to cut a deep furrow with a plow, lay de soldiers head to head, and plow de dirt back on dem.

About a year after de War started de master got one of dese A.W.O.L.'s from de army so we could come to Miller County, where he bought de place on Red River now known as de Adams Farm. When we first came here dis place, as well as de rest of de valley, was just a big canebrake — nothin' lived in dere but bears, wolves, and varmints. Why, de master would have to round up de livestock each afternoon, put dem in pens, and den put out guards all night to keep de wolves and bears from gettin' 'em. De folks didn't go gallivantin' round nights like dey do now or de varmints would get them. But den we didn't stay here but a few months until de master's A.W.O.L. was up, so we had to go back and join de army. We fought in Mississippi, Alabama, Georgia, and South Carolina.

When de War ended, de master moved us to Miller County, but not on de Adams farm. For de man what used to own de farm said Uncle Sam hadn't made any such money as was paid him for de farm, so he wanted his farm back. Dat Confederate money wasn't worth de paper it was printed on, so de master had to give him back de farm. Poor Massa Ogburn—he didn't live long after dat. He and his wife are buried side by side in Rondo Cemetery.

Not long after de Negroes was freed, I took eighty-six of dem to de votin' place at Homan and voted 'em all straight Democratic. On my way back home dat evenin' five Negroes jumped from de bushes and stopped me. Dey 'splained dat I was too influential with de Negroes and proceeded to string me up by de neck. I hollers as loud as I could, and Roy Nash and Hugh Burton, de election officers, just happened to be comin' down de road and hear me yell. Dey run off de niggers and cut me down, but by dat time I had passed out. It was several weeks before I got well, and I can still feel dat rope round my neck. Iffen dey had known how to tie a hangman's knot I wouldn't be here to tell you about it.

It wasn't long after dis dat I joined Colonel Baker's gang for protection. Colonel Baker was a great and brave man and did more for de white folks of dis country dan any other man. Why, iffen it hadn't been for him, de white folks couldn't have lived in dis country, de Negroes was so mean. Dey was so mean dat dey tied heavy plow shares around de necks of two little white boys and threw dem in de lake. I was dere.

And another time I was with a bunch of niggers when dey was plannin' on killin' a white man who was a friend of mine. As soon as I could I slips away and tips him off. When I got back one of dem niggers looks at me suspicious like and asks, "Where you been, nigger?" I was shakin' like a leaf in a storm, but I says: "I ain't been nowhere—just went home to get some cartridges to help kill dis white man."

Not long after I joined Colonel Baker's gang, we was comin' from Fulton to Clipper through de Red River bottoms. De river was overflowin' and as we was crossin' a deep, swift slough, Colonel Baker and his horse got tangled up in some grapevines. Colonel Baker yelled, and I turned my mule around and cut all de grapevine loose with my bowie knife. Dere ain't nothing like a mule for swimmin'. Dey can swim circles around any horse. As long as he lived, Colonel Baker was always grateful to me for savin' his life.

De Colonel hated de sight of mean niggers. We would ride up to a Negro settlement and tell de niggers we was organizing a colored militia to catch Colonel Baker and his gang. Most of de Negroes would join, but some of dem had to be encouraged by Colonel Baker's big gun. De recruits would be lined up in an open field for drilling. And dey sure was drilled. Colonel Baker and his men would shoot them by the score. Dey killed fifty-three at Homan, Arkansas, eighty-six at Rocky Comfort, Arkansas, six near Ogden, Arkansas, six on de Temple place, sixty-two at Jefferson, Texas, one hundred at North Louisiana, seventy-three at Marshall, Texas, and several others.

All of de big planters was friendly to Colonel Baker. I have carried supplies many times from de big plantation—Harvey, Class, and others —to Colonel Baker. De colonel always carried a big double-barrel shotgun. It must have been de biggest shotgun in de world, not less dan a number eight size. He whipped sixteen soldiers at Old Boston with dis gun one time.

I saw Colonel Baker killed. We had just arrived at his father-in-law's house and I was in the horse lot, about fifty yards from de house, when Joe Davis, Thomas Orr, and some more men rode up. De Colonel was standin' by de chimney and did not see dem come around de house. Dey killed him before he knew dey was around. One of de men asked Mr. Foster, "Where at dat damn nigger?" I ducked down and crawled in under de rail fence and ran—I didn't stop till I was deep in the Sulphur River bottoms. Every minute my heart seemed like it was goin' to jump right out of my mouth. I was the worst scared nigger that ever lived.

CHANEY RICHARDSON

Interviewed at Fort Gibson, Oklahoma
Interviewer not identified
Age when interviewed: 85

I WAS BORN in the old Caney settlement southeast of Tahlequah on the banks of the Caney Creek. Off to the north we could see the big old ridge of Sugar Mountain when the sun shine on him first thing in the morning when we all getting up.

I didn't know nothing else but some kind of war until I was a grown woman, because when I first can remember my old master, Charley Rogers, was always on the lookout for somebody or other he was lined up against in the big feud. My master and all the rest of the folks was Cherokees, and they'd been killing each other off in the feud ever since long before I was borned and just because Old Master have a big farm and three-four families of Negroes them other Cherokees keep on pestering his stuff all the time. Us children was always a-feared to go any place lessen some of the grown folks was along. We didn't know what we was a-feared of, but we heard the master and mistress keep talking about "another party killing" and we stuck close to the place.

Old Mistress' name was Nancy Rogers, but I was a orphan after I was a big girl and I called her "Aunt" and "Mamma" like I did when I was little. You see my own mammy was the house woman and I was raised in the house and I heard the little children call old Mistress "Mamma" and so I did too. She never did make me stop.

My pappy and mammy and us children lived in a one-room log cabin close to the creek bank and just a little piece from Old Master's house.

My pappy's name was Joe Tucker and my mammy's name was Ruth Tucker. They belonged to a man named Tucker before I was born and he sold them to Master Charley Rogers and he just let them go on by the same name if they wanted to, because last names didn't mean nothing to a slave anyways. The folks just called my pappy "Charley Rogers' boy Joe."

I already had two sisters, Mary and Mandy, when I was born, and purty soon I had a baby brother, Louis. Mammy worked at the Big House and took me along every day. When I was a little bigger I would help hold the hank when she done the spinning and Old Mistress done a lot of the weaving and some knitting. She just set by the window and knit most all of the time. When we weave the cloth we had a big loom out on the gallery, and Miss Nancy tell us how to do it.

Mammy eat at our own cabin, and we had lots of game meat and fish the boys get in the Caney Creek. Mammy bring down deer meat and wild turkey sometimes, that the Indian boys get on Sugar Mountain. Then we had corn bread, dried bean bread, and green stuff outen Master's patch. Mammy make the bean bread when we get short of cornmeal and nobody going to the mill right away. She take and boil the beans and mash them up in some meal and that make it go a long ways.

The slaves didn't have no garden 'cause they work the old master's garden and make enough to have some anyway.

When I was about ten years old the feud got so bad the Indians was always talking about getting their horses and cattle killed and their slaves harmed. I was too little to know how bad it was until one morning my own mammy went off somewhere down the road to get some stuff to dye cloth and she didn't come back. Lots of the young Indian bucks on both sides of the feud would ride around the woods at night, and Old Master got powerful uneasy about my mammy and had all the neighbors and slaves out looking for her, but nobody find her. It was about a week later that two Indian men rid up and ask Old Master wasn't his gal Ruth gone. He says yes, and they take one of the slaves along with a wagon to show where they seen her. They find her in some bushes where she'd been getting bark to set the dyes, and she been dead all the time. Somebody done hit her in the head with a club and shot her through and through with a bullet too. She was so swole up they couldn't lift her up and just had to make a deep hole right alongside her and roll her in it she was so bad mortified. Old Master nearly go crazy he was so mad, and the young Cherokee men ride the woods every night for about a month, but they never catch on to who done it.

I think Old Master sell the children or give them out to somebody then, because I never see my sisters and brother for a long time after the Civil War, and for me, I have to go live with a new mistress that was a Cherokee neighbor. Her name was Hannah Ross, and she raised me until I was grown. I was her home girl, and she and me done a lot of spinning and weaving too. I helped the cook and carried water and milked. I carried the water in a homemade piggin set on my head. Them piggins was kind of buckets made out of staves set around a bottom and didn't have no handle.

I can remember weaving with Miss Hannah Ross. She would weave a strip of white and one of yellow and one of brown to make it pretty. She had a reel that would pop every time it got to a half skein so she would know how to stop and fill it up again. We used copperas and some kind of bark she bought at the store to dye with. It was cotton clothes winter and summer for the slaves, too, I'll tell you.

When the Civil War come along we seen lots of white soldiers in them brown butternut suits all over the place, and about all the Indian men was in it too. Old master Charley Rogers' boy Charley went along too. Then pretty soon—it seems like about a year—a lot of the Cherokee men come back home and say they not going back to the War with that General Cooper, and some of them go off the Federal side because the captain go to the Federal side too. Somebody come along and tell me my own pappy have to go in the War and I think they say he on the Cooper side, and then after while Miss Hannah tell me he got kilt over in Arkansas.

I was so grieved all the time I don't remember much what went on, but I know pretty soon my Cherokee folks had all the stuff they had et up by the soldiers and they was just a few wagons and mules left. All the slaves was piled in together and some of the grown ones walking, and they took us way down across the big river and kept us in the bottoms a long time until the War was over. We lived in a kind of a camp, but I was too little to know where they got the grub to feed us with. Most all the Negro men was off somewhere in the War.

Then one day they had to bust up the camp and some Federal soldiers go with us and we all start back home. We got to a place where all the houses is burned down and I ask what is that place. Miss Hannah say: "Skullyville, child. That's where they had part of the War."

All the slaves was set out when we got to Fort Gibson, and the soldiers say we all free now. They give us grub and clothes to the Negroes at that place. It wasn't no town but a fort place and a patch of big trees. Miss Hannah take me to her place and I work there until I was grown. I didn't get any money that I seen, but I got a good place to stay.

Pretty soon I married Ran Lovely and we lived in a double log house here at Fort Gibson. Then my second husband was Henry Richardson, but he's been dead for years, too. We had six children, but they all dead but one.

I didn't want slavery to be over with, mostly because we had the War I reckon. All that trouble made me the loss of my mammy and pappy, and I was always treated good when I was a slave. When it was over I had rather be at home like I was. None of the Cherokees ever whipped us, and my mistress give me some mighty fine rules to live by to get along in this world, too.

BETTY ROBERTSON

Interviewed at Fort Gibson, Oklahoma
Interviewer not identified
Age when interviewed: 93

I WAS BORN close to Webbers Falls, in the Canadian District of the Cherokee Nation, in the same year that my pappy was blowed up and killed in the big boat accident that killed my old master.

I never did see my daddy excepting when I was a baby and I only know what my mammy told me about him. He come from across the water when he was a little boy and was grown when Old Master Joseph Vann bought him, so he never did learn to talk much Cherokee. My mammy was a Cherokee slave, and talked it good. My husband was a Cherokee born Negro, too, and when he got mad he forget all the English he knowed.

Old Master Joe had a mighty big farm and several families of Negroes, and he was a powerful rich man. Pappy's name was Kalet Vann, and Mammy's name was Sally. My brothers was named Sone and Frank. I had one brother and one sister sold when I was little and I don't remember the names. My other sisters was Polly, Ruth, and Liddie. I had to work in the kitchen when I was a gal, and they was ten or twelve children smaller than me for me to look after, too. Sometime Young Master Joe and the other boys give me a piece of money and say I worked for it, and I reckon I did, for I have to cook five or six times a day. Some of the master's family was always going down to the river and back, and every time they come in I have to fix something to eat. Old Mistress had a good cookin' stove, but most Cherokees had only a big fireplace and pot hooks. We had meat, bread, rice, potatoes, and plenty of fish and chicken. The springtime give us plenty of green corn and beans, too. I couldn't buy anything in slavery time, so I just give the piece of money to the Vann children. I got all the clothes I need from Old Mistress, and in winter I had high top shoes with brass caps on the toe. In the summer I wear them on Sunday, too. I wore loom cloth clothes, dyed in copperas what the old Negro women and the old Cherokee women made.

The slaves had a pretty easy time, I think. Young Master Vann never was very hard on us and he never whipped us, and Old Mistress was a widow woman and a good Christian and always kind. I sure did love

249

her. Maybe Old Master Joe Vann was harder, I don't know, but that was before my time. Young Master never whip his slaves, but if they don't mind good he sell them off sometimes. He sold one of my brothers and one sister because they kept running off. They wasn't very big either, but one day two Cherokees rode up and talked a long time, then Young Master came to the cabin and said they were sold because Mammy couldn't make them mind him. They got on the horses behind the men and went off.

Old Master Joe had a big steamboat he called the *Lucy Walker*, and he run it up and down the Arkansas and the Mississippi and the Ohio river, Old Mistress say. He went clean to Louisville, Kentucky, and back. My pappy was kind of a boss of the Negroes that run the boat, and they all belong to Old Master Joe. Some had been in a big runaway and had been brung back, and wasn't so good, so keep them on the boat all the time mostly. Mistress say Old Master and my pappy on the boat somewhere close to Louisville and the boiler bust and tear the boat up. Some niggers say my pappy kept hollering, "Run it to the bank! Run it to the bank!" but it sunk and him and Old Master died.

Old Master Joe was a big man in the Cherokees, I hear, and was good to his Negroes before I was born. My pappy run away one time, four or five years before I was born, Mammy tells me, and at that time a whole lot of Cherokee slaves run off at once. They got over in the Creek country and stood off the Cherokee officers that went to get them, but pretty soon they give up and come home. Mammy say they was lots of excitement on Old Master's place and all the Negroes mighty scared, but he didn't sell my pappy off. He just kept him and he was a good Negro after that. He had to work on the boat, though, and never got to come home but once in a long while.

Young Master Joe let us have singing and be baptized if we want to, but I wasn't baptized till after the War. But we couldn't learn to read or have a book, and Cherokee folks was afraid to tell us about the letters and figures because they have a law you go to jail and a big fine if you show a slave about the letters.

When the War come they have a big battle away west of us, but I never see any battles. Lots of soldiers around all the time, though.

One day Young Master come to the cabins and say we all free and can't stay there less'n we want to go on working for him just like we'd been, for our food and clothes. Mammy got a wagon and we traveled around a few days and go to Fort Gibson. When we get to Fort Gibson they was a lot of Negroes there, and they had a camp meeting and I was baptized. It was in the Grand River close to the ford and winter time. Snow on the ground and the water was muddy and all full of pieces of ice. The place was all woods, and the Cherokees and the soldiers all come down to see the baptizing.

We settled down a little ways above Fort Gibson. Mammy had the wagon and two oxen, and we worked a good size patch there until she died, and then I get married to Cal Robertson to have somebody to take care of me. Cal Robertson was eighty-nine years old when I married him forty years ago, right on this porch. I had on my old clothes for the wedding, and I ain't had any good clothes since I was a little slave girl. Then I had clean warm clothes and I had to keep them clean, too!

I got my allotment as a Cherokee freedman, and so did Cal, but we lived here at this place because we was too old to work the land ourselves. In slavery time the Cherokee Negroes do like anybody else when they is a death—just listen to a chapter in the Bible and all cry. We had a good song I remember. It was "Don't Call the Roll, Jesus, Because I'm Coming Home." The only song I remember from the soldiers was: "Hang Jeff Davis to a Sour Apple Tree," and I remember that because they said he used to be at Fort Gibson one time. I don't know what he done after that.

I been a good Christian ever since I was baptized, but I keep a little charm here on my neck anyways, to keep me from having the nosebleed. It's got a buckeye and a lead bullet in it. I had a silver dime on it, too, for a long time, but I took it off and got me a box of snuff. I'm glad the War's over and I am free to meet God like anybody else, and my grandchildren can learn to read and write.

HARRIETT ROBINSON

Interviewed at Oklahoma City, Oklahoma
Interviewer not identified
Age when interviewed: 94

I WAS BORN September 1, 1842, in Bastrop, Texas, on Colorado River. My pappy was named Harvey Wheeler and my mammy Carolina Sims. My brothers and sisters was named Alex, Taylor, Mary, Cicero, Tennessee, Sarah, Jeff, Ella, and Nora. My sister Liza, was mulatto and Master Colonel Sims' son had three chillen by her. We never seen her no more after her last child was born. I found out, though, that she was in Canada.

I nursed three white chillen, Lulu, Helen Augusta, and Lola Sims. I done this before the War that set us free. We kids used to make extra money by toting gravel in our aprons. They'd give us dimes and silver nickels.

We lived in cedar log houses with dirt floors and double chimneys, and doors hung on wooden hinges. One side of our beds was bored in the walls and had one leg on the other. Them white folks give each nigger family a blanket in winter.

Our clothes was wool and cotton mixed. We had red rustic shoes, soles one-half inch thick. They'd go a-whick-a-wack. The mens had pants with one seam and a right-hand pocket. Boys wore shirts.

We ate hominy, mush, grits, and pone bread for the most part. Many of them ate out of one tray with wooden spoons. All victuals for field hands was fixed together.

Women broke in mules, throwed 'em down, and roped 'em. They'd do it better'n men. While Mammy made some hominy one day both my foots was scalded, and when they clipped them blisters, they just put some cotton round them and catched all dat yellow water and made me a yellow dress out of it. This was 'way back yonder in slavery, before the War.

Whenever white folks had a baby born, den all de old niggers had to come through the room and the master would be over behind the bed and he'd say, "Here's a new little mistress or master you got to work for." You had to say, "Yessir, Master," and bow real low or the overseer would crack you. Them was slavery days, dog days.

My mammy belonged to Master Colonel Sam Sims and his old mean wife, Julia. My pappy belonged to Master Meke Smith and his good wife, Harriet. She was sure a good woman. I was named after her. Master Sam and Master Meke was partners. Every year them rich men would send so many wagons to New Mexico for different things. It took six months to go and come.

Slaves was punished by whip and starving. Decker was sure a mean slaveholder. He lived close to us. Master Sam didn't never whip me, but Miss Julia whipped me every day in the morning. During the War she beat us so terrible. She say, "Your master's out fighting and losing blood trying to save you from them Yankees, so you can get your'n here." Miss Julia would take me by my ears and butt my head against the wall.

She wanted to whip my mother, but Old Master told her, "No sir." When his father done give my mammy to Master Sam, he told him not to beat her, and if he got to where he just had to, just bring her back and place her in his yard from where he got her.

White folks didn't allow you to read or write. Them what did know come from Virginny. Mistress Julia used to drill her chillen in spelling any words. At every word them chillen missed, she gived me a lick across the head for it. Meanest woman I ever seen in my whole life.

This skin I got now, it ain't my first skin. That was burnt off when I was a little child. Mistress used to have a fire made on the fireplace and she made me scour the brass round it and my skin just blistered. I just had to keep pulling it offen me.

We didn't had no church, though my pappy was a preacher. He preached in the quarters. Our baptizing song was "On Jordan's Stormy Bank I Stand" and "Hark from the Tomb." Now all dat was before the War. We had all our funerals at the graveyard. Everybody, chillen and all, picked up a clod of dirt and throwed in on top the coffin to help fill up the grave.

Talking about niggers running away, didn't my step-pappy run away? Didn't my uncle Gabe run away? The frost would just bite they toes most nigh off, too, whiles they was gone. They put Uncle Isom, my step-pappy, in jail and while's he was in there he killed a white guardsman. Then they put in the paper, "A nigger to kill," and our master seen it and bought him.

He was a double-strengthed man, he was so strong. He'd run off, so help you God. They had the bloodhounds after him once and he caught the hound what was leading and beat the rest of the dogs. The white folks run up on him before he knowed it and made them dogs eat his ear plumb out. But don't you know he got away anyhow.

One morning I was sweeping out the hall in the Big House and somebody come a-knocking on the front door and I goes to the door. There was Uncle Isom with rags all on his head. He said, "Tell Old Master here I am." I goes to Master's door and says, "Master Colonel Sam, Uncle Isom said here he am." He say, "Go round to the kitchen and tell black mammy to give you breakfast."

When he was through eating they give him three hundred lashes and, bless my soul, he run off again.

When we went to a party the nigger fiddlers would play a tune dat went like this:

> I fooled Old Master seven years,
> Fooled the overseer three;
> Hand me down my banjo,
> And I'll tickle your bel-lee.

We had the same doctors the white folks had and we wore asafetida and garlic and onions to keep from taking all them ailments.

I 'member the battle being fit. The white folks buried all the jewelry and silver and all the gold in the Blue Ridge Mountains, in Orange, Texas. Master made all us niggers come together and get ready to leave 'cause the Yankees was coming. We took a steamer. Now this was in slavery time, sure 'nough slavery. Then we got on a steamship and pulled out to Galveston. Then he told the captain to feed we niggers. We was on the bay, not the ocean. We left Galveston and went on trains for Houston.

After the War, Master Colonel Sims went to get the mail and so he call Daniel Ivory, the overseer, and say to him, "Go round to all the quarters and tell all the niggers to come up, I got a paper to read to 'em. They're free now, so you can get another job, 'cause I ain't got no more niggers which is my own." Niggers come up from the cabins nappy-headed, just like they gwine to the field. Master Colonel Sims say: "Caroline (that's my mammy), you is free as me. Pa said bring you back and I'se gwine do just that. So you go on and work and I'll pay you and your three oldest chillen ten dollars a month a head and four dollars for Harriet," that's me, and then he turned to the rest and say "Now all youuns will receive ten dollars a head till the crop is laid by." Don't you know before he got halfway through, over half them niggers was gone.

Them Klu Klux Klans come and ask for water with the false stomachs and make like they was drinking three bucketsful. They done some terrible things, but God seen it all and marked it down.

We didn't had no law, we had "bureau." Why, in them days if somebody stole anything from you, they had to pay you and not the law. Now they done turned that round and you don't get nothing.

One day whiles Master was gone hunting, Mistress Julia told her brother to give Miss Harriett (me) a free whipping. She was a nigger killer. Master Colonel Sam come home and he said, "You infernal sons o' bitches, don't you know there is three hundred Yankees camped out here and if they knowed you'd whipped this nigger the way you done, they'd kill all us. If they find it out, I'll kill all you all." Old rich devils, I'm here but they is gone.

TOM ROBINSON
Interviewed near Hot Springs, Arkansas
Interviewed by Mary D. Hudgins
Age when interviewed: 88

IT's MY UNDERSTANDING that I was born in Catawba County, North Carolina. As far as I remember, Newton was the nearest town. I was born on a place belonging to Jacob Sigmans. I can just barely remember my mother. I was not eleven when they sold me away from her. I can just barely remember her. But I do remember how she used to take us children and kneel down in front of the fireplace and pray. She'd pray that the time would come when everybody could worship the Lord under their own vine and fig tree—all of them free. It's come to me lots of times since. There she was a-praying, and on other plantations women was a-praying. All over the country the same prayer was being prayed. Guess the Lord done heard the prayer and answered it.

Old man Sigmans wasn't a bad master. Don't remember so much about him. I couldn't have been eleven when he sold me to Pinkney Setzer. He kept me for a little while and then he sold me to David Robinson. All three of them lived not so far apart in North Carolina.

But pretty soon after he bought me old man Dave Robinson moved to Texas. We was there when the War started. We stayed there all during the War. I was set free there.

We lived in Cass County. It was pretty close to the Arkansas border, and 'twasn't far from Oklahoma. I remember well when they was first gathering them up for the War. We used to hear the cannon often. To be sure I was scared, right at first. Pretty soon we got used to it. Somebody even made up a song, "Listen to the Homemade Thunder." They'd sing it every time the cannon started roaring. There never was any fighting right around us. I never really saw any fighting.

Old man Dave Robinson was good to me. He didn't have a big farm—just owned me. Treated me almost like I was one of his own children. 'Course, I had to work. Sometimes he whipped me—but no more than he had to. I was just a child and any child has got to be made to mind. He was good to me, and old Miss was good to me. All my masters was pretty good to me—lots better than the usual run. I kept the name Robinson, and I named my son Dave, so you might know which one I think the most of.

One day I was out milking the cows. Mr. Dave come down into the field, and he had a paper in his hands. "Listen to me, Tom," he said. "Listen to what I reads you." And he read from a paper all about how I was free. You can't tell how I felt. "You're jokin' me," I says. "No, I ain't," says he, "you're free." "No," says I, "it's a joke." "No," says he, "Its a law that I got to read this paper to you. Now listen while I read it again."

But still I wouldn't believe him. "Just go up to the house," says he, "and ask Mrs. Robinson. She'll tell you." So I went. "It's a joke," I says to her. "Did you ever know your master to tell you a lie?" she says. "No," says I, "I ain't." "Well," she says, "the War's over and you're free."

By that time I thought maybe she was telling me what was right. "Miss Robinson," says I, "can I go over to see the Smiths?"—they was a colored family that lived nearby. "Don't you understand," says she, "you're free. You don't have to ask me what you can do. Run along, child." And so I went. And do you know why I was a going? I wanted to find out if they was free too. I just couldn't take it all in. I couldn't believe we was all free alike.

Was I happy? Lord! You can take anything. No matter how good you treat it—it wants to be free. You can treat it good and feed it and give it everything it seems to want—but if you open the cage—it's happy?

After the War was over I farmed. I farmed all my life, till I got too old. I stopped three-four years ago. I didn't sharecrop, except just at first to get a start. I rented. I paid thirds and fourths. I always rented. I wasn't a sharecropper. Now I lives with my son—Dave Robinson—the one I named for my master. It was awful hard going after the War. But I got me a place—had to sharecrop for a year or two. But I worked hard and saved all I could. Pretty soon I had me enough that I could rent. I always raised the usual things—cotton and corn and potatoes and a little truck and that sort of thing—always raised enough to eat for us and the stock, and then some cotton for a cash crop.

My first wife, well, it was kind of funny. I wasn't more than nineteen. She had eleven children. Some of them was older than I was. But it wasn't too hard on me. They was all old enough to take care of themselves. I lived with that woman for seventeen years. Then she died.

I been married five times. Three of my children are living. One lives here in Hot Springs. Then there's one in Texarkana and there's one in Kansas City. Two of my children are dead. The youngest died just about last year. All my wives are dead.

FEREBE ROGERS

Interviewed at Milledgeville, Georgia
Interviewed by Ruth Chitty
Age when interviewed: 100+

I 'MEMBERS a whole heap about slavery times. When freedom come I had five chillen. Five chillen and ten cents. Dey says I'm a hundred and eight or nine years old, but I don't think I'm quite as old as dat. I knows I'se over a hundred, though. I was bred and born on a plantation on Brier Creek in Baldwin County. My old marster was Mr. Sam Hart. He owned my mother. She had thirteen chillen. I was de oldest, so I took devil's fare.

My daddy was a old-time free nigger. He was a good shoemaker and could make as fine shoes and boots as every you see. But he never would work till he was plumb out o' money—den he had to work. But he quit just soon as he made a little money. Mr. Chat Morris—he had a regular shoe shop—offered him steady work makin' boots and shoes for him. Was goin' pay him three hundred dollars a year. But he wouldn't take it. Was too lazy. De old-time free niggers had to tell how dey make day livin', and if dey couldn't give satisfaction about it, dey was put on de block and sold to de highest bidder. Most of 'em sold for three years for fifty dollars. My daddy brought one hundred dollars when he was sold for three or four years.

I was on de block twice myself. When de old head died dey was so many slaves for de chillen to draw for, we was put on de block. Mr. John Bagget bought me den, and said I was a good breedin' woman. Den later, one de young Hart marsters bought me back.

All de slaves had different work to do. My auntie was one de weavers. Old Miss had two looms goin' all de time. She had a old loom and a new loom. My husband made de new loom for old Miss. He was a carpenter and he worked on outside jobs after he'd finished tasks for his marster. He used to make all de boxes dey buried de white folks and de slaves in, on de Hart and Golden plantations. Dey was pretty as you see, too.

I was a field hand myself. I come up twixt de plow handles. I weren't de fastest one with a hoe, but I didn't turn my back on nobody plowin'. My marster had over a thousand acres o' land. He was good to us. We had plenty to eat, like meat and bread and vegetables. We raised everything on de plantation—wheat, corn, potatoes, peas, hogs, cows, chickens, sheep—just everything.

All de clothes was made on de plantation, too. Dey spun de thread from cotton and wool, and dyed it and wove it. We had cutters and dem dat done de sewin'. I still got de first dress my husband give me. My husband was Kinchen Rogers. His marster was Mr. Bill Golden, and he lived about four miles from where I stayed on de Hart plantation.

Us slaves went to de white folks church a-Sunday. Marster, he was a Primitive Baptist, and he try to keep his slaves from goin' to other churches. We had baptizin's first Sundays. Back in dem days dey baptized in de creek, but at de windin' up o' freedom dey dug a pool. I went to church Sundays, and dat's where I met my husband. I been married just one time. He de daddy o' all my chillen. I had fifteen in all.

Young marster was fixin' to marry us, but he got cold feet, and a nigger by name o' Enoch Golden married us. He was what we called a "double-headed nigger"—he could read and write, and he knowed so much. On his dyin' bed he said he been de death o' many a nigger 'cause he taught so many to read and write.

Me and my husband couldn't live together till after freedom 'cause we had different marsters. When freedom come, Marster wanted all us niggers to sign up to stay till Christmas. After dat we worked on shares on de Hart plantation; den we farmed four-five years with Mr. Bill Johnson.

I'm goin' to tell you de truth. I don't tell no lies. Dese has been better times to me. I think it's better to work for yourself and have what you make dan to work for somebody else and don't get nothin' out of it. Slavery days was mighty hard. My marster was good to us (I mean he didn't beat us much, and he give us plenty plain food), but some slaves suffered awful. My aunt was beat cruel once, and lots de other slaves. When dey got ready to beat you, dey'd strip you stark mother naked and dey'd say, "Come here to me, God damn you! Come to me clean! Walk up to dat tree, and damn you, hug dat tree!" Den dey tie your hands round de tree, den tie your feets; den dey'd lay de rawhide on you and cut your buttocks open. Sometimes dey'd rub turpentine and salt in de raw places, and den beat you some more. Oh, it was awful! And what could you do? Dey had all de advantage of you. I never did get no beatin' like dat, but I got whippin's—plenty o' 'em. I had plenty o' devilment in me, but I quit all my devilment when I was married. I used to fight—fight with anything I could get my hands on.

You had to have passes to go from one plantation to another. Some de niggers would slip off sometime and go without a pass, or maybe Marster was busy and dey didn't want to bother him for a pass, so dey go without one. In every district dey had about twelve men dey call patterrollers. Dey ride up and down and round looking for niggers without passes. If dey ever caught you off your plantation with no pass, dey beat you all over. I 'member a song about—

> Run, nigger, run, de patterroller get you,
> Slip over de fence slick as a eel.
> White man catch you by de heel,
> Run, nigger, run!

When slaves run away, dey always put de bloodhounds on de tracks. Marster always kept one hound named Rock. I can hear him now when dey was on de track, callin', "Hurrah, Rock, hurrah, Rock! Catch him!" Dey always send Rock to fetch him down when dey found him. Dey had de dogs trained to keep dey teeth out you till dey told 'em to bring you down. Den de dogs would go at your throat, and dey'd tear you to pieces, too. After a slave was caught, he was brung home and put in chains.

De marsters let de slaves have little patches o' land for deyselves. De size o' de patch was accordin' to de size o' your family. We was allowed about four acres. We made about five hundred pounds o' lint cotton, and sold it at Warrenton. Den we used de money to buy stuff for Christmas. But Christmas weren't no different from other times. We used to have quiltin' parties, candy pullin's, dances, corn shuckin's, games like thimble and such like.

Course dey had doctors in dem days, but we used mostly homemade medicines. I don't believe in doctors much now. We used sage tea, ginger tea, rosemary tea—all good for colds and other ailments, too. We had men and women midwives. Dr. Cicero Gibson was with me when my first baby come. I was twenty-five years old den. My baby child seventy-five now.

I had my right arm cut off at de elbow if I'd tried to learn to read and write. If dey found a nigger what could read and write, dey'd cut your arm off at de elbow, or sometimes at de shoulder.

I don't believe in no conjures. One conjure-man come here once. He try his best to overcome me, but he couldn't do nothin' with me. After dat, he told my husband he couldn't do nothin 'to me, 'cause I didn't believe in him, and dem conjure-folks can't hurt you lessen you believe in 'em. He say he could make de sun stand still, and do wonders, but I knowed dat weren't so, 'cause can't nobody stop de sun 'cept de man what made it, and dat's God. I don't believe in no conjures. I don't pay much attention to times o' de moon to do things, neither. I plants my garden when I gets ready. But bunch beans does better if you plants 'em on new moon in April. Plant butter beans on full moon in April—potatoes first o' March.

When de War broke out de damn Yankees come to our place. Dey done everything dat was bad. Dey burn everything dey couldn't use, and dey took a heap o' corn. Marster had some corn pens on de river, dough, dey didn't find. I just can't tell you all dey done.

De goodness o' de Lord is de reason I live so long, I reckon. I worked hard all my life, and always tried to do right.

GEORGE ROGERS
Interviewed in North Carolina
Interviewed by Pat Matthews
Age when interviewed: 94

GEORGE ROGERS is the name I has carried for ninety-four years and over. I will be ninety-five the first day of this comin' August. Louis Rogers was my father. My mother was Penny Rogers. All my brothers and sisters are dead except one sister. She is livin' in Buffalo, New York. She is somewhere round seventy years old. She was the baby in our home. My mother and father and all of us belonged to Felix Rogers. He lived in the edge of Wake County next to Greenville County. My mother came from Canada. My marster came here from Canada and married here. He married old man Billy Shipp's daughter. Her name was Matilda Shipp.

I cannot read and write. Dey did not allow no niggers to handle no papers in dem days. Marster had three plantations and about one hundred slaves. We had good houses and plenty to eat. My marster was a good man. We had no church on the plantation, but we had prayer meeting in our houses. He allowed dat and when dey had a big meeting, he made us all go. We had dances or anything else we wanted to at night. We had corn shuckings, candy pullings, and all the whiskey and brandy we wanted. My daddy didn't do nothin' but still for him. Whiskey was only ten cents a quart den.

I have never seen him really whip a slave any more dan he whipped his own chillens. He whipped us all together when we stole watermelons and apples. He made us chillen, white and black, eat together at a big table to ourselves. We had ordinary clothes, but we all went alike. In the summer and winter we all went barefooted and in our shirttails most of de time. His chillens was just as bad for goin' barefooted as we niggers was.

We had our patches, and he allowed us to have the money we made on 'em. Our houses were called slave quarters. Our marster's house was a big fine two story house. We slaves called it "de Great House." None of de slaves from Marster Roger's plantation never run away.

We chillen played de games of marbles, cat ball, and we played base, prison base. At night we all played peep squirrel in the house. We played blindfold and tag. We fished a lot in Briar Creek. We caught a lot of fish. Sometimes we used pin hooks we made ourselves. We would trade our fish to missus for molasses to make candy out of.

When we got sick we had a doctor. His name was Dr. Hicks. I never was sick, but some of de rest was. We had an old colored man who doctored on all us chillen. He gave us roots and herbs.

I have seen slaves sold. My marster died the year the War started; den dey had a big sale at our house. Dey had a sale, and old man Askew bought a whole lot of our niggers. I don't know his name, only dey called him "old man Askew." Old man Askew was a slave speculator. He didn't do nothin' but buy up slaves and sell 'em. He carried de ones he bought at our house to Texas. He bought my half-sister and carried her to Texas. After de surrender I saw her in Texas once, never no more.

When de War begin dey carried Young Marster off. His name was William Rogers, and dey sent me to wait on him. I was in camp with him up here by de old fair grounds. After we got there I seed old Colonel Farrabow, he was colonel of dat regiment. We all left Raleigh on wagons, and I don't know where we went after we left Raleigh; I was lost. We got on de train at Fayetteville, where dey kept de rations. We went to a place where dere was a lot of water. I don't know its name. We were dere about three days when dey had a battle, and den Colonel Farrabow come round and told me Marster was gone. He told us to go to the breastworks and work. I stayed dere three years and eight months. Den dey had another battle dere just before I left, and de Yankees took de place.

I went to de Yankees den. Dey give me clothes, shoes, somethin' to eat, and some money too. I worked for 'em while dey were camped in Raleigh. Dey were camped on Newbern Avenue and Tarboro Street and all out in Gatlin' Field in de place now called Lincoln Park. De Yankees when dey took us, told us to come on with 'em. Dey told us to get all de folk's chickens and hogs. We was behind 'em, and we had plenty. Dey made us steal and take things for 'em. Wheeler's cavalry went before us, dat's why dey was so rich. Dey got all de silver, and we got de chickens and hogs.

De Yankees skinned chickens and geese. Dey cut hogs and cows up and den skinned 'em. Dey took just part of a cow sometimes, just de hind quarters and left de rest. We went to one place, and de white woman only had one piece of meat and a big gang of little chillen. I begged de Yankees to let dat piece of meat alone, she was so poor, but de officer told 'em to take it, and dey took her last piece o' meat.

I stayed with de Yankees two years after de surrender. Dey carried me to Florida when I left Raleigh. When I left 'em in Florida I went to Texas to mind cattle. I stayed in Texas seven years. Den Mr. Hardie Pool from down here at Battle Bridge, Wake County, come out dere. When he started home I couldn't stand it no longer, and I just told him I was goin' back home to North Carolina. No sir, when I got home, I would not go back. No more mindin' cattle in Texas for me. I married after I come back here. I married Polly Bancomb first, den a woman named Betsy Maynard, and last, Emily Walton.

When de surrender come Marster was dead, but he left it so dat all his slaves who had families got a piece of land. Dere were four of 'em who got land. He was dead, but Missus done like he had it fixed.

We had white overseers. Old man John Robinson stayed there till de surrender; den he left. We used to kill squirrels, turkeys, and game with guns. When Marster went off some of us boys stole de guns, and away we went to de woods huntin'. Marster would come back drunk. He would not know, and he did not care, neither, about we huntin' game. We caught possums and coons at night with dogs. Marster and Missus was good to us.

ALICE SEWELL
Interviewed at St. Louis, Missouri
Interviewer not identified
Age when interviewed: 86

I WAS BORN in Montgomery, Alabama, November 13, 1851, the daughter of Rhoda and Edmond Carey. I have three brothers and two sisters dead. I am the only living child. I ain't never been in a schoolhouse in my life and I never did learn how to read or write.

I recollect three of my overseers. The first one's name Elik Clayton, the second one named Mofield, and the third one named Pierson. I was thirteen years old when the third one got me and de War had started, so we had to pack all de cotton up in bales and in sun face houses and sun face cribs to be out of the weather. The seed cotton was kept in de gin house, 'cause dey didn't had no time to fool with dat. Den dey up and bought spinning wheels and cards, so us women could spin it to make cloth and make clothes at home and would not have to go to de factory to buy clothes.

Dey had to keep de money to care for de families de soldiers left behind and send corn by de loads to de battlefield to feed de horses. Dey stopped raising cotton after de War started and just raised foodstuff 'cause dey had to send food to de battlefield for de soldiers. De poor white folks what lived up in de hilly country, too poor to own slaves, while de War was going on had to come down out of the hilly country. Dey lived on government land and dey had to have food for dem and de children. Deir menfolks was taken away from dem to war. Dey was called counterscript soldiers, and if dey refused to go to War dey got shot down like a dog. So de most of 'em rather go and take chances of de War missing 'em dan get shot without a doubt. Dey used to say dey had to go and fight a rich man's war but dey couldn't help demselves no better'n us slaves could.

My owner was very rich. He owned four plantations of slaves. He had two plantations on de Calopoosa River, one named Jedkins upper ferry plantation and de other Jedkins Mill place and the third plantation was called the Bradshaw place. It was out from de river and de fourth one was called de High Long plantation.

He was always fairly kind to his slaves. He didn't believe in abusing dem 'less he couldn't help it, and when he'd find out de overseers beat 'em without a cause, he'd fire 'em right away and get somebody else. Dat's why he so prosperous, 'cause he was fair. He never even allowed overseers on his plantation what had grown boys, to be runnin' round amongst his slaves neither, no he didn't.

Dey didn't allow us to sing on our plantation 'cause if we did we just sing ourselves happy and to shouting and dat would settle de work.

Dey did allow us to go to church on Sunday about two miles down de public road, and dey hired a white preacher to preach to us. He never did tell us nothing but "Be good servants, pick up old marse and old misses' things about de place, don't steal no chickens or pigs, and don't lie about nothing." Den dey baptize you and call dat you got religion. Never did say nothing about a slave dying and going to Heaven. When we die, dey bury us next day and you is just like any of the other cattle dying on de place. Dat's all 'tis to it and all 'tis of you. You is just dead, dat's all. De old lady dat raised my mother, she was a black mammy. She done all de burying of de niggers, said de funeral sayings by herself. She knew it by heart.

Dey swapped my grandmother away 'cause she didn't bear children like dey wanted her to, so de man dey swapped her off to come back two months later and told our owner dat Grandmama was heavy with child. Den he wanted to buy her back 'cause she was a good worker, but her new owner would not let him have her back and she had thirteen children after dat. Our old owner surely was sick of dat swap. My mother was only three years old when dey sold her mother to another marster and she never saw her again till she had all dem thirteen children.

Dis is how Mother found Grandmother. Our owner bought a slave what come off a plantation dat my grandmother was on. She was turned

over to dis slave owner to satisfy a gambling debt left unpaid by de
dead husband. So she told my mother all about de deal and all de
children mother had never seen. My mother had three children of her
own, at dat time. De slave dat brought de news name was Elsie. So
Elsie had lots of relatives on dis plantation she was sold off of. Well, she
had to have a pass every time she want to go visit her folks. So she tells
my mother next time I get a pass to go see my people, you ask Old Boss
for one too so you can go see you mamma and sisters and brothers you
never seen.

Mamma did and when Mamma got to old John Beasley's plantation
on Lime Creek Mamma didn't know Grandmother Sallie and grandmother Sallie didn't know her daughter till Elsie introduced 'em to each
other. Dey was so glad dey just hugged and kissed plenty. De War
was going on den and dey fought four years and two months.

De first year after de War my father and mother kept us children
and stayed right on with our owner and done sharecropping till Father
was able to buy stock of his own, but he did not buy no property. When
I got eighteen years old I married, but I stayed right on with my mother
and father just de same, and my children buried both my mother and
father. My mother lived to be a hundred years old and my father was
between eighty and ninety when he died.

We used to slip off in de woods in de old slave days on Sunday evening
way down in de swamps to sing and pray to our own liking. We prayed
for dis day of freedom. We come from four and five miles to pray together
to God dat if we don't live to see it, to please let our chillen live to see a
better day and be free, so dat dey can give honest and fair service to de
Lord and all mankind everywhere. And we'd sing "Our little meetin's
about to break, chillen, and we must part. We got to part in body, but
hope not in mind. Our little meetin's bound to break." Den we used to
sing "We walk about and shake hands, fare you well my sisters, I am
going home."

I never did hear nothing about what de niggers 'specked from de white
folks. We was so glad to get loose, we didn't 'speck nothing but get
out of bondage.

Dey didn't even give us time off to wash our clothes. We had to wash
'em at night when we ought to been resting our old backs what was so
tired. We liked to go to de field clean in de mornings. Dat's de only way
we had of doing it.

I left Montgomery, Alabama, de last of 1902 when Louis was only
eleven years old and came to Morouse, Alabama, and stayed five years
after dat. I moved to Arkansas, stayed quite a while, don't know how
long. All dat time I made my living washing and ironing and picking
cotton from farm to farm. My husband died twenty-eight years ago last
March. I been in St. Louis now between twelve and thirteen years.

I owned a nice home in Warren, Arkansas. I sold it to come up here.
De folks down dere said dey would sure miss seeing me walking around

down dere with my white apron on, but I believed in immigration like de Bible said. So I just immigrated from de South up here to de North. God said de plantations would grow up and de hoot owls would have 'em and dey is doin' it. Growin' up into wilderness. God planned dem slave prayers to free us like he did de Israelites, and dey did.

ROBERT SHEPHERD
Interviewed at Athens, Georgia
Interviewed by Grace McCune
Age when interviewed: 91

MARSE JOE, he had three plantations, but he didn't live on none of 'em. He lived in Lexin'ton. He kept a overseer on each one of his plantations and dey had better be good to his niggers, or else Marse Joe would sure get 'em away from dere. He never allowed 'em to work us too hard, and in bad or real cold weather us didn't have to do no outside work 'cept everyday chores what had to be done, come rain or shine, like milkin', tendin' de stock, fetchin' in wood, and things like dat. He seed dat us had plenty of good somepin' to eat and all de clothes we needed. Us was lots better off in dem days dan us is now.

Old Marster, he had so many niggers dat he never knowed 'em all. One day he was a-ridin' along towards one of his plantations and he met one of his slaves, named William. Marse stopped him and asked him who he was. William said: "Why, Marster, I'se your nigger. Don't you know me?" Den Marster, he just laughed and said: "Well, hurry on home when you gets what you is gwine after." He was in a good humor dat way most all de time. I can see him a-ridin' dat little hoss of his'n what he called Button, and his little dog hoppin' along on three legs right side of de hoss. Dere weren't nothin' de matter with dat little dog; walkin' on three legs was just his way of gettin' round.

Marster never let none of de slave chillen on his plantation do no work, till dey got fifteen—dat was soon 'nough, he said. On all of his plantations dere was one old woman dat didn't have nothin' else to do but look after and cook for de nigger chillen whilst dey mammies was at work in de fields. Aunt Viney took care of us. She had a big old horn what she blowed when it was time for us to eat, and us knowed better dan to get so far off us couldn't hear dat horn, for Aunt Viney would sure tear us up. Marster had done told her she better fix us plenty to eat and give it to us on time.

Dere was a great long trough what went plum across de yard, and dat was where us et. For dinner us had peas or some other sort of vegetables, and corn bread. Aunt Viney crumbled up dat bread in de trough and poured de vegetables and pot likker over it. Den she blowed de horn and chillen come a-runnin' from every which way. If us et it all up, she had to put more victuals in de trough. At nights, she crumbled de corn bread in de trough and poured buttermilk over it. Us never had nothin' but corn bread and buttermilk at night. Sometimes dat trough would be a sight, 'cause us never stopped to wash our hands, and before us had been eatin' 'more dan a minute or two what was in de trough would look like real mud what had come off our hands. Sometimes Aunt Viney would fuss at us and make us clean it out.

Dere was a big sand bar down on de crick what made a fine place to play, and wadin' in de branches was lots of fun. Us frolicked up and down dem woods and had all sorts of good times—anything to keep away from Aunt Viney 'cause she was sure to have us fetchin' in wood or sweepin' 'de yards if us was handy where she could find us. If us was out of her sight she never bothered about dem yards and things.

Us was scared to answer dat horn when us got in Marster's tobacco. He raised lots of tobacco and rationed it out to mens, but he never 'lowed chillen to have none till dey was big enough to work in de fields. Us found out how to get in his tobacco house and us kept on gettin' his tobacco before it was dried out till he missed it. Den he told Aunt Viney to blow dat horn and call up all de chillen. "I'se gwine to whip every one of 'em," he would declare. After us got dere and he seed dat green tobacco had done made us so sick us couldn't eat, he just couldn't beat us. He just laughed and said: "It's good enough for you."

Aunt Martha, she done de milkin' and helped Aunt Nancy cook for de slaves. Dey had a big long kitchen up at de Big House where de overseer lived. De slaves what worked in de field never had to do deir own cookin'. It was all done for 'em in dat big kitchen. Dey cooked some of de victuals in big old washpots and dere was sure a plenty for all. All de cookin 'was done in big fireplaces what had racks made inside to hang pots on and dey had big old ovens for bakin' and thick iron skillets, and long-handled fryin' pans. You just can't imagine how good things was cooked dat way on de open fire. Nobody never had no better hams and other meat dan our marster kept in dem big old smokehouses, and his slaves had meat just like white folks did. Dem cooks knowed dey had to cook a plenty and have it ready when it was time for de slaves to come in from de fields. Miss Ellen, she was de overseer's wife, went out in de kitchen and looked over everything to see that it was all right and den she blowed de bugle. When de slaves heared dat bugle, dey come in a-singin' from de fields. Dey was happy 'cause dey knowed Miss Ellen had a good dinner ready for 'em.

De slave quarters was long rows of log cabins with chimblies made out of sticks and red mud. Dem chimblies was all de time catchin' fire. Dey didn't have no glass windows. For a window dey just cut a openin' in a log and fixed a piece of plank across it so it would slide when dey wanted to open or close it. Doors was made out of rough planks, beds was rough homemade frames nailed to de side of de cabins, and mattresses was coarse, home-wove ticks filled with wheat straw. Dey had good homemade cover. Dem beds slept mighty good.

Dere weren't many folks sick dem days, especially amongst de slaves. When one did die, folks would go twelve or fifteen miles to de buryin'. Marster would say: "Take de mules and wagons and go; but mind you, take good care of dem mules." He never seemed to care if us went— fact was, he said us ought to go. If a slave died on our place, nobody went to de fields till after de buryin'. Master never let nobody be buried till dey had been dead twenty-four hours, and if dey had people from some other place, he waited till dey could get dere. He said it weren't right to hurry 'em off into de ground too quick after dey died. Dere warn't no undertakers dem days. De homefolks just laid de corpse out on de coolin' board till de coffin was made. A coolin' board was made out of a long straight plank raised a little at de head and had legs fixed to make it set straight. Dey wrapped woman corpses in windin' sheets. Uncle Squire, de man what done all de wagon work and buildin' on our place, made coffins. Dey was just plain wood boxes dat dey painted to make 'em look nice.

White preachers conducted the funerals, and most of de time our own marster done it, 'cause he was a preacher hisself. When de funeral was done preached, dey sung "Harps from de Tomb." Den dey put de coffin in a wagon and drive slow and careful to de graveyard. De preacher prayed at de grave and de mourners sung, "I'se Born to Die and Lay Dis Body Down." Dey never had no outside box for de coffin to be set in, but dey put planks on top of de coffin before dey started shovellin' in de dirt.

Fourth Sundays was our meetin' days, and everybody went to church. Us went to our white folks' church and rode in a wagon behind deir carriage. Dere was two Baptist preachers—one of 'em was Mr. John Gibson and de other was Mr. Patrick Butler. Marse Joe was a Methodist preacher hisself, but dey all went to de same church together. De niggers set in de gallery. When dey had done give de white folks de sacrament, dey called de niggers down from de gallery and give dem de sacrament, too. Church days was sure 'nough big meetin' days 'cause everybody went. Dey preached three times a day: at eleven in de mornin', three in de evenin', and den again at night. De biggest meetin' house crowds was when dey had baptizin', and dat was right often. Dey dammed up de crick on Saturday so as it would be deep enough on Sunday and dey done de baptizin' before dey preached de three o'clock sermon. At dem baptizin's dere was all sorts of shoutin', and dey would sing "Roll Jordan, Roll," "De Livin' Waters," and "Lord I'se Comin' Home."

When de crops was laid by and most of de hardest work of de year done de baptizin' before dey preached de three o'clock sermon. At dem times in August. Dat was when us had de biggest times of all. Dey had great big long tables and just everything good to eat. Dey would kill five or six hogs and have 'em carried dere to be barbecued, and Marster carried his own cooks along. After de white folks et dey fed niggers, and dere was always a plenty for all. Marster sure looked after all his niggers good at dem times.

When de camp-meetin' was over, den come de big baptizin': white folks first, den niggers. One time dere was a old slave woman what got so scared when dey got out in de crick dat somebody had to pull her foots out under her to get her under de water. She got out from dere and testified dat it was de devil a-holdin' her back.

De white ladies had nice silk dresses to wear to church. Slave womans had new calico dresses what dey wore with hoopskirts dey made out of grapevines. Dey wore poke bonnets with ruffles on 'em and if de weather was sort of cool, dey wore shawls. Marster always wore his linen duster. Dat was his white coat, made cutaway style with long tails. De cloth for most all of de clothes was made at home. Marse Joe raised lots of sheep and de wool was used to make cloth for de winter clothes. Us had a great long loom house where some of de slaves didn't do nothin' but weave cloth. Some carded bats, some done de spinnin', and dere was more of 'em to do de sewin'.

Miss Ellen, she looked after all dat, and she cut out most of de clothes. She seed dat us had plenty to wear. Sometimes Marster would go to de sewin' house, and Mist'ess would tell him to get on away from dere and look after his own work, dat her and Aunt Julia could run dat loom house. Marster he just laughed den and told us chillen what was hangin' around de door to just listen to dem womans cackle.

Us had water buckets, called piggens, what was made out of cedar and had handles on de sides. Sometimes us sawed off little vinegar kegs and put handles on 'em. Us loved to drink out of gourds. Dere was lots of gourds raised every year. Some of 'em was so big dey was used to keep eggs in and for lots of things us uses baskets for now. Dem little gourds made fine dippers.

Dem corn shuckin's was sure 'nough big times. When us got all de corn gathered up and put in great long piles, den de gettin' ready started. Why, dem womans cooked for days, and de mens would get de shoats ready to barbecue. Marster would send us out to get de slaves from de farms round about dere. De place was all lit up with light-wood knot torches and bonfires, and dere was 'citement a-plenty when all niggers get to singin' and shoutin' as dey made de shucks fly.

One of dem songs went somethin' like dis: "Oh! my head, my poor head, Oh! my poor head is affected." Dere weren't nothin' wrong with our heads—dat was just our way of lettin' our overseer know us wanted some liquor. Purty soon he would come 'round with a big horn of whiskey, and dat made de poor head well, but it weren't long before it got worse again, and den us got another horn of whiskey. When de corn was all shucked, den us et all us could and, let me tell you, dat was some good eatin's. Den us danced de rest of de night.

Next day when us all felt so tired and bad, Marster, he would tell us about stayin' up all night, but Mist'ess took up for us, and dat tickled Old Marster. He just laughed and said: "Will you listen to dat woman?" Den he would make some of us sing one of dem songs us had done been singin' to dance by. It goes sort of like dis: "Turn your pardner round! Steal round de corner, 'cause dem Johnson gals is hard to beat! Just glance round and have a good time! Dem gals is hard to find!"

Us had big possum hunts, and us sure catched a heap of 'em. De gals cooked 'em with 'taters and dey just made your mouth water. I sure wish I had one now. Rabbits was good, too. Marster didn't allow no huntin' with guns, so us just took dogs when us went huntin'. Rabbits was kilt with sticks and rocks 'cept when big snow come. Dey was easy to track to dey beds den, and us could just reach in and pull 'em out. When us catch 'nough of 'em, us had big rabbit suppers.

I didn't have no sure 'nough weddin'. Me and Julie just jumped over de broom in front of Marster and us was married. Dat was all dere was to it. Dat was de way most of de slave folks got married dem days. Us knowed better dan to ask de gal when us wanted to get married. Us just told our Marster and he done de askin'. Den, if it was all right with de gal, Marster called all de other niggers up to de big house to see us jump over de broom.

If a slave wanted to get married to somebody on another place, den he told Marster and his marster would talk to de gal's marster. Whatever dey agreed on was all right. If neither one of 'em would sell one of de slaves what wanted to get married, den dey let 'em go ahead and jump over de broom, and de man just visited his wife on her marster's place, mostly on Wednesday and Saturday nights. If it was a long piece off, he didn't get dere so often. Dey had to have passes den, 'cause de patterrollers would get 'em sure if dey didn't. Dat meant a thrashin' and dey didn't miss layin' on de sticks when dey catch a nigger.

De big war was about over when dem Yankees come by our place and just went through everything. Dey called all de slaves together and told 'em dey was free and didn't belong to nobody no more. And said de slaves could take all dey wanted from de smokehouses and barns and de Big House, and could go when and where dey wanted to go. Dey tried to hand us out all de meat and hams, but us told 'em us weren't hungry, 'cause Marster had always done give us all us wanted. When dey couldn't make none of us take nothin', dey said it was de strangest thing dey had done ever seed and dat dat man Echols must have sure been good to his niggers.

When dem Yankees had done gone off Marster come out to our place. He blowed de bugle to call us all up to de house. He couldn't hardly talk, 'cause somebody had done told him dat dem Yankees couldn't talk his niggers into stealin' nothin'. Marster said he never knowed before how good us loved him. He told us he had done tried to be good to us and had done de best he could for us and dat he was mighty proud of de way every one of us had done behaved ourselfs. He said dat de War was over now and us was free and could go anywhere us wanted to, but dat us didn't have to go if us wanted to stay dere. He said he would pay us for our work and take care of us if us stayed or, if us wanted to work on shares, he would allow us to work some land dat way. A few of dem niggers drifted off, but most of 'em stayed right dere till dey died.

Me, I stayed right dere till after Marster died. He was sick a long, long time and one morning Old Mist'ess, she called to me. "Robert," she said, "you ain't gwine to have no Marster long, 'cause he's about gone." I called all de niggers up to de Big House and when dey was all in de yard, Mist'ess, she said: "Robert, you been with us so long, you can come in and see him before he's gone for good." When I got in dat room I knowed de Lord had done laid His hand on my good old marster, and he was a-goin' to dat home he used to preach to us niggers about, and it appeared to me like my heart would just bust. When de last breath was done gone, I went back out in de yard and told de other niggers, and dere was sure cryin' and prayin' amongst 'em, 'cause all of 'em loved Marster. Dat was sure one big funeral. Mist'ess said she wanted all of Marster's old slaves to go, 'cause he loved 'em so, and all of us went. Some what had done been gone years come back for Master's funeral.

Next day, after de funeral was over, Mist'ess, she said: "Robert, I want you to stay on with me 'cause you know how he wanted his work done." Den Mist'ess daughter and her husband Mr. Dickenson, come dere to stay. None of de niggers liked dat Mr. Dickenson and so most of 'em left and den, about two years after Marster died, Mist'ess went to Atlanta to stay with another of her daughters, and she died dere. When Mist'ess left, I left too and come on here to Athens, and I been here ever since.

MORRIS SHEPPARD
Interviewed at Fort Gibson, Oklahoma
Interviewer not identified
Age when interviewed: 85

OLD MARSTER tell me I was borned in November, 1852, at de old home place about five miles east of Webber's Falls, mebbe kind of northeast, not far from de east bank of de Illinois River. Master's name was Joe Sheppard, and he was a Cherokee Indian. Tall and slim and handsome. He had black eyes and mustache, but his hair was iron gray, and everybody liked him because he was so good-natured and kind.

I don't remember old Mistress' name. My mammy was a Crossland Negro before she come to belong to Master Joe and marry my pappy, and I think she come with old Mistress and belong to her. Old Mistress was small and mighty pretty too, and she was only half Cherokee. She inherit about half a dozen slaves, and say dey was her own and Old Master can't sell one unless she give him leave to do it.

Dey only had two families of slaves with about twenty in all, and dey only worked about fifty acres, so we sure did work every foot of it good. We got three or four crops of different things out of dat farm every year, and something growing on dat place winter and summer.

Pappy's name was Caesar Sheppard and Mammy's name was Easter. Dey was both raised round Webber's Falls somewhere. I had two brothers, Silas and George, dat belong to Mr. George Holt in Webber's Falls town. I got a pass and went to see dem sometimes, and dey was both treated mighty fine.

The Big House was a double log house with a big hall and a stone chimney but no porches, with two rooms at each end, one top side of de other. I thought it was mighty big and fine. Us slaves lived in log cabins dat only had one room and no windows, so we kept de doors open most of de time. We had homemade wooden beds with rope springs and de little ones slept on trundle beds dat was homemade too.

At night dem trundles was just all over de floor, and in de morning we shove dem back under de big beds to get dem outen de way. No nails in none of dem nor in de chairs and tables. Nails cost big money and Old Master's blacksmith wouldn't make none 'cepting a few for Old Master now and den, so we used wooden dowels to put things together.

They was so many of us for dat little field we never did have to work hard. Up at five o'clock and back in sometimes about de middle of de evening, long before sundown, unless they was a crop to get in before it rain or something like dat. When crop was laid by, de slaves just work round at dis and dat and keep tolerable busy. I never did have much of a job, just tending de calves mostly. We had about twenty calves and I would take dem out and graze 'em while some grown-up Negro was grazing de cows so as to keep de cows' milk. I had me a good blaze-faced horse for dat.

One time Old Master and another man come and took some calves off and Pappy say Old Master taking dem off to sell. I didn't know what "sell" meant and I asked Pappy, "Is he going to bring 'em back when he get through selling them?" I never did see no money either, until time of de War or a little before.

Master Joe was a good provider, and we always had plenty of corn pone, sow belly and greens, sweet potatoes, cow peas, and cane molasses. We even had brown sugar and cane molasses most of de time before de War. Sometimes coffee, too.

De clothes wasn't no worry neither. Everything we had was made by my folks. My aunt done de carding and spinning and my mammy done de weaving and cutting and sewing, and my pappy could make cowhide shoes with wooden pegs. Dey was for bad winter only. Old Master bought de cotton in Fort Smith because he didn't raise no cotton, but he had a few sheep and we had wool-mix for winter.

Everything was stripedy 'cause Mammy like to make it fancy. She dye with copperas and walnut and wild indigo and things like dat, and make pretty cloth. I wore a stripedy shirt till I was about eleven years old, and den one day while we was down in de Choctaw Country Old Mistress see me and nearly fall offen her horse! She holler, "Easter, you go right now and make dat big buck of a boy some britches!"

We never put on de shoes until about late November when de frost begin to hit regular and split our feet up. Den when it get good and cold and de crop all gathered in anyways, they is nothing to do 'cepting hog killing and a lot of wood chopping, and you don't get cold doing dem two things.

De hog killing mean we gets lots of spareribs and chitlings, and somebody always get sick eating too much of dat fresh pork. I always pick a whole passel of muscadines for Old Master and he make up sour wine, and dat helps out when we get the bowel complaint from eating dat fresh pork. If somebody bad sick he get de doctor right quick, and he don't let no Negroes mess around with no poultices and teas and such things like cupping-horns neither!

Us Cherokee slaves seen lots of green corn shooting and de like of dat, but we never had no games of our own. We was too tired when we come in to play any games. We had to have a pass to go any place to have singing or praying and den they was always a bunch of patrollers around to watch everything we done. Dey would come up in a bunch of about nine men on horses, and look at all our passes, and if a Negro didn't have no pass dey wore him out good and made him go home. Dey didn't let us have much enjoyment.

Right after de War de Cherokees that had been with de South kind of pestered the freedmen some, but I was so small dey never bothered me, just de grown ones. Old Master and Mistress kept on asking me did de night riders persecute me any but dey never did. Dey told me some of dem was bad on Negroes but I never did see none of dem night riding like some said dey did.

Old Master had some kind of business in Fort Smith, I think, 'cause he used to ride in to dat town about every day on his horse. He would start at de crack of daylight and not get home till way after dark. When he get home he call my uncle in and ask about what we done all day and tell him what we better do de next day. My uncle Joe was de slave boss and he tell us what de master say do.

When dat Civil War come along I was a pretty big boy, and I remember it good as anybody. Uncle Joe tell us all to lay low and work hard and nobody bother us, and he would look after us. He sure stood good with de Cherokee neighbors we had, and dey all liked him. There was Mr. Jim Collins, and Mr. Bell, and Mr. Dave Franklin, and Mr. Jim Sutton, and Mr. Blackburn that lived around close to us and dey all had slaves. Dey was all with the South, but dey was a lot of dem Pin Indians all up on de Illinois River and dey was with de North and dey taken it out on de slave owners a lot before de War and during it too. Dey would come in de night and hamstring de horses and maybe set fire to de barn, and two of 'em named Joab Scarrel and Tom Starr killed my pappy one night just before de War broke out. I don't know what dey done it for, only to be mean, and I guess they was drunk.

Them Pins was after Master all de time for a while at de first of de War, and he was afraid to ride into Fort Smith much. Dey come to de house one time when he was gone to Fort Smith and us children told dem he was at Honey Springs, but they knowed better and when he got home he said somebody shot at him and bushwhacked him all the way from Wilson's Rock to dem Wildhorse Mountains, but he run his horse like de devil was setting on his tail and dey never did hit him. He never seen them neither. We told him about de Pins coming for him and he just laughed.

When de War come Old Master seen he was going into trouble and he sold off most of de slaves. In de second year of de War he sold my mammy and my aunt dat was Uncle Joe's wife and my two brothers and my little sister. Mammy went to a mean old man named Pepper Goodman and he took her off down de river and pretty soon Mistress tell me she died 'cause she can't stand de rough treatment.

When Mammy went Old Mistress took me to de Big House to help her, and she was kind to me like I was part of her own family. I never forget when they sold off some more Negroes at de same time, too, and put dem all in a pen for de trader to come and look at. He never come until the next day, so dey had to sleep in dat pen in a pile like hogs. It wasn't my Master done dat. He done already sold 'em to a man and it was dat man was waiting for de trader. It made my Master mad, but dey didn't belong to him no more and he couldn't say nothing.

The man put dem on a block and sold 'em to a man dat had come in on a steamboat, and he took dem off on it when de freshet come down and de boat could go back to Fort Smith. It was tied up at de dock at Webber's Falls about a week and we went down and talked to my aunt and brothers and sister. De brothers was Sam and Eli. Old Mistress cried just like any of de rest of us when de boat pull out with dem on it.

Pretty soon all de young Cherokee menfolks all gone off to de War, and de Pins was riding round all de time, and it ain't safe to be in dat part round Webber's Falls, so Old Master take us all to Fort Smith where they was a lot of Confederate soldiers. We camp at dat place a while and Old Mistress stay in de town with some kinfolks. Den Old Master get three wagons and ox teams and take us all way down on Red River in de Chocktaw Nation. We went by Webber's Falls and filled de wagons. We left de furniture and only took grub and tools and bedding and clothes, 'cause they wasn't very big wagons and was only single-yoke. We went on a place in de Red River bottoms close to Shawneetown and not far from de place where all de wagons crossed over to go into Texas. We was at dat place two years and made two little crops.

One night a runaway Negro come across from Texas and he had de bloodhounds after him. His britches was all muddy and tore where de hounds had cut him up in de legs when he clumb a tree in de bottoms. He come to our house and Mistress said for us Negroes to give him something to eat and we did. Then up come de man from Texas with de hounds and with him was young Mr. Joe Vann and my uncle that belong to young Joe. Dey called young Mr. Joe "Little Joe Vann" even after he was grown on account of when he was a little boy before his pappy was killed. His pappy was old Captain "Rich Joe" Vann, and he been dead ever since long before de War. My uncle belong to old Captain Joe nearly all his life.

Mistress try to get de man to tell her who de Negro belong to so she can buy him, but de man say he can't sell him and he take him on back to Texas with a chain around his two ankles. Dat was one poor Negro dat never got away to de North, and I was sorry for him 'cause I know he must have had a mean master, but none of us Sheppard Negroes, I mean the grown ones, tried to get away.

I never seen any fighting in de War, but I seen soldiers in de South army doing a lot of blacksmithing alongside de road one day. Dey was fixing wagons and shoeing horses.

After de War was over, Old Master tell me I am free but he will look out after me 'cause I am just a little Negro and I ain't got no sense. I know he is right, too. Well, I go ahead and make me a crop of corn all by myself and then I don't know what to do with it. I was afraid I would get cheated out of it 'cause I can't figure and read, so I tell Old Master about it and he bought it offen me. We never had no schools in slavery and it was agin' the law for anybody to even show a Negro de letters and figures, so no Cherokee slave could read.

We all come back to de old place and find de Negro cabins and barns burned down and de fences all gone and de field in crab grass and cockleburs. But de Big House ain't hurt 'cepting it need a new roof. De furniture is all gone, and some said de soldiers burned it up for firewood. Some officers stayed in de house for a while and tore everything up or took it off.

Master give me over to de National Freedmen's Bureau and I was bound out to a Cherokee woman name Lizzie McGee. Then one day one of my uncles named Wash Sheppard come and tried to get me to go live with him. He say he wanted to get de family all together again. He had run off after he was sold and joined de North army and discharged at Fort Scott in Kansas, and he said lots of freedmen was living close to each other up by Coffeyville in de Coo-ee-scoo-ee district.

I wouldn't go, so he sent Isaac and Joe Vann dat had been two of old Captain Joe's Negroes to talk to me. Isaac had been Young Joe's driver, and he told me all about how rich Master Joe was and how he would look after us Negroes. Dey kept after me 'bout a year, but I didn't go anyways. But later on I got a freedman's allotment up in dat part close to Coffeyville, and I lived in Coffeyville awhile but I didn't like it in Kansas.

I lost my land trying to live honest and pay my debts. I raised eleven children just on de sweat of my hands and none of dem ever tasted anything dat was stole. When I left Mrs. McGee's I worked about three years for Mr. Sterling Scott and Mr. Roddy Reese. Mr. Reese had a big flock of peafowls dat had belonged to Mr. Scott and I had to take care of dem. I would have to tromp seven miles to Mr. Scott's house two or three times a week to bring back some old peafowl dat had got out and gone back to de old place!

Poor Old Marster and Mistress only lived a few years after de War. Master went plumb blind after he moved back to Webber's Falls and so he move up on de Illinois River about three miles from de Arkansas, and there Old Mistress take de white swelling and die and den he die pretty soon. I went to see dem lots of times and they was always glad to see me.

I would stay around about a week and help 'em, and dey would try to get me to take something, but I never would. Dey didn't have much and couldn't make any more and dem so old. Old Mistress had inherited some property from her pappy and dey had de slave money, and when dey turned everything into good money after de War dat stuff only come to about six thousand dollars in good money, she told me. Dat just about lasted 'em through until dey died, I reckon.

By and by I married Nancy Hildebrand what lived on Greenleaf Creek, about four miles northwest of Gore. She had belonged to Joe Hildebrand and he was kin to old Steve Hildebrand dat owned de mill on Flint Creek up in de Going Snake District. She was raised up at dat mill, but she was borned in Tennessee before dey come out to de Nation. Her master was white but he had married into de Nation and so she got a freedmen's allotment too. She had some land close to Catoosa and some down on Greenleaf Creek.

We was married at my home in Coffeyville, and she bore me eleven children and then went on to her reward. A long time ago I came to live with my daughter Emma here at dis place, but my wife just died last year. She was eighty-three. I reckon I wasn't cut out on de church pattern, but I raised my children right. We never had no church in slavery, and no schooling, and you had better not be caught with a book in your hand even, so I never did go to church hardly any.

Of course I hear about Abraham Lincoln and he was a great man, but I was told mostly by my children when dey come home from school about him. I always think of my Old Master as de one dat freed me, and anyways Abraham Lincoln and none of his North people didn't look after me and buy my crop right after I was free like Old Master did. Dat was de time dat was de hardest and everything was dark and confusion.

BILL SIMMS

Interviewed in Ottawa, Kansas
Interviewed by Leta Gray
Age at interview: 97

M Y NAME IS Bill Simms. I was born in Osceola, Missouri, March
16, 1839. I lived on the farm with my mother and my master,
whose name was Simms. I had an older sister, about two years older
than I was. My master needed some money so he sold her, and I have
never seen her since except just a time or two.

On the plantation we raised cows, sheep, cotton, tobacco, corn, which
were our principal crops. There was plenty of wild hogs, turkey, and
deer, and other game. The deer used to come up and feed with the
cattle in the feed yards, and we could get all the wild hogs we wanted
by simply shooting them in the timber.

A man who owned ten slaves was considered wealthy, and if he got
hard up for money, he would advertise and sell some slaves, like my
oldest was sold on the block with her children. She sold for eleven
hundred dollars, a baby in her arms sold for three hundred dollars.
Another sold for six hundred dollars and the other for a little less than
that. My master was offered fifteen hundred dollars for me several times,
but he refused to sell me, because I was considered a good, husky slave.
My family is all dead, and I am the only one living.

The slaves usually lived in a two-room house made of native lumber.
The houses were all small. A four or five room house was considered a
mansion. We made our own clothes, had spinning wheels and raised
and combed our own cotton, clipped the wool from our sheeps' backs,
combed and spun it into cotton and wool clothes. We never knew what
boughten clothes were. I learned to make shoes when I was just a boy
and I made the shoes for the whole family. I used to chop wood and
make rails and do all kinds of farm work.

I had a good master. Most of the masters were good to their slaves.
When a slave got too old to work they would give him a small cabin
in the plantation and have the other slaves to wait on him. They would
furnish him with victuals and clothes until he died.

Slaves were never allowed to talk to white people other than their
masters or someone their masters knew, as they were afraid the white

man might have the slave run away. The masters aimed to keep their slaves in ignorance and the ignorant slaves were all in favor of the Rebel army. Only the more intelligent were in favor of the Union army.

When the War started, my master sent me to work for the Confederate Army. I worked most of the time for three years off and on, hauling cannons, driving mules, hauling ammunition and provisions. The Union Army pressed in on us and the Rebel army moved back. I was sent home. When the Union Army came close enough I ran away from home and joined the Union Army. There I drove a six-mule team and worked at wagon work, driving ammunition and all kinds of provisions until the war ended.

Then I returned home to my old master, who had stayed there with my mother. My master owned about four hundred acres of good land, and had had ten slaves. Most of the slaves stayed at home. My master hired me to work for him. He gave my mother forty acres of land with a cabin on it and sold me forty acres, for twenty dollars, when I could pay him. This was timbered land and had lots of good trees for lumber, especially walnut. One tree on this ground was worth one hundred dollars. If I could only get it cut and marketed, I could pay for my land.

My master's wife had been dead for several years and they had no children, the nearest relative being a nephew. They wanted my master's land and was afraid he would give it all away to us slaves, so they killed him, and would have killed us if we had stayed at home. I took my mother and ran into the adjoining Claire County. We settled there and stayed for some time, but I wanted to see Kansas, the state I had heard so much about.

I couldn't get nobody to go with me, so I started out afoot across the prairies for Kansas. After I got some distance from home it was all prairie. I had to walk all day long following buffalo trail. At night I would go off a little ways from the trail and lay down and sleep. In the morning I'd wake up and could see nothing but the sun and prairie. Not a house, not a tree, no living thing, not even could I hear a bird.

I had little to eat. I had a little bread in my pocket. I didn't even have a pocket knife, no weapon of any kind. I was not afraid, but I wouldn't start out that way again. The only shade I could find in the daytime was the rosinweed on the prairie. I would lay down so it would throw the shade in my face and rest, then get up and go again.

It was in the spring of the year in June. I came to Lawrence, Kansas, where I stayed two years working on the farm. In 1874 I went to work for a man by the month at thirty-five dollars a month and I made more money than the owner did, because the grasshoppers ate up the crops. I was hired to cut up the corn for him, but the grasshoppers ate it up first. He could not pay me for some time. Grasshoppers were so thick you couldn't step on the ground without stepping on about a dozen at each step. I got my money and come to Ottawa in December, 1874, about Christmas time.

My master's name was Simms and I was known as Simms' Bill, just like horses. When I came out here I just changed my name from Simms' Bill, to Bill Simms. Ottawa was very small at the time I came here, and there were several Indians close by that used to come to town.

The Indians held their war dance on what is now the courthouse grounds. I planted the trees that are now standing on the courthouse grounds. There were few farms fenced and what were, were on the streams. The prairie land was all open. Ottawa didn't have many business houses. There was also an oil mill where they bought castor beans and made castor oil. There was one hotel, which was called Leafton House.

The people lived pretty primitive. We didn't have kerosene. Our only lights were tallow candles, mostly grease lamps. They were just a pan with grease in it, and one end of the rag dragging out over the side which we would light. There were no sewers at that time. I had no chance to go to school when a boy, but after I came to Kansas I was too old to go to school, and I had to work, but I attended night school, and learned to read and write and figure.

The farm land was nearly all broke up by ox teams, using about six oxen on a plow. In Missouri we lived near the Santa Fe Trail, and the settlers traveling on the trail used oxen, and some of them used cows. The cows seem to stand the road better than the oxen and also gave some milk. The travelers usually aimed to reach the prairie states in the spring, so they could have grass for their oxen and horses during the summer.

I have lived here since I came here. I was married when I was about thirty years old. I married a slave girl from Georgia. Back in Missouri, if a slave wanted to marry a woman on another plantation, he had to ask the master, and if both masters agreed they were married. The man stayed at his owner's, and the wife at her owner's. He could go to see her on Saturday night and Sunday. Sometimes only every two weeks.

If a man was a big strong man, neighboring plantation owners would ask him to come over and see his gals, hoping that he might want to marry one of them, but if a Negro was a small man he was not cared for as a husband, as they valued their slaves as only for what they could do, just like they would horses. When they were married and if they had children they belonged to the man who owned the woman.

Osceloa is where the saying originated, "I'm from Missouri, show me." After the War the smart guys came through and talked the people into voting bonds, but there was no railroad built. Most counties paid their bonds, but the county in which Osceola stands refused to pay for their bonds because there was no railroad built, and they told the collectors to "show me the railroad and we will pay," and that is where "show me" originated.

My wife died when we had three children. She had had to work hard all her life and she said she didn't want her children to have to work as hard as she had, and I promised her on her death bed, that I would educate our girls. So I worked and sent the girls to school.

My two girls both graduated from Ottawa University, the oldest one being the first colored girl to ever graduate from that school. After graduation she went to teach school in Oklahoma, but only got twenty-five dollars a month, and I had to work and send her money to pay her expenses. The younger girl also graduated and went to teach school, but she did not teach school long, until she married a well-to-do farmer in Oklahoma. The older girl got her wages raised until she got one hundred and twenty-five dollars per month.

I have worked at farm work and tree husbandry all my life. I have been living alone about twenty-five years. I don't know how old I was, but my oldest daughter had written my mother before she died, and got our family record, which my mother kept in her old Bible. Each year she writes me and tells me on my birthday how old I am.

JANE SIMPSON
Interviewed at St. Louis, Missouri
Interviewer not identified
Age at interview: 90

I WAS BORN more than ninety years ago down in Burkersville, Kentucky. My memory' not so good, 'cause I been sick more than twenty years, so I might tell my story scatterin' like. I'll do the best I can. I been sold six times in my life, first to Christ Ellis, second, to John Emerson, and my third owner was Jessie Cook.

I wasn't old enough to be much help, till I come the property of Marse Cook. Den I was big enough to pick up chunks in de field, set brush heap afire, burn up rubbish, pull weeds, and de like. He sold me to Dr. Hart around de age of ten to be his house girl. De doctor kept me till de Civil War was in de air and dey started running de slaves to Texas 'cause dey thought de Yankees couldn't make it plumb to Texas, but dey did. By de time we got as far as Crowlers Ridge, peace was declared.

My father's owner was old Bill Cuington, de meanest slave owner in de county. Dey made him go to war, so when he come back, he told my papa dat he was free as him now, and he could go if he wanted to, or stay, he didn't care which, but if he stayed he wouldn't get nothing for his work.

A white neighbor friend heard Marse Bill say it. He told my father to come to his place with him down de road apiece where he was clearing up land, but if he got caught, don't ever tell he helped him get away 'cause some of the land he was clearing up was owned by Cuington, and

Cuington would fire him if he knowed he helped one of his ex-slaves in any way.

So papa taken my mother and us four children de route dis white friend helped him to go, to Clarington, Arkansas. He got us a job on a farm owned by his friend, Jerry Diles. Our whole family went to work on Mr. Diles' farm and we made a good crop. Mama milked, I cooked, de rest of de family farmed; and we stayed there more'n four years. When we left we had money enough to buy us a farm and stock of our own.

I 'member well when I was a child how dey wouldn't allow us chillen nothin' to eat but pumkin and mush.

We didn't own no clocks dem days. We just told de time by de sun in de day and de stars at night. If it was clouded we didn't know what time it was. De white folks didn't want to let de slaves have no time for deir self, so de old folks used to let us chillen run and play at night, while de folks sleep and dey watch de stars to tell about what time to call us in and put us to bed, before de white folks know we was out.

I been sold six times in my life, but I never got more dan three or four whippings, but dey cut de blood out of me every one of dem times. If Old Miss got mad about something, just anything at all, she'd have you whipped, when maybe you had not done a thing, just to satisfy her spite feeling.

I never can forget, I was sitting upstairs in Old Miss' house quilting when de first Yankee army boat went to Vicksburg, Mississippi. Old Miss made me get right up and go get her children out of school and bring 'em right home. She's scared to death most, but de boat went right on. It didn't even stop.

I had to take her children back and forth to school every day. Dey was mighty nice children. Dem very white children taught me to read and write, but I been sick so bad and so long I done forgot every bit of it.

My first old master never was married and he only bought two slaves in his whole life and had between fifty and a hundred slaves, all kin-folks. Dey raised children on his plantation worse dan flies. I never had a child in my life but I raised a host of other folks' chillen.

I had an uncle who was buying his freedom from Marse Chris and was almost paid out when Marse Chris died, but he didn't know nothing about keeping receipts, so he was put on the auction block and sold again.

Old Master was a drunkard. He fell off a rock one night and broke his hip. He died from dat fall. Before he died he told Papa he knew he was goin' to die, and he had been so mean to his old slaves dat he wanted to do somethin' for 'em, and no one never knew where he kept his money.

My grandpapa, Meridie, and grandmother, Juda, was de only two slaves he ever bought and all de rest come from dem two. Old Marse Chris told Grandfather before he died that there was a keg buried at de foot of de cliff with all his money in it, for he was very rich. My old grandfather told de overseer about it. Dey wouldn't dare to dig and find anything on de owner's plantation without de overseer let 'em, especially when de boss is dead, and de overseer, of course, said he looked for de keg and didn't find nothing.

I never even heard of white folks giving niggers nothing. Most of de time dey didn't even give 'em what dey 'spose to give 'em after dey was free. Dey was so mad 'cause dey had to set 'em free, dey just stayed mean as dey would allow 'em to be anyhow, and is yet, most of 'em. I used to hear old slaves pray and ask God when would de bottom rail be de top rail, and I wondered what on earth dey talkin' about. Dey was talkin' about when dey goin' to get from under bondage. 'Course I know now.

My mama and daddy had thirteen children and they is everyone dead but me. My papa's name was Dave Bedford. He was 103 years old when he died in Holly Grove, Arkansas. My sister died and left nine children and I raised every one of dem. One boy is deaf and dumb, and lives in Little Rock, Arkansas, and is one of the best paperhangers down there.

My husband was a farmer. He has been dead so long. I can't tell when he died. While my husband lived we farmed all de time and lived well. When he died I had four thousand dollars in de bank at Mound Bayou, Mississippi. De bank went down and I been a beggar ever since. Never did get one penny of dat money. I been here in St. Louis so long, I don't know how long I been here.

GUS SMITH
Interviewed at Rolla, Missouri
Interviewer not identified
Age when interviewed: 92

I WAS BORN IN 1845, on de fourth of July, near Rich Fountain, Osage County, Missouri, not far from Jefferson City. My father's name was Jim Messersmith, and my mother's maiden name was Martha Williams. I was called August Messersmith until I was old enough to vote, den I changed it to plain Gus Smith. My friends nicknamed me "Chinie" and I am called dat today.

My master's name was Bill Messersmith and he called hisself a Pennsylvania Dutchman. His father settled in Missouri, near Jefferson City, many years before de War. He owned 1,500 acres of land. The old man, my master's father, had a good many slaves but de chillen didn't have so many after de old man died. Rufus, the old man's son and my master's brother, took one of de Negro boys; his sister, Manisee, took a Negro girl. These two, Rufus and Manisee, never married and lived with my master. Zennie, another sister, took a girl and a boy. She married a man by de name of Goodman and my master took my father and my mother.

My master's father, before he died, told his chillen dat at his death he wanted each child to put their slaves out to work until dey earned eight hundred dollars apiece, to earn their own freedom; in dat way each slave paid it demselves. He did not believe it was right to keep dem in slavery all their lives. But de War came and dey were free without having to work it out.

We all wore homespun clothes, made of wool mostly. Mother carded, spun, and wove all our clothes. My master let us come and go pretty much as we pleased. In fact we had much more freedom dan de most of de slaves had in those days. He let us go to other places to work when we had nothing to do at home and we kept our money we earned, and spent it to suit ourselves. We had it so much better dan other slaves dat our neighbors would not let their slaves associate with us, for fear we would put devilment in their heads, for we had too much freedom. My father and mother had their own cabin to live in with their family, but de rest of de slaves stayed with our mistress. My father's relations lived within ten miles of us. Dey come to see us but dat was about all de company we had.

We used to sing all the old plantation songs, but my father and mother were not such good singers. We all had good times along with de work. During Christmas time and de whole month of January, it was de rulin' to give de slaves a holiday in our part of de country. A whole month, to go and come as much as we pleased and go for miles as far as we wanted to, but we had better be back by de first of February. If we wanted to go through a territory where it was hard to travel, or get by, we got a pass from our master.

We had quiltin's, dancin', makin' rails, for days at a time. We don't have nothin' to eat now like we did then. All kinds of game, wild ducks, geese, squirrels, rabbits, possum, pigeons, and fried chicken. My, women in those days could cook'. Great big pound cakes a foot and a half high. You don't see such things, nowadays.

I remember my father shooting so many pigeons at once that my mother just fed dem to the hogs. Just shoot the game from our back yard. I have seen de wild pigeons so thick dey looked like storm clouds coming. I've seen dem so thick dey broke tree limbs down. Ducks and geese de same way. We could kill dem by tow sacks full, with clubs. White folks and colored folks came to these gatherings, from miles around, sat up all night dancin', and drinkin'. People kept whiskey by de barrel in those days. You see in those days dey just loaded up ten or twelve bushel of corn, took it to de "still-house" and traded it for a barrel of whiskey. Not much selling in those days, everything was traded, even to labor. Our folks would tell us to go and help so and so and we done it.

Mother was de cook in those days at our place. De hewed log house we lived in was very big, about five or six rooms. In times of our holidays, we always had our own musicians. Sometimes we sent ten or twelve miles for a fiddler. He'd stay a week or so in one place and den he would go on to de next farm, maybe four or five miles away, and dey had a good time for a week. When we didn't have much work, we would get up about five o'clock every morning, but in busy season we had to be up and ready to work at daybreak. There was plenty of work for every one den, even to de little darkies, if only to pull weeds. We raised wheat, corn, cotton, tobacco, cabbage, potatoes, sheep hogs, and cattle. Had plenty of everything to eat.

Our closest neighbors was de Thorntons. Old man Thornton did not allow his slaves to go no place. He was a rough man, a low heavy set fellow, weighed about one hundred and sixty pounds. He was mean to his slaves. He whipped dem all de time. I've seen their clothes sticking to their backs, from blood and scabs, being cut up with de cowhide. He just whipped dem because he could. Us used to say he always give his niggers a "breakfast spell ever' mornin'!" Dat is he whipped dem every morning. I remember he had a nigger woman about seventy years old on his place. De Thorntons did not feed their slaves; dey was nearly starved. One night that old woman was so hungry she stole a chicken from her master, Old Thornton, and was cooking it in her cabin. He found it out some way and started to her cabin and caught her, while she had it on boiling. He was so mad, he told her to get a spoon and eat every bite before she stopped. It was scalding hot but he made her do it. She died right away; her insides was burned.

Why, Old Thornton was dat mean dat he killed his own son. He just beat him to death with de whip stock of dat cowhide, a whip made of buckskin. It was like dis. De boy had a girl he was courtin' in another town. He started to see her on Saturday noon. His daddy told him to be back by Sunday night. But de boy did not get back before Monday morning, ten o'clock. His father was in de field working and saw him coming down de road. He went to meet him and met him at de gate. He asked why he did not get back sooner and lit into beating him with the whip stock, de part dat would be de whip handle. He beat him so hard dat de boy died in after ten hours. It aroused de neighborhood and dey began to plan a lynching party. He got wind of it some way and got all his slaves together and pulled out. He left dat place and no one ever knowed where he went. Dat happened before de end of de War.

There was a lot of runaway slaves in those days. I never see any of dem but I heard de folks talk about dem. Many passed through our part of de country. In time of slavery, people were sold like cattle or hogs. There was no sale bills dat we seen, because folks in dem days was usually honest and did not have a lot of red tape in buying and selling. Our master would not sell any of us. He did not believe in separating us, and tried to keep us together. He didn't have any trouble with his slaves at all. He was as good a man as ever lived and we did pretty much as we pleased.

He married before de War, but his first wife died a few months later. He married a year after his wife died. He went to Pennsylvania and came back and went to California for about a year. Before he left he made my father boss. My father stayed on de place and took care of everything. He was boss all during de War.

When the battle of Wilson Creek was fought up near Springfield, most all soldiers passed by our house. After dey passed den came de bushwhackers. Dey stole all de niggers dey could, running dem down South to sell. Dey came to our place in de morning; it must have been about 1862–63. De whole family of colored folks was home, 'cepting my father. Dey looked across de road and seen another house and asked us whose house it was. We told dem it was our master's house. Dey saw we had a mare in de yard and told us to saddle her up. And dey told my oldest brother to be ready to go with dem when dey come back. Dey went halfway to my master's house and for some reason wheeled and came back. My mother looked out de door and seen them coming and said: "Here they come."

She said to my oldest bother, "Get under dat puncheon floor, maybe dey won't take August," meaning me. I was about twelve or thirteen years old den. We had a great big hearth, de rocks and puncheon came right up to it. My mother raised de one end of a puncheon and my brother hid there under de floor. De bushwhackers came back to de house and searched everywhere, failed to find him, even raised de floor and looked under, but my brother had crawled so far up in de corner dey did not see him. Dey asked my mother where he was and said, "By God! We want to know." Mother answered and said she sent him down to de field to get some corn for de hogs and told me to run down there and look for him.

Well I did. I run down in dat field and am going yet. I stayed out in dat woods for four days and nights with nothing to eat but what wild grapes and hazel nuts I could find. I knew better dan to go back dere, but I did not know where to go. I fell on a plan to go to my young misus, Zennie. Dey lived off de main road, two miles from where we lived. When I got to her home, it was in de evening about four o'clock. I saw my cousin, Melie, fifteen or sixteen years old, but was afraid to speak to her. I saw her out a piece from de barn, but I wouldn't let her see me. I stayed all night in de barn, and next morning I peeped out de window and saw her again. She was picking beans. I hollered and she recognized me and asked me if I wasn't August. I said yes. She told me to come on out and go with her, dat my mother and all of dem was at their house den. My oldest brother, Jim, was there too. He was four years older dan me.

Den I went down to de house and dey soon fixed me something to eat. But only a little because dey were afraid it might make me sick.

My mother told me to stay with Miss Zennie. Miss Zennie had married de second time to a man by de name of George McGee. Her first husband, Dave Goodman, was killed right at de start of de War by a gang of robbers something like de bushwhackers, who went in gangs of ten and fifteen, stealing niggers or anything else dey could get their hands on.

George McGee and my brother Jim hid out in de bluffs at Rollin's Ferry, a place where ferryboats ran. George McGee hid because he did not want to go in de army. So he takes my brother and hides in de bluffs. Dey both came to de house for provisions about twelve o'clock dat night and took me with dem. We camped out dat night and next morning dey said to me: "You stay here. Dey is out of meat at de house." So dey went back to de house and killed and dressed a young heifer and came back at night to get me. We had a good time eating supper and playing.

Along in de night I heard something like horses hoofs hitting de ground. I told my mother and she said, "You don't hear nothing." George McGee, de young marster said, "Wait, he is right. I hears something too!" We jumped up and went out and down a steep hollow and made it back to our camp dat night yet. Next morning we wondered who it could have been dat we heard. Dat night we went back to see how de folks was getting on and found out it was my own father and our own marster who had come a-hunting for us. If we had known, we would not have run.

My master told his sister, Miss Zennie, to keep us hid out of de way, that we were doing all right. I stayed in dat bluff about two years, until de close of de War. I never saw my father and master for over a year. I saw my mother every time I went to de house for something to eat, about twelve o'clock at night. My father had to hide out too. He kept de stock out in de bushes, watching after de master's affairs while he was away.

We stayed hid until dey took General Lee. Den we went back to Old Master's house and it was not long until peace was declared. Our house was about a quarter of a mile from de master's, on a farm he had bought from an old Dutchman, about one hundred and sixty acres. One morning, Old Master come over early and said: "Jim, by God! You are a free man dis morning, as free as I am. I can't hold you any longer. Now take your family and go over on dat hundred and sixty acres I bought and go to work." He was giving us all a chance to pay out de farm for ourselves a home. My father said, "There's nothing to go with it to help clear it and live." To which Old Master answered: "There's de smokehouse, take all you want and I'll furnish you with everything else you need for a year, until you get a start." He allowed us to use anything to work with he had on his place.

Den we went to work. Old Master said, "I've got all de land my heart could wish but none of it is cleared off. Go down dere with your boys and I'll send two men, both white (Irishmen, Jim and Tom Norman) and all of you clear off dat land. I'll give you five years lease to clear all you can. All you clear, you can have half." Well, we cleared fifty acres dat winter. We made rails, fenced it, and put it all in corn dat first year. There was six of us to do dis; my cousin joined my father, brother, and myself, and de two white men.

We had it cleared by the first of March—all ready to plow in 1865. My father raised his own sheep and cotton, and from dis my mother made our clothes. Father cleared thirty acres on his place de same year and sowed it all in wheat. De first year we got 817 bushels of wheat and 1,500 bushel of corn, it was all new land. Corn really growed in dem days. We hoed it by hand. You don't see corn like dat now. We worked out every little weed. Every little darky worked in dem days.

My grandad, Godfry, owned a place called de old Potter's place, near Vichey Springs, Vichey, Missouri, not far from where we lived. He bought it from a man who used to make pottery. Grandfather made his own mill to grind grain for bread. In dose days there was no steam operated mills and few water mills. Sometimes we had to go as much as twenty miles to grind corn. So grandfather made his own burr to grind corn and wheat. It was as big as any burr in de large mills, but it was turned by hand power. It was made of limestone rock, a great big stone about two and a half foot across. De top burr would probably weigh about three or four hundred pounds. De bottom case would weigh a thousand pounds or more. There was a hole in de top stone, where de grain flowed freely to de bottom and ground out on the big thick stone below. I ground many a bushel of meal on it myself. I don't know how Grandfather got de large stones in place, for it was there as long as I could remember. I just wonder if it isn't some place there yet. I would like to go and find out and see de old burr again.

Those were hard days, when folks had to go on foot twenty miles to mill. I remember in my early days, we used cattle for teams to haul, start at four o'clock in de morning, drive all day, stay overnight and grind de next day. Sometimes de crowd ahead of us was so big we had to stay over for three or four days. Sometimes we would be until eleven or twelve at night getting home. Gone at least two days and one night. I had to make trips like dis many times.

Sometimes we could take a couple of bushel of corn and go horse-back, but twice a year, spring and fall, we would take eight or ten bushel of wheat, and six or eight bushel of corn or, according to what we needed, and take de cattle and a old wooden axle wagon, walking and driving de cattle all de way there and back. We drove or led dem with only a rope around dem.

De last trip I made millin', I drove for Bill Fannins, a yoke of young three-year old cattle. Wasn't even broke. Went twenty-five miles, drove all de way, walking, while he sat up in de wagon. Sometimes de wagon dragged in de mud—de old wooden axle burying so deep we couldn't hardly get it out—going through timber and dodging brush. Some folks went even further dan dat. Sometimes a mill might be four or five miles from you but dey got out of fix and you would have to go to another one. Maybe twenty-five miles or more.

There was not many good doctors in those days, but my grandfather was an old fashioned herb doctor. I remember him well. I was about twenty-five years old when he died. Everybody knew him in dat country and he doctored among a white people, one of de best doctors of his kind. He went over thirty miles around to people who sent for him. He was seldom at home. Lots of cases dat other doctors gave up, he went and raised them. He could cure anything.

When I was sick one time, I was den about eighteen or nineteen years old, my folks had Dr. Boles, from Lane's Prairie and Dr. Mayweather from Vichey, to come and tend me. Dey both gave me up. I had typhoid and pneumonia. Dese doctors were de best to be found but dey could do nothing and said I was as good as dead. My grandfather was gone, had come to Rolla, doctoring Charley Stroback's child whose clothes had caught fire and he was burned badly. Grandfather could "blow out" fire.

He got home about four o'clock in de morning after de doctors had done give me up. He felt my pulse and said he didn't know whether I was dead or alive. No pulse, but he said I felt warm. He asked my grandmother if she had any light bread baked. She said yes and got it for him. He told her to butter it and lay the butter side down on my mouth and if it melted I was still living. She did this and soon she said, "Yes, he is still alive." He said, "Now go to work and get a little whiskey and butter and beat it together good and drop just two drops in his mouth, and in four hours drop two more." He sat beside me, laid his hands on my breast and about ten o'clock de next day I began to come around. I realized he was there and he asked me if I knew him, which I did.

In "blowing fire," my grandfather simply blew on de burn and de fire and pain was gone. It was a secret charm, handed down from generation to generation. He said only one could be told. He told my Aunt Harriet and she could "blow fire" de same as my grandfather.

I remember one good old doctor in dis part of de country. Old Dr. Stark. He was as good a doctor, de finest we had in those days. He could chew tobacco and spit enough to drown a dog. A lot of de old herb remedies my grandfather used, I can still remember. He used one called "white root." It is a bush dat grows here. In de spring of de year, when its leaves bloom out, in de morning house, when de sun shines on it, it looks just like bright light. It has an awful bitter taste. It was used for mighty near any ailment. He had another herb, he used, called "remedy weed." It is a bright green looking weed dat grows around springs. It is also used for many ailments. Another one was sarsaparilla root. It grows here, lots of it. He went to de woods and gathered it all hisself getting wild cherry bark, ditney, pennyroyal, and camomile root. Others he gathered and dried; some to make teas and others to put in whiskey.

Dogwood buds, some kind of a medicine used as a laxative. Ginseng was another remedy. I do not know what it was used for, but it was powerful good and one remedy he used was called "spicewood." It was also a healthful drink, like store tea. You gather it in de fall, using de stem or stocky part, break it up and dry it. I used it all de time while I worked on de river, at de tourist camps. It has a fine flavor and it's good for you.

Indian turnip grows by de thousands in de woods here. Great places of it, looks like turnips, grows in big bunches and bright red. Colored folks used to use de Indian turnip in slave times. Dey would take dis and dry it, pulverize it, and tie it in big quantities around their feet to keep off de trail of bloodhounds. No bloodhound could trail a bit further after smelling it. It was strong like red peppers, burns like everything, and colored folks running away used it all de time.

Grandfather also used "butternut root," some call it white walnut. You take one dose of dis and it will cure de worst case of chills, no matter how bad. Take two tablespoons for a dose. It is as severe as croton oil. By Golly, it won't leave a thing in you, clears you out, and one dose does de work. Oh man, but it is bitter.

He used golden seal, a medicine found in places here, very costly, worth seven dollars to eight dollars a pound now. I don't know what he used dem all for, but I do remember him getting dem in their proper seasons, and kept dem always on hand.

For sore throat or quinsy, he had some sort of tea. He used onion tea too. He took an onion, roasted it in its hull in ashes, squeezed out de juice, and added a little sugar, and gave it to de patient. For rheumatism, he used poke root, dried it and put it in whiskey. De only thing dat is good for rheumatics. There were many more remedies, but I can't recall them now.

JORDON SMITH
Interviewed at Marshall, Texas
Interviewer not identified
Age when interviewed: 86

I'SE BORN IN GEORGIA, next to the line of North Carolina, on Widow Hick's place. My papa died before I'se borned but my mammy was called Aggie. My old missus died and us fell to her nephew, Ab Smith. My gramma and grampa was full-blooded Africans and I couldn't understand their talk.

My missus was borned on the Chattahoosa River and she had two thousand acres of land in cultivation, a thousand on each side of the river, and owned five hundred slaves and two hundred fifty head of work mules. She was the richest woman in the whole county.

Us slaves lived in a double row log cabins facin' her house and our beds was made of rough plank and mattresses of hay and lynn bark and shucks, made on a machine. I'se spinned many a piece of cloth and wove many a brooch of thread.

Missus didn't allow her niggers to work till they's twenty-one, and the chillen played marbles and run round and kick their heels. The first work I done was hoeing and us worked long and as we could see a stalk of cotton or hill of corn. Missus used to call us at Christmas and give the old folks a dollar and the rest a dinner. When she died me and my mother went to Ab Smith at the dividement of the property. Master Ab put us to work on a big farm he bought and it was hell among the yearlin's if you crossed him or Missus, either. It was double trouble and a cowhidin' whatever you do. She had a place in the kitchen where she tied their hands up to the wall and cowhided them and sometimes cut they back almost to pieces. She made all go to church and let the women wear some her old, fine dresses to hide the stripes where she'd beat them. Mammy say, that to keep the folks at church from knowin' how mean she was to her niggers.

Master Ab had a driver, and if you didn't do what the driver say, Master say to him, "Boy, come here and take this nigger down, a hundred licks this time." Sometimes us run off and go to a dance without a pass and about time they's clickin' they heels and getting set for the big time, in come a patterroller and say, "Havin' a big time, ain't you? Got a pass?" If you didn't, they'd get four or five men to take you out and when they got through you'd sure go home.

Master Ab had hundreds acres wheat and made the woman stack hay in the field. Sometimes they got sick and wanted to go to the house, but he made them lay down on a straw pile in de field. Lots of chillen was borned on a straw pile in the field. After the chile was borned he sent them to the house. I seed that with my own eyes.

They was a trader yard in Virginia and one in New Orleans and sometimes a thousand slaves was waitin' to be sold. When the traders knowed men was comin' to buy, they made the slaves all clean up and greased they mouths with meat skins to look like they's feedin' them plenty meat. They lined the women up on one side and the men on the other. A buyer would walk up and down 'tween the two rows and grab a woman and try to throw her down and feel of her to see how she's put up. If she's purty strong, he'd say, "Is she a good breeder?" If a gal was eighteen or nineteen and put up good she was worth 'bout fifteen hundred dollars. Then the buyer'd pick out a strong, young nigger boy about the same age and buy him. When he got them home he'd say to them, "I want you two to stay together. I want young niggers."

If a nigger ever run off the place and come back, Master'd say, "If you'll be a good nigger, I'll not whip you this time." But you couldn't believe that. A nigger run off and stayed in the woods six month. When he come back he's hairy as a cow, 'cause he lived in a cave and come out at night and pilfer round. They put the dogs on him but couldn't catch him.

Finally he come home and Master say he won't whip him and Tom was crazy 'nough to believe him. Master say to the cook, "Fix Tom a big dinner." And while Tom's eatin', Master stand in the door with a whip and say, "Tom, I'se change my mind. You have no business runnin' off and I'se gwine take you out just like you come into the world."

Master gits a bottle whiskey and a box cigars and have Tom tied up out in the yard. He takes a chair and say to the driver, "Boy, take him down two hundred and fifty licks this time." Then he'd count the licks. When they's one hundred and fifty licks it didn't look like they is any place left to hit, but Master say, "Finish him up." Then he and the driver sat down, smoke cigars, and drink whiskey, and Master tell Tom how he must mind he master.

Then he lock Tom up in a log house and Master tell all the niggers if they give him anything to eat he'll skin 'em alive. The old folks slips Tom bread and meat. When he gets out, he's gone to the woods again. They's plenty niggers what stayed in the woods till surrender.

I heard some slaves say they white folks was good to 'em, but it was a tight fight where us was. I'se thought over the case a thousand times and figured it was 'cause all men ain't made alike. Some are bad and some are good. It's like that now. Some folks you works for got no heart and some treat you right. I guess it always will be that way.

They was more ghosts and haunts them days than now. It look like when I'se comin' up, they was as common as pig tracks. They come in different forms and shapes, sometimes like a god or cat or goat or like a man. I didn't believe in 'em till I seed one. A fellow I knowed could see 'em every time he went out. One time us walkin' 'long a country land and he say, "Jordon, look over my right shoulder." I looked and see a man walkin' without a head. I broke and run plumb off from the man I'se with. He wasn't scared of 'em.

I'se refugeed from Georgia To Anderson County, Texas, before the War. I see Abe Lincoln once when he come through, but didn't none of us know who he was. I heared the President wanted 'em to work the young niggers till they was twenty-one but to free the growed slaves. They say he give 'em thirty days to consider it. The white folks said they'd wade blood saddle deep before they'd let us loose. I don't blame 'em in a way, 'cause they paid for us. In another way it was right to free us. We was brought here and no person is supposed to be made a brute.

After surrender, Master Ab call us and say we could go. Mammy stayed but I left with my uncles and aunts and went to Shreveport where the Yanks was. I didn't hear from my mammy for the next twenty years.

In Ku Klux times they come to our house and I stood tremblin', but they didn't bother us. I heared 'em say lots of niggers was took down in Sabine River and Kluxed, just 'cause they wanted to get rid of 'em. I think it was desperadoes what done that, 'stead of the Ku Klux. That was did in Panola County, in the Bad Lands. Bill Bateman and Hulon Gresham and Sidney Farney was desperadoes and would kill a nigger just to get rid of him. 'Course, lots of folks was riled up at the Kluxers and blamed 'em for everything.

After surrender I went to Shreveport and steamboated from there to New Orleans, then to Vicksburg. Old hands was paid fifteen dollars a trip. I come here in 1872 and railroaded thirty years, on the section gangs and in the shops. Since then I farmed and I'se had three wives and nineteen chillen and they are scattered all over the state. Since I'se too old to farm I work at odd jobs and get a ten dollars a month pension.

SUSAN SNOW
Interviewed at Meridian, Mississippi
Interviewed by William B. Allison
Age at interview: 87

I WAS BORN in Wilcox County, Alabama, in 1850. W. J. Snow was my old marster. He bought my ma from a man named Jerry Casey. Venus was her name, but dey mostly called her "Venie."

I'se workin' now for one o' my old folks. I can't work much—just carries things to her and such. She's my old mistis' own daughter and she's got grandchillun grown and married. All de chillen dat's livin' is older'n me. When her pa bought my mammy, I was a baby. Her pa owned a heap o' niggers. I'se de only one still hangin' around.

My ma was a black African and she sure was wild and mean. She was so mean to me I couldn't believe she was my mammy. Dey couldn't whip her. Dey used to say she was a "conger" and dey was all scared of till de next day to get somebody to help tie her up, den he'd forget to whip her. Dey used to say she was a "conger" and dey was all scared of her. But my ma was scared o' "congers," too.

All de niggers on de place was born in de family and was kin 'cept my ma. She told me how dey brought her from Africa. You know, like we say "President" in dis country, well dey call him "Chief" in Africa. Seem like de chief made 'rangements with some men and dey had a big goober grabbin' for de young folks. Dey stole my ma and some more and brung 'em to dis country.

I don't 'member nothin' about havin' no pa. You know, in dem days husbands and wives didn't belong to de same folks. A man didn't get to see his wife 'cept twice a week. Dat was Wednesday and Saturday night. De woman had to walk a chalk line. I never heard tell o' wives runnin' round with other men in dem days. My ma say her husband was so mean dat after us left Alabama she didn't want to marry no more.

I was raised in Jasper County. Marster bought land from everybody round till he had a big plantation. He had niggers, horses, mules, cows, hogs, and chickens. He was a rich man, den.

Every nigger had a house o' his own. My ma never would have no board floor like de rest of 'em, on 'count she was a African—only dirt. Dey say she was 108 year old when she died.

Us went to church with de white folks if us wanted to. Dey didn't make us. I didn't go much, 'cause I didn't have religion den. Us didn't have no schoolin'. Us could go to school with de white chillen if us wanted to, but didn't nobody teach us. I'se educated, but I ain't educated in de books. I'se educated by de licks and bumps I got.

My white folks was good people and didn't whip nobody, unless dey needed it. Some o' de niggers was sure 'nough bad. Dey used to take de marster's horses out at night and ride 'em down. One nigger, Sam, got dat mad at a mule for grabbin' at cotton he cut his tongue out. 'Course, Marster whipped him, but when he went to look for him about a hour after, he found him asleep. Said he ought to kill him, but he didn't.

When we was sick dey had a doctor for us just like dey done for deyselves. Dey called him in to prescribe for us. I was snake bit when I was eight year old. Dey used to be a medicine named lobelia. De doctor give me dat and whiskey. My ma carried me up to de Big House every mornin' and left me and carried me home at night. Old Miss would watch over me in de daytime. My young marster told me dat when I got to be ten year old, I'd have a snake coiled up on my liver. Dat scared me most to death till I was past ten year old.

Dey made all de niggers' clothes on de place. Homespun, dey called it. Dey had spinnin' wheels and cards and looms at de Big House. All de women spinned in de winter time.

I never knowed what it was to wear more dan one garment till I was most grown. I never had a pair o' shoes o' my own. Old Miss let me wear her'n sometimes. Dey had shoes for de old folks, but not for de chillen.

I got more whippin's dan any other nigger on de place, 'cause I was mean like my mammy. Always a-fightin' and scratchin' with white and black. I was so bad Marster made me go look at de niggers dey hung to see what dey done to a nigger dat harm a white man.

I'se gwine tell dis story on myself. De white chillen was a-singin' dis song:

> Jeff Davis, long and slim,
> Whipped old Abe with a hickory limb.

> Jeff Davis is a wise man, Lincoln is a fool,
> Jeff Davis rides a gray, and Lincoln rides a mule.

I was mad anyway, so I hopped up and sung dis one:

> Old Gen'l Pope had a shotgun,
> Filled it full o' gum,
> Killed 'em as dey come.

> Called a Union band,
> Make de Rebels understand
> To leave de land,
> Submit to Abraham.

Old Miss was a-standin' right behind me. She grabbed up de broom and laid it on me. She made *me* submit. I caught de feathers, don't you forget it. I didn't know it was wrong. I'd heared de niggers sing it and I didn't know dey was a-singin' in dey sleeves. I didn't know nothin' about Abe Lincoln, but I hear'd he was a-tryin' to free de niggers and my mammy say she want to be free.

De young folks used to make up a heap o' songs, den. Dey'd compose dey own songs and sing 'em. I never will forget one song dey sung when dey buried anybody. It made Old Marster, Mistis, and all of 'em cry. Us chillen cried, too. It went like dis:

> My mother prayed in de wilderness,
> In de wilderness,
> In de wilderness.
> My mother prayed in de wilderness,
> And den I'm a-goin' home.

Chorus
> Den I'm a-goin' home,
> Den I'm a-goin' home.
> We'll all make ready, Lord,
> And den I'm a-goin' home.

> She plead her cause in de wilderness,
> In de wilderness,
> In de wilderness.
> She plead her cause in de wilderness,
> And den I'm a-goin' home.

Old Aunt Hannah fell to my marster from his daddy. She had twelve chillen a-workin' on de place. De oldest was named Adam and de littlest was named Eve. She had two twins what was named Rachel and Leah. Dey nursed my mistis' two twins. Dey kept one a-nursin' most all de time.

My ma was de cause o' my marster a-firin' all de overseers. Dey blamed everything on her 'cause she was de only bought nigger. Marster say she a valuable nigger, but she was so mean he was afraid dey'd kill her. He say, "She'll work without no watchin' and overseers ain't nothin', nohow."

Dey was a white man—I ain't lyin'—I know him and I seen him. He had nigger hounds and he made money a-huntin' runaway niggers. His own niggers kilt him. Dey hung 'em for it. Two was his niggers and one belong to somebody else.

My young marster used to work in de field with us. He'd boss de niggers. Dey called him Bud, but us all called him Babe. I sure did love dat boy. When de War come dey used to tease him and say, "Bud, why don't you go to de War?" Dey laughed and teased him when he went. But 'tweren't no laughin' when he come home on a furlough and went back. Dey was cryin' den. And well dey might cry, 'cause he never come back no more. He was kilt in de War.

My ma was de first to leave de plantation after de surrender. All de other niggers had a contract to stay, but she didn't. She went to Newton County and hired out. She never wanted to stay in one place, nohow. If she had a crop half made and somebody made her mad, she'd up and leave it and go somewheres else.

You know, dey was mighty strict, about den, with cullud folks, and white people, too. De Kloo Kluxes was out nights. I heared tell about 'em whippin' people. But dey never bothered me. Dey was speakers gwine around, tellin' de niggers what dey was gwinea get. Dey never got nothin' to my knowledge, 'cept de government let 'em homestead land. My ma homesteaded a place close to Enterprise, Scott County, but she got mad and left it like she always done.

She was a-gettin' long in years afore she got religion. She was good to me after dat. She couldn't learn de Lord's Prayer, but she used to pray, "Our Father, Which are in Heaven; Hallowed be Thy name. Thy mercy, Lord, You've showed to others; That mercy show to me. Amen." She went to rest in it, too.

I went to Enterprise, den to Meridian, nursin' (wet-nursin' when I could) and workin' out. I never worked in de field, if I could help it. (Old Miss hired me out as a nurse first when I was eight year old.) When I come to Meridian, I cut loose. I'se a woman, but I'se a prodigal. I used to be a old drunkard. My white folks kept tellin' me if I got locked up one more time dey wouldn't pay my fine. But dey done it again and again.

De niggers called me "Devil." I was a devil till I got religion. I weren't baptized till 1887. Den I found peace. I had a vision. I told it to a white lady and she say, "Susie, dat's religion a-callin' you." But you know white folks' religion ain't like niggers' religion. I know a woman dat couldn't 'member de Lord's Prayer, and she got religion out o' prayin', "January, February, March." I didn't join de church till 1891, after I had a second vision. I'se a member in good standin' now. I done put all my badness behind me, 'cept my temper. I even got dat under more control.

RIA SORRELL

Interviewed at Raleigh, North Carolina
Interviewed by Pat Matthews
Age when interviewed: 97

I JUST LACK three years of bein' one hundred years old. I belonged to Jacob Sorrell. His wife was named Elizabeth. My age was give to me by Mr. Bob Sorrell, the only one of Old Marster's chillens dat is livin' now.

Dey had four boys, Marcillers, Bob, Adolphus, and Dr. Patrick Sorrell. Dey had three girls, Averada and two other ones dat died before dey was named. I was born on Marster's plantation near Leesville, in Wake County, North Carolina. Dat's been a long time ago. I can't get around now like I could when I was on de plantation.

Dere was about twenty-five slaves on de place and Marster just wouldn't sell a slave. When he whipped one he didn't whip much. He was a good man. He seemed to be sorry every time he had to whip any of de slaves. His wife was de pure devil. She just enjoyed whippin' Negroes. She was tall and sparemade, with black hair and eyes. Over both her eyes was a bulge place in her forehead. Her eyes set way back in her head. Her jaws were large like a man's and her chin stuck up. Her mouth was large and her lips thin and seemed to be closed like she had somethin' in her mouth most all de time.

When Marster come to town she raised old scratch with de slaves. She whipped all she could while Marster was gone. She tried to boss Marster but he wouldn't allow dat. He kept her from whippin' many a slave. She just wouldn't feed a slave and when she had her way our food was bad. She said underleaves of collards was good enough for slaves. Marster took feedin' in his hands and fed us plenty at times. He said people couldn't work without eatin'.

Our houses was good houses, 'cause Marster seed to it dey was fixed right. We had good beds and plenty of cover. De houses was called de nigger houses. Dey was about two hundred yards from de big house. Our houses had two rooms and Marster's had seven rooms.

We didn't have any overseers. Marster said he didn't believe in 'em and he didn't want any. De oldest slaves on the place woke us up in the morning and acted as foreman. Marster hardly ever went to de field. He told Squire Holman and Sam Sorrell, two old slaves, what he wanted

294

done and dey told us and we done it. I worked at de house as nurse and house girl most of de time.

Mother and Father worked in de field. Mother was named Judy and Father was named Sam. You sees Father was a slave foreman. Marster bought Squire Holman from de Holmans and let him keep his name. Dat's why he was called dat.

We worked from sunup till sunset with a rest spell of two hours at twelve o'clock. He give us holidays to rest in. That was Christmas, a week off den, den a day every month, and all Sundays. He said he was a Christian and he believed in givin' us a chance. Marster died of consumption. He give us patches and all dey made on it. He gives slaves days off to work deir patches.

I sure believes Marster went to heaven, but Missus, well I don't know. Don't know about her, she was so bad. She would hide her baby's cap and tell me to find it. If I couldn't find it, she whipped me. She would call Marster, and I doin' de best I could to please her, and say, "Come here, Jacob, and whip dis nigger," but Marster paid no attention to her. He took our part. Many was de meals he give us unbeknown to his wife. Dere was no mixin' white and black on Marster's place, no sir, nothin' like dat. He was like a father to us. Sometimes he brought hog haslets and good things to de nigger house and told us to cook it. When it was done he come and et all he wanted, got up and said, "I'm goin' now," and you didn't see him no more till next day.

We had prayer meetin' anytime and we went to the white folks church. Dere was no whiskey on de place. Now at corn shuckin's dey had a big supper and all et all dey wanted. I'll tell you Jake Sorrell was all right. We didn't have any dances no time. Some nights Marster would come to our cabins, call us all into one of 'em and pray with us. He stood up in de floor and told us all to be good and pray. I saw him die. I saw him when de breath went out of him. De last word he said was, "Lord, do your will, not mine." Den he breathed twice and was no more.

Missus died since de surrender. When she got sick she sent for me to go and wait on her. I went and cleaned her like a baby, waited on her till de evenin' she died dat night. I went off dat evenin' late to spend de night and next mornin' when I got dere she was dead. I just couldn't refuse Missus when she sent for me even if she had treated me bad.

My grandmother was as white as you is. She was Lottie Sorrell. Marster bought my grandmother. I do not know my grandfather's name. Grand-mother was a cook and she told me the reason she was so white was 'cause she stood over de fire so much. Ha, ha, dats what she told me. She had long straight hair. I 'members her well.

I 'members de Yankees. De Southern, our folks, was in front. Dey come along a road right by our house. Our folks was goin' on and de Yankees right behind. You could hear 'em shootin'. Dey called it skirmishin'. It was rainin' and our folks was goin' through de mud and slush. Dey had wagons and some would say, "Drive up, drive up, Goddamn it! Drive up, de damn Yankees right behind us." Dey had turkeys and chickens on de wagons and on deir hosses. Dey got things out of de houses and took de stock. Dey searched de houses and took de quilts and sheets and things.

De Yankees was soon dere and dey done de same thing. Dat was a time. They took all dey could find and dere weren't much left when all got through. De Yankees poured out 'lasses and stomped down things dey could not carry off. I was afraid of de Yankees. Dey come up and said, "Hain't you got some money round here?" I told 'em I knowed nothin' about money. Dey called me "Auntie" and said "Auntie, tell us where de money is, you knows." I says "Dey don't let me see everything around here, no, dat dey don't."

Dere was one thing dey wouldn't allow. Dat was books and papers. I can't read and write. I heard talk of Abraham Lincoln comin' through when talk of de War come about. Dey met, him and Jeff Davis, in South Carolina. Lincoln said, "Jeff Davis, let dem niggers go free." Jeff Davis told him, "You can't make us give up our property." Den de War started.

When dey told us we was free we stayed right on with Marster. We got crackers and meat from de Yankees and when de crop was housed in de fall Marster gave us part of all we made. We come to Raleigh on on a old steer cart to get our crackers and meat dat was our allowance. We stayed at Marster's till Father died. I married there. We finally moved to the Page place about eleven miles north of Raleigh. We been farmin' with de white folks ever since, till we got so we couldn't work.

I married Buck Sorrell since de surrender. We had four boys and two girls, six children in all. Dey are all dead, 'cept one, her name is Bettie.

A lot of de niggers in slavery time worked so hard dey said dey hated to see de sun rise in de mornin'. Slavery was a bad thing, 'cause some white folks didn't treat deir niggers right.

ELIZABETH SPARKS

Interviewed at Matthews Court House, Virginia
Interviewed by Claude Anderson
Age when interviewed: 95

M Y MISTRESS' name was Miss Jennie Brown. She died about four years ago, Bless her. She was a good woman. Course I mean she'd slap and beat you once in a while but she weren't no woman for fightin', fussin', and beatin' you all day like some I know. She was too young when de War ended for that. Course no white folks perfect. Her parents a little rough. I wasn't born then but my parents told me.

Miller was my master. His old father, he was a tough one. Lord! I've seen him kill 'em. He'd get the meanest overseers to put over 'em. Why, I 'member time after he was dead when I'd peep in the closet and just see his old clothes hangin' there and just fly. Yessir, I'd run from them clothes and I was just a little girl then. He was that way with them black folks. No, he ain't in heaven! Went past heaven. He was clerk and was he tough! Sometimes he beat 'em until they couldn't work. Give 'em more work than they could do. They'd get beaten if they didn't get work done. Bought my mother, a little girl, when he was married. She was a real Christian and he respected her a little. Didn't beat her so much. 'Course he beat her once in a while. Shep Miller was terrible. There was no end to the beatin'. I saw it with my own eyes.

He beat women as well as men. Beat women just like men. Beat women naked and wash 'em down in brine. Sometimes they beat 'em so bad they just couldn't stand it and they run away to the woods. If you get in the woods, they couldn't get you. You could hide and people slip you somethin' to eat. Then he call you every day. After while he tell one of colored foreman tell you come on back. He ain't a-goin' beat you anymore. They had colored foreman but they always have a white overseer. Foreman get you to come back and then he beat you to death again.

They worked six days from sun to sun. If they forcin' wheat or other crops, they start to work long before day. Usual work day began when the horn blew and stop when the horn blew. They got off just long 'nough to eat at noon. Didn't have much to eat. They get some suet and slice of bread for breakfast. Well, they give the colored people an allowance every week. For dinner they'd eat ash cake baked on blade of a hoe.

I lived at Seaford then and was round fifteen or sixteen when my mistress married. Shep Miller lived at Springdale. I 'member just as well when they gave me to Jennie. We was all in a room helpin' her dress. She was soon to be married, and she turns round and says to us, "Which of you niggers think I'm gonna get when I get married?" We all say, "I don't know." And she looks right at me and point her finger at me like this and sayed, "You!" I was so glad. I had to make her believe I was cryin', but I was glad to go with her. She didn't beat. She was just a young thing. 'Course she take a whack at me sometimes, but that weren't nothin'. Her mother was a mean old thing. She'd beat you with a broom or a leather strap or anything she'd get her hands on.

She used to make my Aunt Caroline knit all day and when she get so tired after dark that she'd get sleepy, she'd make her stand up and knit. She work her so hard that she'd go to sleep standin' up and every time her head nod and her knees sag, the lady'd come down across her head with a switch. That was Miss Jennie's mother. She'd give the cook just so much meal to make bread from and if she burnt it, she'd be scared to death 'cause they'd whip her. I 'member plenty of times the cook ask: "Marsa, please 'scuse dis bread; it's a little too brown." Yes sir! Beat the devil out her if she burn dat bread.

I went with Miss Jennie and worked at house. I didn't have to cook. I got permission to get married. You always had to get permission. White folks would give you away. You jump 'cross a broomstick together and you was married. My husband lived on another plantation. I slept in my mistress' room but I ain't slept in any bed. No, sir! I slept on a carpet, an old rug, before the fireplace. I had to get permission to go to church, everybody did. We could set in the gallery at the white folks' service in the mornin' and in the evenin' the folk held baptize service in the gallery with white folks present.

Shep went to war but not for long. We didn't see none of it, but the slaves knew what the War was about. After the War they tried to fool the slaves about freedom and wanted to keep 'em workin' but the Yankees told 'em they was free. They sent some of the slaves to South Carolina when the Yankees came near to keep the Yankees from gettin' 'em. Sent Cousin James to South Carolina. I never will forget when the Yankees came through. They was takin' all the livestock and all the men slaves back to Norfolk with 'em to break up the system. White folks was just goin' to keep on havin' slaves. The slaves wanted freedom, but they's scared to tell the white folks so. Anyway, the Yankees was givin' everything to the slaves. I can hear 'em tellin' Old Missy now. "Yes! give'er clothes. Let her take anything she wants." They even took some of Miss Jennie's things and offered 'em to me. I didn't take 'em, though, 'cause she'd been purty nice to me.

What tickled me was my husband, John Sparks. He didn't want to leave me and go 'cause he didn't know where they's takin' 'em nor what they's gonna do, but he wanted to be free; so he played lame to keep from goin'. He was just a limpin' round. It was all I could do to keep from laughin'. I can hear Miss Jennie now yellin' at them Yankees. "No, who are you to judge? I'll be the judge. If John Sparks wants to stay here, he'll stay." They was gonna take him anyhow and he went inside to pack and the baby started cryin'. So one of 'em said that as long as he had a wife and a baby that young they guess he could stay. They took all the horses, cows, and pigs and chickens and anything they could use and left.

I was about nineteen when I married. I was married in 1861, my oldest boy was born in 1862, and the fallin' of Richmond came in 1865.

Before Miss Jennie was married she was born and lived at her old home right up the river here. You can see the place from outside here. On the plantation my mother was a house woman. She had to wash white folks' clothes all day and hers after dark. Sometimes she'd be washin' clothes way up round midnight. Couldn't wash any niggers' clothes in daytime. My mother lived in a big one room log house with an upstairs.

Sometimes the white folks give you about ten cents to spend. A woman with children would get about half a bushel of meal a week; a childless woman would get about a peck and a half of meal a week. If you was workin', they'd give you shoes. Children went barefooted the year round. The men on the road got one cotton shirt and jacket.

Once in a while they was free niggers come from somewhere. They could come see you if you was their folks. Niggers used to go way off in quarters and slip and have meetins'. They called it stealin' the meetin'. The children used to teach me to read. There weren't no schools for niggers. Slaves went to bed when they didn't have anything to do. Most time they went to bed when they could. Sometimes the men had to shuck corn till eleven and twelve o'clock at night.

If you went out at night, the patrollers would catch you if you was out after time without a pass. Most of the slaves was a-feared to go out. Plenty of slaves ran away. If they catch 'em they beat 'em near to death. But you know dey's good and bad people everywhere. That's the way the white folks was. Some had hearts; some had gizzards 'stead o' hearts.

When my mother's master died, he called my mother and brother Major and get religion and talked so purty. He say he so sorry that he hadn't found the Lord before and had nothin' 'gainst his colored people. He was sorry and scared, but confessed. My mother died twenty years since then at the age of seventy-four. She was religious and all the white folks set store to her.

Old Massa done so much wrongness I couldn't tell you all of it. Slave girl Betty Lilly always had good clothes and all the privileges. She was a favorite of his'n. But cain't tell all! God's got all! We used to sing a song when he was shippin' the slaves to sell 'em about "Massa's Gwine Sell Us Tomorrow."

My husband lived on the plantation next to my mistress. He lived with a bachelor master. He tell us once when he was a pickinnany Old Marse Williams shot at him. He didn't shoot 'em; he just shoot in the air and my old man was so scared he ran home and got in his mammy's bed. Massa Williams used to play with 'em; then dey got so bad that dey'd run and grab his legs so's he couldn't hardly walk, so when he sees 'em he just shoots in de air.

Old Massa, he just come on up to the cabin and say, "Mammy, where dat boy?" She say, "In dere under the bed. You done scared him to death!" Old Massa go in and say, "Boy! What's the matter with you?" Boy say, "You shot me, Master, you shot me." Master say, "Ah, go on! Get up and come along. I ain't shot you. I just shot and scared you. Heh! Heh! Heh!" Yes sir my old husband sayed he sure was scared that day.

LOUIS THOMAS

Interviewed at St. Louis, Missouri
Interviewer not identified
Age when interviewed: 93

I WAS BORN in Pickens County, Alabama, May 9, 1844. My mother's name was Tama and my father's was Thomas Windom. Our owner was Levy Windom. I had two sisters and two brothers. I married Caroline Windom. She was owned by the same folks I was. We had eleven children but only two is living. The oldest one, Laura Richardson, I am living with. The other daughter's name is Evergreen Richardson, who also lives in St. Louis. Dey are both Richardsons but deir husbands are not related.

I been living in St. Louis since 1923. When I was a slave, I had to plow barefooted, hooked to a double horse plow. For eight or ten years of dat time we had a white overseer in de summer. I did not only plow barefooted but naked as well. In de winter dey allowed me a few clothes but not many. I worked from daylight until dark; I didn't know nothing about time.

Making and gathering crop was my biggest task. We made five hundred bales of cotton a year, besides growing wheat, potatoes, and other vegetables for the hands. I stayed on de plantation till way after de Civil War was fought. If de slaves could get as near as East St. Louis and Ohio without getting caught, dey would join de Yankees and help fight for freedom. But the Rebs wouldn't think of giving slaves any guns, as mean as they had been to us.

Dey knew too well we would shoot dem first thing. I remember well I was in Tuscaloosa, Alabama, and dere was a speech made dere by General Forest on a Sunday. He said, "Dere ain't a Yankee in five hundred miles of Tuscaloosa, Alabama." So de Rebs was so happy about dat dey started early de very next morning putting de flooring back in de bridge dey done took out so de Yankees couldn't cross and get to them.

The following Tuesday night, de very next day, I mean, dem Yankees come in our town cross dat very bridge. That same night Old Marse made us hitch up all his horses and get up all de flour, meat, and everything we done raised, and carry it up Tom Bilby River, which was a swamp, to hide it from de Yankees. But dat didn't do a bit of good. Dem Yankees got all our stuff and us, too, and destroyed everything he had. Us slaves was so mad at Old Marse, we helped 'em get rid of everything. Den we went on back home, 'cause we had nowhere else to go and de War wasn't over and we hadn't nary a penny of money.

I made my last crop in 1867 on dat very plantation where I lived all my days. Of course we was free den or supposed to be free. Dey promised to pay us, but we never got nothin', least not yet, Marse ain't paid me, and he's dead now.

In March, 1868, dey sent to de field for all us hands to come up to de house to sign a contract. We all went. We was so used to minding Old Marse when he sent for us we just mind right on like it was still slavery. So I had always been mighty handy about most things so he wanted me above de others, so he took my hand, put it on his pen and held it right dere and signed my name hisself. I got mad as a wet hen about dat agreement he read to me. So he tried to make me feel good saying he was goin' to give me half. I knowed better.

I felt dere was going to be some trouble up to de house, so I had a pistol in my pocket, that had been dropped by the Yankees on purpose to help us slaves shoot our way out. So I just told my old boss I ain't goin' to do it, and when he raised up at me I just whipped out dat pistol and everything in sight got out of my way. I was mad a-plenty, and I already always had plenty of temper. So while I had everybody scared and excited I left and never did go back. I went to Columbus, Mississippi, and stayed until 1923. All dat time I done sharecropping farming and made good. When I left dere I came to St. Louis and have not worked since. I was too old for a job, but I worked many a day for two bits a day and churned all day to get milk to drink 'cause I couldn't get no other food. I cut grass and mowed after sharecropping days were over.

I never had any schooling. What learning I got I picked up hearing the children. I have twenty-two grandchildren, nine great-grandchildren.

J. T. TIMS
Interviewed at Little Rock, Arkansas
Interviewed by Samuel S. Taylor
Age when interviewed: 86

I WAS BORN in Jefferson County, Mississippi, in 1853. That would make me eighty-six years old. I was born six miles from Fayette— six miles east of Fayette. I was eighty-six years old the eleventh day of September. My father's name was Daniel Tims, and my mother's name was Ann Tims. My mother was born in Lexington, Kentucky. Ma's been dead years and years ago, and my father is gone too. I don't know the name of my mother's master. But my father's master was named Blount Steward. Pa was born on Blount's plantation and Blount bought my ma because they brought her from Kentucky for sale. They had her for sale just like you would sell hogs and mules. Then my father saw her and liked her and married her. She was a slave too.

Blount Steward was kind of good. He was very well till the War started—the Federal war. Miss Ann went to whip me for nothing. I was carrying her daughter to school every day except Saturdays and Sundays. One day, Miss Ann was off and I was at the back steps playin' and she decided to whip me. I told her I hadn't done nothin', but she put my head between her legs and started to beatin' me. And I bit her legs. She let me loose and hollered.

Then she called for William to come and beat me. William was one of the colored slaves. William come to do it. Ma had been peeping out from the kitchen watchin' the whole thing. When William come up to beat me, she come out with a big carving knife and told him, "That's my child and if you hit him, I'll kill you."

Then she sent for Tully to come and whip me, I mean to whip my mother. Tully was my young master. Tully come and said to my mother, "I know you ain't done nothin' nor your child neither, but I'll have to hit you a few light licks to satisfy Ma." Blount come the next day and went down to where Pa was making shoes. He said, "Daniel, you're looking mighty glum." Pa said, "You'd be lookin' glum too if your wife and child had done been beat up for nothin'."

When he said that, Blount got mad. He snatched up a shoe hammer and hit Pa up side the head with it. Pa said, "By God, don't you try it again!" Blount didn't hit him again. Pa was ready to fight, and he wasn't sure that he could whip him. Pa said, "You won't hit me no more." The War was goin' on then.

The following Sunday night, twelve head of us left there. My ma and pa and me and our whole fmily and some more besides was along. We went from the plantation to Rodney, Mississippi, first, trying to get on a steamboat—gunboat. The gunboat wouldn't take us for fear we would get hurt. The War was goin' on then. So we just transferred down the river and went on to Natchez. We went there walking and wading. We was from Sunday night to Sunday night gettin' there. We didn't have no trouble 'cept that the hounds was runnin' us. But they didn't catch us—they didn't catch none of us. My ma and my pa and my brothers and sisters besides me was all in the crowd, and we all go to Natchez. They are all dead and gone to Judgment now but me.

At Natchez, Ma didn't do anything. We children didn't do nothin' there, either. But Pa joined the army. He joined it the next day after he got there. Then I went to work waiting on the Sixty-fourth—let me see— yes, it was the Sixty-fourth Brass Epaulettes. I was waiting on one of the sergeants. He was a Yankee sergeant. The sergeant's name was Josephus, and the captain of the company was Lieutenant Knowles.

I was with them two years and six months. I never did get hurt. When they went to fight at New Orleans, the captain wouldn't let me take part in it. He said I was so brave he was afraid I might get hurt.

Me and my father were the only ones working in the family at that time. I stayed right in Natchez, but my father didn't. My father's first stop was in Bullocks Bar right above Vidalia. That was where his company was stationed first. He went from there to Davis Bend. I wasn't with him. He was in a colored regiment. I was with a white regiment. He left Davis Bend and went to Vicksburg. His next trip was up the Sunflower River. Then his next trip he went from there up to De Valls Bluff. That is where he come free. That was the end of the fighting there—right there.

From there he came back to Rodney. We all went to Davis Bend while Pa was there. When he left and went to De Valls Bluff, Ma went to Rodney. I stayed with the soldiers two years and a half down there at Natchez. That's as far as I went with them. When they left I stayed. I went to Rodney with my mother and stayed with her and the rest of the children till she died. My ma died in 1874. My father died down here in Pine Bluff several years ago. After Ma died, Pa married another woman. He went back to Pine Bluff and was killed by a train when he was crossing a trestle.

Blount Steward was the only master any of us ever had, outside of my ma's first master—the one in Kentucky. I don't know anything about them. I was eight years old when the War began and twelve years old when it ended. I must have been older than that because I was twelve years old when I was serving them soldiers. And I had to come away from them before the War was over.

The first work I ever did in slave time was dining-room service. When I left the dining-room table, I left carrying my young mistress to school six miles from Fayette. They give me to Lela, my young mistress. She was the young girl I was carrying to school when I got the whipping. When Old Miss was whippin' me, I asked her what she was whipping for, and she said, "Nothin', 'cause you're mine, and I can whip you if I want to." She didn't think that I had done anything to the girl. She was just mad that day, and I was around, so she took it out on me. After that, I never did any more work as a slave, because the whole family ran away about that time. I don't reckon Pa would ever have run off if Old Miss hadn't whipped me and if Old Master hadn't struck him. They was good till then, but it looked like the War made them mean.

They had patrols going round watching the colored people to keep them from running off. That's all I know about them. I don't remember hearin' anything about the jayhawkers. But I heard lots about the Ku Klux. They were terrible. The white folks had one another goin' round watching and keeping them from runnin' off. The Ku Klux would whip people they caught out. They would whip them just because they could, because they called themselves bosses, because they was white and the colored people was niggers. They didn't do nothin' but just keep the slaves down. It was before the War that I knew about the Ku Klux. There wasn't no difference between the patrollers and the Ku Klux that I knows of. If they'd catch you, they all would whip you. I don't know nothin' about the Ku Klux Klan after the War. I know they broke them up.

Before the War, we lived in a old log house. It had one window, one door, and one room. Colored people didn't have no two or three-room houses before the War. I'll tell you that right now. All de furniture we had was bed stools and quilts. 'Course we had them old stools that Pa made. We kept food right there in the house where we was in one corner. We didn't have no drawers—nothing like that.

The white folks fed us. They give us as much as they thought we ought to have. Every Saturday night you would go to the smokehouse and get your meat and meal and your molasses. Didn't get no flour, no coffee, no sugar. Pa was an ox driver and when he would go to Rodney to carry cotton, he would buy sugar and coffee for himself. You see, they would slip and kill a couple of hogs and carry them along with them. That was the only way they could get a little money. My pa's main work was shoemaking, but he worked in the field too. He was a driver chiefly when he was out in the fields. He hoed and plowed. He was the leader of the gang. He never got a chance to make no money for hisself before the War. Nope, the colored people didn't have no money at all lessen they slipped and got it.

Say I wanted this woman for my wife. We would just put down the broom and step over it and we would be married. That is all there was to it before emancipation. Didn't have no matrimony read nor nothing. You were married when you stepped over the broom handle. That was your wife.

They say Abe Lincoln come down in this part of the country and asked for work. He had his little grip. The man said, "Wait till I go to dinner." Didn't say, "Come to dinner," and didn't say nothin' about, "Have dinner." Just said, "Wait till I go eat my dinner." When he come back, Abe Lincoln was up there looking over his books. He'd done changed his clothes and everything. He had guards with him but they didn't see 'em. That is the story I heard them tell.

When the slaves got freed, they wasn't expecting to get nothing that I knows of 'cept what they worked for. They weren't spectin' no forty acres and a mule. Who was goin' to give it to 'em? The Rebs? They didn't give 'em nothin' but what they could put on their backs—I mean lashes.

Blount had stocks that he used to put them in. The stocks had hinges on one side and latches on the other. The nigger would put his head in one hole and his arms through the others, and the old man would beat on the other end. Your feet would be stretched out and you would be layin' on your belly.

Blount whipped me once because I wouldn't go to the cow barns to get the milk to put in the coffee that morning. I didn't have time. They had given me to Lela, and I had to take her to school. I was responsible if she was late. He had give me to Lela. Next morning with her, and we didn't come back till Friday evening. She went down to her Aunt Leona Harrison's and carried me with her. She was mad because they whipped me when I belonged to her.

After slavery, we worked by the month on people's plantations. I did that kind of work till after awhile the white people got so they rented the colored people land and selled them mules for their work. Then some worked on shares and some rented and worked for theirselves. Right after the War most of the farms were worked on shares. We were lucky to be able to get to work by the month.

I went to school in Natchez, Mississippi. My teacher came from the North, I suppose. But those I had in Rodney, I know they come from the North. Miss Mary—that's all the name I knowed—and Miss Emma were my teachers in Rodney. They come from Chicago. I never went to school here. I didn't get no further than the second grade. I stopped school to go work when the teacher went back to Chicago. After that I went to work in the field and made me a living. I hadn't done but a little work in the field helping Pa now and then before that.

They tried to whip me once since freedom. A man tried to whip me down in Stoneville because another man give me a drink. He tried to cut me with his knife. I knocked him down. I told him I could kill him, but I just didn't want to. While I was swearing out a warrant to get him arrested, he went and got a gun somewheres. He came right on in with his pistol and struck me with it. I knocked him down again, and he was dead for twenty-five minutes. They didn't have to go nowheres to serve the warrant on him. Nobody did anything to me about it.

I come to Little Rock fifty years ago or more. I farmed as long as I was able. Doctor stopped me when I began to fall out. I cooked for Dr. Stone and his wife for ten years in Greenville, Mississippi. Then I come to Pine Bluff on a vacation. The next time they give me a vacation, I stayed away for eleven years.

I went to get some money Dr. Stone owed me for some work I had done for him once and he wanted me to come back and cook again. I didn't do that and he died without paying me for the work. He said it was his brother that owed me. But it was him that hired me. I attended to some mules for nine months at four dollars a week. I never got but one four dollars. The mules belonged to him and his brother both, but it was him that hired me. It wasn't Captain Stone, his brother. It was him, and I looked to the man that hired me for my money. I didn't have nothing to do with nobody but him. It was him promised to pay me.

JOHN WHITE

Interviewed at Sand Springs, Oklahoma
Interviewer not identified
Age when interviewed: 121

OF ALL MY MAMMY'S CHILDREN I am the first born and the longest living. The others all gone to join Mammy. She was named Mary White, the same name as her mistress, the wife of my first master, James White.

About my pappy, I never hear his name and I never see him, not even when I was the least child around the Old Master's place way back there in Georgia more'n one-hundred twenty years ago! Mammy try to make it clear to me about my daddy. She married like the most of the slaves in them days. He was a slave on another plantation. One day he come for to borrow something from Master White. He sees a likely looking gal, and the way it work out that gal was to be my mammy. After that he got a paper saying it was all right for him to be off his own plantation. He come a-courting over to Master White's. After a while he talks with the master. Says he wants to marry the gal, Mary. The master says it's all right if it's all right with Mary and the other white folks. He finds out it is and they makes ready for the wedding. Mary says a preacher wedding is the best but Master say he can marry them just as good. There wasn't no Bible, just an old Almanac. Master White read something out of that. That's all and they was married. The wedding was over!

Every night he gets a leave paper from his master and come over to be with his wife, Mary. The next morning he leaves her to work in the fields. Then one night Mammy says he don't come home. The next night is the same, and the next. From then on Mammy don't see him no more—never find out what happen to my pappy.

When I was born Mammy named me John—John White. She tells me I was the blackest "white" boy she ever see! I stays with her till I was eleven year old. The master wrote down in the book when I was born, April 10, 1816, and I know it's right. Mammy told me so, and Master told me when I was eleven and he sold me to Sarah Davenport.

Mistress Sarah lived in Texas. Master White always selling and trading to folks all over the country. I hates to leave on account of Mammy and the good way Master White fared the slaves—they was good people.

Mammy cry but I has to go just the same. The tears are on my face a long time after the leaving. I was hoping all the time to see Mammy again, but that's the last time.

We travels and travels on the stagecoach. Once we cross the Big River—Mississippi—on the boat and pick up the horses on the other side. A new outfit, and we rides some more. Seems like we going to wear out all the horses before we gets to the place.

The Davenport plantation was way north of Linden, Texas, up in the Red River country. That's where I stayed for thirty-eight years. There I was drug through the hackles by the meanest master that ever lived. The mistress was the best white woman I ever know but Master Presley used his whip all the time, reason or no reason, and I got scars to remember by!

I remembers the house. A heavy log cabin with a gallery clear across the front. The kitchen was back of the house. I work in there and I live in there. It wasn't built so good as the master's house. The cold winds in the winter go through the cracks between the logs like the walls was somewheres else, and I shivers with the misery all the time. The cooking got to be my job. The washing too. Washday come around and I fills the tub with clothes. Puts the tub on my head and walks half a mile to the spring where I washes the clothes. Sometimes I run out of soap. Then I make ash soap right by the spring. I learns to be careful about streaks in the clothes. I learns by the bullwhip. One day the master finds a soapy streak in his shirt. Then he finds me.

The Military Road goes by the place and the master drives me down the road and ties me to a tree. First he tears off the old shirt and then he throws the bullwhip to me. When he is tired of beating me more torture is a-coming. The salt water cure. It don't cure nothing but that's what the white folks call it. "Here's at you," the master say, and slap the salt water into the bleeding cuts. "Here's at you!" The blisters burst every time he slap me with the brine. Then I was loosened to stagger back into the kitchen. The mistress couldn't do nothing about it 'cept to lay on the grease thick, with a kind word to help stop the misery.

Ration time was Saturday night. Every slave get enough fat pork, corn meal, and such to last out the week. I reckon the master figure it to the last bite because they was no leavings over. Most likely the shortage catch them! Sometimes they'd borrow, sometimes I'd slip some things from out the kitchen. The single womenfolks was bad that way. I favors them with something extra from the kitchen. Then they favors me—at night when the overseer thinks everybody sleep in they own places!

I was always back to my kitchen bed long before the overseer give the get-up-knock. I hear the knock, he hear me answer. Then he blow the horn and shout the loud call, "ARE YOU UP," and everybody knows it was four o'clock and pour out of the cabins ready for the chores.

Sometimes the white folks go around the slave quarters for the night. Not on the Davenport plantation, but some others close around. The slaves talked about it amongst themselves. After a while they'd be a new baby. Yellow. When the child got old enough for chore work the master would sell him—or her. No difference was it his own flesh and blood—if the price was right!

I traffic with lots of women but never marries. Not even when I was free after the War. I sees too many married troubles to mess up with such doings!

Sometimes the master sent me alone to the grinding mill. Load in the yellow corn, hitch in the oxen, I was ready to go. I gets me fixed up with a pass and takes to the road. That was the trip I like best. On the way was a still. Off in the brush. If the still was lonely I stop, not on the way but on on the way back. Mighty good whiskey, too! Maybe I drinks too much, then I was sorry. Not that I swipe the whiskey, just sorry because I gets sick!

Then I figures a woods camp meeting will steady me up and I goes. The preacher meet me and want to know how is my feelings. I says I is low with the misery and he say to join up with the Lord. I never join because he don't talk about the Lord. Just about the master and mistress. How the slaves must obey around the plantation—how the white folks know what is good for the slaves. Nothing about obeying the Lord and working for him. I reckon the old preacher was worrying more about the bullwhip than he was the Bible, else he say something about the Lord! But I always obeys the Lord—that's why I is still living!

The slaves would pray for to get out of bondage. Some of them say the Lord told them to run away. Get to the North. Cross the Red River. Over there would be folks to guide them to the free state—Kansas. The Lord never tell me to run away. I never tried it, maybe, because mostly they was caught by patrollers and fetched back for a flogging—and I had whippings enough already!

Before the Civil War was the fighting with Mexico. Some of the troops on they way south passed on the Military Road. Wasn't any fighting around Linden or Jefferson during the time. They was lots of traveling on the Military Road. Most of the time you could see covered wagons pulled by mules and horses, and sometimes a crawling string of wagons with oxen on the pulling end. From up in Arkansas come the stagecoach along the road. To San Antonio. The drivers bring news the Mexicans just about all killed off and the white folks say Texas was going to join the Union. The country's going to be run different they say, but I never see no difference. Maybe because I ain't white folks.

Wasn't many Mexicans around the old plantation. Come and go. Lots of Indians—Cherokees and Choctaws—living in mud huts and cabin shacks. I never see them bother the whites; it was the other way around.

During the Civil War, when the Red River was bank high with muddy water the Yankees made a target of Jefferson. That was a small town down south of Linden. Down the river come a flat barge with cannon fastened to the deck. The Yankee soldiers stepped across the river from Jefferson and the shooting started. When the cannon went to popping the folks went a-running—hard to tell who run the fastest, the whites or the blacks! Almost the town was wiped out. Buildings was smashed and big trees cut through with the cannon balls. And all the time the Yankee drums was a-beating and the soldiers singing:

> We'll hang Jeff Davis on a sour apple tree,
> As we go marching on!

Before the Civil War everybody had money. The white folks, not the Negroes. Sometimes the master take me to the town stores. They was full of money. Cigar boxes on the counter, boxes on the shelf, all filled with money. Not the crinkley paper kind, but hard, jingley gold and silver! Not like these scarce times!

After the War I stay on the plantation till a soldier man tells me of the freedom. The master never tell us—Negroes working just like before the War. That's when I leave the first time. Slip off, saying nothing, to Jefferson. There I found some good white folks going to New Orleans. First place we go is Shreveport, by wagon. They took me because I fix up with them to do the cooking. On to the Big River—Mississippi—and boards a river steamboat for New Orleans. Lots of Negroes going down there—to work on the canal.

The whole town was built on logs covered with dirt. Trying to raise itself right out of the swamp. Sometimes the water get high and folks run for the hills. When I got there almost was I ready to leave.

I like Texas the best. Back to Jefferson is where I go. Fifteen-twenty mile below Linden. Almost the first person I see was Master Davenport. He says, "Black rascal, you is coming with me." And I do. He tried to keep his slaves and just laugh when I tell him about the freedom. I worked for food and quarters till his meanness come cropping out again. That wasn't long and he threatened me with the whip and the buck and gag. The buck and gag was maybe worse. I got to feeling that iron stick in my mouth, fastened around my head with chains, pressing hard on my tongue. No drinking, no eaing, no talking!

So I slip off again. That night I goes through Linden. Crawling on my hands and knees! Keeping in the dark spots, hiding from the whites, till I pass the last house, then my feets hurries me to Jefferson, where I gets a ride to Arkansas. In Russelville is where I stop. There I worked around in the yards, cutting the grass, fancying the flower beds, and earned a little money for clothes and eats, with some of it spent for good whiskey.

That was the reason I left Arkansas. Whiskey. The law got after me to tell where was a man's whiskey still. I just leave so's I won't have to tell.

But while I was making a little money in Russelville, I lose out on some big money, account some white folks beat me to it. I was out in the hills west of town, walking along the banks of a little creek, when I heard a voice. Queer like. I called out, "Who is that talking?" And I hears it again. "Go to the white oak tree and you will find ninety thousand dollars!" what I hear. I look around, nobody in sight, but I see the tree. A big white oak tree standing taller than all the rest round about. Under the tree was a grave. An old grave. I scratched around but finds no money and thinks of getting some help.

I done some work for a white man in town and told him about the voice. He promised to go with me, but the next day he took two white mens and dug around the tree. Then he says they was nothing to find. To this day I know better. I know wherever they's a ghost, money is around someplace! That's what the ghost come back for. Somebody dies and leaves buried money. The ghost watches over it till it sees somebody it likes. Then ghost shows himself—let's know he's around. Sometimes the ghost tells where is the money buried, like that time at Russelville.

That ain't the only ghost I've seen or heard. I see one around the yard where I is living now. A woman. Some of these times she'll tell me where the buried money is. Maybe the ghost woman thinks I is too old to dig. But I been a-digging all these long years. For a bite to eat and a sleep— under cover. I reckon pretty soon she's going to tell where to dig. When she does, then old Uncle John won't have to dig for the eats no more!

MINGO WHITE

Interviewed at Burleson, Alabama
Interviewed by Levi D. Shelby, Jr.
Age when interviewed: 85–90

I WAS BORN IN CHESTER, South Carolina, but I was mostly raised in Alabama. When I was about four or five years old, I was loaded in a wagon with a lot more people in it. Where I was bound I don't know. Whatever become of my mammy and pappy I don't know for a long time. I was told there was a lot of slave speculators in Chester to buy some slaves for some folks in Alabama. I 'members dat I was took up on a stand and a lot of people come round and felt my arms and legs and chest, and ask me a lot of questions. Before we slaves was took to de tradin' post Old Marsa Crawford told us to tell everybody what asked us if we'd ever been sick dat us'd never been sick in our life. Us had to tell 'em all sorts of lies for our marsa or else take a beatin'.

I was just a li'l thing, tooked away from my mammy and pappy, just when I needed 'em most. The only carin' that I had or ever knowed anything about was give to me by a friend of my pappy. His name was

John White. My pappy told him to take care of me for him. John was a fiddler and many a night I woke up to find myself 'sleep 'twixt his legs whilst he was playin' for a dance for de white folks. My pappy and mammy was sold from each other, too, de same time as I was sold. I used to wonder if I had any brothers or sisters, as I had always wanted some. A few years later I found out I didn't have none.

I'll never forget de trip from Chester to Burleson. I wouldn't 'member so well, I don't guess, 'ceptin' I had a big old sheep dog named Trailer. He followed right in back of de wagon dat I was in. Us had to cross a wide stream what I took to be a river. When we started cross, old Trailer never stopped followin'. I was watchin' him close so if he gived out I was goin' to try to get him. He didn't give out; he didn't even have to swim. He just walked along and lapped de water like a dog will.

John took me and kept me in de cabin with him. De cabin didn't have no furniture in it like we has nowadays. De bed was one-legged. It was made in de corner of de room, with de leg settin' out in de middle of de floor. A plank was runned 'twixt de logs of de cabin and nailed to de post on de front of de bed. Across de foot another plank was runned into de logs and nailed to de legs. Den some straw or corn shucks was piled on for a mattress. Us used anything what we could get for cover. De table had two legs, de legs set out to de front whilst de back part was nailed to de wall. Us didn't have no stove. There was a great big fireplace where de cookin' was done. Us didn't have to cook, though, lessen us got hungry after supper been served at de house.

I weren't nothin' but a child endurin' slavery, but I had to work de same as any man. I went to de field and hoed cotton, pulled fodder and picked cotton with de rest of de hands. I kept up, too, to keep from gettin' any lashes dat night when us got home. In de winter I went to de woods with de menfolks to help get wood or to get sap from de trees to make turpentine and tar. Iffen us didn't do dat we made charcoal to run de blacksmith shop with.

De white folks was hard on us. Dey would whip us about de least li'l thing. It wouldn'ta been so bad iffen us had a had comforts, but to live like us did was 'nough to make anybody soon as be dead. De white folks told us dat us born to work for 'em and dat us was doin' fine at dat.

De next time dat I saw my mammy I was a great big boy. Dere was a woman on de place what everybody called "Mammy"—Selina White. One day Mammy called me and said, "Mingo, your mammy is comin'." I said, "I thought dat you was my mammy." She said, "No, I ain't your mammy. Your mammy is away from here." I couldn't believe dat I had another mammy and I never thought about it anymore.

One day I was sittin' down at de barn when a wagon come up de lane. I stood round like a child will. When de wagon got to de house, my mammy got out and broke and run to me and throwed her arms round my neck and hug and kiss me. I never been put my arms round her or nothin' of de sort. I just stood dere lookin' at her. She said, "Son, ain't you glad to see your mammy?" I looked at her and walked off. Mammy

Selina call me and told me dat I had hurt my mammy's feelins', and dat dis woman was my mammy.

I went off and studied and I begins to 'member things. I went to Selina and asked her how long it been since I seen my mammy. She told me dat I had been away from her since I was just a li'l chile. I went to my mammy and told her dat I was sorry I done what I did and dat I would like for her to forget and forgive me for de way I act when I first saw her. After I had talked with my real mammy, she told me of how de family had been broke up and dat she hadn't seed my pappy since he was sold.

My mammy never would of seen me no more if de Lord hadn'ta been in de plan. Tom White's daughter married one of Mr. Crawford's sons. Dey lived in Virginia. Back den it was de custom for women to come home whenever dey husbands died or quit 'em. Mr. Crawford's son died and dat forced her to come home. My mammy had been her maid, so when she got ready to come home she brung my mammy with her.

It was hard back in dem days. Every mornin' before daybreak you had to be up and ready to get to de field. It was de same every day in de year 'cept on Sunday, and den we was gettin' up earlier dan de folks do now on Monday. De drivers was hard, too. Dey could say whatever dey wanted to and you couldn't say nothin' for yourself. Somehow or other us had a instinct dat we was goin' to be free.

In de event when de day's work was done de slaves would be found locked in deir cabins prayin' for de Lord to free dem like he did de chillen of Israel. Iffen dey didn't lock up, de marsa or de driver would of heard 'em and whipped 'em. De slaves had a way of puttin' a wash pot in de door of de cabin to keep de sound in de house.

I 'members once old Ned White was caught prayin'. De drivers took him de next day and carried him to de pegs, what was four stakes drove in de ground. Ned was made to pull off everything but his pants and lay on his stomach between de pegs whilst somebody strapped his legs and arms to de pegs. Den dey whipped him till de blood run from him like he was a hog. Dey made all of de hands come and see it, and dey said us'd get de same thing if us was cotched. Dey don't allow a man to whip a horse like dey whipped us in dem days.

After my mammy come where I was I helped her with her work. Her task was too hard for any one person. She had to serve as maid to Mr. White's daughter, cook for all of de hands, spin and card four cuts of thread a day, and den wash. Dere was one hundred and forty-four threads to de cut. If she didn't get all of dis done she got fifty lashes dat night. Many de night me and her would spin and card so she could get her task de next day. No matter what she had to do de next day she would save to get dem cuts of thread, even on wash day.

Wash day was on Wednesday. My mammy would have to take de clothes about three-quarters of a mile to de branch where de washin' was to be done. She didn't have no washboard like dey have nowdays. She had a paddle what she beat de clothes with. Everybody knowed when wash day was 'cause dey could hear de paddle for about three or four miles. "Pow-pow-pow," dats how it sound. She had to iron de clothes de same day dat she washed and den get dem four cuts of thread.

Lots of times she failed to get 'em and got de fifty lashes. One day when Tom White was whippin' her she said, "Lay it on, Marsa White, 'cause I'm goin' to tell de Yankees when dey come." When Mammy got through spinnin' de cloth she had to dye it. She used sumac berries, indigo, bark from some trees, and dere was some kind of rock what she got red dye from. De clothes wouldn't fade, neither.

De white folks didn't learn us to do nothin' but work. Dey said dat us weren't supposed to know how to read and write. Dere was one feller name E. C. White what learned to read and write endurin' slavery. He had to carry de chillen's books to school for 'em and go back after dem. His young marsa taught him to read and write unbeknownst to his father and de rest of de slaves.

Us didn't have nowhere to go 'cept church and we didn't get no pleasure outen it 'cause we weren't allowed to talk from de time we left home till us got back. If us went to church de drivers went with us. Us didn't have no church 'cept de white folks church.

After old Ned got such a terrible beatin' for prayin' for freedom he slipped off and went to de North to join de Union Army. After he got in de army he wrote to Marsa Tom. In his letter he had dese words: "I am layin' down, Marsa, and gettin' up, Marsa," meaning dat he went to bed when he felt like it and got up when he pleased to. He told Tom White dat iffen he wanted him he was in the army and dat the could come after him.

After old Ned had got to de North, de other hands begin to watch for a chance to slip off. Many a one was cotched and brung back. Dey knowed de penalty what dey would have to pay, and dis cause some of 'em to get desperate. Druther dan to take a beatin' dey would choose to fight it out till dey was able to get away or die before dey would take de beatin'.

Lots of times when de patterrollers would get after de slaves dey would have de worse fight and sometimes de patterrollers would get killed. After de War I saw Ned, and he told me de night he left the patterrollers runned him for four days. He say de way he hid to keep dem from catchin' him was he went by de woods. De patterrollers come in de woods lookin' for him, so he just got a tree on 'em and den followed. Dey figured dat he was headin' for de free states, so dey headed dat way too, and Ned just followed dem far as dey could go. Den he clumb a tree and hid whilst dey turned round and come back. Ned went on without any trouble much. De patterrollers used to be bad. Dey would run de folks iffen dey was caught out after eight o'clock in de night, iffen dey didn't have no pass from de marsa.

After de day's work was done there weren't anything for de slaves to do but go to bed. Wednesday night they went to prayer meetin'. We had to be in de bed by nine o'clock. Every night de drivers come round to make sure dat we was in de bed. I heerd tell of folks goin' to bed and den gettin' up and goin' to another plantation.

On Saturday de hands worked till noon. Dey had de rest of de time to work dey gardens. Every family had a garden of deir own. On Saturday nights the slaves could frolic for a while. Dey would have parties sometimes and whiskey and home-brew for de servants. On Sundays we didn't do anything but lay round and sleep, 'cause we didn't like to go to church. On Christmas we didn't have to do no work, no more'n feed the stock and do de li'l work round de house. When we got through with dat we had de rest of de day to run round wherever we wanted to go. 'Course, we had to get permission from de marsa.

De owners of slaves used to give corn shuckin' parties, and invite slaves from other plantations. Dey would have plenty of whiskey and other stuff to eat. De slaves would shuck corn and eat and drink. Dey used to give cotton pickin's de same way. All of dis went on at night. Dey had jacklights in de cotton patch for us to see by. De lights was made on a forked stick and moved from place to place whilst we picked. De corn shuckin' was done at de barn, and dey didn't have to have lights so dey could move dem from place to place.

I was pretty big boy when de War broke out. I 'member seein' de Yankees cross Big Bear Creek bridge one day. All of de soldiers crossed de bridge but one. He stayed on de other side till all de rest had got across, den he got down offen his horse and took a bottle of somethin' and strewed it all over de bridge. Den he lighted a match to it and followed de rest. In a few minutes de Rebel soldiers come to de bridge to cross but it was on fire and dey had to swim across to de other side. I went home and told my mammy dat de Rebels was chasin' de Union soldiers, and dat one of de Unions has poured some water on de bridge and set it afire. She laugh and say: "Son, don't you know dat water don't make a fire? Dat musta been turpentine or oil."

I 'member one day Mr. Tom was havin' a big barbecue for de Rebel soldiers in our yard. Come a big roarin 'down de military road, and three men in blue coats rode up to de gate and come on in. Just as soon as de Rebels saw 'em dey all run to de woods. In about five minutes de yard was full of blue coats. Dey et up all de grub what de Rebels had been eatin'. Tom White had to run away to keep de Yankees from gettin' him. Before de Yankees come, de white folks took all dey clothes and hung 'em in de cabins. Dey told de colored folks to tell de Yankees dat de clothes was deir'n. Dey told us to tell 'em how good dey been to us and dat we liked to live with 'em.

De day dat we got news dat we was free, Mr. White called us niggers to the house. He said: "You are all free, just as free as I am. Now go and get yourself somewhere to stick your heads."

Just as soon as he say dat, my mammy hollered out: "Dat's 'nough for a yearlin'." She struck out across de field to Mr. Lee Osborn's to get a place for me and her to stay. He paid us seventy-five cents a day, fifty cents to her and two bits for me. He gave us our dinner along with de wages. After de crop was gathered for that year, me and my mammy cut and hauled wood for Mr. Osborn. Us left Mr. Osborn dat fall and went to Mr. John Rawlins. Us made a sharecrop with him. Us'd pick two rows of cotton and he'd pick two rows. Us'd pull two rows of corn and he'd pull two rows of corn. He furnished us with rations and a place to stay. Us'd sell our cotton and open corn and pay Mr. John Rawlins for feedin' us. Den we moved with Mr. Hugh Nelson and made a sharecrop with him. We kept movin' and makin' sharecrops till us saved up 'nough money to rent us a place and make a crop for ourselves.

Us did right well at dis until de Ku Klux got so bad, us had to move back with Mr. Nelson for protection. De mens that took us in was Union men. Dey lived here in the South but dey taken us part in de slave business. De Ku Klux threat to whip Mr. Nelson, 'cause he took up for de niggers. Heap of nights we would hear of de Ku Klux comin' and leave home. Sometimes us was scared not to go and scared to go away from home.

One day I borrowed a gun from Ed Davis to go squirrel huntin'. When I taken de gun back I didn't unload it like I always been doin'. Dat night de Ku Klux called on Ed to whip him. When dey told him to open de door, he heard one of 'em say, "Shoot him time he gets de door open." "Well," he says to 'em, "Wait till I can light de lamp." Den he got de gun what I had left loaded, got down on his knees and stuck it through a log and pull de trigger. He hit Newt Dobbs in de stomach and kilt him.

He couldn't stay round Burleson any more, so he come to Mr. Nelson and got 'nough money to get to Pine Bluff, Arkansas. The Ku Klux got bad sure 'nough den and went to killin' niggers and white folks, too.

I married Kizi Drumgoole. Reverend W. C. Northcross perform de ceremony. Dere weren't nobody dere but de witness and me and Kizi. I had three sons, but all of 'em is dead 'ceptin' one and dat's Hugh. He got seven chillens.

LIZZIE WILLIAMS

Interviewed at Asheville, North Carolina
Interviewed by Marjorie Jones
Age when interviewed: 90

I'SE BORN in Selma, Alabama, I can't mind how long ago, but just about ninety years. I come to dis country about 1882. I'se purty poorly dese days and I'se gettin' homesick for my old home.

I'se born and live on old man Billy Johnson's plantation—thousands acres of ground and plenty of niggers. My pappy, he always belong to old man Billy. He not such a bad man but de Lord knows I'se seed better ones. When I'se right smart size, Missy Mixon, she was Marse Billy's wife's sister, she get Marse Billy to let her have me. She was a good woman. She took me to town to live and make a little white girl out of me. Y'all knows what I means. I got treated more like de white folks dan de rest of de niggers.

But 'twarn't long afore Missy send me to New Orleans to nurse de sick child of her sister. I never was satisfied down dere. Everybody so different. But de next year we go back to Alabama.

I went to Marse Ellis Mixon's. He terrible mean to his niggers. But I belong to de missus, she always treat me good. All de little niggers have to learn to work when dey little; get out and pull weeds. Dey never had no time to play. Most dem niggers was scared to death, just like de ones on Billy Johnson's plantation. Dey know dey get whipped just like a mule if dey act like dey don't wanna work. Dey never get much to eat, just side meat, corn bread and 'lasses. Old Billy he had overseers what was mean to de poor niggers. Sometime dey ties dem up and dey strip dem and dey whips dem with cowhide, else dey lets other niggers do it.

All de niggers have to go to church, just like de white folks. Dey have a part of de church for demselfs. After de War we have a church of our own. All de niggers love to go to church and sing. I mind a lot of de songs we used to sing in de fields. I mind my pappy used to sing in de field: "Get on Board, Little Chillen, Get on Board." Sometimes dey baptize in de river. Den dey sing:

> I wanna be ready,
> I wanna be ready,
> I wanna be ready, good Lord, to walk in Jerusalem just like John.
> John say de city was just four square,
> To walk in Jerusalem just like John,
> But I'll meet my mother and father dere,
> To walk in Jerusalem, just like John.

I 'members about de patterollers. De niggers have to get a pass from de massa or de missus if dey go anywhere. De patterollers just like police. About dozen of dem ride along together. First thing dey say: "Where you pass?" Den if you have one dey lets you go but if you don't have one dey strips you to de waist and dey lams you good till de blood comes. Sometimes dey rolls you over a barrel and lams you while de barrel rolls.

I mind a tale my pappy tell about one time he see de patterollers comin'. He scared to death 'cause he didn't have no pass. He know if dey finds him what dey do. So Pappy he gets down in de ditch and throw sand and grunts like a hog. Sure 'nough, dey thinks he a hog and dey pass on, 'cept one who was behind de others. He say, "Dat am de gruntin'est old hog I ever hear. I think I go see him." But de others dey say: "Just let dat old hog alone and mind you own business." So dey pass on. Pappy he laugh about dat for long time.

I mind old Mose, he have monthly pass from de massa but he forget it one day and de patterrollers whip him and throw him in de calaboose. In de mornin' when de massa wake and find no fresh water and no fire in de stove and de cows not milked, he say: "I know Mose in de calaboose," and he have to go after Mose.

Lots of de poor niggers run away, but 'twarn't no use. Dere weren't no place to go. Dey was always lookin' for you and den you had to work harder dan ever, besides all kinds of punishment you got. Den dey nearly starve you to death, just feed you on bread and water for long time.

De niggers never know nothin' about learnin', just work all dey's fit for. De only thing I ever do with a book is just to dust it off. I mind two little niggers whose missy teach dem to read. Emily, she look like a white gal. She was treated just like she white. Her daddy was a white man. Emily was a smart gal. She belong to one of de Johnson mens. She do all de sewin' for her missy. When de missy go to buy clothes for de chillen she always take Emily along. Her pappy pay no more attention to her dan to de rest of de niggers. But de missy she was good to her. She never stay in de quarters; she stay in de house with de white folks. But Emily had de saddest look on her yaller face 'cause de other niggers whisper about her pappy. Many de poor nigger women have chillen for de massa, dat is if de massa a mean man. Dey just tell de niggers what to do and dey know better dan to fuss.

Old Missus she good to me. I mind one time I got terrible mad and say some ugly words. Marse Ellis he come up behind me and he say: "Lizabeth I gwine to wallop you good for dat." I commence cryin' and run to de missus and she say: "Look here, Ellis Mixon, y'all mind you own business and look after you own niggers. Dis one belongs to me." Just de same, when de missus went upstairs Marse Ellis take me in de smokehouse and start to hit me. I yell for de missus and when she come she plenty mad. Marse say he never meant to whip me, just scare me a little.

I mind about de War. We niggers never know what it about. We just go on and work. Never see nothin', never hear nothin', never say nothin', but de War all round. Every day we hear dat de Yankee soldiers comin'. De plantations was gettin' robbed. Everybody kept a-hidin' things. It was a terrible time. I mind plain when dey comes to Selma. All de folks was at church when de Yankees come. Dey weren't no fightin' much, dey didn't have time. Dey just march in and take de town. But Oh lordy, dat night dey burn de stores and houses and take all de things dey want. Cannons and guns all round, it was terrible sight.

Marse Ellis' plantation about fifteen mile from Selma on Pea Ridge. I mind one night Marse come home from town and he say: "'Lizabeth." I say, "Yes sir." He say: "Bring me some fresh water from de spring." I run as fast as I can and bring de water and give it to him. Den he say: "'Lizabeth, de Yankees am comin' soon, and I knows you's gwine to tell 'em where I hide all my belongings, guns and everything."

"No," I says, "just why would I tell where you hide you guns and things?" Missy come in den and she say: "Go on and let Lizzie alone, better be feared dem niggers you done so mean to gwine tell, dat's all you got to be feared of. But you let Lizzie alone, she belong to me."

Marse Ellis he go out and hide some more stuff. Dat night de soldiers burn Selma. Dat were on Sunday. Next night we wake up in de middle of de night and de house where we keep de best carriage and horse was a-burnin'. De poor horse done break out of de barn and was a-runnin' round all over de place a-screamin' with her poor back burnt terrible. We never find out if de Yankees set de barn fire or not. Guess dey did. Dey done set Marse Hyde's house afire and burn it to de grownd with Marse Hyde in it. Marse Hyde, he had plantation in New Orleans and when de Yankees take de town Marse Hyde, he promise not to leave, but when de soldiers know he escape dey come to his house on Pea Ridge. When de Yankees find him here, dey burn him in de house with all his belongings.

On de Tuesday mornin' after dey burn Selma I wake up to see Marse Ellis' plantation all surrounded with Yankee soldiers. I was nigh scared to death. I so afraid dey hurt me and Missy but dey didn't, dey just march through de house and when dey see Marse Ellis dey ask him for he guns and things dey want. Marse Ellis show dem where de things were. 'Twarn't no use to do anything else. I take Marse Frank's tobacco and hide it in de missus' trunk. Den when de soldiers get what dey want dey laugh and march away on de hill.

After de surrender all de niggers just lost. Nowhere to go, nothin' to do, unless dey stay with de massa. Nobody have anything but 'Federate money and it was no good. My pappy had about three hundred dollars but 'twarn't no good at all.

All some of de white folks think of was killin' de poor niggers what worked for dem for years. Dey just scour de country and shoot dem, especially de young men. One day dey come down de road towards my pappy. Dey start askin' questions about what he gwine to do now he free. "What I gwine to do?" says Pappy. "What can I do? I just stay on de plantation and help Old Massa if I can get an old mule and a piece of an old plow." One of de boys look at Pappy and say "I like take you head for a target," but de old man with dem say, "No," so dey leave my pappy alone.

Dey have de commissary where de folks get food; it belong to de Yankee soldiers. Food scarce like everything. Folks say now dey have hard times; dey won't know nothin' about hard times 'less day live in wartime and be slave to white folks.

Den dey was de Ku Klux Klan. Dey were frightful lookin' critters. My pappy say dey go out in de country and tie poor niggers to de tree and beat 'em to death. Dey dress all kinds of fashions. Most of dem look like ghosts. Dey never go like de patterrollers; dey just sneak round at night when de poor niggers in bed. Den about twelve o'clock dey tie up all de niggers dey catch and after dey through beatin' 'em, dey leaves dem with dey hands tied in de air and de blood a-streamin' out of dey backs.

After freedom I come here to live with my folks de Williams. Dat's how I come to be Williams. Never had no chillen of my own. Dey calls me 'Lizbeth Johnson before I went to live with de Mixons. Den I be one of de Mixon niggers, den later I be a Williams. Don't guess names matter much no way.

WILLIS
Interviewed in Georgia
Interviewer not identified
Age when interviewed: 101

I WAS THIRTY-FIVE years old when freedom declared. I belonged to a doctor who had three or four plantations in Burke County. I work in de field and I drove de doctor thirty years. He owned three hundred slaves. I never went to school a day in my life, 'cept Sunday school, but I took de doctor's sons four miles every day to school. Guess he had so much business in hand he thought de chillen could walk. I used to sit down on de school steps till dey turn out. I got way up de alphabet by listenin', but when I went to courtin' I forgot all dat.

Marster had a carriage and a buggy, too. My father drive de doctor. Sometimes I was fixin' to go to bed and had to hitch up my horse and go five or six mile. I had a regular saddle horse, two pair of horses for carriage. Doctor were a rich man. Richest man in Burke County. He made his money on his farm. When summertime come, I went with him to Bath, when he had a house on Tena Hill. We drive down in de carriage. Sundays we went to church when Dr. Goulding preach. De darkies went in de side door. I hear him preach many times.

De Big House was set in half acre yard. About fifty yards on one side was my house, and fifty yards on de other side was de house o' Granny, a woman what tended de chillen and had charge o' de yard when we went to Bath. Back yonder was de quarters, half a mile long; dey was one room across, and some had shed room. When any of 'em got sick, Marster would go round to see 'em all.

When darky wouldn't take whippin' from de overseer, he had to carry dem to de boss. And if we needed any brushin' de marster brush 'em. Why, de darkies would whip de overseer!

Dey made dey own money. In slavery time, if you wanted four-five acre of land to plant you anything on, Marster give it to you and what-ever dat land make, it belong to you. You could take dat money and spend it any way you wanted. Still he give you somethin' to eat and clothe you, but dat patch you make cotton on, sometimes a whole bale, dat money yours.

When de soldiers come through, dey didn't burn dat place, but dey went in dere and took out everything dey want and give it to de cullud people. Dey kept it till dey get free. De soldiers took de doctor's horses and carry 'em off. Got in de crib and took de corn. Got in de smokehouse and took de meat out. Old Marster bury his money and silver in an iron chest. Dey took it three hundred yards away to a clump o' trees and bury it. It took four men to carry it. Dere was money without mention in dat chest! After de soldiers pass through dey went down and got it back.

When freedom was declared, I went down to Augusta to de Freed-man's Bureau to see if 'twas true, we was free. I reckon dere was over a hundred people dere. De man got up and stated to de people: "You all is just as free as I am. You ain't got no mistis and no marster. Work when you want." On Sunday morning Old Marster sent de house gal and tell us to all come to de house. He said: "What I want to send for you all is to tell you dat you are free. You have de privilege to go anywhere you want, but I don't want none o' you to leave me now. I wants you-all to stay right with me. If you stay, you must sign to it."

I asked him: "What you want me to sign for? I is free." "Dat will hold me to my word and hold you to your word," he say. All my folks sign it, but I wouldn't sign. Marster call me up and say: "Willis, why wouldn't you sign?" I say: "If I is already free, I don't need to sign no paper. If I was workin' for you and doin' for you before I got free, I can do it still, if you wants me to stay with you."

My father and mother tried to get me to sign, and I wouldn't sign. My mother said: "You ought to sign. How you know Marster gwine pay?" I say: "Den I can go somewhere else."

Marster pay first class hands fifteen dollars a month, other hands ten dollars, and den on down to five and six dollars. He give rations like dey always have. When Christmas come, all come up to be paid off. Den he calls me. Ask where is me? I was standin' round de corner of de house. "Come up here, Willis," he say. "You didn't sign dat paper but I reckon I have to pay you too." He paid me and my wife a hundred and eighty dollars. I said: "Well, you-all thought he wouldn't pay me, but I got my money too."

I stayed to my marster's place one year after de War, den I left dere. Next year I decided I would quit dere and go somewhere else. It was on account o' my wife. You see, Marster bought her off, as de highest bidder, down at Waynesboro, and she ain't seen her mother and father for fifteen years. When she got free, she went down to see 'em. Weren't willin' to come back. 'Twas on account o' Mistis and her. Dey both had chillens, five-six year old. The chillens had disagreement. Mistis slap my gal. My wife sass de mistis. But my marster, he was as good a man as ever born. I wouldn't have left him for nobody, just on account of his wife and her fell out.

I quit then and goes over three miles to another widow lady's house and make bargain with her. I pass right by de door. Old Boss sitting on de piazza. He say: "Hey, boy, where you gwine?" I say: "I decided to go." I was a foreman o' de plow hands den. I saw to all de locking up, and things like dat. He say: "Hold on dere." He come out to de gate. "Tell you what I give you to stay here. I give you five acre of as good land as I got, and thirty dollars a month, to stay here and see to my business." I say: "I can't, Marster. It don't suit my wife round here. She won't come back, I can't stay." He turn on me den, and busted out crying. "I didn't thought I could raise up a darky dat would talk dat-a-way," he said.

Well, I went on off. I got de wagon and come by de house. Marster say: "Now, you gwine off but don't forget me, boy. Remember me as you always done." I said: "All right."

I went over to dat widow lady's house and work. Along about May I got sick. She say: "I going send for de doctor." I say: "Please ma'am, don't do dat." I thought maybe he kill me 'cause I left him. She say: "Well, I gwine send for him." I in desperate condition. When I know anything, he walk up in de door. I was layin' with my face toward de door, and I turn over.

Doctor come up to de bed. "Boy, how you gettin' on?" "I bad off," I say. He say: "I see you is. Yes." Lady say: "Doctor, what you think of him?" Doctor say: "Mistis, it most too late, but I do all I can." She say: "Please do all you can. He about de best hand I got."

Doctor fix up medicine and told her to give it to me. She say, "Uncle Will, take dis medicine." I afraid to take it. Afraid he was tryin' to kill me. Den two men, John and Charlie, come in. Lady say: "Get dis medicine in Uncle Will." One o' de men hold my hand and dey gag me and put it in me. Next few days I can talk and ask for something to eat so I get better. I say: "Well, he didn't kill me when I took de medicine!"

I stayed dere with her. Next year I move right back in two miles, other side where I always live, with another lady. I stayed dere three years. Got along all right. When I left there, I left dere with three hundred dollars and plenty corn and hog. Everything I want, and three hundred cash dollars in my pocket! Fourth year I left and went down to another place near de creek. I stay dere thirty-three years in dat one place.

LULU WILSON

Interviewed at Dallas, Texas
Interviewer not identified
Age when interviewed: 97

I'SE BORN IN SLAVERY, ageable as I am, I'm a old time, slavery woman and the way I been through the hackles, I got plenty to say about slavery. I know they ain't no good in it, and they better not bring it back.

My paw weren't no slave. He was a free man, 'cause his mammy was a full blood Creek Indian. But my maw was born in slavery, down on Wash Hodges' paw's place, and he give her to Wash when he married. That was the only woman slave what he had and one man slave, a young buck. My maw say she took with my paw and I'se born, but a long time passed and didn't no more younguns come, so they say my paw am too old and wore out for breedin' and wants her to take with this here buck. So the Hodges set the nigger hounds on my paw and run him away from the place and Maw always say he went to the free state. So she took with my step-paw and they must of pleased the white folks what wanted niggers to breed like livestock, 'cause she birthed nineteen chillen.

When I'se li'l I used to play in that big cave they calls Mammoth and I'se so used to that cave it didn't seem like nothin' to me. But I was real li'l then, for soon as they could they put me to spinnin' cloth. I 'members plain, when I was li'l there was talk of war in them parts, and they put me to spinnin' and I heared 'em say it was for soldiers. They marched round in a li'l, small drove and practiced shootin'.

Now, when I was li'l they was the hardest times. They'd nearly beat us to death. They taken me from my mammy, out the li'l house built onto they house and I had to sleep in a bed by Missus Hodges. I cried for my maw but I had to work and wash and iron and clean and milk cows when I was most too li'l to do it.

The Hodges had three chillens and the oldest one they was mean to, 'cause she so thickheaded. She couldn't learn nothin' out of a book but was kinder and more friendly like than the rest of the lot. Wash Hodges was just mean, pore trash and he was a bad actor and a bad manager. He never could make any money and he starved it outen the niggers. For years all I could get was one li'l slice of sowbelly and a puny, li'l piece of bread and a 'tater. I never had 'nough to stave the hungriness outen my belly.

My maw was cookin' in the house and she was a clink, that am the best of its kind. She could cuss and she warn't afraid. Wash Hodges tried to whip her with a cowhide and she'd knock him down and bloody him up. Then he'd go down to some his neighbor kin and try to get them to come help him whip her. But they'd say, "I don't want to go up there and let Chloe Ann beat me up." I heared Wash tell his wife they said that.

When Maw was in tantrum, my step-paw wouldn't partialize with her. But she was a religious woman and believed time was comin' when niggers wouldn't be slaves. She told me to pray for it. She seed a old man what the nigger dogs chased and et the legs near off him. She said she was chased by them bloody hounds and she just picked up a club and laid they skull open. She say they hired her out and sold her twice but always brung her back to Wash Hodges.

Now, Missus Hodges studied about meanness more'n Wash done. She was mean to anybody she could lay her hands to, but special mean to me. She beat me and used to tie my hands and make me lay flat on the floor and she put snuff in my eyes. I ain't lying before God when I say I knows that's why I went blind.

I did see white folks sometimes what spoke right friendly and kindly to me.

I gets to thinkin' how Wash Hodges sold off Maw's chillen. He'd sell 'em and have the folks come for 'em when my maw was in the fields. When she'd come back, she'd raise a ruckus. Then many the time I seed her plop right down to a settin' and cry about it. But she allowed they weren't nothing could be done, 'cause it's the slavery law. She said, "Oh Lord, let me see the end of it before I die, and I'll quit my cussin' and fightin' and rarin'." My maw say she's part Indian and that account-able for her ways.

One day they truckled us all down in a covered wagon and started out with the family and my maw and step-paw and five of us chillen. I know I'se past twelve year old. We come a long way and passed through a free state. Some places we drove for miles in the woods 'stead of the big road, and when we come to folks they hid us down in the bed of a wagon. We passed through a li'l place and my maw say to look, and I seed a man goin' up some steps, totin' a bucket of water. She say, "Lulu, that man's your paw." I ain't never think she's as considerable of my step-paw as of my paw, and she give me to think as much. My step-paw never did like me, but he was a fool for his own younguns, 'cause at the end of the wars when they set the niggers free he tramped over half the country, gatherin' up them younguns they done sold away.

We went to a place called Wadefield, in Texas, and settled for some short passin' of time. They was a Baptist church next our house and they let me go twice. I was fancified with the singin' and preachin'. Then we goes on to Chatfield Point and Wash Hodges built a log house and covered it with weather boarding and built my maw and paw quarters to live in. They turned in to raisin' corn and 'taters and hogs. I had to work like a dog. I hoed, and milked ten cows a day.

Missus told me I had ought to marry. She said if I'd marry she'd togger me up in a white dress and give me a weddin' supper. She made the dress and Wash Hodges married me outen the Bible to a nigger belongin' to a nephew of his'n. I was 'bout thirteen or fourteen. I know it weren't long after that when Missus Hodges got a doctor for me. The doctor told me lessen I had a baby, old as I was and married, I'd start in on spasms. So it weren't long till I had a baby.

In 'twixt that time, Wash Hodges starts layin' out in the woods and swamps all the time. I heared he was hidin' 'out from the War and was supposed to go, 'cause he done been a volunteer in the first war and they didn't have no luck in Kentucky. One night when we was all asleep, some folks whooped and woke us up. Two soldiers come in and they left more outside. They found Wash Hodges and said it was midnight and to get 'em something to eat. They et and some more come in and et. They tied Wash's hands and made me hold a lamp in the door for them to see by. They had some more men in the wagon, with they hands tied. They drove away and in a minute I heared the reports of the guns three or four times. Next day I heared they was soldiers and done shot some conscripts in the bottoms back of our place.

Wash Hodges was gone away four years and Missus Hodges was meaner'n the devil all the time. Seems like she just hated us worser than ever. She said blabber-mouth niggers done cause a war. Well, now, things just kind of drifts along for a spell and then Wash Hodges come back and he said, "Well, now, we done whip the hell out them blue bellies and that'll learn 'em a lesson to leave us alone."

Then my step-paw seed some Federal soldiers. I seed them, too. They drifted by in droves of fifty and a hundred. My step-paw allowed as how the Feds done told him they ain't no more slavery, and he tried to point it out to Wash Hodges. Wash says that's a new ruling and it am that growed-up niggers is free, but chillen has to stay with they marsters till they's of age. I don't never recall just like, the passin' of time. I know I had my little boy youngun and he growed up, but right after he was born I left the Hodges and felt like it's a fine, good riddance.

If they ain't no more slavery, and if they'll pay folks liveable wages, they'll be less stealin' and slummerin' and goin's on. I worked so hard. For more'n fifty years I waited as a nurse on sick folks. I been through the hackles if any mortal soul has.

SARAH WILSON

Interviewed at Fort Gibson, Oklahoma
Interviewer not identified
Age when interviewed: 87

I WAS A CHEROKEE SLAVE and now I am a Cherokee freedwoman, and besides that I am a quarter Cherokee my own self. And this is the way it is. I was born in 1850 along the Arkansas River about halfway between Fort Smith and old Fort Coffee and the Skullyville boat landing on the river. The farm place was on the north side of the river on the old wagon road what run from Fort Smith out to Fort Gibson, and that old road was like you couldn't hardly call a road when I first remember seeing it. The ox teams bog down to they bellies in some places, and the wagon wheel mighty nigh bust on the big rocks in other places. I remember seeing soldiers coming along that old road lots of times, and freighting wagons, and wagons what we all know carry mostly whiskey, and that was breaking the law, too! Them soldiers catch the man with that whiskey they sure put him up for a long time, lessen he put some silver in they hands. That's what my Uncle Nick say. That Uncle Nick a mean Negro and he ought to know about that.

Like I tell you, I am quarter Cherokee. My mammy was named Adeline and she belong to Old Master Ben Johnson. Old Master Ben bring my grandmammy out to that Sequoyah district way back when they call it Arkansas. Mammy told me, and God only know who my mammy's pa is, but mine was Old Master Ben's boy, Ned Johnson.

Old Master Ben come from Tennessee when he was still a young man, and bring a whole passel of slaves and my mammy say they all was kin to one another, all the slaves, I mean. He was a white man that married a Cherokee woman, and he was a devil on this earth. I don't want to talk about him none.

White folks was mean to us like the devil, and so I just let them pass. When I say my brothers and sisters, I mean my half brothers and sisters, you know, but maybe some of them was my whole kin anyways, I don't know. They was Lottie, that was sold off to a Starr because she wouldn't have a baby, and Ed, Dave, Ben, Jim, and Ned.

My name is Sarah now but it was Annie until I was eight years old. My old mistress' name was Annie and she name me that, and Mammy

325

was afraid to change it until Old Mistress died, then she change it. She hate Old Mistress and that name too. Lottie's name was Annie, too, but Mammy changed it in her own mind but she was afraid to say it loud, a-feared she would get a whipping. When sister was sold off Mammy tell her to call herself Annie when she was leaving but call herself Lottie when she get over to the Starrs. And she done it too, I seen her after that and she was called Lottie all right.

The Negroes lived all huddled up in a bunch in little one-room log cabins with stick and mud chimneys. We lived in one, and it had beds for us children like shelves in the wall. Mammy used to help us up into them.

Grandmammy was mighty old and Mistress was old too. Grandmammy set on the Master's porch and minded the baby mostly. I think it was Young Master's. He was married to a Cherokee girl. They was several of the boys but only one girl, Nicie. The old master's boys were Aaron, John, Ned, Cy, and Nathan. They lived in a double log house made out of square hewed logs, and with a double fireplace out of rock where they warmed theirselves on one side and cooked on the other. They had a long front porch where they set most of the time in the summer, and slept on it, too.

There was over a hundred acres in the master's farm, and it was all bottom land too, and maybe you think he let then slaves off easy! Work from daylight to dark! They all hated him and the overseer too, and before slavery ended my grandmammy was dead and Old Mistress was dead and Old Master was mighty feeble and Uncle Nick had run away to the North soldiers and they never got him back. He run away once before, about ten years before I was born, Mammy say, but the Cherokees went over in the Creek Nation and got him back that time.

The way he made the Negroes work so hard. Old Master must have been trying to get rich. When they wouldn't stand for a whipping he would sell them. I saw him sell a old woman and her son. Must have been my aunt. She was always pestering around trying to get something and put it inside her apron. He flew at her and cussed her, and started like he was going to hit her but she just screamed out loud and run at him with her fingers stuck out straight and jabbed him in the belly. He had a big soft belly, too, and it hurt him. He seen she wasn't going to be afraid, and he set out to sell her. He went off on his horse to get some men to come and bid on her and her boy, and all us chillen was mighty scared about it.

They would have hangings at Fort Smith courthouse, and Old Marster would take a slave there sometimes to see the hanging, and that slave would come back and tell us all scary stories about the hanging. One time he whipped a whole bunch of the men on account of a fight in the quarters, and then he took them all to Fort Smith to see a hanging. He tied them all in the wagon, and when they had seen the hanging he asked them if they was scared of them dead men hanging up there.

They all said yes, of course, but my old Uncle Nick was a bad Negro and he said, "No, I ain't a-feared of them nor nothing else in this world," and Old Master jumped on him while he was tied and beat him with a rope, and then when they got home he tied old Nick to a tree and took his shirt off and poured the cat-o-nine-tails to him until he fainted away and fell over like he was dead. I never forget seeing all that blood all over my uncle, and if I could hate that old Indian any more I guess I would, but I hated him all I could already I reckon.

Old Master wasn't the only hellion neither. Old Mistress just as bad, and she took most of her wrath out hitting us children all the time. She was afraid of the grown Negroes, afraid of what they might do while Old Master was away, but she beat us children all the time. She would call me, "Come here, Annie!" and I wouldn't know what to do. If I went when she called "Annie" my mammy would beat me for answering to that name, and if I didn't go Old Mistress would beat me for that. That made me hate both of them, and I got the devil in me and I wouldn't come to either one. My grandmammy minded the master's yard, and she set on the front porch all the time, and when I was called I would run to her and she wouldn't let anybody touch me.

When I was eight years old Old Mistress died, and Grandmammy told me why Old Mistress picked on me so. She told me about me being half Mister Ned's blood. Then I knowed why Mister Ned would say, "Let her alone, she got big, big blood in her," and then laugh.

Young Mister Ned was a devil, too. When his mammy died he went out and "blanket married." I mean he brung in a half white and half Indian woman and just lived with her.

The slaves would get rations every Monday morning to do them all week. The overseer would weigh and measure according to how many in the family, and if you run out you just starve till you get some more. We all know the overseer steal some of it for his own self but we can't do anything, so we get it from the old master some other way.

One day I was carrying water from the spring and I run up on Grandmammy and Uncle Nick skinning a cow. "What you-all doing?" I say, and they say keep my mouth shut or they kill me. They was stealing from the master to piece out down at the quarters with. Old Master had so many cows he never did count the difference.

I guess I wasn't any worse than any the rest of the Negroes, but I was bad to tell little lies. I carry scars on my legs to this day where Old Master whip me for lying, with a rawhide quirt he carry all the time for his horse. When I lie to him he just jump down offen his horse and whip me good right there.

In slavery days we all ate sweet potatoes all the time. When they didn't measure out enough of the tame kind we would go out in the woods and get the wild kind. They growed along the river sand between where we lived and Wilson's Rock, out west of our place.

Then we had boiled sheep and goat, mostly goat, and milk and wild greens and corn pone. I think the goat meat was the best, but I aint had no teeth for forty years now, and a chunk of meat hurts my stomach. So I just eats grits mostly.

Besides hoeing in the field, chopping sprouts, shearing sheep, carrying water, cutting firewood, picking cotton, and sewing I was the one they picked to work Mistress' little garden where she raised things from seed they got in Fort Smith. Green peas and beans and radishes and things like that. If we raised a good garden she give me a little of it, and if we had a poor one I got a little anyhow even when she didn't give it.

For clothes we had homespun cotton all the year around, but in winter we had a sheepskin jacket with the wool left on the inside. Sometimes sheepskin shoes with the wool on the inside, and sometimes real cow leather shoes with good peggings for winter, but always barefooted in summer, all the men and women too.

Lord, I never earned a dime of money in slave days for myself but plenty for the old master. He would send us out to work the neighbor's field and he got paid for it, but we never did see any money.

I remember the first money I ever did see. It was a little while after we was free, and I found a greenback in the road at Fort Gibson and I didn't know what it was. Mammy said it was money and grabbed for it, but I was still a hell cat and I run with it. I went to the little sutler store and laid it down and pointed to a pitcher I been wanting. The man took the money and give me the pitcher, but I don't know to this day how much money it was and how much was the pitcher, but I still got that pitcher put away. It's all blue and white stripedy.

Most of the work I done off the plantation was sewing. I learned from my granny and I loved to sew. That was about the only thing I was industrious in. When I was just a little bitsy girl I found a steel needle in the yard that belong to Old Mistress. My mammy took it and I cried. She put it in her dress and started for the field. I cried so Old Mistress found out why and made Mammy give me the needle for my own.

We had some neighbor Indians named Starr, and Mrs. Starr used me sometimes to sew. She had nine boys and one girl, and she would sew up all they clothes at once to do for a year. She would cut out the cloth for about a week, and then send the word around to all the neighbors, and Old Mistress would send me because she couldn't see good to sew. They would have stacks of drawers, shirts, pants, and some dresses all cut out to sew up. I was the only Negro that would set there and set in that bunch of women, and they always talked to me nice. And when they eat I get part of it too, out in the kitchen. One Negro girl, Eula Davis, had a mistress sent her too, one time, but she wouldn't sew. She didn't like me because she said I was too white and she played off to spite the white people. She got sent home, too.

When Old Mistress die I done all the sewing for the family almost. I could sew good enough to go out before I was eight years old, and when I got to be about ten I was better than any other girl on the place—for sewing. I can still quilt without my glasses, and I have sewed all night long many a time while I was watching Young Master's baby after Old Mistress died.

They was over a hundred acres in the plantation, and I don't know how many slaves, but before the War ended lots of the men had run away. Uncle Nick went to the North and never come home, and Grandmammy died about that time.

We was way down across the Red River in Texas at that time, close to Shawneetown of the Choctaw Nation but just across the river on the other side in Texas bottoms. Old Master took us there in covered wagons when the Yankee soldiers got too close by in the first part of the War. He hired the slaves out to Texas people because he didn't make any crops down there, and we all lived in kind of camps. That's how some of the men and my Uncle Nick got to slip off to the North that way.

Old Master just rant and rave all the time we was in Texas. That's the first time I ever saw a doctor. Before that when a slave sick the old women give them herbs, but down there one day Old Master whip a Negro girl and she fall in the fire, and he had a doctor come out to fix her up where she was burnt. I remember Granny giving me clabber milk when I was sick, and when I was grown I found out it had had medicine in it. Some Negroes believed in buckeyes and charms but I never did. Old Master had some good boys, named Aaron, John, Ned, Cy and Nat, and they told me the charms was no good. Their sister Nicie told me too, and said when I was sick just come and and tell her.

Before freedom we didn't have no church but slipped around to the other cabins and had a little singing sometimes. Couldn't have anybody show us the letters either, and you better not let them catch you pick up a book even to look at the pictures, for it was against a Cherokee law to have a Negro read and write or to teach a Negro. They didn't tell us anything about Christmas and New Year either, and all we done was work.

When the War ended we was still in Texas, and when Old Master got a letter from Fort Smith telling him the slaves was free he couldn't read, and Young Miss read it to him. He went wild and jumped on her and beat the devil out of her. Said she was lying to him. It near about killed him to let us loose, but he cooled down after awhile and said he would help us all get back home if we wanted to come. Mammy told him she could bear her own expenses. I remember I didn't know what "expenses" was, and I thought it was something I was going to have to help carry all the way back.

It was a long time after he knew we was free before he told us. He tried to keep us, I reckon, but had to let us go. He died pretty soon after he told us, and some said his heart just broke and some said some Negroes poisoned him. I didn't know which.

Anyways we had to straggle back the best way we could, and me and Mammy just got along one way and another till we got to a ferry over the Red River and into Arkansas. Then we got some rides and walked some until we got to Fort Smith. They was a lot of Negro camps there and we stayed awhile and then started out to Fort Gibson because we heard they was giving rations out there. Mammy knew we was Cherokee anyway, I guess.

That trip was hell on earth. Nobody let us ride and it took us nearly two weeks to walk all that ways, and we nearly starved all the time. We was skin and bones and feet all bloody when we got to the Fort. We come here to Four Mile Branch to where the Negroes was all setting down, and pretty soon Mammy died.

I married Oliver Wilson on January 2, 1878. He used to belong to Mr. DeWitt Wilson of Tahlequah, and I think the old people used to live down at Wilson Rock because my husband used to know all about that place and the place where I was borned. Old Mister DeWitt Wilson give me a pear tree the next year after I was married, and it is still out in my yard and bears every year.

I was married in white and black checkedy calico apron that I washed for Mr. Tim Walker's mother Lizzie every day for many years over close to Fort Gibson, and I was sure a happy women when I married that day. Him and me both got our land on our Cherokee freedman blood and I have lived to bury my husband and see two great-grandchildren so far.

I heard a lot about Jefferson Davis in my life. During the War we hear the Negroes singing the soldier song about hang Jeff Davis to a apple tree, and Old Master tell about the time we know Jeff Davis. Old Master say Jeff Davis was just a dragoon soldier out of Fort Gibson when he bring his family out here from Tennessee, and while they was on the road from Fort Smith to where they settled young Jeff Davis and some more dragoon soldiers rid up and talked to him a long time. He say my grandmammy had a bundle on her head, and Jeff Davis say, "Where you going, Aunty?" And she was tired and mad and she said, "I don't know, to hell I reckon," and all the white soldiers laughed at her amd made her that much madder.

WILLIS WINN
Interviewed near Marshall, Texas
Interviewer not identified
Age when interviewed: 115

THE ONLIEST STATEMENT I can make about my age is my old master, Bob Winn, always told me if anyone ask me how old I is to say I'se borned on March 10, in 1822. I'se knowed my birthday since I'se a shirttail boy, but can't figure in my head.

My pappy was Daniel Winn and he come from Alabama, and I

'member him always sayin' he'd like to go back there and get some chestnuts. Mammy was named Patsy and they was nine of us chillen. The five boys was me and Willie and Hosea and two Georges, and the gals was Carolina and Dora and Anna and Ada, and all us lived to be growed and have chillen.

Massa Bob's house faced the quarters where he could hear us holler when he blowed the big horn for us to get up. All the houses was made of logs and we slept on shuck and grass mattresses what was always full of chinches. I still sleep on a grass mattress, 'cause I can't rest on cotton and featherbeds.

We et yellow bread and greens and black-eyed peas and pot likker and sopped 'lasses. Us and the white folks all cooked in fireplaces. A big iron pot hung out in the yard for to boil greens and hog jowl and such like. We didn't know nothin' about bakin' powder and made our soda from burnt cobs. That's just as good soda as this Arm and Hammer you get in the store. We et flour bread Sundays, but you darsn't get cotch with flour dough 'cept on that day. Mammy stole lots of it, though. She rolled it up and put it round her head and covered it with her head rag.

Wild game was all over the country—buffalo and bears and panthers and deer and possum and coon. The squirrels almost run over you in the woods. We et at a long, wooden trough, and it was always clean and full of plenty grub. We used buffalo and fish bones for spoons, and some et with they hands. The grub I liked best was whatever I could get.

Us slaves didn't wear nothing but white lowell cloth. They give us pants for Sunday what had a black stripe down the leg. The chillen wore wool clothes in winter, but the big folks wore the same outfit the year round. They didn't care if you froze.

I can show you right where I was when the stars fell. Some say they covered the ground like snow, but nary one ever hit the ground. They fell in about twelve feet of the ground. The chillen jumped up and tried to catch them. I don't 'member how long they fell, but they was shootin' through the air like skyrockets for quite a spell.

Missy Callie had one gal and two boys and Massa Bob had three overseers. He didn't have nigger drivers, but had his pets. We called them pimps 'cause they was always tattlin' when we done anything. His place was just as far as you could let your eyes see, about 1,800 or 1,900 acres, and he owned more'n five hundred niggers.

I still got the bugle he woke us with at four in the mornin'. When the bugle blowed you'd better go to hollerin', so the overseer could hear you. If he had to call you, it was too bad. The first thing in the mornin' we'd go to the lot and feed, then to the woodpile till breakfast. They put out grub in the trough and give us so long to eat. Massa hollered if we was slow eating, "Swallow that grub now and chaw it tonight. Better be in that field by daybreak." We worked from see to can't.

I'se seed many a nigger whipped on a "buck and gag bench." They buckled 'em down hard and fast on a long bench, gagged they mouth with cotton and when Massa got through layin' on the cowhide, the blood was runnin' off on the ground. Next mornin' after he whip you, he'd come to the quarters when you get up and say, "Boy, how is you feelin'?" No matter how sore you is, you'd better jump and kick you heels and show how lively you is. Massa hated me to he dying day, 'cause I told Missy about him whippin' a gal scandalously in the fields, 'cause she want to go to the house to her sick baby. Missy Callie didn't whip us, but she'd twist our noses and ears nearly off. Them fingers felt like a pair of pinchers. She stropped on her guns and rode a big bay horse to the field.

Massa had a gin and I hauled cotton to Port Caddo, on Caddo Lake. I drove eight mules and hauled eight bales of cotton. Massa followed me with two mules and two bales of cotton. I usually had a good start of him. The patterrollers has cotched me and unhitched my mules and drove 'em off, leavin' me in the middle of the road. They'd start back home, but when they overtook Massa they stopped, 'cause he drove the lead mules. He fetched 'em back and say, "Willie, what happen?" He sure cussed them patterrollers and said he'll get even yet.

They was sellin' slaves all the time, puttin' 'em on the block and sellin' 'em, accordin' to how much work they could do in a day and how strong they was. I'se seed lots of 'em in chains like cows and mules. If a owner have more'n he needed, he hit the road with 'em and sold 'em off to adjoinin' farms. None of 'em ever run off. They couldn't get away. I'se seed too many try it. If the patterrollers didn't cotch you, some white folks would put you up and call your massa. They had a 'greement to be on the watch for runaway niggers. When the massa get you back home and get through with you, you'd sure stay home.

In slavery time the niggers wasn't allowed to look at a book. I learned to read and write after surrender in the jail at Hot Springs, in Arkansas.

They give us cake at Christmas and eggnog and "silly-bug." Eggnog is made from whites of eggs and "silly-bug" from yallers. You have to churn the whiskey and yallers to make "silly-bug."

Corn shuckin's was the things them days. I liked to see 'em come. They cooked up guineas and ducks and chickens and sometimes roast a pig. Massa kept twenty, thirty barrels whiskey round over the place all the time, with tin cups hangin' on the barrels. You could drink when you want to, but sure better not get drunk. Massa have to watch he corners when corn shuckin' am over, or us niggers grab him and walk him around in the air on their hands.

When some of the white folks died every nigger on the place had to go to the grave and walk round and drop in some dirt on him. They buried the niggers any way. Dig a ditch and cover 'em up. I can show you right now down in Louisiana where I was raised, forty acres was nothin' but niggers buried on 'em.

I 'member lots about the War but can't tell you all, 'cause every war has its secrets. That war had four salutes, and you'd better give the right one when you meet the captain. I'se heared the niggers sing, "Gonna hang Jeff Davis to a sour apple tree." My pappy fought in the last battle, at Mansfield, and so did Massa Bob.

When the 'Federates come in sight of Mansfield they was carryin' a red flag, and kept it raised till surrender. When the Yanks come in sight they raised a white flag and wanted the 'Federates to surrender, but they wouldn't answer. It wasn't long till the whole world round there smelt like powder. Nowadays guns just goes "pop-pop," but them guns sounded like thunder.

After surrender Massa freed the men and Missy freed the women, but he didn't let us loose when he ought. They wasn't no places divided with niggers as I heared about. Niggers in Louisiana say Queen Elizabeth sent a boatload of gold to America to give the free men, but we never seed any of it. Massa give us each a barrel meal, a barrel flour, a side of meat, and then gallons 'lasses, and tell us we can work for who we pleases. Daddy bought two cows and a horse, eight hogs and a goat, from Massa on credit and we moved and made three crops.

The Yanks stayed round Louisiana a long time after surrender. They come to white folks' houses what hadn't freed they slaves and busted they meal and flour barrels and burn they meat and say, "If we have to face you again, we'll sweep you from the cradle up."

I'se been cotched by them Ku Kluxers. They didn't hurt me, but have lots of fun makin' me cut capers. They pulls my clothes off once and make me run about for a hundred yards and stand on my head in the middle the road.

They is plenty niggers in Louisiana that is still slaves. A spell back I made a trip to where I was raised, to see my old missy before she died, and there was niggers in twelve or fourteen miles of that place that they didn't know they is free. They is plenty niggers round here what is same as slaves, and has worked for white folks twenty and twenty-five years and ain't drawed a five cent piece, just old clothes and somethin' to eat. That's the way we was in slavery.

About four years after surrender Pappy say he heared folks say gold was covering the ground at Hope, Arkansas, so we pulled up and moved there. We found lots of money where they'd been a big camp, but no gold. We lived there sixteen years, and then I come to Texarkana and worked twelve years for a sawmill. I never married till I was old, in Little Washington, Arkansas, and lived with my wife thirty-six years before she died. We raised eighteen chillen to be growed and nary one of 'em was arrested.

I was always wild and played for dances but my wife was religious, and after I married I quieted down. When I joined the church, I burned my fiddle up. I always made a livin' from public road work since I left Texarkana, till I got no 'count for work. The only time I voted was in Hope, and I voted the Republican ticket and all my folks got mad.

If it wasn't for the good white folks, I'd starved to death. Before I come here, I was livin' in a shack on the T & P tracks and I couldn't pay no rent. I was sick and the woman made me get out. Master Vestals found me down by the tracks, eatin' red clay. I'd lived for three days on six tomatoes. I et two a day. Master Vestal went home and his wife cooked a big pot of stew, with meat and potatoes, and fetched it to me. Then they built a house down behind their back yard and I'se lived with 'em ever since.

CLARA C. YOUNG
Interviewed at Monroe County, Mississippi
Interviewer unidentified
Age when interviewed: Approximately 95

I DON'T KNOW when I was born, but I do know dat I'se seventeen years old when I was first sold. Dey put me and my brother up on de auction block at de same time. He brung fourteen hundred dollars but I dis'members 'zackly what dey paid for me. Weren't dat much, though, for big strong mens brung more dan womens and gals.

I was born in Huntsville, Alabamy, and my mammy and pappy was named Silby and Sharper Conley. Dey took de last name from de old marster dat owned 'em. I lived dere with 'em till de chillen drew dey parts and us was divided out. While I was with Old Marster, he let Miss Rachel—dat was his wife—have me for de house. She learned me how to cook and wait on de table and, I declare, she call me her very smartest gal! Sometimes, though, I wouldn't come right quick like when she ring de bell for me, and she'd start ringin' it harder and harder. I knowed den she was mad. When I'd get dere, she'd fuss at me and turn my dress up and whip me—not hard 'cause she weren't so strong— but I'd holler some!

Dey had a nigger woman to teach all de house darkies how to read and write and I larned how to sign my name and got as far as b-a-k-e-r in de blue-back speller.

Marse Conley and Miss Rachel had four chillen, Miss Mary, Miss Alice, Miss Willie, and Marse Andrew. When de time come, dey give me to Marse Andrew. He carried me and de rest out to Texas where he thought he would go and get rich. We never stayed long, though, for lots of de niggers runned away to de free states and Marse Andrew didn't like dat.

It was when he brought us back to Huntsville dat I was sold. All de white folks was a-gettin 'scared dey was gwine to lose dey slaves and dere was a powerful lot of nigger sellin' goin' on den. Marse Ewing bought me from him and carried me to his plantation near Aberdeen, Mississippi. Den I started to workin' in de field with de rest of de hands.

De overseer dat we had was right mean to us when we didn't work our rows as fast as de others, and sometime he whip us, women and all. When he did dat some of us most nigh always tell de marster and he would jump on de overseer and tell him to lay off de women and chillen. Dey was always sort of thoughtful of us and we loved Old Marster.

I heard tell one time, though, of de hired man (he was a nigger) and de overseer whippin' one of my cousins till she bled. She was just seventeen years old and was in de family way for de first time and couldn't work as hard as de rest. Next mornin' after dat she died. De hired man told de rest if dey said anything about it to de marster, he'd beat dem to death, too, so everybody kept quiet and de marster never knowed.

We worked hard in de field all day, but when dark come we would all go to de quarters and after supper we would set round and sing and talk. Most of de time we had good food to eat 'cause most of us had our gardens, and de quarters cook would fix what we wanted if we brung it to her. Durin' de last years before de surrender, we didn't have much to eat, though, and made out de best we could.

De most fun we had was at our meetin's. We had dem most every Sunday and dey lasted way into de night. De preacher I liked de best was named Matthew Ewing. He was a comely nigger, black as night, and he sure could read out of his hand. He never learned no real readin' and writin' but he sure knowed his Bible and would hold his hand out and make like he was readin' and preach de purtiest preachin' you ever heard. De meetin's last from early in de mornin' till late at night. When dark come, de men folks would hang up a wash pot, bottom upwards, in de little brush church house us had, so's it would catch de noise and de overseer wouldn't hear us singin' and shoutin'. Dey didn't mind us meetin' in de daytime, but dey thought iffen we stayed up half de night we wouldn't work so hard de next day—and dat was de truth.

You shoulda seen some of de niggers get religion. De best way was to carry 'em to de cemetery and let 'em stand over a grave. Dey would start singin' and shoutin' about seein' fire and brimstone. Den dey would sing some more and look plumb sanctified.

When us had our big meetin's, dere would always be some darkies from de plantations around to come. Dey would have to slip off 'cause dey marsters was afraid dey would get hitched up with some other black boy or gal on de other plantation and den dey would either have to buy or sell a nigger before you could get any work out of him.

We never knowed much about de War, 'cept dat we didn't have as much to eat or wear, and de white menfolks was all gone. Den, too, Old Miss cried a lot of de time.

De Yankees come round after de War and told us we's free and we shouted and sang, and had a big celebration for a few days. Den we got to wonderin' about what good it did us. It didn't feel no different. We all loved our marster and missus and stayed on with 'em just like nothin' had happened. De Yankees tried to get some of de men to vote, too, but not many did 'cause dey was scared of de Ku Kluxers. Dey would come at night all dressed up like ghosts and scare us all. We didn't like de Yankees anyway. Dey weren't good to us. When dey left we would always sing dat little song what go like dis:

> Old Mister Yankee, think he is so grand,
> With his blue coat tail a-draggin' on de ground!

I stayed on with Old Marster after de surrender, with de rest, till I met Joshua. Joshua Young was his name and he belonged to de Youngs what lived out at Waverly. I moved out dere with him after we married. We didn't have no big weddin' 'cause dere weren't much money den. We had a preacher, though, and den went along just like we had always been married.

Josh, he's been dead for a long time now but we had a good life out at Waverly and many a night stood outside de parlor door and watch de white folks at dey big dances and parties. De folks was powerful nice to us and we raised a passel of chillen out dere.

LITT YOUNG
Interviewed near Marshall, Texas
Interviewer not identified
Age when interviewed: 87

I'SE BORN in 1850 in Vicksburg, and belonged to Missy Martha Gibbs. Her place was on Warner Bayou and the old battlefield was right there in her field. She had two husbands, one named Hockley and he died of yellow fever. Then she marries a Dr. Gibbs, what was a Yankee, but she didn't know it till after the War. Massa Hockley bought my daddy from a nigger trader up North somewheres, but my mammy always belonged to the Gibbs' family. I had a sister and two brothers, but the Gibbs sold them to the Simmons and I never seed 'em any more.

Old Missy Gibbs had so many niggers she had to have lots of quarters. They was good houses, weatherboarden with cypress and had brick chimneys. We'd pull green grass and bury it awhile, then boil it to make mattresses. That made it black like in auto seats. Missy was a big, rich Irishwoman and not scared of no man. She lived in a big, fine house, and buckled on two guns and come out to the place most every morning. She out-cussed a man when things didn't go right. A yellow man drove her down in a two-horse avalanche. She had a white man for overseer what live in a good house close to the quarters. It was whitewashed and had glass windows. She built a nice church with glass windows and a brass cupola for the blacks. A yellow man preached to us. She had him preach how we was to obey our master and missy if we want to go to heaven, but when she wasn't there, he come out with straight preachin' from the Bible.

Good gracious, what we had to eat! They give us plenty—turnip greens and hog jowl and peas and corn bread, and milk by the barrels. Old women what was too old to work in the field done the cookin' and tended the babies. They cooked the corn bread in a oven and browned it like cake. When they pulled it out, all the chillen was standin' round, smackin' they lips. Every Christmas us got a set of white lowell clothes and a pair brogan shoes and they done us the whole year, or us go naked.

When that big bell rung at four o'clock you'd better get up, 'cause the overseer was standin' there with a whippin' strap if you was late. My daddy got a whippin' most every morning for oversleeping. Them mules was standin' in the field at daylight, waitin' to see how to plow a straight furrow. If a nigger was a five hundred pound picker and didn't weigh up that much at night, that was not getting his task and he got a whipping. The last weighing was done by lightin' a candle to see the scales.

Us have small dances Saturday nights and ring plays and banjo and fiddle playin' an knockin' bones. There was fiddles make from gourds and banjoes from sheep hides. I 'member one song, "Coffee grows on white oak trees, River flows with brandy-o." That song was started in Vicksburg by the Yankee soldiers when they left to go home, 'cause they so glad war was over.

Missy have a big, steam sawmill there on Warner Bayou, where the steamboats come up for lumber. It was right there where the bayou empties in the Mississippi. I 'member seein' one man sold there at the sawmill. He hit his massa in the head with a single tree and kilt him and they's fixin' to hang him, but a man promised to buy him if he's promise to be good. He give five hundred dollars for him.

Dr. Gibbs was a powerful man in Vicksburg. He was the occasion of them Yanks takin' advantage of Vicksburg like they done. Before the War he'd say to Missy, "Darling, you oughtn't whip them poor, black folks so hard. They is gwine be free like us some day." Missy say, "Shut up. Sometimes I believe you is a Yankee, anyway."

Some folks say Dr. Gibbs was workin' for the North all the time before the War, and when he doctored for them durin' the War, they say they knowed it. The 'Federates have a big camp there at Vicksburg and cut a big ditch out at the edge of town. Some say General Grant was knowin' all how it was fixed, and that Dr. Gibbs let him know.

The Yankees stole the march on the 'Federates and waited till they come out the ditch and mowed 'em down. The 'Federates didn't have no chance, 'cause they didn't have no cannon, just cap and ball rifles. The main fight started about four in the morning and held on till about ten. Dead soldiers was layin' thick on the ground by then. After the fight, the Yanks cut the buttons off the coats of them that was kilt.

I seed the Yankee gunboats when they come to Vicksburg. All us niggers went down to the river to see 'em. They told us to get plumb away 'cause they didn't know which way they was gwine to shoot. General Grant come to Vicksburg and he blowed a horn and them cannons began to shoot and just kept shootin'. When the Yankee come to Vicksburg, a big, red flag was flyin' over the town. Five or six hours after them cannons started shootin' they pulled it down and hoisted a big, white one. We saw it from the quarters.

After surrender the Yanks arrested my old missy and brought her out to the farm and locked her up in the black folks' church. She had a guard day and night. They fed her hardtack and water for three days before they turned her a-loose. Then she freed all her niggers. About that time Massa Gibbs run out of corn to feed the stock and he took my daddy and a bunch of niggers and left to buy a boatland of corn. Missy seized a bunch us niggers and starts to Texas. She had Irishmen guards, with rifles, to keep us from runnin' 'way. She left with ten six-mule teams and one ox cook wagon. Them what was able walked all the way from Vicksburg to Texas. We camped at night and they tied the men to trees. We couldn't get away with them Irishmen havin' rifles. Black folks naturally scared of guns, anyway. Missy finally locates about three miles from Marshall and we made her first crop and on June 19, the next year after emancipation, she set us free.

Dr. Gibbs followed her to Texas. He said the Yanks captured his niggers and took his load of corn as they was comin' down the Tennessee River, where it joins the Mississippi. Me and Mammy stayed in Texas, and never did see Daddy again. When us freed the last time us come to Marshall and I works in a grist mill and shingle mill. I cut ties for fifteen cents apiece. I cut wood for the first engines and they paid me a dollar twenty-five cents a cord. I got where I cut three cords a day. I helped clear all the land where Texarkana is now. When the railroads quit using wood, I worked as section hand for a dollar twenty-five cents a day. I farmed five years and never made a cent and went back to the railroad.

I marries in Marshall so long ago I done forgot. I raises six gals and has three grandchillen. They's all livin' 'cept one. Since my wife died and I'se too ailing to work, I'se been kept by the pension.

A Photo Essay of Former Slaves

These photographs are of actual slaves, although they do not represent any of the persons whose interviews appear in this book. They were photographed during the period from about 1861 to 1935 in Virginia, South Carolina, North Carolina, and Washington, D.C.

The sensitivity of these portraits, their honesty and forthrightness, correspond to the candid nature of the narratives.

Many of the photographs were taken by the father and son team of George and Huestis Cook and were obtained from the Valentine Museum in Richmond, Virginia. The collodion or "wet plate" method which came into use in 1851—ten years before the start of the Civil War—and which succeeded the daguerreotype was used for most of these photographs.

While George Cook was primarily a studio portraitist, his son Huestis, the baby seen in the picture on the following page, was one of the first of the "field" photographers who packed his buggy with cameras, glass plates, plate holders, collodion, silver nitrate, plus his tent or "darkroom" and all his developing supplies and took photography to the back roads.

These particular photographs were chosen not only because it was felt they would help in bringing the personal narratives of the ex-slaves to life, but also because a quality exists in each of them that marks them as an interesting composition and a work of art in their own right.

Cook Collection, Valentine Museum, Richmond, Va.

New York Historical Society

New York Historical Society

BY
HEWLETT & BRIGHT.

SALE OF

VALUABLE
SLAVES,

(On account of departure)

The Owner of the following named and valuable Slaves, being on the eve of departure for Europe, will cause the same to be offered for sale, at the NEW EXCHANGE, corner of St. Louis and Chartres streets, on *Saturday,* May 16, at Twelve o'Clock, *viz.*

1. **SARAH**, a mulatress, aged 45 years, a **good cook** and accustomed to house work in general, is an excellent and faithful nurse for sick persons, and in every respect a first rate character.

2. **DENNIS**, her son, a mulatto, aged 24 years, **a first rate cook and stew-** ard for a vessel, having been in that capacity for many years on board one of the Mobile packets; is strictly honest, temperate, and a first rate subject.

3. **CHOLE**, a mulatress, aged 36 years, she is, without execption, one of the most competent servants in the country, a first rate washer and ironer, does up lace, a good cook, and for a bachelor who wishes a house-keeper she would be invaluable; she is also a good ladies' maid, having travelled to the North in that capacity.

4. **FANNY**, her daughter, a mulatress, aged 16 years, speaks French and English, is a superior hair-dresser, (pupil of Guilliac,) a good seamstress and ladies' maid, is smart, intelligent, and a first rate character.

5. **DANDRIDGE**, a mulatoo, aged 26 years, a first rate dining-room ser- vant, a good painter and rough carpenter, and has but few equals for honesty and sobriety.

6. **NANCY**, his wife, aged about 24 years, a confidential house servant, good seamstress, mantuamaker and tailoress, a good cook, washer and ironer, etc.

7. **MARY ANN**, her child, a creole, aged 7 years, speaks French and English, is smart, active and intelligent.

8. **FANNY or FRANCES**, a mulatress, aged 22 years, is a first rate washer and ironer, good cook and house servant, and has an excellent character.

9. **EMMA**, an orphan, aged 10 or 11 years, speaks French and English, has been in the country 7 years, has been accustomed to waiting on table, sewing etc.; is intelligent and active.

10. **FRANK**, a mulatto, aged about 32 years speaks French and English, is a first rate hostler and coachman, understands perfectly well the management of horses, and is, in every respect, a first rate character, with the exception that he will occasionally drink, though not an habitual drunkard.

☞ All the above named Slaves are acclimated and excellent subjects; they were purchased by their present vendor many years ago, and will, therefore, be severally warranted against all vices and maladies prescribed by law, save and except FRANK, who is fully guaranteed in every other respect but the one above mentioned.

TERMS:—One-half Cash, and the other half in notes at Six months, drawn and endorsed to the satisfaction of the Vendor, with special mortgage on the Slaves until final payment. The Acts of Sale to be passed before WILLIAM BOS- WELL, *Notary Public,* at the expense of the Purchaser.

New-Orleans, May 13, 1835.

PRINTED BY BENJAMIN LEVY.

Cook Collection

Cook Collection

Cook Collection

Cook Collection

Cook Collection

Cook Collection

Cook Collection

Confederate Museum, Richmond, Va.

Cook Collection

Cook Collection

Cook Collection

Virginia State Library, Richmond, Va.

Cook Collection

Cook Collection

Cook Collection

Library of Congress

THE BACKGROUND OF THE SLAVE NARRATIVE COLLECTION[1]

THE SLAVE Narrative Collection represents the culmination of a literary tradition that extends back to the eighteenth century, when the earliest American slave narratives began to appear. The greatest vogue of this genre occurred during the three decades of sectional controversy that preceded the Civil War. The avowed intention of the publication of the antebellum narrative was to challenge the roseate portrait of slavery painted by its apologists. The proslavery justification of the "peculiar institution" alleged that it was a benevolent system and that the position of the slave was more secure than that of the Northern wage earner. The slave, according to George Fitzhugh, one of the most vigorous of the proslavery propagandists, "was happy as a human can be."[2]

But the stereotype of the "contented slave" was contradicted by the many fugitive slaves who sought refuge from bondage in the North and in Canada. Their often sensational revelations of the realities of slave life provided a persuasive challenge to southern justifications of slavery. During the antebellum period several thousand autobiographical and biographical accounts of slave experiences, generally promoted and distributed by abolitionist propagandists, were published. These narratives enjoyed immense popularity, were eagerly sought for publication by abolitionist journals, and proved financially successful.[3] While it is difficult to weigh precisely the influence on the antislavery crusade exerted by these tracts, the conclusion that they proved effective counterpropaganda to that disseminated by the proponents of slavery is inescapable.

[1] "The Background of the Slave Narrative Collection" was first published in slightly different form in 1967 in *American Quarterly*, XIX: 3, pp. 534–553. Copyright, 1967. Trustees of the University of Pennsylvania.

[2] George Fitzhugh, *Sociology for the South, or the Failure of Free Society* (Richmond, Va., 1854), p. 246.

[3] Charles H. Nichols, "Who Read the Slave Narratives," *Phylon Quarterly*, XX (Summer 1959), 149–62. Marion Wilson Starling, "The Slave Narrative: Its Place in American Literary History" (Unpublished doctoral dissertation, New York University, 1946).

The vogue of the slave narrative waned after the Civil War. The typical antebellum narrative had served as an exposé of the horrors of the "peculiar institution." But the Civil War settled the issue of slavery and destroyed the narrative's *raison d'être*. The sensational narrative of prewar vintage lingered on, but its publication after the war failed to elicit the sympathy and enthusiasm which it had earlier. A nation weary of war and intent upon reconciliation expressed little desire to be reminded of the realities of life before the war. Most of the narratives that did appear in the half-century following Reconstruction—their number meager when compared to the plethora of antebellum narratives—reflected a radically different conception of slave life. Now the narratives were employed almost exclusively as a nostalgic and sentimental reaffirmation of the "plantation legend" popularized by Southern local colorists.[4] While local color treatment of the oral tradition of the ex-slave helped to sustain an interest in Black folklore during the early years of the twentieth century, this alone proved insufficient to arouse a more general interest in recording the ex-slave's account of life under slavery. As the ranks of former slaves dwindled, so also did the possibility of preserving the "inside view" of slavery that their testimonies provided.

This trend was rather dramatically reversed during the late twenties and the decade of the thirties, which witnessed a revival of interest in the slave narrative. During this period several independent projects to secure ex-slave testimonies were initiated. What most clearly distinguished these from earlier efforts was their sociological character. While ideological factors were never totally eliminated and, indeed, often inspired interest in their collection, the single-minded moralism that had pervaded earlier narratives was substantially diminished. The typical supplanted the dramatic as the primary focus of inquiry; detailed questionnaires were designed in order to obtain a catalogue of information on the daily round of slave life. The primary goal in each instance was simply to get these aged Blacks to discuss the range of their experiences and impressions of life under the slave regime as fully and as freely as possible. The Federal Writers' Project study that produced the Slave Narrative Collection was the most ambitious and comprehensive of these several efforts.

The sources of this resurgence of interest in the slave narrative are both numerous and complex, and several of the more salient of these factors should be noted. By 1930 the number of surviving ex-slaves was diminishing, and the time was imminent when their testimonies could no longer be secured. However, this fact, often cited as a motivating factor by those compiling the narratives, was significant in an immediate sense only. That the ranks of former slaves were being rapidly depleted goes far toward explaining the sense of urgency that inspired the several efforts to gather the narratives, but this fact alone is insufficient to account for the heightened awareness of their value at this particular

[4] Richard M. Dorson, *American Folklore* (Chicago, 1959), 175–177.

time. The underlying sources of this interest must be sought elsewhere.

As the antebellum narrative had gained prominence in reaction to the Southern defense of slavery, so interest in the latter-day slave narrative was stimulated by the attitude toward the slave regime that prevailed following World War I. Seldom before or since has racism been so pervasive and so academically respectable in America as during the early years of the twentieth century. The assumption of the innate and inherited inferiority of non-Anglo Saxon racial and ethnic groups permeated and dominated intellectual as well as popular thought. Social, scientific, and historical thought both mirrored and reinforced this racism.

By far the most profound influence upon the historical study of slavery during this period was exerted by the writings of Ulrich B. Phillips, whose monumental *American Negro Slavery*[5] established him as the leading authority on the subject. *American Negro Slavery* was so comprehensive, its scholarship so exacting, and its racial assumptions so closely attuned to those then prevailing, that it "succeeded in neutralizing almost every assumption of the anti-slavery tradition."[6] The portrait of slavery that emerged bore a striking resemblance to that espoused by proslavery apologists before the Civil War. The severity of American slavery was minimized, its civilizing and Christianizing functions extolled; the notion that the slave was submissive rather than defiant was reasserted. The overall effect was a verification of the "plantation myth" and a confirmation of what Stanley M. Elkins has termed the "Sambo" image of the slave.[7]

The revival of interest in the slave narrative reflected a post-World War I revitalization of Black culture, which was instituted and promoted in large measure by Blacks themselves. This was marked by the advent of a concerted quest for a "usable" past, one that would impart a sense of self-respect and identity to Black Americans. One of the forms it assumed was the serious study of Black history, spearheaded by the unremitting efforts and inspiration of the fiery W. E. B. DuBois and Carter G. Woodson, the energetic founder, editor, and moving spirit behind the *Journal of Negro History*. The emergence of an increasing number of Black scholars signaled the demise of Black acquiescence to the prevailing White interpretations of the Black past.

The authority of Phillips' interpretation of slavery therefore did more than rekindle interest in the subject. Although accepted as authoritative in most academic circles, this sympathetic view of slavery was indignantly contested by the new generation of Black scholars who, as blood descendants, did not approach the subject in the spirit of erudition alone. As Phillips' Southern background and heritage had exerted a profound

[5] Ulrich B. Phillips, *American Negro Slavery, A Survey of the Supply, Employment, and Control of Negro Labor as Determined by the Plantation Regime* (New York, 1918).
[6] Stanley M. Elkins, *Slavery: A Problem in American Institutional and Intellectual Life* (Chicago, 1959), p. 11.
[7] Elkins.

and pervasive influence upon his perspective of slavery, so the portrait espoused by Black students was derived from a tradition perpetuated and enriched by the accounts of those who had experienced life under the slave regime. When Phillips spurned the use of ex-slave reminiscenses as reliable sources of historical data, he rejected the validity of the very source upon which many of the basic assumptions of the Black scholar were ultimately founded. Black scholars were quite understandably convinced that Phillips' interpretations was unsound.

Phillips' aversion to the slave narrative, moreover, precluded the study of slavery written from the standpoint of the slave. In rejecting the use of the slave narrative and reminiscences, therefore, Phillips should also have refrained from making judgments about the experiential world of the slave, since the sources he did employ were inadequate to provide definitive answers to the questions "What was it like to be a slave?" It was a recognition of the fact that only an individual who had lived under the slave regime could adequately answer this question that contributed substantially to the surge of interest in the slave narrative.

The discovery of Black culture engaged the attention of a growing number of Whites as well. White writers found in Black life a fresh source of artistic materials, and serious treatment of Blacks was a distinguishing feature of the Southern literary renaissance that flourished in the twenties.[8] Interest in Black art and entertainment was reflected in the acceptance of jazz by White musicians and its popularization among White audiences.[9] The fascination with Black folklore, which extended back to the nineteenth century, increased significantly during the twenties and was enlivened by innovations such as the unique brand of folk sociology pioneered by Howard W. Odum at the University of North Carolina.[10]

This burgeoning interest in Black people was enhanced immeasurably by the attention given by the rapidly expanding disciplines of anthropology and sociology. While social scientific thought was not immune to the popular racial preconceptions of the day, the authority of such doctrines was weakened by the impact of intellectual currents from within the social sciences themselves. The concept of culture, more than any other single idea, contributed to the erosion of racist respectability. Although explicitly accepted only in avant-garde circles during the twenties, the culture concept had been an implicit and sometimes contradictory component of the working assumptions of many social scientists even at the zenith of the vogue of racism. Facilitated by the decline of racialist explanations and by an increased sophistication in methodological techniques, social scientific attention accorded the phenomenon of race and Blacks in American culture steadily increased

[8] Willard Thorp, *American Writing in the Twentieth Century* (Cambridge, 1960), pp. 258–262.
[9] Neil Leonard, *Jazz and the White Americans: The Acceptance of a New Art Form* (Chicago, 1962).
[10] Dorson, *American Folklore*, pp. 176–177.

throughout the twenties and thirties.[11] The convergence of these several currents fostered a climate receptive to efforts to obtain personal testimonies concerning antebellum slave life, and it was from within this cultural milieu that interest in the collection of ex-slave narratives was spurred.

The earliest of these endeavors to secure interviews with ex-slaves was initiated in 1929 under private auspices, when separate and independent projects were simultaneously begun at Fisk University and at Southern University. The project at Southern was directed by John B. Cade, a historian whose interest in the utilization of the accounts of ex-slaves was initially aroused by the controversy over the nature of the slave regime and, in particular, by Phillips' contention that the slave had been contented with his lot. A preliminary study conducted at Southern during the years 1929–1930 was expanded during the early years of the depression under Cade's direction, and the results of these interviews were later summarized in Cade's article "Out of the Mouths of Ex-Slaves."[12] The success of this project stimulated a similar attempt by Cade at Prairie View State College during the years 1935–1938, which produced over four hundred interviews from slaves in thirteen states. Unfortunately, the results of these interviews remain unpublished.[13]

The Fisk collection of slave narratives evolved as an unanticipated consequence of research efforts directed by Charles S. Johnson, who in 1928 had established the Social Science Institute at Fisk. The influence of Johnson's research training at the University of Chicago's renowned Department of Sociology was reflected in one of his earliest studies, which involved an extensive community study of the Fisk University environs. Johnson's research design in this study relied heavily upon personal interviews, and a large number of former slaves were among those interviewed by Ophelia Settle of the Institute's research staff. Johnson quickly recognized the value of preserving these firsthand accounts of slave life before they were lost and urged that a concerted effort be made to obtain them.[14] In addition to those secured in Nashville, interviews were conducted in rural Tennessee and Kentucky and later as an integral aspect of the study of Macon County, Alabama, which formed the substance of Johnson's analysis of the plantation as an institution.[15] These interviews proved so satisfactory that Johnson anticipated publication of a volume based on an analysis of the 100

[11]Ethel Shanas, "The American Journal of Sociology Through Fifty Years," *American Journal of Sociology*, L (May 1945), 522–533.

[12]John B. Cade, "Out of the Mouths of Ex-Slaves," *Journal of Negro History*, XX (July 1935), 294–337.

[13]John B. Cade to author, July 30, 1965. Cade to T. R. Griffith of Prairie View State College, February 13, 1935, Letter in Cade's possession. The materials obtained in the Prairie View studies are housed in the Southern University Archives.

[14]Mrs. Ophelia Settle Egypt to author, interview, September 16, 1965.

[15]Charles S. Johnson, *Shadow of the Plantation* (Chicago, 1934); see also E. Franklin Frazier, *The Negro Family in the United States* (Chicago, 1939).

documents Miss Settle had obtained.[16] Although this proposal was never realized, approximately one-third of these narratives have been reproduced in the Institute's *Unwritten History of Slavery.*[17]

Private efforts to preserve the life histories of former slaves accounted for only a small portion of the narratives collected during this period, however. The advent of the New Deal marked a new phase in these efforts, for it was under New Deal employment programs for jobless white-collar workers that these efforts were most fully realized. The suggestion that the goals of the Federal relief program might be adapted to a project designed to interview ex-slaves was first advanced in 1934 by Lawrence D. Reddick, then a member of the faculty of Kentucky State College, who had studied under Charles S. Johnson at Fisk and had participated in the efforts of the Social Science Institute to secure ex-slave testimonies in rural areas of Tennessee. A receptivity on the part of Federal Emergency Relief Administation officials to white-collar projects encouraged him to propose the idea of expanding the collection of ex-slave data as part of the relief program. The project was a "natural," for aside from its intrinsic historical value, it would provide employment for unemployed Black college graduates, who had, Reddick asserted, "been left out generally in the program of recovery."[18]

Before presenting his proposal for the project to FERA officials, Reddick conferred with Charles S. Johnson and Carter Woodson and secured their support for the venture. Johnson's enthusiasm for the collection of this data has already been noted. Woodson, likewise sensitive to the importance of preserving accounts of slave life by former slaves themselves, had hoped to have The Association for the Study of Negro Life and History undertake such a project, but here, as in numerous other instances, research he envisioned was frustrated by inadequate financial resources.[19] The possibility of having this activity conducted under the aegis of the FERA therefore appealed to him, and the association was officially recorded as a "co-operating sponsor" of the project that was instituted as a result of Reddick's proposal.[20] The support of these two eminent scholars, conspicuously designated in Reddick's project proposal as the

[16]Johnson memorandum in the possession of B. A. Botkin, undated.

[17]Ophelia Settle Egypt, J. Masuoka and Charles S. Johnson, *Unwritten History of Slavery: Autobiographical Accounts of Negro Ex-Slaves,* Social Science Source Documents No. 1 (Nashville, 1945). Those narratives not included in this volume remain in the personal possession of Mrs. Egypt.

[18]Lawrence D. Reddick to author, interview, July 20, 1965, September 23, 1965. Reddick to Harry L. Hopkins, Federal Relief Administrator, June 14, 1934, Correspondence Relative to Ex-Slave Interviews in possession of B. A. Botkin.

[19]Alfred E. Smith, former FERA Advisor on Negro Affairs, to author, interview, Aug. 10, 1965.

[20]Reddick to Hopkins, June 14, 1934; Reddick to Clark Foreman, Advisor on the Economic Status of Negroes, Department of Interior, May 15, 1934; Reddick to Forrester B. Washington, Advisor on Negro Affairs, FERA, May 21, 1934, Correspondence Relative to Ex-Slave Interviews.

project's "continual advisors," was more than nominal; while their endorsement was designed to enhance chances of obtaining official approval of the project, it was an undertaking that both men were vitally interested in seeing successfully inaugurated.

Reddick proposed that a regional unit composed of twelve Black college graduates be established to gather the personal testimonies of ex-slaves in the "Valley of the Ohio River," including Kentucky, Tennessee, West Virginia, Ohio, and southern Indiana and Illinois. This project was conceived as a pilot study preliminary to a far more ambitious Southern regional project designed to employ 500 Black white-collar workers in systematically interviewing the surviving ex-slave population.[21] The reaction to the pilot proposal was generally favorable, and the first units conducted under Reddick's supervision were begun in Indiana and Kentucky in September, 1934, and were in operation through July of 1935. During this brief period of activity approximately two hundred and fifty interviews were obtained. However, the pilot project was plagued by a dearth of qualified personnel almost from its inception. Although the proposal had been designed to employ Blacks with college training, the exigencies of the relief program dictated the employment of individuals who had little and sometimes no college training and interviewing experience. The failure of this project to approach its early promise, coupled with a lack of coordination inherent in the administrative structure of FERA, and the uncertainty of the future of FERA arts programs under its successor, Works Progress Administration, prevented the more comprehensive Southern regional project from progressing beyond the planning stage under FERA.[22]

While the FERA project was the first attempt to interview ex-slaves under governmental auspices, the influence it exerted upon the development of later programs has been exaggerated. The impression of continuity between this project and the later Slave Narrative Collection under WPA was more apparent than real; the FERA project did not, as has been asserted elsewhere,[23] serve as a precedent for the establishment of such a project under the Writers' Project. Indeed, rather than spur their further collection, the example of the FERA project may have temporarily forestalled the adoption of a similar study under the Writers' Project. The response of Henry G. Alsberg, National Director of the Writers' Project, to a Georgia Writers' Project request to undertake the collection of ex-slave reminiscences is revealing in this regard.

[21]Reddick to Hopkins, June 14, 1934.

[22]William F. McDonald, "Federal Relief Administration and the Arts" (Unpublished manuscript prepared under the sponsorship of the American Council of Learned Societies, 1949), pp. 87–88. WPA "Index of Research Records," Unit reports, September 15, 1934–July 11, 1935, Correspondence Relative to Ex-Slave Interviews. Reddick to author, July 20, 1965. These narratives remain in Reddick's possession.

[23]Benjamin A. Botkin, *Lay My Burden Down*, p. x; McDonald, "Federal Relief Administration and the Arts," pp. 734–735.

I think your plan for write-ups of the stories of ex-slaves is fine. There was a project of this type under CWA and FERA. It was started in Kentucky, but for some reason was not well conducted and therefor discontinued. Indeed, I think in all the southern states and some of the border northern states a project of this type could be undertaken if it were wisely handled.[24]

The several attempts to gather ex-slave data under the Writers' Project were independent and spontaneous, although they were undertaken in response to the same cultural factors that elicited similar studies earlier.

On the other hand, while the lead initiated by Reddick was not continued under the Writers' Project, the type of problems he encountered contributed to the growing awareness of the inadequacies of establishing cultural projects within the existing structure of FERA and the necessity of developing an organization devoted solely to the cultivation of the arts. In this sense, the FERA and interim Civil Works Administration experiences proved invaluable in the formation of the WPA, in which white-collar projects figured prominently. The relief functions for which these earlier agencies had been created were now broadened and better coordinated. The several WPA Arts projects were designed to combat the changing character of the relief rolls, which were increasingly being frequented by white-collar workers whose savings had been exhausted.

The spirit of innovation and experimentation, which proved the hallmark of the New Deal, was nowhere revealed more clearly than in the establishment of Federal Project Number One, better known as the Federal Arts Project, which included the Federal Art, Music, Theatre, and Writers' Projects. With its organization the Federal government embarked upon an unprecedented program of support for artistic and cultural endeavors. The Arts Project called for the creation of a separate and distinct agency to coordinate and direct activities in each of the respective areas. These organizations were headed by personnel who were professionally qualified to assess the value and promise of project proposals and to provide competent direction to the activities undertaken.[25]

The primary task of the Federal Writers' Project, as originally conceived, was the preparation of a comprehensive and panoramic *American Guide*, a geographical-social-historical portrait of the states, cities, and localities of the entire United States. The original idea of a single multivolume national guide ultimately gave way to *The American Guide*

[24]Henry G. Alsberg to Carolyn Dillard, July 7, 1936, Correspondence Pertaining to Ex-Slave Studies, Records of the Federal Writers' Project, Works Progress Administration, National Archives, Record Group 69. Since all the materials here used from the National Archives are from the Records of the Federal Writers' Project, they will hereafter be indicated by the symbol NA. Correspondence Pertaining to Ex-Slave Studies will hereafter be cited as Ex-Slave Studies.

[25]McDonald.

Series, composed of a number of state and local *Guides.*[26] The concept of a national guide had been expressed in several proposals submitted to FERA, but it was shaped in large measure by the National Director of the Writers' Project, Henry G. Alsberg, a man of diverse talents whose background and experience included a Columbia law degree and subsequent legal practice, work as a foreign correspondent, and the directorship of the Provincetown Theatre. More importantly, Alsberg brought to his position a tempered liberalism sympathetic to the aspirations of the New Deal and a receptivity toward innovation that helped pave the way for the Slave Narrative Collection.[27]

As the Writers' Project became more firmly established and its research potential became more apparent, the scope of its efforts broadened and deepened from its exclusive concern with the *Guides.* Activities initially associated only with the compilation of the *Guides* soon assumed a significance in their own right. The collections of folklore, life-histories, and materials on Black life, among others, provided considerable breadth and a characteristic flavor to the Writers' Project as well as considerable impetus toward the collection of slave narratives. But none of these several supplemental activities supplanted the priority accorded the compilation of the state and local *Guides,* which persisted throughout the life of the Writers' Projects as its overriding objective. Especially in the early stages of the program, the more competent writers were most often assigned to the *Guide* projects, while less skilled writers were involved in other activities. While the emphasis placed upon the collecting of the narratives varied considerably from state to state, the efforts expended to secure them and the quality of the materials obtained were directly influenced by this scale of priorities.[28]

A new appreciation of the indigenous and folk elements in American society fostered by the depression was reflected in the emphases of the Writers' Project. The program and personnel of the Writers' Project presented an exceptional and unique opportunity to pursue folklore research on a national basis, and the emphasis upon the collection of folklore materials that evolved became one of its most characteristic and productive features. To direct activities in this area, the Writers' Project recruited John A. Lomax, honorary curator of the Archives of American Folk Song in the Library of Congress and one of the foremost figures in the development of American folklore. Lomax was especially intrigued by the spontaneity and uniqueness of Black lore, and he was singularly successful in the discovery of new and vital sources of Black folk materials.[29] Although the soundness of his theory and practice has been questioned, Lomax's contribution to folklore research was enormous. His

[26]McDonald, pp. 721–749.
[27]McDonald, pp. 750–753.
[28]McDonald, pp. 790–870; Carolyn Dillard, former Director of the Georgia Writers' Project, to author, August 9, 1965.
[29]John A. Lomax, *Adventures of a Ballad Hunter* (New York, 1947).

pioneer efforts established him as "the greatest popularizer and one of the greatest field collectors of American folksong." [30]

Lomax's tenure with the Writers' Project was relatively brief, but his impact upon its program and especially upon the formation of the Slave Narrative Collection was enduring. His early direction of the Project's folklore research mirrored his personal interest in Southern and rural materials.[31] The interview method of collecting folklore and a corollary emphasis upon the collection of life-history materials, both of which he introduced, became a hallmark of Writers' Project research. The life-history approach was utilized in several unpublished Writers' Project studies besides the Slave Narrative Collection, such as the autobiographies of Texas and Kansas range pioneers.[32] The technique was later most fully developed in the highly original and widely acclaimed *These Are Our Lives*, a series of life histories of varied inhabitants of the southeastern United States.[33]

An awakened appreciation during the depression of the richness of the cultural diversity of the American people quickened interest in and sympathy for American minority groups. The broad equalitarianism of the New Deal both reflected and inspired this attitude. The Roosevelt administration proved more responsive to the needs and demands of Blacks than any previous administration since Lincoln's; Blacks, in turn, became an important element in the New Deal coalition. This climate was fostered by the efforts of a handful of prominent administration spokesmen and by the pressures Blacks themselves exerted to obtain representation in New Deal programs. Through these efforts, Blacks were appointed to positions of responsibility within numerous governmental agencies. The basic function of these members of the "Black Cabinet" or "Black Brain Trust," a vocal and articulate group of highly trained and politically astute Black intellectuals who spearheaded the struggle for civil rights during the thirties, was to serve, officially and unofficially, as an agency's "race relations advisor" and "to look out for the Negro interests." Discrimination still flourished, for this representation of Blacks in the New Deal was largely token. But compared to the indifference of previous administrations, it was a significant departure.[34]

Black participation on the Writers' Project was achieved only after the

[30]Donald K. Wilgus, *Anglo-American Folksong Scholarship Since 1898* (New Brunswick, N. J., 1959), p. 157.

[31]McDonald, pp. 838–857.

[32]Harold C. Evan, Acting State Director of the Kansas Writers' Project to George Cronyn, Associate Director of the FWP, April 19, 1937, "Ex-Slave Studies," NA, B. A. Botkin, "We Called It Living Lore," *New York Folklore Quarterly*, XIV (Fall 1958), 189–201.

[33]Federal Writers' Project, *These Are Our Lives* (Chapel Hill, N. C., 1939).

[34]Arthur M. Schlesinger, Jr., *The Politics of Upheaval* (Boston, 1960), pp. 424–438; John Hope Franklin, *From Slavery to Freedom* (rev. ed.; New York, 1964), pp. 512–533; Allen F. Kifer, "The Negro Under the New Deal, 1933–1941" (Unpublished doctoral dissertation, University of Wisconsin, 1961).

lack of Black personnel had been scored by vigilant Black leaders. Alsberg, sympathetic throughout to the problems of Black employment in the Writers' Project, was receptive to suggestions that a Black be placed in a high administrative position.[35] Following the predictable New Deal pattern, an Office of Negro Affairs, which played a vital role in the Writers' Project program, was created. Sterling A. Brown, Washington, D. C., poet and a member of the Howard University English faculty, was enlisted, with "Black Cabinet" support, to insure that "the Negro [was] not neglected in any of the publications written by or sponsored by the Writers' Project." [36]

While its primary official responsibilities were editorial, the Office of Negro Affairs also served as watchdog over the personnel practices of the Writers' Project. In this its course of action was limited since personnel policies were largely determined by the participating states, and the national office could do little more than deplore the discrimination that existed [37] and recommend the addition of qualified Black writers. Black participation was in many instances circumscribed by the fact that Southern mores dictated the establishment of separate units for White and Black, the cost of which was often prohibitive.[38] Moreover, state Writers' Project officials were extremely sensitive to local White public opinion and were reluctant to take any action that might endanger their already tenuous status in the eyes of the White community. When individual Blacks were hired in states lacking separate Black units, their terms were often of short duration; the familiar pattern of "last hired, first fired" is amply documented in FWP records.[39] Yet the record of the FWP on this score is a mixed one. While Blacks were virtually excluded from Writers' Projects in several Southern states, this pattern was not universal. In several states—notably Virginia, Louisiana, and Florida—ambitious Black units flourished; in several others the number of Black workers fluctuated in response to work quotas. The energies of the Black writers were directed almost exclusively to the collection of materials pertaining to Black culture.

When considered in terms of the relative paucity of Black personnel on the Writers' Project, their accomplishments are impressive. In addition to the collection and preparation of materials for inclusion in the state

[35]Alsberg to Aubrey Williams, National Youth Administrator, December 16, 1935, Records of Henry G. Alsberg, NA.

[36]Eugene C. Homes, Assistant Editor for Negro Affairs to the Editor, *The Spokesman*, San Francisco, April 10, 1938, Negro Studies File, NA. Sterling A. Brown to author, interview, July 20, 1965.

[37]Response to inquiry by Alsberg to all state directors, January 7, 1936, Negro Studies File, NA. Microfilmed personnel records of the Works Progress Administration, Federal Records Center, St. Louis.

[38]Exempli gratia, Edwin Bjorkman, North Carolina State Director, to Alsberg, January 11, 1936, Negro Studies File, NA.

[39]Exempli gratia, Memo from the Office of Negro Affairs to W. T. Couch, Writers' Project Regional Director, October 19, 1938, Negro Studies File, NA.

Guides, Black workers in Arkansas, Louisiana, Florida, and Virginia were engaged in research studies pertaining to aspects of Black history and culture. In addition, the Washington office of the FWP contemplated publication of a history of the antislavery struggle, "from the Negro point of view"; a comprehensive bibliography of writings on Black culture; and the compilation of a documentary record of events in the history of the "underground railroad." Sterling A. Brown, whose unstinting support and encouragement sustained each of these efforts, had personally formulated plans for the publication of a volume that would draw substantially upon Writers' Project materials obtained by Black researchers.[40] These studies were curtailed and publication plans based upon them thwarted, however, by the abrupt termination of the Writers' Project in 1939. Only *The Negro in Virginia,* a product of that state's Black unit directed by Roscoe E. Lewis and one of the outstanding achievements of the Writers' Project, achieved publication.[41]

Preliminary plans for the Writers' Project made no provision for collecting slave autobiographies and reminiscences. Interviews with former slaves were undertaken spontaneously after the inception of the FWP and were included among the activities of several Southern Writers' Projects for almost a year before these largely desultory efforts were transformed into a concerted regional project coordinated by the Washington office. Project records reveal that a small number of interviews had been sporadically conducted, often by a single Black employee, in Alabama, Arkansas, Florida, Georgia, South Carolina, Texas, and Virginia without explicit direction or apparent recognition from Washington before the collection of narratives was officially inaugurated by the national headquarters of the FWP in April of 1937.[42]

The first systematic effort to obtain slave autobiographies under the auspices of the Federal Writers' Project was begun in Georgia. In July, 1936, Reverend J. C. Wright, an official of the Atlanta Urban League, proposed to Carolyn Dillard, Georgia Writers' Project Director, a project to compile the autobiographies of former slaves as a means of involving unemployed Blacks in the program of the Writers' Project. Mrs. Dillard, receptive to the idea, secured approval of the project from the Washington office. Black and White interviewers obtained over one hundred interviews, samples of which were forwarded to Washington for evaluation

[40]Ex-Slave Studies, Negro Studies File, NA.

[41]Virginia Writers' Project, *The Negro in Virginia* (New York, 1940). Roscoe Lewis evinced a keen interest in the tales of former slaves, both in this and in his later research activities. His efforts to obtain slave narratives continued after the Writers' Project was terminated. At the time of his death in 1961 he had begun a systematic analysis of the more than 200 life histories he had collected. His papers and the records of these interviews remain in the possession of his son, Roger Lewis.

[42]Mabel Montgomery, South Carolina State Writers' Project Director, to Alsberg, May 27, 1936, August 21, 1936; Bernice Babcock, Arkansas State Director, to Alsberg, December 18, 1936, Negro Studies File, NA. J. Frank Davis, Texas State Supervisor, to Cronyn, April 7, 1937, Ex-Slave Studies, NA. Alabama and Virginia narratives are dated.

and editorial comment.[43] Since the Office of Negro Affairs was responsible for all materials pertaining to Black people, the narratives were reviewed by Sterling Brown, who characterized them as "colorful and valuable" and urged their continued collection.[44] Yet, despite recognition of their value as sociohistorical data by social scientists outside the Writers' Project[45], they failed to provoke any comparable enthusiasm from other members of the Project's editorial staff or to stimulate the suggestion that their collection might be extended to the remaining Southern and border states with large populations of ex-slaves.

It was a group of ex-slave narratives submitted by the Florida Writers' Project that directly sparked the establishment of a regional study under FWP auspices. The Florida narratives had been independently undertaken under the direction of the State Director of the Florida Writers' Project, Carita Doggett Corse, who had earlier glimpsed the potential value of such interviews while engaged in research on a history of the picturesque Fort George Island. When Mrs. Corse was appointed Director of the Florida Writers' Project in the fall of 1935, the recollection of her conversations with an aged ex-slave who had vividly recalled much of the Island's romantic past, coupled with the Writers' Project emphasis upon personal history and interview methods of data collection, suggested the possibility of utilizing Project personnel to interview ex-slaves.[46] In 1936 employees of the active Black unit, which included novelist-anthropologist Zora Neale Hurston, interviewed a substantial number of former slaves as an integral part of their quest for indigenous Negro folklore materials. These activities were nominally associated with the compilation of the *Florida Guide*, and the narratives obtained were later considered for inclusion in a projected volume entitled *The Negro in Florida*, which was never completed.[47]

In March of 1937 several of the Florida interviews were forwarded to Washington for editorial comment, where they were reviewed by John A. Lomax and George Cronyn, Associate Director of the FWP, as well as by Sterling A. Brown. Lomax was intrigued by the narratives and immediately discerned the value of preserving them. That he was unaware of previous attempts to gather them is revealed by the fact that he erroneously credited Mrs. Corse with initiating these activities. Commending Mrs. Corse for her imaginative efforts, Lomax wrote:

> I have enjoyed very much reading this batch of reminiscences from ex-slaves. It seems to me that they are of very great value and I con-

[43]Extensive correspondence in Georgia Folder, Ex-Slaves Studies, NA.

[44]Memo "Report from the Editor on Negro Affairs," February 1937, Negro Studies File, NA.

[45]Georgia Folder, Ex-Slave Studies, NA. This included efforts by the Department of Sociology at the University of Chicago to obtain them.

[46]Carita Doggett Corse to author, July 12, 1965; see her *The Key to the Golden Islands* (Chapel Hill, N. C., 1931).

[47]Corse to Alsberg, June 15, 1938; Alsberg to Corse, June 3, 1939; Negro Studies File, NA.

gratulate you on being the first to open up, as you have done, this field of investigation.[48]

Lomax was chiefly responsible for the inclusion of this activity as an integral aspect of the FWP program. Excited by the possibilities afforded by the structure and emphases of the Writers' Project for large-scale collection of the narratives, he proposed that these efforts should be extended on a more systematic basis to the remaining Southern and border states. On April 1, 1937, these activities were formally initiated with the dispatch of instructions to each of these states to direct their workers to the task of interviewing former slaves.[49]

Reflecting Lomax's interest and influence, the primary responsibility for the direction and coordination of the study was delegated to the Folklore Division of the Project, which Lomax headed, rather than to the Office of Negro Affairs. Lomax seized the initiative for its direction from its inception and remained the guiding spirit behind the collection of the autobiographies until his resignation from the Writers' Project several months later. The project assumed a form and a scope that bore Lomax's imprint and reflected his experience and zeal as a folklore collector. His sense of urgency inspired the efforts in several states. And his prestige and personal influence enlisted the support of many Project officials, particularly in the deep South, who might otherwise have been unresponsive to requests for materials of this type.[50]

The wisdom of selecting Lomax, a White Southerner, to direct a project involving the collection of data from Black former slaves might be questioned. While his background may have influenced his other folklore experiences, any racial preconceptions Lomax may have held do not appear to have had an appreciable effect upon the Slave Narrative Collection. The instructions drawn by Lomax relative to the conduct of the interviews stressed the necessity of obtaining a faithful account of the ex-slave's version of his experience.

> It should be remembered that the Federal Writers' Project is not interested in taking sides on any question. The worker should not censor any materials collected regardless of its nature.[51]

Lomax constantly reiterated his insistence upon the importance of recording interview conversations verbatim, with no holds barred. In his editorial capacity he closely adhered to this dictum, making only minor grammatical corrections, never altering the substance of the narratives.

---

[48]Lomax to Corse, April 6, 1937, Ex-Slave Studies, NA.

[49]Cronyn to FWP Directors in all Southern and border states, April 1, 1937, Ex-Slave Studies, NA.

[50]Botkin, Unpublished manuscript, May 26, 1941, Records of the Library of Congress Project, Writers' Unit, NA.

[51]"Supplementary Instructions #9E to the 'American Guide Manual.'" April 22, 1937. Records of the Library of Congress Project, Writers' Unit, NA.

Narratives were never rejected or revised because their authenticity was questioned.

On the other hand, while Lomax was keenly sensitive to the importance of establishing adequate rapport with these aged Blacks, the possibility that this might have been accomplished more effectively by Black rather than White interviewers does not appear to have been seriously considered. Earlier evaluations of the Georgia narratives had reported that Black interviewers appeared "able to gain better insight" than Whites and that the interviews obtained by Blacks were "less tinged with glamour."[52] Nevertheless, no special attempt was made, as had been the case in the earlier efforts in Georgia, Florida, and several other states, to assign Blacks to this task. Indeed, those employed in securing interviews after direction was assumed by the national office of the FWP were almost exclusively Whites,[53] and it is probable that in many instances caste etiquette led many ex-slaves to tell White interviewers "what they wanted to hear." Lomax's personal success in obtaining Black folklore may have blinded him to the effects that the race of the interviewer might have exerted upon the interview situation. But Lomax alone should not be held responsible for the paucity of Black interviewers employed in this task; his duties were editorial and not administrative. The dearth of Black representation derived primarily, as noted above, from the inability of Washington officials to obtain the inclusion of Black personnel in local and state units of the Writers' Project.

The response to the request for ex-slave materials was extremely varied. Interviews were conducted in all the Southern and most of the border states, as well as in New York and Rhode Island. Alabama, North Carolina, South Carolina, and Texas sponsored especially productive projects, but the achievement of the Arkansas Project, whose Director, Bernice Babcock, had a special interest in the slave narrative, exceeded that of any other state. Although the Arkansas narratives are often marred by brevity, over seven hundred, or almost one-third of the entire Collection, were obtained here. One writer, Irene Robertson, alone interviewed 286 former slaves. Here, as in numerous other instances in the history of the Writers' Project, projected plans for publication were frustrated by the termination of the FWP.[54]

Most of the narratives were compiled in 1937 and early 1938. Several factors dictated that interview activities finally should be curtailed. Most compelling was the fact that they could not be maintained indefinitely, because the FWP had embarked upon several other projects, in addition to the preparation of the *Guides*, which competed for the time and energies of its personnel. Uncertainty about the ultimate disposition of the narratives curbed interest as well. Mrs. Dillard expressed this complaint.

[52]Dillard to Alsberg, October 15, 1936, December 11, 1936, Ex-Slave Studies, NA.
[53]Survey of personnel from microfilmed personnel records of the Works Progress Administration, Federal Records Center, St. Louis.
[54]Arkansas Folder, Ex-Slave Studies, NA.

> Enthusiasm about making these interviews has somewhat waned since we had no definite plans for publication, and the assignments seemed more like fill in time when there was nothing to be done on the Guide.[55]

Many officials felt, moreover, that the repetition that characterized the narratives was a defect and that a point of diminishing returns had been reached.[56] Finally, many felt, erroneously it now appears, that the supply of ex-slaves had been exhausted. By the spring of 1939 the collecting of slave narratives had ceased.

After interviewing had ended, the narratives lay dormant for several years. It appeared that they might be relegated to permanent archival oblivion in each of the respective states. Upon the termination of the FWP, however, the responsibility for the final disposition of the narratives was assumed by the Writers' Unit of the Library of Congress Project, which was concerned primarily with the conservation of Writers' Project materials not intended for publication by the individual states. Approximately twenty-three hundred narratives, as well as a thousand related documents and other "non-narrative materials" (newspaper advertisements of slave auctions and runaways, state laws and bills pertaining to slavery, tax enumerations on slaves, copies of bills of sale, etc.) were among the materials called in from the states for permanent storage in the Library of Congress. The processing of these materials was directed by Benjamin A. Botkin, a noted folklorist who had succeeded John A. Lomax as Folklore Editor of the Writers' Project.

Botkin was the individual chiefly responsible for the preservation of the narratives in a permanent collection, for without his sensitivity to the value of this collective portrait and without his concern for its preservation and utilization the narrative materials would probably have never been put to use. It was Botkin who appropriately subtitled the Collection, "A Folk History of Slavery in the United States," and whose *Lay My Burden Down* later directed scholarly attention to the collection.

The task of processing the narratives initially involved their appraisal, indexing, and arrangement alphabetically by individual informant and state. The appraisal of each individual narrative proved an excessively elaborate procedure and was abandoned after nearly four-fifths of the entire Collection had been evaluated. Unfortunately, the important task of indexing the Collection was suspended as well, thus depriving scholars of a feature which would have greatly facilitated its use. Botkin then completed the arrangement of the narratives for inclusion in the Rare Book Room of the Library of Congress.[57] With the exception of a number of the Virginia narratives used in the preparation of *The Negro in Virginia*

---

[55]Dillard to Alsberg, April 15, 1937, Ex-Slave Studies, NA.

[56]Memo from Alan and Elizabeth Lomax to Alsberg, September 9, 1938, Ex-Slave Studies, NA.

[57]Records of the Library of Congress Project, Writers' Unit, NA. The "non-narrative materials" which accompanied the narratives are deposited in the Archives of Folk Song in the Library of Congress.

and not forwarded to Washington, all of the others were presented in bound volumes to the Library of Congress in 1941.[58]

The collection today stands as a tribute to the Federal Writers who undertook the task of preserving these unique accounts of a most significant era. But above all the Collection stands as a monument to the former slaves, whose collective testimony surpasses in vividness and freshness many other efforts to reconstruct antebellum life. The narratives, above all, illumine the personal reality of slave life. Their value is perhaps best summarized in the following passage from the introduction to the Collection: "Beneath all the surface contradictions and exaggerations, the fantasy and flattery, [the narratives] possess an essential truth and humanity which surpasses as it supplements history and literature." [59]

[58]Louisiana was the sole Southern state that did not participate in the Writers' Project ex-slave study. Narratives were collected in Louisiana after the termination of the Writers' Project and were employed in the writing of the Louisiana Writers' Program's *Gumbo Ya-Ya* (Boston, 1945), a miscellany of Louisiana folklore. Carbon typescripts of the original narratives are deposited in the Louisiana State Library, Baton Rouge.

[59]Federal Writers' Project, *Slave Narratives*, p. x.

APPENDIX I

State	Narratives
Alabama	129
Arkansas	677
Florida	67
Georgia	184
Indiana	62
Kansas	3
Kentucky	34
Maryland	22
Mississippi	26
Missouri	84
North Carolina	176
Ohio	32
Oklahoma	75
South Carolina	274
Tennessee	26
Texas	308
Virginia	15

APPENDIX II
Race of Interviewers*

BLACK

Interviewer	State
Claude Anderson	Virginia
Edwin Driskell	Georgia
David Hoggard	Virginia
Augustus Ladsen	South Carolina
——Rogers	Maryland
Levi D. Shelby, Jr.	Alabama
Samuel S. Taylor	Arkansas
Grace E. White	Missouri

WHITE

Interviewer	State
William B. Allison	Mississippi
Ruth Chitty	Georgia
Cecil Copeland	Arkansas
Annie D. Dean	Alabama
W. W. Dixon	South Carolina
Margaret Fowler	Alabama
Leta Gray	Kansas
Beulah Sherwood Hagg	Arkansas
Sarah H. Hall	Georgia
Mary Hicks	North Carolina
Mary D. Hudgins	Arkansas
Marjorie Jones	North Carolina
Travis Jordan	North Carolina
Grace McCune	Georgia
Watt McKinney	Arkansas
Pat Matthews	North Carolina
Ila B. Prine	Alabama
Irene Robertson	Arkansas
Caldwell Sims	South Carolina
Geneva Tonsill	Georgia
C. E. Wells	Mississippi
Daisey Whaley	North Carolina

*The race of those interviewers whose names are not on this list could not be determined.

INDEX OF
PROPER NAMES

SUBJECT INDEX

Africa, 45, 50, 54, 89, 175, 192, 198, 228, 287, 290, 291

Agriculture and agricultural techniques, 8, 9, 19, 30, 76, 87, 235, 262, 277, 282, 284, 297, 300. *See also* Cotton; Corn; Tobacco; Rice; Wheat.

Alcoholic beverages, 15, 21, 62, 71, 77, 78, 80, 83, 95, 96, 119, 124, 141, 161, 164, 169, 200, 205, 218, 221, 232, 259, 267, 271, 281, 286, 289, 295, 308, 309, 314, 332

Apache Indians, 43

Artisans, 24, 93, 95, 103, 116, 135, 141, 158, 161, 198, 208, 228, 234, 250, 256, 257, 302

Auctions, slave. *See* Markets, slave.

Baptists, 13, 18, 85, 88, 102, 111, 117, 176, 177, 189, 193, 222, 238, 257, 266, 323. *See also* Religion, organizations.

Beatings. *See* Whippings.

Beds. *See* Housing.

Big House. *See* Housing, master.

Bloodhounds. *See* Dogs.

Boats. *See* Navigation.

Buildings, 15, 22, 28, 43, 62, 64, 67, 96, 103, 104, 120, 122, 123, 148, 149, 151, 156, 165, 168, 178, 199, 200, 205, 209, 213, 224, 242, 243, 265, 267, 268, 272, 284, 317, 320, 336, 337, 338. *See also* Housing.

Burials. *See* Funeral ceremonies.

Babies. *See* Child and infant care and activities.

Cabins, slave. *See* Housing, slave.

Cajuns, 10

Camp meetings. *See* Religion.

Cat-o-nine-tails. *See* Whippings.

Catholics, 238

Cattle, 9, 40, 41, 43, 47, 50, 51, 57, 70, 91, 95, 103, 120, 123, 141, 150, 161, 163, 182, 190, 209, 210, 237, 255, 261, 270, 275, 277, 285, 304

Celebrations, 17, 98, 99

Charms. *See* Voodoo.

Cherokee Indians, 83, 154, 186, 201, 234, 246, 247, 248, 249, 250, 251, 269–273, 308, 324, 329, 330

Cheyenne Indians, 43, 44

Chickasaw Indians, 83, 207, 208, 210

Chickens, 12, 23, 86, 102, 178, 183, 215, 234

Child and infant care and activities, 20, 40, 62, 64, 66, 71, 72, 104, 105, 112, 117, 124, 141, 145, 167, 168, 191, 192, 200, 202, 216, 227, 249, 264, 265, 279, 288, 316, 322, 327, 338

Childbirth, 45, 47, 55, 64, 71, 217, 252, 288

Chocktaw Indians, 72, 127, 207, 213, 234, 271, 272, 308, 329

Christmas. *see* Rest days.

Churches. *See* Religion, organizations.

Civil War, 8, 9, 14, 17, 23, 26, 28, 32, 34, 35, 38, 41, 46, 51, 55, 65–68, 70, 73, 74, 77, 79, 82, 83, 85–87, 92, 94, 96, 101, 103, 105, 107, 110, 112–114, 117, 118, 120, 125, 128, 130, 133–135, 137, 138, 142, 143, 147, 148, 153, 155, 156, 158, 159, 161, 162, 165, 170, 172, 173, 175, 181, 182, 186, 187, 190, 197, 201–206, 209, 211, 216, 219–223, 230, 231, 233–235, 238, 240, 244, 247, 248, 250–252, 259–261, 263, 268, 271–274, 276–278, 281–284, 293–296, 298, 300–304,